DRESSAGE 101

101
DRESSAGE

**The Ultimate Source of Dressage Basics
in a Language You Can Understand**

JANE SAVOIE

Photographs by Jayson Benoit
Illustrations by Susan E. Harris and Patricia Peyman Naegeli

T **S**
TRAFALGAR SQUARE

This edition published in 2025 by
Trafalgar Square Books
An imprint of the Stable Book Group, Brooklyn, New York

Material first published in two volumes in 1998: *Cross-Train Your Horse* and *More Cross-Training*
Original paperback edition published in 2011 by Trafalgar Square Books, North Pomfret, Vermont

Disclaimer of Liability
The author and publisher shall have neither liability nor responsibility to any person or entity with respect to any loss or damage caused or alleged to be caused directly or indirectly by the information contained in this book. While the book is as accurate as the author can make it, there may be errors, omissions, and inaccuracies.

Trafalgar Square Books encourages the use of approved safety helmets in all equestrian sports and activities.

Trafalgar Square Books certifies that the content in this book was generated by a human expert on the subject, and the content was edited, fact-checked, and proofread by human publishing specialists with a lifetime of equestrian knowledge. TSB does not publish books generated by artificial intelligence (AI).

ISBN: 9781646012381
Library of Congress Cataloging-in-Publication Data is available on file.

All photographs by Jayson Benoit
Illustrations by Susan E. Harris and Patricia Peyman Naegeli
Book design by Lauryl Eddlemon
Index by Andrea Jones (JonesLiteraryServices.com)
Cover design by RM Didier

Printed in China

10 9 8 7 6 5 4 3 2 1

In loving memory of Jane Savoie
1948–2021

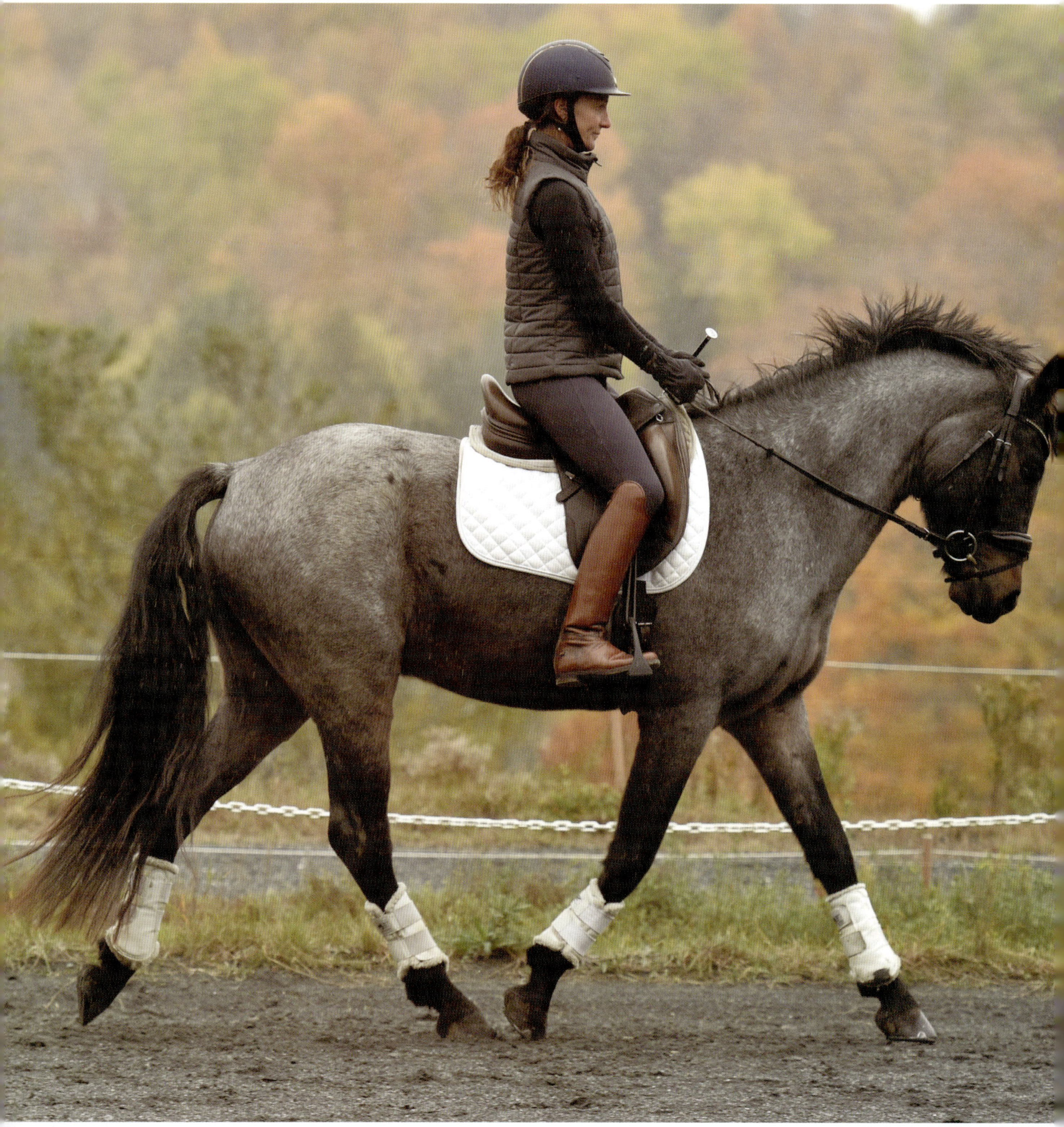

CONTENTS

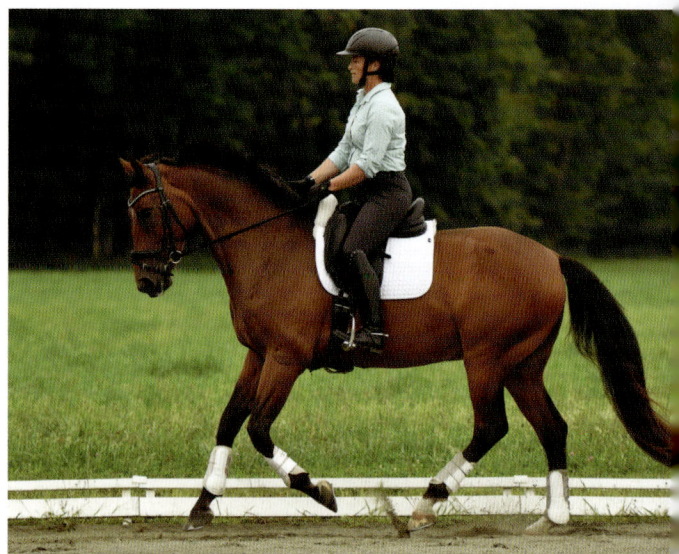

FOREWORD

from the Publisher

In 1998, Trafalgar Square Books published two books by US Equestrian Team dressage rider Jane Savoie: *Cross-Train Your Horse* and *More Cross-Training.* These weren't our first books with Jane—in 1992 *That Winning Feeling!* had broken new ground as the first sport psychology book geared specifically for equestrians. We knew Jane had a distinctive voice, dedication to the industry, and fierce passion for teaching others. These qualities came together in her *Cross-Training* books to provide the most complete, classically correct references on basic dressage ever available in print, and all delivered in her trademark style of taking knowledge seriously but approaching it *joyfully.*

A little more than a decade later, the demand for the clear, detailed explanations and step-by-step photographs Jane had worked so hard to compile remained, and so we combined the two *Cross-Training* books into a single illustrated manual. We entitled the book *Dressage 101,* because at its heart, that's what it was—a complete introductory course to dressage movements and dressage training. *Dressage 101* went on to become a consistent bestseller and was reprinted many times.

Now we are more than *another* decade later. The world is a very changed place from when Jane first sat down next to Trafalgar Square

Books Founder Caroline Robbins in the company's farmhouse office and worked through every line of explanation in her manuscripts to ensure the reader could both understand and practice the skills she described. Few books are edited with such meticulousness today, and you would be hard-pressed to find a professional rider and trainer at the Olympic level willing to commit the time needed to record the amount of knowledge contained in these pages. It is safe to say that *Dressage 101* is now *the only book in print* where individuals can find content of the highest quality from a universally trusted and much-loved source.

In 2021, we lost Jane, our remarkably talented author and dear friend, to the cancer she had fought for many years. Knowing that Jane had devoted much of her career to teaching others, that sharing her knowledge was the spark that "lit her fire," we felt that her books, and *Dressage 101,* in particular, needed to remain available. With Jane's husband Rhett's blessing, we set about finding a photographer and team of model riders to reshoot *Dressage 101's* images so Jane's original captions could remain intact. The project was blessed with the talents and time of Jayson Benoit, Bekki Read, and their team of riders and horses, as well as their beautiful Round Robin Farm in Tunbridge,

Vermont, only a few miles from the original photoshoot's Huntington Farm location in Strafford. In addition, two riders featured in the original *Cross-Training* books—Deborah Dean-Smith and Carole Ann ("Pinky") Tullar—appear again in this new edition, demonstrating that even more than 25 years later, dressage is not a pursuit we "age out of," and Jane's lessons are as applicable now as they were back when she was representing the United States in international competition.

It is deeply meaningful to us to be able to see this new edition of *Dressage 101* to fruition. We were infinitely changed by the time we shared with Jane Savoie—we learned about horses,

riding, writing, and ourselves. We learned about friendship, and the give and take that allows one to span decades. It is our hope that this book will keep Jane's voice alive and present in the industry she loved, and that generations to come can learn from her, preserving her place as an unparalleled teacher of equestrianism, and a remarkable human being.

Caroline Robbins, *Founder,*
Trafalgar Square Books

Martha Cook, *Publisher*

Rebecca Didier, *Managing Editor*

AUTHOR'S NOTE

Thanks to all of you who wrote asking me to compile the information from my two books *Cross-Train Your Horse* and *More Cross-Training* into one volume so you can find everything you need in one place. I'm absolutely delighted to be able to do this for you in *Dressage 101*.

I chose the title *Dressage 101* because in this book you're getting the building blocks to create a solid foundation for training your horse. That firm foundation is based on clear communication and clarity of aids. After all, a house built on a poor foundation will topple in a storm, so it's essential that, no matter what type of riding you do, your basics are solid and correct.

From those basics, you can either go on to more advanced dressage work or successfully specialize in other disciplines. For example, as I watched the riders in the World Equestrian Games in Kentucky, it became increasingly apparent to me that the champions who excelled in every discipline recognize that a solid foundation based on classical training principles is essential.

At these World Championships, it was exciting to see that the level of communication and the quality of training in all the disciplines far surpasses what was commonly seen years ago. As Olympic show jumper Anne Kursinski says, "What I do is 'dressage with jumps in the way!'"

All this training not only makes for champions at the highest level of the sport, but also makes for happier horses—and riders who just have more fun with their horses whether or not they ever plan to step into a competitive ring.

Now don't panic when you see how much information is in *Dressage 101*. You don't need to absorb it all at once. Concentrate on the section you are working on with your horse and move forward through the book at your horse's pace; the information is all presented in a progressive manner.

I'm pleased you've chosen me to guide you through your horse's dressage education. I'll be here on these pages for each step of your journey. Remember to have fun!

PREFACE

Welcome to the fascinating world of classical training—that is, training your horse the way it has been done for hundreds of years. This book is not only for the dressage enthusiast, but also for those of you who have no intention of ever setting foot inside a competitive dressage arena, but want to do dressage to help you clearly communicate with your horse and develop his body and movement so that over time he becomes more beautiful and athletic.

I want you to have the tools to give your horse a solid foundation from which you either go on to compete up through the dressage levels or easily branch off into any riding discipline with a new edge to excel in your chosen specialty. All riders will find that this is a simple, non-mysterious system of training that places a high priority on the horse's physical and mental well-being.

Here's what's in store for you: In chapter 1 I describe the three golden rules—*clarity, consistency,* and *kindness.* These principles form the basis of the philosophy that permeates this book. And in chapter 2, I explain how dressage promotes physical and emotional therapy. Chapter 3 starts your horse's formal education with a discussion of longeing technique and your job as rider and trainer. I am making certain

assumptions, even at this initial stage, about the level of training of both you and your horse. Specifically, I'm addressing horses that have been started under saddle and riders who have some control over their position as well as the skill to comfortably walk, trot, and canter.

Starting in chapter 5, I explore the heart of training work under saddle. Here, I introduce the first two of my Four Stages of training. The information in Stages One and Two is for all riders, and every horse regardless of his natural ability, talent, or eventual career.

I call Stage One "Dressage 101," because it is reminiscent of my freshman year in college when my schedule was filled with introductory (101) courses. As with any good introductory course, its discussion of "the basics" provides you with a solid background from which you can easily progress to the next level.

Stage Two includes the "nuts and bolts" of training—all the transitions, school figures, and movements. Note: I have provided diagrams for setting up small- and standard-size dressage arenas in chapter 22, though you can practice most of the basic work from Stages One and Two anywhere, whether out on the trail or in a field. However, for some of the exercises described in "nuts and bolts" you will find it helpful to set up a rectangle and some markers when you work in your ring, arena, field, or schooling area. You don't need to outline the entire perimeter of your rectangle—you can just define the corners with some poles or perhaps mow a rectangular area in your field so that the taller grass forms a clear boundary. Then designate the middle of each short and long side with four markers, such as small road cones or plastic milk containers filled with sand and you are open for business.

Some riders are perfectly content to stop at the end of Stage Two. After all, at this point, you should have a happy, responsive horse who knows quite a lot: he understands about going forward and being straight; he accepts a contact with your hands so you can communicate with him through the reins; he moves in a regular rhythm and a steady tempo in all three paces; he can do transitions, circles and turns, back up, lengthen his stride, and go sideways. You've also learned how to use all these movements to solve some simple training problems.

However, I hope you will continue on to Stage Three, where you'll learn about "The Professional's Secret." This secret is the *half-halt*. With it, you'll soon be able to put your horse "on the bit," which will add a whole new dimension to your training; it will enhance everything you already know how to do by making both you and your horse more physically comfortable. Once he is on the bit, your horse's back will feel springy and easier to sit on, he'll move more fluidly, and this "connection" from his back end to his front end will set up both of you for even greater things.

Then, once you're really bitten by the bug, I know you'll want to learn what you can do next

so I've included some "fancy stuff" in Stage Four. This material is well within the capacity of most horses. A word of caution here, though: You'll probably find that the more you know about dressage, the more you'll want to know. So, although the whole process of training classically can become endlessly fascinating and addictive, bear in mind that no horse should be schooled in a ring every day. All horses need play days and trail days to preserve their sanity and their joy in their work.

This final stage addresses the issue of self-carriage, which is the ultimate goal of dressage. Self-carriage enables you to bring back, to the ridden horse, the beauty of movement he has when he's at liberty. Your half-halt allows you to rebalance him so that his forehand is lighter and freer, thus making his movement just as expressive as he is when out cavorting in his field.

The information in Stage Four brings you through the work that is required in the United States Equestrian Federation's (USEF) dressage tests at Third Level. This includes collected, medium, and extended gaits, advanced lateral movements, and flying changes. I stop here in this book, because that's all you'll really need to know to incorporate classical training into your regular program so you have a calm horse responding happily and willingly to the most invisible of cues. If you decide to continue on to the higher levels—canter pirouettes, piaffe and passage—you will have already laid the solid foundation needed for this more advanced work.

I do have a few additional comments. First, you'll discover that in running text, I refer to all riders as "she" and all horses as "he." I'm hoping my male readers and mare owners will not take offense at my arbitrary choice of pronouns. I am not being sexist here! I'm simply trying to avoid cumbersome references to "he and she" and the impersonal sound of calling your horse "it."

Also, in the interest of clarity, you'll notice that nearly all of the movements and exercises are described with your horse traveling to the left—that is, counterclockwise. When you go to the right, all you need to do is reverse the aids. I say "nearly" because toward the end of the book, there are some exceptions.

I believe that you'll find the explanations and descriptions "reader-friendly." They are basically a reflection of my own learning style. By nature I'm a very left-brained, methodical, analytical person who eventually learned how to unleash and blend some right-brained creativity into my established system. So that's what you'll find when you get to the movements. Every exercise will be broken down and clearly explained in a step-by-step manner.

And if some of the words and expressions sound new or foreign, don't worry, because you'll find a glossary of terms in an appendix (p. 377). In fact, each time I introduce a new dressage word or phrase, I put it in bold type so you'll know that the term is defined in the glossary.

You'll also find lots of imaging in this book to help you tap into your creative side and strive for peak performance. After all, practice doesn't make perfect. *Perfect practice makes perfect.* And in your imagination, you never miss!

Whether you're a recreational rider or an aspiring professional, dressage can give you a choice. You don't need to be victimized by a tense, flighty, uncooperative horse or a lazy, sullen, heavy-on-the-forehand type who you have to kick and pull to make stop, go, and turn. You can discover the joy of riding a calm, responsive animal who responds happily and willingly to the most invisible cues.

Convinced? I hope so because you're about to embark on an exciting adventure of a lifetime of learning. Any horse with three acceptable paces—one that can walk, trot, and canter in a regular rhythm—can do this program. And, don't panic. There aren't any secrets or complicated theories to absorb. What I do is simply training—clearly presented and kindly executed. I'll be giving you a clear-cut, non-hocus-pocus system that's straightforward and easy to learn. Ready? Have fun!

J.S.

SETTING THE STAGE FOR DRESSAGE TRAINING

1

DRESSAGE

What's in It for You

IS DRESSAGE FOR YOU?

According to the United States Equestrian Federation (USEF) rulebook, the ultimate purpose of dressage is *the harmonious development of the physique and ability of a horse.* It makes a horse calm, supple, attentive and keen, thus closer to achieving perfect understanding with his rider. Does this sound like something that might appeal to you?

Would you like your horse to be relaxed, obedient, and more of a pleasure to ride? Wouldn't it be fun to have a horse that willingly and enthusiastically responds to refined, invisible signals? Dressage will enable you to develop a nonverbal language—a way to clearly communicate with your equine partner so you begin to function as one.

Is the idea of helping your horse become more of an athlete appealing? Consider a horse when he's free. Even the most common animal is fascinating and beautiful to watch when he gets the wind under his tail on a crisp spring morning or when he cavorts with his friends while being pursued by imaginary enemies.

The catch here, however, is that horses aren't designed to be ridden. And as much as you might love your horse, you really are a burden to him. You bring this proud creature in from the field, put a saddle and your weight on his back, and suddenly he doesn't move in the same lofty way. Instead of showing himself off with a "Hey! Look at me! I'm hot stuff!" attitude, he either lazily shuffles along or stiffens his body and moves with tension. Fortunately, this is where dressage holds the key to unlock his potential; you can give the beauty of movement the horse has when he's at liberty back to the horse that is being ridden.

Now let's consider some physical and balance problems. Is your horse ever so sore, stiff, or weak that he can't do his job? I'm not talking about fancy maneuvers here. I mean real nitty-gritty stuff like the quality of the basic paces—such as the horse that is so unathletic he can barely canter and ends up switching leads behind, dragging his hind feet along the ground or simply breaking back into the trot. With a program of systematic training like the one presented in this book, a horse like that can become a strong and capable athlete.

Are you a jumper rider who finds that your horse is so "locked" or "blocked" in his body that he's difficult to turn? He's so hard, in fact, that you wonder if you'll be able to stay in the ring, let alone negotiate a corner in order to have a decent approach to the next fence. Or maybe you go for a so-called "pleasure" ride and return exhausted because your horse has been pulling your arms out of their sockets for an hour? Cross-training with dressage enables you to become your horse's physical therapist, so you can loosen, strengthen, unlock, unblock, supple, rebalance, and teach your friend to carry himself.

If all this doesn't entice you, consider the fact that proper physical training can prolong your horse's useful years. Most of the world's top dressage horses peak in their teens when many other competitive types are getting ready to retire.

You'll also discover the joys of learning from, and communicating with, your partner. Horse people often say, "I wish my horse could talk so he could tell me what's wrong." Well, horses do talk. We just need to learn how to listen to what they're saying—that is, we need to learn how to interpret their body language and behavior. Dressage training creates a mutual awareness that improves performance in whatever is your chosen discipline.

BEGINNING AT THE END

Before we get started with the specifics of training, let's examine the ultimate aim which, for me, is the development of a happy, athletic horse. I'm convinced that dressage provides the system and technique to do just that for horses of all ages, shapes, sizes, and abilities.

The proof of this for me was that when I started teaching, I began to see all different types of horses, from many diverse backgrounds, change right before my eyes. Tense horses became relaxed. Stiff horses became more supple. Tight horses started taking longer, looser strides and swinging through their backs.

What fun! I was inspired and thus began my new mission. My goal during lessons and now with this book is to give riders in all disciplines the tools they needed to develop happy and athletic horses. I want them to understand and appreciate their horse's uniqueness while bringing out the personal best in each.

Dressage can show you how to build the self-esteem of the shy horse and make him feel as if he can do anything. It can help the lazy horse discover that going forward is fun. It encourages the tense horse to put his trust in his rider and learn to relax, nurses the timid fellow along until he becomes more confident and brave, and even transforms the rogue into an agreeable, cooperative sort.

I have found that to reach this goal, training needs to follow three golden rules: Clarity, Consistency, and Kindness. These form the basis of the philosophy you'll find permeating this book. Occasionally, force or domineering styles of training will produce competent athletes, but I'd be willing to bet that these approaches rarely create happy horses that have joyful partnerships with their riders.

CLARITY

When I first started teaching lessons and clinics, I found that there was a distinct advantage to my left-brained, list-making learning style. Since I had needed to break things down into a step-by-step process for myself, I was able to do the same thing for others.

I discovered that many riders were confused about the "how to" of things. As a result, their horses often struggled to understand what they wanted. Signals for movements seemed to be chosen by "multiple choice" and responses were, inevitably, haphazard.

I found out just how vague riders were because I'd ask them questions like, "How do you ask for a transition to the canter?" They'd reply, "Well...." and then there would be a long pause. Or they'd say, "Sometimes I'll do this and sometimes I'll try that." No wonder it took so long to train—there was no clarity or consistency in the language between horse and rider. In response I started to use "recipe riding" to teach: if you blend this with this and then add a pinch of that, you'll get a certain result! I wanted my students to understand cause and effect before they tried to get creative.

I discovered that with my formulas I was able to make things clear enough to riders that they

could follow through with a program after I had left. This was important to me if the clinics were going to have any value. I thought it was fairly useless to stand in the middle of the ring and say, "Now use your left leg" or "Slow down there." That might help for the moment, but would not leave a rider understanding why or when to do anything when she was on her own.

"I discovered that many riders were confused about the 'how to' of things."

• • • • •

I tried to get the point across that training questions shouldn't have multiple choice answers. One signal means one, and only one, thing. When you want to ask for something else, you must have a completely different cue. With this kind of clarity, you can eliminate a lot of confusion, and training can progress more smoothly.

You start by teaching the young or un-schooled horse basic "words" like "go," "stop," "turn left," "turn right." Then, you develop his vocabulary one word at a time. Eventually he has an extensive understanding of a nonverbal language that allows you to communicate through subtle variations of signals.

CONSISTENCY

If communicating can be so straightforward and clear, you might wonder why it takes one rider three times as long as another equally able rider to train her animal. It often boils down to consistency. It's important to understand that every second you're on your horse you're either *training* or *"untraining"* him.

For example, if one day you insist that your horse walk energetically under his own steam without any urging from you, and then the next day you start using alternate leg aids to keep him going, you're being inconsistent. Or, let's say you've decided to train your horse to slow down when you brace your back; you do your homework diligently while in the ring, and he's really starting to understand what it means when you "still" your seat. But then you head off on a trail ride and find yourself pulling on the reins to slow him down instead of using your back. This is the kind of inconsistency that *"untrains"* him.

KINDNESS

The signals that you use to communicate with your horse are called "aids", and that's exactly how I'd like you to think of them. You'll communicate with your horse by *aiding* or *helping* him to understand rather than regarding your signals as rigid commands.

To explain what the aids mean, you'll need to use the basic principles of behavior modification.

This is a method that can be used to train any animal most efficiently. When you shape behavior, you give a stimulus—the aid—which the animal will respond to with either a correct or an incorrect response. You must reward the correct response or "punish" the incorrect one.

Since you presumably want the correct behavior to be repeated, reward this response. You can do this in any number of ways—patting, verbally praising with a "Good boy!" or "Good girl!", or taking a short break by walking on a long rein. My system emphasizes training with reward because I believe that this is the way to nurture a happy and cooperative partnership.

In order to change the incorrect response, you "punish" your horse. I must stress, however, that the word "punish" does not imply severity in any way. Punishment can be as mild as simply repeating an exercise or perhaps as strong as a few taps with the whip, but it should never be harsh or abusive.

It's important to keep in mind that when you're teaching a new behavior you must reward every slight effort your horse makes toward doing it right, or else you'll discourage him. *Absence of reward* is the same as punishment: it will take him much longer to understand what you want if you skimp on the praise.

Robert Dover, a four-time Olympian in dressage, says, "Remain patient, reward your horse's every effort, and every day look for harmony and joy in your ride. If you do, you will be rewarded by his becoming ever more beautiful."

KEY POINTS

■ No matter what type of riding you do, there is a place for dressage in your program.

■ Dressage can help your horse become relaxed, obedient, fun to ride, more athletic, and it can prolong his useful life.

■ To develop a happy, athletic horse, training should be *clear, consistent,* and *kind.*

2

Just What the
DOCTOR ORDERED

In this chapter, you'll have a chance to see one of the many uses of dressage: as physical and emotional therapy for horses. It can help any horse become stronger, more comfortable, and more athletic, as well as calm, confident, and secure.

PHYSICAL THERAPY

Several years ago a student brought her combined training horse to me for some lessons. This horse had a chronic sore back, and his rider was at a loss as to how to make him better. She had explored several different avenues—injecting his back, massage, therapeutic pads, and different saddles. Everything helped a little, but she was determined to get him one hundred percent pain-free.

She knew that all of the "solutions" she had tried were merely "band-aids." If she was going to make him totally comfortable, she'd have to stop treating the symptoms and pay closer attention to the cause.

I looked at his physique and guessed that his weak and underdeveloped back muscles were the source of his problem. Strengthening these muscles became our objective. To do this, we worked him with his hindquarters coming well under his body and his head and neck placed very long and low. Initially, we kept him in that "deep" position (which I more thoroughly explain on p. 258) for the entire session. All of his school figures, transitions, and movements were done in this frame. While "deep," his back was raised rather than dropped and hollow, so the right muscles developed. Within a couple of months, his back was so much stronger that he was able to do his work easily.

The physical therapy was a temporary measure. Eventually his rider was able to ride him "deep" for just his warm-up and cool-down. The rest of his work was done in a frame appropriate for the work he was doing in competition.

A SWAN EMERGES

If you really need to be convinced that dressage is great physical therapy, you need to meet Judi Whipple and Homer. Judi's first love was dressage but she was horseless until a kindly neighbor gave her his pet. The first time I saw Homer, I groaned (inwardly) for Judi. What a project! This nine-year-old Appaloosa had no paces. He crawled in the walk, shuffled in the trot and was so unbalanced in the canter that he couldn't make it around one large circle without breaking to the trot or cross-cantering. Plus, he was very weak behind, had no desire to go forward, and all these problems were complicated by his quick temper.

But Judi was up to the challenge. She worked her "dressage magic," and within a relatively short period of time, Homer was transformed. I still shake my head in wonder every time I see him. This "90-pound weakling" blossomed into "The Incredible Hulk!" His body is muscular and strong and he is willingly schooling some fairly advanced dressage movements. He goes sideways easily and his extensions are developing. But the most amazing thing is to see this horse—who couldn't even canter—now doing a balanced counter-canter and starting flying changes.

THE COLLECTION CONNECTION

By first **connecting** your horse—also known as putting him **"on the bit"** and later **collecting** him—that is, asking him to carry himself by shifting his center of gravity more toward his hind legs—you can help him become more of an athlete. Although I don't get into the actual aids and exercises to produce these two important qualities until Stage Three, I want to introduce them to you and discuss them a little

here to give you an inkling of what they can do for your horse.

Learning to connect your horse is desirable because it makes your horse more physically comfortable (and more comfortable for you to sit on!), as well as better able to do many of the things you'll want to do with him. Plus, connection is a prerequisite if you want to go on to the ultimate athletic goal of collecting your horse.

Collection, or **self-carriage,** is the icing on the cake. Not only does it allow you to prolong the useful life of your horse by transferring some of his weight off his front legs, but it also makes him more maneuverable, athletic, and easier to ride.

Before I get ahead of myself with this talk about *collection,* let's first take a look at *connection.*

WHAT'S THE CONNECTION?

Think of connection as the concept of the horse's back being the "bridge" between his hind legs and his front legs. The horse's power, his "engine," is in the hindquarters. You need to connect him over his back so that the energy can travel from the hind legs, over the back, through his neck, into the rider's hands, and then be recycled back to the hind legs.

We dressage riders call this connection phenomenon **"on the bit."** You might also hear connection being described as **"throughness," "roundness,"** "packaged," "over the back," "round outline, shape, or **frame,"** or "moving from the hind legs into the hands." These are phrases that sometimes create a lot of confusion. (To add to the mix-up, we also have all sorts of ways to describe a horse who isn't connected such as "disconnected," "hollow," "in two parts," "dropping his back,", or "off the bit.")

Basically, a horse's **frame** (which is the outline or silhouette of his body) is described as **round** when his hind legs step well under his body so that his back is raised and looks convex rather than dropped and concave, his neck is long and arched, and he stretches toward the contact. The top of his body resembles the curve of a bow when it is tightly strung (photos 2.1 and 2.2).

All riders should strive to build a better equine athlete. It's a fact that "use makes the muscle" and the horse that's connected or on the bit will develop a rounded, muscular, and

2.1 Compare the frame (outline or silhouette) of Cady O'Daly Class Pet (also known as Maeve) in this photo to the one on the facing page. In this photo, Maeve is not connected. Her hind legs are lazy, her back is low and hollow, and her neck is high.

therefore beautiful "topline." The horse that carries himself with a stiff, hollow back and an upside-down neck will develop the muscles under the neck and the "bottom line." At best, this can lead to the horse moving with choppy, short strides that are uncomfortable for both horse and rider. At worst, the horse's back becomes weak and eventually painful.

COLLECTION: THE ULTIMATE GOAL

As I said earlier, collection is the icing on the cake. Only when a horse is in self-carriage is he able to dance. As Sally Swift said in her wonderful book *Centered Riding*, "When the horse has self-carriage, with each stride he reaches the hind leg well under his belly, giving the body increased support, thus lightening the whole

2.2 Here, Maeve is connected, and her frame is "round." Her hind legs step well under her body, her back just behind the saddle looks raised and convex, her neck is long and arched, and she is seeking a comfortable contact with rider Bekki Read's hands.

forehand and lending liveliness and gaiety to his appearance and movements."

The difficulty in achieving self-carriage is that by nature a horse's center of gravity is more towards his front legs. But when a rider starts to collect a horse, she shifts his center of gravity more toward the hindquarters. The horse does this through **engagement**—bending and flexing the joints of the hind legs. This flexing and closing of the joints causes the hindquarters to lower and a corresponding elevation and lightening of weight on the forehand. When the horse is correctly collected, you'll notice that a comparison of the relative height of the horse's withers to the croup shows that the withers look higher.

Collection helps the endurance horse to lighten his forehand so there are fewer front-end injuries caused by pounding along the miles; it helps the jumper to turn handily and to rock back on his hocks so he can propel himself over fences; it enables the dressage horse to become more beautiful and expressive in his movement; and lets the pleasure horse carry himself so that the contact with the rider's hand is light and pleasant.

This last benefit reminds me of a rider I met at one of my teaching clinics. This girl was obviously not a dressage rider so I asked her why she was there. She explained that her horse was so heavy on the forehand that riding him made her arms and back sore. He really wasn't much of a pleasure to take out on a ride. So we discussed the idea of self-carriage as a long-range goal. And, in order to reach it, we decided on exercises and short-term goals that would head her horse on that path.

She left the clinic armed with exercises to help her balance her horse and with full knowledge that it would take time to develop the strength of his hindquarters. Since the horse wasn't used to carrying weight behind, the muscles would have to be built up very gradually. She needed to understand that to demand immediate results would be like expecting herself to do five hundred deep knee bends while carrying one hundred and fifty pounds on her back. By the time she reached seventy-five (or even twenty-five!), her muscles would be screaming, and she'd be unable to do even one more.

I saw this girl and her horse a year later. She had done her homework, and her horse had been transformed. Through her diligence and patience, her partner was now light in her hands and truly fun to ride.

I'll explain the technique to produce collection in detail starting on page 239, but I'd like to share what Dennis Reis, who once upon a time earned his living on the Professional Rodeo Cowboys Association circuit, says about connection and self-carriage (fig. 2.4).

Dennis was a cowboy who trained horses for a living and discovered he had been doing dressage without knowing it. As his ability to communicate with his animals evolved and his talent was noticed by his neighbors, who were mostly dressage riders, he found himself in the unusual position of being asked to reschool upper-level dressage horses who were brought to him with specific problems. The dressage riders sought him out even though he had no classical training himself.

When asked about collection, Dennis is quick to point out that it's not just a "head-set." "Collection isn't conforming to a preconceived notion of a frame or a picture of what it should look like. It's not a reduction in speed or a shortening of frame. It's a posture that generates deep inside the body. The horse is round, balanced, engaged, off the forehand, and his back and neck are turned off—not braced." In dressage terms, when the horse's back and neck are "turned off," the energy that originates in the hindquarters can flow to the forehand without meeting any stiffness or restriction caused by the sustained contraction of the back muscles.

Dennis is enthusiastic about the joys of riding a horse that is in self-carriage. "The movements are fluid and elastic, transitions are flowing and soft, the horse is light and easy to guide and willingly yields his body to the rider."

EMOTIONAL THERAPY

I could go on and on with stories about how dressage is useful for every horse physically. I've seen horses with one weak hind leg develop strength and become even behind, and I've seen horses who just wouldn't turn become handy and maneuverable. But, I don't want to ignore the emotional benefits of dressage for horses. Not only can it turn an insecure, dangerous animal into a calm and confident partner, as you'll see in the story of Eli that follows, but it can add to your horse's fun by giving him a base from which he can enjoy a wide variety of activities.

A ROGUE TURNED PARAGON

The greatest example of what dressage can do for a horse's brain is illustrated by the story of Sue and Eli. The first time I saw Eli he was six years old and standing on his hind legs. According to the man who was riding him, he was a rogue who had temper tantrums and rearing was part of his repertoire. I found out he had been sent up and down the East Coast. At each new home the rider became discouraged and he'd be shuffled off cheaply to another barn.

Sue went to see him because the price was right and she was struck by the fact that he was attractive and had three good paces. She felt she might be able to overcome his bad habits. When the curious asked her about her new horse, she would laughingly call him her "reclaimer."

The first four months were a delicate balance between gently but firmly explaining to Eli that he wasn't going to get his way while not pushing him to the point of a "mental meltdown" by keeping his beginning work very basic and simple. She made a huge effort to be very consistent and build a language between them one word at a time. Every slightly cooperative effort on his part was lavishly rewarded.

When Sue first asked me to help her with basic dressage, it was easy for me to tell from the ground when Eli was on the verge of one of his fits because I would see his eye roll around. This was not the sort of horse you'd want to challenge head-on since he was used to fighting for his life. I suggested that Sue always work him a little below his pressure threshold; I wanted to keep him happy and Sue safe.

Over the course of those first four months, I watched Eli slowly change. He began to trust Sue. He knew he could count on her being absolutely consistent in her behavior: her aids were always given in the same way; he was always rewarded for trying; and there were no surprises.

Within the year a wonderful partnership was born. Eli's eye always remained calm and confident. He had learned to trust Sue so much that if she pressured him, he took it and responded positively. As their relationship strengthened, Sue was able to go beyond the basic work very quickly. And the proof of Eli's emerging self-assurance was that at his first dressage competition not only did he behave like a paragon, but he also was the high score champion.

Here was a lovely animal that in someone else's hands would most likely have become increasingly dangerous to the point of having to be destroyed. But he found his niche, and under Sue's guidance he was able to fulfill his potential.

No matter what riding you do, dressage techniques can help your horse become a willing partner and an able athlete. But before I get started with the horse's actual primary education, I'd like to spend some time explaining how to longe your horse and how to improve your riding skills. In chapter 3, I'll discuss the purpose and basic technique of longeing, and in chapter 4, I'll look at you as the rider: the development of your seat and the right attitude toward training.

KEY POINTS

- Although not every horse can become a dressage specialist, every horse can benefit from dressage training.

- Dressage increases communication and establishes a foundation from which a horse can excel in any other discipline.

- Dressage can help you deal with a horse's physical problems, such as stiffness, soreness, and unathletic movement, as well as mental problems such as tension, disobedience and inattentiveness.

3

LONGEING

Riding from the Ground

To longe or not to longe? As with most training questions, there are different schools of thought as to whether the advantages of training on the longe outweigh the disadvantages of wear and tear on the horse's body. I agree that trotting endlessly around on small circles can be tough on legs and joints. However, I do think that longeing my horses for short periods (fifteen minutes or so) can be very useful for a variety of reasons that I'll get into shortly.

Think of longeing as riding from the ground. I longe a young horse to get some basic rules established. I teach him the simple voice commands like slow, whoa, walk, trot, and canter, which I'll also use when I start riding. I explain that the reins (the longe line) mean stop and that the driving aids (the whip) mean go forward. He becomes attentive and tunes into me for all his instructions—not only voice commands but also subtle changes in my body position and the way I use the longe whip. When it's finally time for mounted work, we have a way to communicate.

The horse experiences contact—the connection from the rider's hand to his mouth that will

happen when being ridden—as he stretches into the side reins (reins that attach from the girth to the bit) and seeks contact with a long neck and a lowered head. Seeking the contact forward and down toward the ground will help him to come into a "round" frame (I introduced the word "round" on page 10)—a very desirable shape to work in to develop his muscles correctly (figs. 3.1 and 3.2).

He also discovers his balance on circles and develops regularity in his gaits without the burden of a rider. For example, let me tell you about Basil. Basil was a big-moving, young horse who managed just fine in walk and trot. When it was time to canter, however, pandemonium broke loose. Because he was gawky and unbalanced when his rider, Leslie, would ask for a depart, he'd leap forward, leaving his hind legs way out behind his body and just go faster and faster.

We helped Basil learn to balance himself in the canter by first letting him canter on the largest circle possible while on the longe, without the additional burden of a rider. To set him up for the canter depart, Leslie drew him onto a

3.1 Don't be fooled by the arched and lowered shape of this horse's neck. Top Scholar (Jax) is avoiding taking a contact with the side reins. If he does this when being longed in side reins, he'll most likely also avoid a contact with the reins when being ridden.

3.2 Because he's being sent more forward, Jax is now starting to stretch into and seek the contact forward and down toward the ground. Note how nicely his hind leg steps under his body. As a result his back is round, his neck is longer, and he takes a definite contact with the side reins.

slightly smaller circle. Next she pushed him back out to the larger circle by pointing the whip toward the girth, while she gave the voice command... "Aaannd canter!" Reducing the size of the circle improved his balance (something he was losing when asked to canter under saddle) while enlarging the circle during the transition ensured that he stayed bent to the inside and increased the likelihood of cantering on the correct lead. With the aid of comfortably adjusted side reins and no interference from a desperate rider, he soon learned how to balance himself.

There are a number of situations where longeing is just plain useful. You can longe a horse for fifteen or twenty minutes to keep him exercised when you're unable to ride or he can't wear a saddle for some reason. The stiff or tight horse often benefits from ten minutes of longeing prior to mounted work. Longeing allows him to loosen, stretch, and warm up before the added weight of the rider on his back. And, because I have a keen sense of self-preservation, I'll longe a fresh horse for a few minutes so he can get the bucks out of his system. Besides the fact that it's not going to do my aging body any good to be bucked off, I never want him to

realize that he is, in fact, capable of depositing me in the dirt! Discretion is certainly the better part of valor.

EQUIPMENT

I'm assuming that your horse is not an unbroken youngster and has already been under saddle. Prepare him for his longeing session by first tacking him up with a bridle and a saddle. Remove the bridle's reins or tie them up out of the way by twisting one rein around the other and feeding the throatlatch through one of the loops. Tie up the stirrups by winding the leathers around them and feeding the free end of the leather through the loop (figs. 3.3 to 3.5).

3.3 To prevent the reins from hanging down when longeing, twist one rein around the other and feed the throatlatch of the bridle through one of the loops in the reins before you fasten it.

3.4 Place the longeing cavesson on your horse's head and secure the noseband first. The cavesson should fit snugly so it doesn't shift and rub your horse's eye.

3.5 Tie the stirrups up out of the way so they don't bang against your horse's sides.

Basic equipment for longeing includes a longeing cavesson, two side reins, a longe line and a whip. It's important for the cavesson to fit securely so it doesn't move around and perhaps rub against his eye. Place the cavesson on his head and secure the noseband first. Then fasten the cavesson's throatlatch. A halter is a poor substitute for a cavesson, but if you opt to use one over the bridle, be sure to adjust it very snugly so it doesn't twist or slide around and rub your horse's outside eye. Never attach your longe line to the bit because it could hurt the bars of your horse's mouth.

I also recommend using gloves because it can be pretty painful to have a fresh horse pull a nylon or web longe line through your hands. Without gloves, rope burn might force you to let go so that your horse ends up running around with a thirty-foot longe line trailing along behind him. If that happens, he might panic and bolt or perhaps get himself tangled up in the line. At best, he'll scare himself, and at worst, he could be badly hurt.

I also like to put boots or bandages on my horse's legs to protect them from damage if they hit each other.

Both the longe line and the longe whip should be long—at least thirty feet long for the line and a minimum of twelve feet, including the lash, for the whip. The line should be long enough so that your horse can make a fairly large circle, yet not so long that you can't influence him with your body, voice and whip. The circle you should make with most horses is twenty meters in diameter (approximately sixty feet).

Hold the longe line in your leading hand (that is the left hand if the horse is tracking to the left), with the slack layered back and forth across the palm of your hand. Never wind the slack around your hand, because it can be dangerous if your horse decides to take off (fig. 3.6).

Hold the longe whip in the other hand. Ideally, the whip needs to be long enough for you to stand in the center of your circle and, if necessary, reach the horse's barrel with the lash. I've been known to put "extenders" like shoe laces on the end of whips to make the lash longer. You see, in order for a circle to be a good gymnastic shape in terms of teaching the horse something about balance, it must be round. You may say, "well, a circle is always round," but it's nearly impossible to make a round circle if you're walking along with the horse because your whip is too short. You need to be able to stand almost

3.6 Safety first: Layer the excess longe line back and forth across your hand. Never wind it around your hand or let it drag on the ground where it could get wrapped around your foot.

3.7 Place the side reins around the back saddle billet to prevent them from slipping down too low on the girth.

still in one spot and just pivot around your leading leg. For example, when your horse is circling to the left, you pivot around your left leg, which remains in the same spot. Stand with your feet apart and your knees slightly bent so that you can absorb any sudden movement.

Side reins, which attach from the girth to the rings of the bit above the reins, can be made of all leather, leather and elastic, or with a round rubber doughnut insert. I personally prefer all leather because some horses feel the "give" in the elastic and test the contact by pulling or snatching at the reins. I don't want them to learn how to do this on the longe because I certainly

don't want them doing it when I ride. The side reins with the rubber doughnut are a good compromise because they provide some give without being too "stretchy."

When I'm ready to use the side reins, I'll attach them to the back billet strap on the saddle. I don't place them around both billets or around the entire girth because I don't want them to slip down too low. As far as the height of the side reins is concerned, a good rule of thumb is that they should be placed at the height of the rider's knee (fig. 3.7).

However, I always lead the horse away from and back to the stable with the side reins unhooked. I do this prior to work because the horse's body is stiff and cold from standing in the stall. I don't want him suddenly to feel restricted or surprised by the side reins while walking out of the barn, because he could run backward or rear and hurt himself seriously. I unhook them after work as a reward.

When I'm in the arena ready to work, I attach the side reins loosely. I adjust them long enough so the horse doesn't feel stifled, restricted, or crammed into a frame, but short enough so that there is a light contact with his mouth and so that his outside shoulder doesn't pop out of the line of the circle (fig. 3.8).

I almost always keep the two side reins the same length. Some people like to have the inside side rein a couple of inches shorter because they believe this helps the horse bend to the inside of the circle. The danger here is that the hindquarters might swing to the outside of the circle in order to avoid the increased bend caused by the shorter inside side rein. If you discover that your horse's tendency is to escape to the outside with his hindquarters, it's best to keep the side reins the same length.

Both the shoulder popping out and the haunches swinging out mean that the horse is crooked. His entire body needs to overlap the line of the circle in order for him to be straight (fig. 3.9). We'll delve more into straightness in chapter 5.

Stand in the center of the circle, pivoting around your leading leg. Stand across from the saddle so there is a triangle formed by the horse's body, the longe line, and the whip (fig. 3.10).

3.8 Make sure that the side reins are adjusted to the same length. They should be short enough to establish a light contact with your horse's mouth but long enough so that he doesn't feel confined.

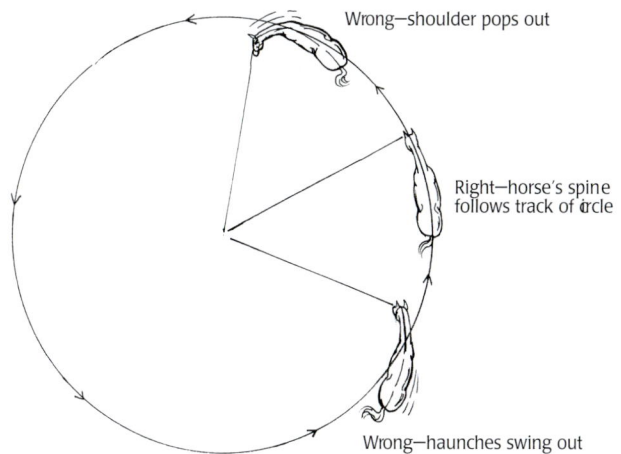

Wrong—shoulder pops out

Right—horse's spine follows track of circle

Wrong—haunches swing out

3.9 Unless the entire body of the horse overlaps the line, or arc, of the circle, the horse is crooked. Here, the horse is first swinging his haunches out, then going straight before his haunches fall in and his shoulders pop out.

3.10 **3.10** The "triangle of control" is formed by the horse's body, the longe line in Bekki's left hand, and the longe whip in her right.

Then you can adjust the horse's speed by the position of your body as well as by the use of the longe whip and longe line. To ask him to slow down, stay equidistant from his body but step laterally more toward the front of his body and give some little tugs on the longe line. To speed him up, stay the same distance away from the horse but step laterally toward the back of his body and raise the whip more toward the hindquarters (fig. 3.11).

Always combine these signals with a voice command so you can develop your horse's knowledge of your vocabulary. Your tone of voice is very important here. For instance, a soothing, quiet tone is appropriate as you say, "Slow" or "Whoa." While you'll want to be more animated as you ask for an upward transition or for more energy as you say something like, "Trot on."

Once he understands basic signals, you can begin to put his body in the desired round, connected frame by combining the aids in the same way that you do when you ride. In other words, at the same moment that you push him forward with the whip, take and give on the longe several times. Then be quiet for a few strides and see if he stretches into the contact. If not, repeat the taking and giving while sending him forward. Be sure to praise him each time you see him even begin to think about stretching toward the contact and becoming rounder in his frame.

Safe is fun. So use your work on the longe to establish obedience to your spoken aids. I remember watching dressage team rider Shelly Francis starting numerous babies on the longe. They knew when she said "Whoa!" they were to stop on a dime. There was no room for discussion. She would say it once, and if she didn't get an immediate response, they'd get several sharp tugs on the longe line. Before she ever set her foot in the stirrups, Shelly was confident from her groundwork that she'd have instant immobility when she said the word "Whoa!"

On the other hand, there are some horses that aren't forward thinkers. They'd rather stop, buck, rear, or wheel around than go forward. Three-day event and dressage trainer Deb Dean-Smith, who is featured in some of the photographs in this book, was training a young stallion who would not go forward when under saddle. So she put him on the longe and laid down the "forward rules" over again while she was safely on the ground. She'd cluck once softly, and if the stallion didn't react immediately, she'd tap him with the whip. She was teaching him to choose to go forward. When he was attentive to the cluck and willing to go forward, Deb praised him with her voice. If he was at all "nappy" when she clucked, she used the whip. He soon decided that going forward was more fun than getting tapped by the whip. Then, if he started thinking backward while she was riding him, all Deb had to do was cluck once, and his automatic, conditioned response was to go forward.

Longeing is an important part of your horse's education. Done correctly, it's a very useful addition to the training and exercising of your horse. Done incorrectly, it can do more harm than good. I've only given you a brief account here in order to get you started on the right

track. For those of you who want to delve deeper into longeing technique, you'll find clear, in-depth explanations in good books like *The Complete Training of Horse and Rider* by Alois Podhajsky and *Horse Training in Hand* by Ellen Schutof-Lesmeister and Kip Mistral.

In the next chapter, I'll discuss your position and your attitude toward riding and training.

Moving backward sends horse forward

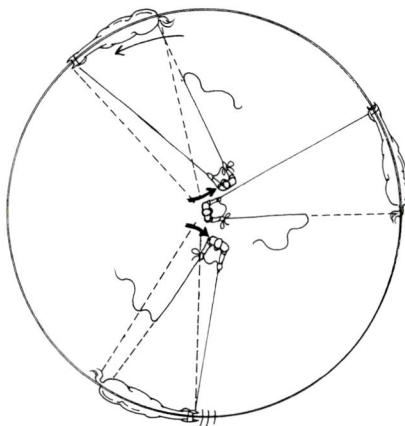

The "longeing triangle" —handler at center

Moving forward to slow horse down

3.11 You can adjust your horse's speed on the longe line by making minor adjustments in the position of your body. Here, if you step to the left, you can slow him down. If you step to the right, you can send him more forward.

KEY POINTS

- Think of longeing as riding and training from the ground. The same guidelines that are used under saddle—moving forward in rhythm, straightness, contact, balance, communication, and obedience.

- Keep longeing sessions brief.

- Basic equipment includes:

HORSE
- Longeing cavesson
- Side reins
- Boots or bandages

RIDER
- Gloves
- Longe whip
- Longe line

4

Let's Get
PERSONAL

Before you begin to do dressage, either for cross-training or as an end in itself, you should take a moment to evaluate yourself as a rider. You need the physical skills that enable you to give commands from an independent seat that is balanced, not only over your center of gravity, but over the horse's center as well. The center of gravity of the horse and the rider is located between the diaphragm and the pelvis. An independent seat means that you can give an aid, or use one part of your body, without causing unwanted motion elsewhere in your body (fig. 4.1).

You'll also need to understand and appreciate your own disposition as well as the nature and character of your partner. This is important because it will enable you to adapt your approach to training to your personality as well as your horse's temperament. For instance, the program for a hot-tempered rider with a flighty horse will be vastly different from the one with the same rider and a phlegmatic horse. And that program will also need to be modified for a passive rider on a lazy horse.

So first we'll discuss your position, and then we'll do an attitude check.

YOUR POSITION

THE IMPORTANCE OF A GOOD SEAT

Picture this. Two riders are getting ready to ask for the canter from the trot. Rider A sits in balance with her feet and legs under her center of gravity, her legs resting quietly on her horse's barrel in a "ready" position. In addition, her center of gravity is directly over that of her horse. Rider B leans behind the motion of the horse, with her legs banging noisily on his sides. Because her center of gravity is behind that of the horse, she sits heavily on his back and hangs onto the reins for balance.

Both riders give the same signal for the canter depart. Rider A's horse obediently steps off into a comfortable canter. Rider B's horse feels those furiously flying legs and just trots off faster. The more he runs, the more his rider loses her balance, until eventually they are so out of sync that Rider B has to stop (if she can) to get reorganized.

Both riders gave the same aid to canter. Why did Rider A succeed and Rider B end up with jostled kidneys? A good seat. All other

4.1 A–H In order to sit in balance, your feet need to be under your center of gravity: (A) Sitting in balance with feet under your center of gravity; (B) in balance even when stool is removed. (C) Sitting out of balance with feet ahead of your center of gravity; (D) out of balance and falling backward when chair is removed. (E) Rider in balance, feet under her center of gravity—dressage seat; (F) in balance, feet under her center of gravity—*jumping seat*. (G) Rider out of balance backward, feet ahead of her center of gravity; (H) out of balance forward, feet *behind* her center of gravity.

things being equal, the rider with the balanced, independent seat will be more effective in communicating her wishes to her horse. Giving signals from a poor or out-of-control position is a wasted effort. You need to sit correctly in order to be effective with your aids. (Which rider were you, by the way?)

A balanced seat looks different in the various riding disciplines. The dressage, Western, and saddle seat riders have long stirrups and sit with their shoulders, hips and heels in a plumb line. Because hunter seat, jumper, and combined training riders use shorter stirrups for jumping, they need to sit with the upper body more forward in order to be in balance. In all cases, however, the riders' shoulders are over their feet. So, good balance for you means balance for the particular type of riding you do. The one

4.2 A–D Balanced seat positions: (A) Hunter seat, (B) dressage, (C) saddle seat, (D) Western.

common requirement for effective riding in all disciplines, however, is having a balanced, independent seat (figs 4.2 and 4.3).

Let's look at how that can be accomplished.

DEVELOPING YOUR POSITION ON THE LONGE

As I explained earlier, an independent seat means that you can use one part of your body without affecting any other part. For example, you can use your right leg without jerking on your right rein. Or you can gently close your right hand without pulling backwards on the

rein. Or you can find your balance without hanging on your horse's mouth.

And since you can't purchase it in a tack store, you might ask how you go about acquiring one of these very desirable independent seats. One of the best ways I know of is for you to be longed on your horse. Now, I know the idea of giving up control of your animal to someone on the ground might not be your method of choice. But look at it this way. You actually get a break from having to control and guide your horse around while arguing with your uncooperative body at the same time. Make it your "quality time"—a golden opportunity to focus totally on yourself and your riding for a while.

The first thing you need is a suitable mount. If your horse is the type that gets hysterical when the tractor starts or takes advantage of you as soon as he feels you coming slightly unglued, it's probably a wise idea to borrow a quiet, generous horse. Find one with comfortable paces who'll go around and around without speeding up or slowing down and won't object to your gyrations.

Limit sessions to fifteen to twenty minutes because all that circling can be tiring for your horse. And be sure to change direction halfway through.

4.3 A–E In addition to being balanced over your own center, you need to be balanced over your horse's center in order to give effective aids and move in harmony with him: (A) Posting *with* the motion; (B) posting *behind* the motion; (C) posting *ahead* of the motion; (D) falling *behind* the motion; (E) falling *ahead* of the motion.

4.4 To prepare the saddle so that you can do exercises on the longe line without stirrups, first pull the buckle on the stirrup leather down a bit so you don't get a bruise on your leg.

4.5 Then cross the stirrups in front of the saddle.

Tack him up with a saddle, bridle, longeing cavesson, and side reins (see chapter 4). Twist the bridle's reins around each other and feed the throatlatch through them so they are out of the way (see photo 3.3 on page 17). Yes, you're going to be riding without reins! Contrary to popular belief, the reins are not your lifelines. You're going to have to learn how to balance yourself without hanging on them.

Adjust the side reins so they are short enough to prevent your horse's shoulder from popping out. The side reins will also help keep him in a rounder frame so his back will be easier to sit on when you trot and canter.

I like to do two kinds of exercises on the longe. The first is designed to develop an independent seat: you move one part of your body while paying close attention that the rest of your body stays still and in the correct position. The second kind of exercise gives you practice sitting perfectly during transitions—both transitions from one pace to another as well as lengthenings and shortenings within the same pace.

EXERCISES TO DEVELOP AN INDEPENDENT SEAT

Keep in mind that you want to make slow, deliberate movements while maintaining control of the parts of your body not directly involved in the exercise.

All these exercises start at the walk. Let the person doing the longeing be responsible for keeping the horse going and making any adjustments. You concentrate solely on yourself.

1. Remove the stirrups from the saddle or cross them over the front of the saddle (figs. 4.4 and 4.5). Place your legs underneath you in correct riding position with your shoulders, hips and feet in a plumb line with a low heel. Place your arms in riding position with your elbows bent at your sides and your hands softly closed around imaginary reins. Now slowly circle your head a few times to the right and then a few times to the left (figs. 4.6 to 4.9). Do a body check. Did your hands stay steady? Did your legs rest quietly on

4.6 Start circling your head by letting your ear drop down toward one shoulder as Lakewin Evans is doing here.

4.7 Continue circling your head slowly until your chin is pointed toward the sky. Do a position check. In this photo there's some tension in the rider's lower back. Also, her lower leg has slipped a bit forward. Her toe should stay directly under her knee.

4.8 As Lakewin continues to circle her head, her back is more relaxed and her lower leg is back in a better position.

4.9 Her back remains relaxed, but her lower leg is slipping forward ever so slightly.

4.10 Circle one arm at a time while the other arm stays in riding position. Always circle backward to open your chest and encourage your shoulders to stay down and back.

4.11 Keep your leg long and relaxed

your horse's sides? Did your upper body remain upright?

2. Arm circles: make slow, big circles with your arms. Always circle backwards so you open your chest. Alternate one arm and then the other, controlling the arm throughout the entire arc of the circle (figs. 4.10 to 4.12). While doing so, run through your checklist to see if the rest of your body stays quiet and controlled.

3. Shoulder rolls: rotate each shoulder up, back and down in the same circling action that you did with your arms (figs. 4.13 and 4.14).

4.12 Release any tension in your shoulders—both the "riding position" arm and the circling arm.

4.13 Next, circle your shoulders only. Drop the fingers of one hand loosely behind your leg. As you circle each shoulder, think, *Up, back, down.*

4.14 Lakewin's upper body looks good here, but her lower leg could be more relaxed.

4.15 The starting position for the waist twist should have your shoulder, hip, and heel in a straight line. Your arms should be out to the sides with palms facing down.

4.16 Twist to each side from the waist, following your back arm with your eyes.

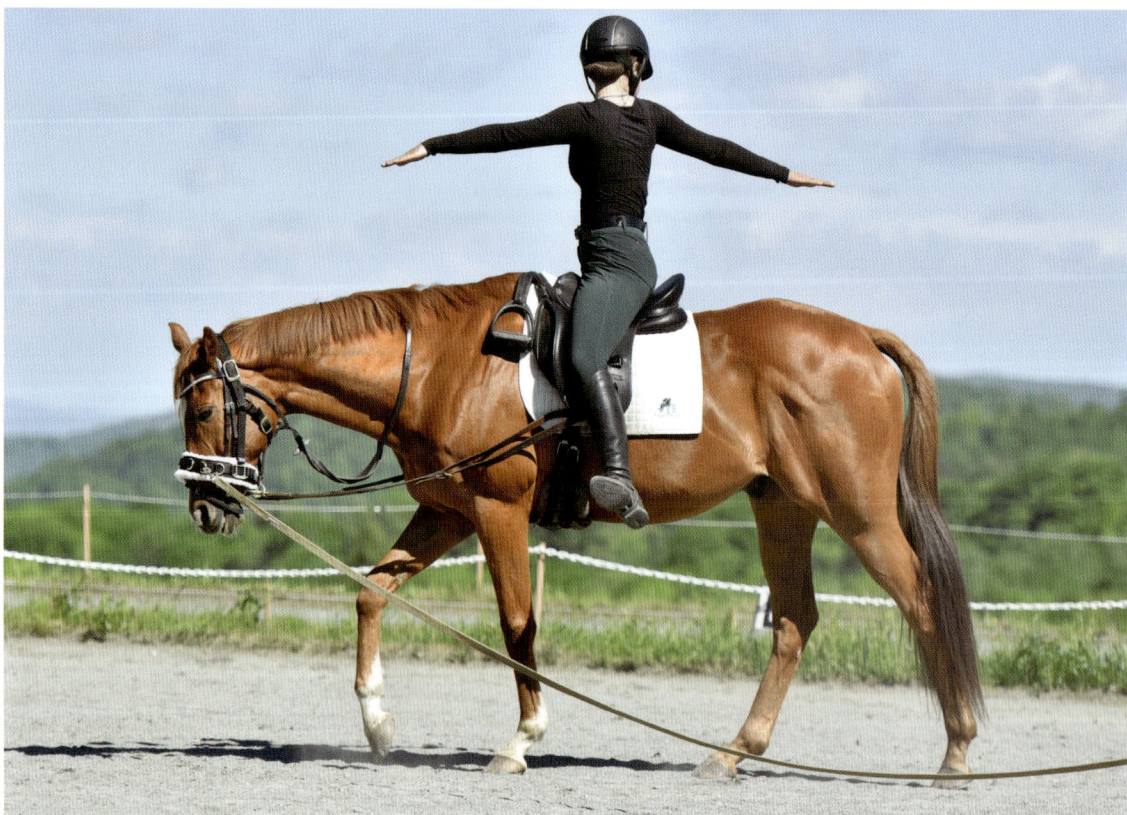

4.17 Slowly twist in the other direction. Here, Lakewin's back arm has dropped slightly. Also, her left toe is turned out, showing that she's looking for balance by gripping with the back of her calf.

4.18 For windmills, stretch both arms straight up over your head with palms facing each other. Keep your elbows beside your ears.

4.19 Slowly lower both arms straight out to the sides.

4. Waist twists: place both arms straight out to the sides and slowly twist your torso left and right. Keep your hips square and your legs still (figs. 4.15 to 4.17).

5. Windmills: stretch both arms straight up over your head, then lower them until they are straight out to the side. Then return to riding position as if holding the reins (figs. 4.18 to 4.20).

6. Scissors: stretch one leg straight forward and one straight back. Point your toes and lock your knees. Then very slowly alternate the position of your legs as if they were a pair of scissors. Keep your hips and torso square (figs. 4.21 to 4.23).

4.20 Return your hands to riding position. Lakewin's upper body is tipped a little forward, and her lower leg has moved a little too far back.

4.21 To do the scissors, straighten your legs and point your toes like a ballet dancer. When your left leg is forward, your right leg is back.

4.22 Very slowly change the position of your legs. Make sure your hips and shoulders stay square. Lakewin should continue looking ahead, between her horse's ears.

4.23 If you feel your body twisting, hold on to the front of the saddle with your outside hand to steady yourself.

4.24 When practicing legs away, sit squarely and symmetrically with equal weight on both seat bones.

4.25 Keep your legs in riding position but lift them away from the saddle so you're balanced on your seat bones.

7. Legs away: put your legs in riding position, then lift your legs off the saddle from your hips so that you're balanced on your seat bones. Be sure not to lean back or round your shoulders (figs. 4.24 and 4.25).

Once you're feeling pretty secure about the exercises, try them in trot and canter. Gulp!

If you momentarily lose your balance, hold onto the front of the saddle and pull yourself down into it until you feel secure again. Then put your hands back in riding position and carry on (fig. 4.26).

4.26 If you feel like you're losing your balance during any of the exercises, hold on to the front of the saddle until you feel secure again. When the particular exercise you're doing gives you a choice, use your outside hand, as this will make it easier to sit with your inside shoulder back so that it is parallel with your horse's inside shoulder as he circles.

MAINTAINING BALANCE DURING TRANSITIONS

Now that we've looked at exercises that will help you develop an independent seat, let's look at the second type of exercise I like to do on the longe: sitting quietly and in perfect balance while the horse is asked to do transitions. Practice transitions from one pace to another as well as lengthenings and shortenings within a pace. Ask the person longeing you for feedback during these transitions. Do your hands stay steady? Do your legs remain softly in contact with your horse's sides? Does your body stay centered or do you lean backward, forward, or sideways?

Transitions on the longe line will teach you to "go with" your horse rather than getting ahead of him or being left behind. You'll be developing some muscle memory for sitting quietly and elegantly, and then you can conjure up that feeling again when you're back in control.

DEVELOPING YOUR POSITION OFF THE LONGE

If being longed is not a viable option because you lack a suitable horse or someone to longe you, you can still pick away at your position faults on your own. It takes approximately three weeks to develop a habit. And that goes for a good habit as well as a bad one. So devote some time each day to working on the areas of your body that need attention.

Since I know I can only concentrate fully on one thing at a time, I work on my position during the first ten minutes of my ride as well as each time I give my horse a break during a training session. During those moments I focus totally on correcting my position. I don't concern myself at all with how the horse is going.

Often I do what I call "extremes." I exaggerate the correction for a few seconds at a time. Then I relax for a bit and repeat the exaggerated correction. Eventually, I let my body find the happy medium.

Let me explain. I had a very difficult time getting my legs underneath me when I started riding dressage. I rode with my legs too forward, my heels jammed down, and my toes stuck out. In order to correct this, each day when I first got on I dropped my stirrups and alternately

4.27 Open your hip joints and stretch your legs as far back as possible.

swung each leg as far back as possible from my hips—much too far back for a good position. Then, I let my legs settle around the horse's barrel several inches behind the perpendicular. When I got to the point that my legs wanted to stay too far back, I stopped working on the exercise and just let them settle into the correct position (figs. 4.27 to 4.29).

One of my students, Joyce, is now a beautiful rider, but that wasn't always the case. She tried so hard to make her position look picture perfect that the effort made her body stiff and rigid. Joyce needed to go to "extremes" to loosen up. We started by focusing on her wrists. She spent time every day making circles with her wrists to unlock them. I'd even see her walking through the barn developing muscle memory by keeping her hands in riding position while softly bobbling her wrists.

Within a few weeks, it became natural for her to ride with relaxed wrists. We systematically worked on the tight parts of her body in this way until she was eventually able to sit in a gracefully controlled way rather than with tension.

So attack your position challenges one at a time by concentrating on "extremes" for several minutes each day. If you tend to lean too far forward, lean too far back. If your heels are up, push them down as far as you can. If your entire arm is too straight and rigid, bend your elbows and hold them back behind your torso. If you tend to be stiff, sit sloppily and loosely instead. If you hunch over, stretch up and try to make yourself four inches taller than you really are. Remember to hold your "extremes" for just a

4.28 Allow your legs to settle around your horse's barrel in this "too-far-back" position.

4.29 Then let gravity take over so that your lower leg comes forward until your toe is directly under your knee.

few seconds and then relax before repeating the exercise. Be creative and play with "extremes" and watch your position improve one piece at a time.

I'd like to mention one other thing at this point about the position of your upper body in the canter. This will be particularly relevant for those of you who want to pursue your dressage education a bit further into the material covered in Stages Three and Four.

It's vital that you learn to sit back in the canter. At the basic levels, if you rock your upper body back so that your seat comes forward with every stride, you'll encourage your horse's hind legs to come more under his body. Then later on, when you are working on self-carriage and the elevation of your horse's forehand, you'll need to sit like this so that your upper body doesn't weight his front end excessively.

To understand the correct placement of your upper body, first halt and imagine a plumb line dropping down from your ear. If you're sitting absolutely straight, that plumb line passes through your shoulder, hip, and heel. I want you to think that no matter where your horse is in his canter stride, your shoulders can never come in front of that plumb line. So during one bound of the canter, your upper body can only rock behind the vertical and then up to the vertical. It never comes in front of that plumb line (figs. 4.30 and 4.31).

4.30 Compare the upper body positions of the two pictures of Bekki at the canter on this page. In the top photo, Bekki's upper body is rocking back behind the vertical, and as a result, her seat comes forward.

4.31 In the second photo, Bekki's upper body is coming in front of the vertical and her seat looks like it's pushing her horse's hind legs backward.

YOUR ATTITUDE DETERMINES YOUR ALTITUDE

In order to invite your horse to dance with you, it's important to examine your attitude objectively. This includes your attitude toward yourself as well as toward your horse. Since I covered this extensively in my book *That Winning Feeling! Program Your Mind for Peak Performance,* I'll just touch on some of the major points in this book.

As you analyze your attitude, ask yourself if you fall into that group of riders who beat themselves up every day. If so, your internal dialogue might sound something like this: "I'm an idiot. When am I ever going to learn how to do this without pulling on my horse's mouth? I'm ruining my horse. I should give him to a professional to ride because he'll never amount to anything with me."

If this sounds like you, you'll need to make some major changes in your self-talk. Denis Waitley, a sports psychologist, says, "It's important for you to realize that the greatest conversation you have every day is the one you have with yourself. So be sure to do it with all due respect."

I know this positive self-talk will be quite a challenge for some of you because we're all raised to be humble. I'm not saying you have to walk around sounding arrogant, but it doesn't hurt to speak highly of yourself to yourself. Since your self-image is always listening to and believing what you say about yourself, all self-criticism is essentially a complete waste of time and counterproductive to training. What good is it going to do to berate yourself with negative comments that only destroy your confidence?

You may not think you see yourself as negative and self-critical. But let's try an experiment and see. For the next twenty-four hours speak to yourself in a positive way only. Keep a note pad handy so you can jot down any self-criticism that slips out, including so-called constructive criticism.

Don't make jokes about yourself such as, "I have a terrible memory. I'd probably forget my head if it weren't attached." The subconscious doesn't have a sense of humor, and if you make fun of yourself, your humorless subconscious mind will simply see what you say as your goal. It's a good idea to ask a friend to keep an eye on you, because chances are you're not even aware of how often you put yourself down. Are you surprised to see how critical you are of yourself?

Okay. You're convinced that sometimes you can be pretty hard on yourself, but you feel embarrassed and self-conscious tooting your own horn. Well, if that's an issue for you, you're just going to have to learn how to lie!

I started lying back in the 1970s when I was showing my crazy Thoroughbred. I used to run around telling everybody who'd listen, "I love to compete!" The truth was, however, that I was actually sick to my stomach. People would ask me if I ever got nervous and I'd proclaim, "No, I never get nervous. In fact, I get a little concerned if I don't have a little extra adrenalin because you need that edge to really do well." (Lie, lie, lie!)

4.32 You need to build the horse's self-esteem. You want him to believe that he can do absolutely everything fabulously!

My subconscious didn't know or care that I was lying. It simply did what it could to help validate my statements. And, amazingly, I eventually loved to compete. My new attitude toward competition became as much a part of my life as my old show nerves had been.

BUILDING SELF-ESTEEM IN HORSE AND RIDER

Years ago I remember bringing a very insecure Zapatero, my Olympic candidate, to Robert Dover for training. Robert Dover, World and Olympic Games Bronze medalist in dressage, is one of our country's most successful and illustrious trainers. Robert rode "Z" and immediately felt how sensitive he was. His comment was, "You need to build this horse's self-esteem.

You want him to believe that he can do absolutely everything fabulously." (fig. 4.32.)

This attitude goes for riders as well.

Now, I realize that sometimes it's a real challenge to stay confident and poised in the face of screaming instructors who belittle and undermine your efforts. I'm not sure why this has become an accepted method of instruction. I've never known sarcasm and shouting at a student to promote understanding. Yet sometimes this is what we're exposed to in the quest for knowledge.

So be sure to take good care of yourself. Ideally, you should find an instructor who will work with you in an atmosphere of mutual respect. If this is impossible, protect yourself emotionally by not taking the criticism personally. Ignore the rudeness (which is actually a reflection of the teacher, not the student) and salvage the information.

Build your self-esteem and your confidence in your abilities. The way to do this is to practice being positive about yourself. Create a mental image of yourself as a patient, capable, brave rider.

If you're obsessing about a potential disaster, visualize the scenario in great detail. But then do some "coping rehearsals" by continuing to play your mental videotape until you see a successful resolution to the situation. Believe that you can handle whatever comes up. Let's look at an example of how this would work.

It's early spring and you're getting ready to take your four-year-old Thoroughbred to his first show. You're really excited all the way up until the time that you hear the weather forecast the day before the show. There's a cold front coming in overnight. The temperature is going to drop twenty-five degrees, the wind will gust up to thirty miles per hour AND your first class is at 7:45 A.M. You think to yourself, "I'm gonna get killed!"

Instead, do "coping rehearsals" several times the night before (fig. 4.33). "See" the scene unfolding in your mind's eye, but be sure it ends on a positive note. You arrive at the showgrounds. The atmosphere is electric. Your horse is very fresh, and his tail is stuck straight up in the air as you head to the warm-up area. He's pretty tight and you feel like you're sitting on a time bomb. He lets out a few bucks, and you see yourself confidently remaining in perfect balance. You're not the least bit unseated by his antics. Your heart rate stays slow and your breathing is deep and regular. After working him for ten minutes, he begins to settle down and becomes attentive and obedient. You see yourself entering the ring and having the performance of your life!

Do you think this is easier said than done? Then start today to reprogram your mind so the new, confident you emerges automatically. But you can't use willpower or iron-jawed determination to achieve this, because the part of your mind that really controls your actions is the subconscious, and in a struggle between the conscious and subconscious mind, the subconscious always prevails. So we are going to direct our efforts toward the subconscious.

4.33 Don't panic when you hear the weather forecast. Instead, "see" yourself entering the arena and having the performance of your life!

Here's your assignment. First, on the left side of a piece of paper, write down a list of all the negative things you believe to be true about your riding, but that you'd like to change. For instance, "I get nervous riding in front of others," "I can't sit the trot," "I always lean to the right," or "My horse takes advantage of me by wheeling around when he sees something scary."

Next, on the right side of the paper, write a replacement for each statement. Word your substitute sentences in the present tense as if you already possess the quality you desire. And use a positive rather than a negative statement. Your paper might look something like this:

I get nervous riding.	I am very focused and relaxed when I ride in front of others.
I can't sit the trot.	I sit deeply and in harmony with my horse in the trot.
I always lean to the right.	I always sit centered and in balance.
My horse takes advantage of me by wheeling around when he sees something different.	My horse is confident, obedient, and submissive even when he sees something that scares him.

Once your list is complete, set aside time at least once a day where you can sit quietly and be uninterrupted for fifteen minutes. Close your eyes and take a few deep breaths. With each breath, feel yourself floating deeper and deeper into relaxation.

Now visualize a computer screen in your mind's eye. You'll be reprogramming yourself by replacing one negative statement at a time with a new, positive affirmation about yourself and your riding skills. Type in one of your negative statements. See the letters as they appear one by one on the screen. For instance, type in "I am a timid rider." Now look at the words and see yourself pressing the button that says "Delete." As you touch the button, the words vanish forever, not only from the screen, but also from your memory. They are no longer a part of you.

Now you are ready for reprogramming. Type in your replacement statement in capital letters. For instance, "I AM CONFIDENT AND BRAVE." Look at the words, and then see yourself pressing the button marked "Save." These are your new instructions to yourself, and they're now stored in your subconscious mind (fig. 4.34).

YOUR ATTITUDE TOWARD YOUR HORSE

By the way, how's your attitude toward your horse? Are you one of those riders who blames the horse when things go wrong?

For example, recently I worked with a green horse and green rider combination. Both of them were struggling with their own lack of balance so neither one could help the other. The woman hadn't ridden for several years and was out of practice as well as out of shape. The horse was a sensitive four-year-old mare who was just barely learning how to balance herself with a rider's weight on her back. All went well in the walk, but every time she was asked to trot, the mare would hop into the canter. The woman's frustrated comment was, "She keeps doing that to me."

I explained that the horse wasn't doing anything to her. The poor horse couldn't trot in a regular rhythm because the rider didn't have an independent seat. During the posting trot, she was using the reins to pull herself up out of the saddle. Since the mare's rhythm and freedom of movement in the trot were being restricted during every stride, she found it easier to hop into the canter.

Another rider I know was upset because her horse was running in the canter and pulling her arms out of their sockets. I had to explain to her that it takes two to pull—so who's hanging on to whom? It took me some time to convince her that she was compounding his balance problem because she was leaning too far forward and hanging on his mouth. Because his hind legs were so far out behind him, it was impossible for him to balance himself. This horse was simply not in a position to slow down. Despite what his rider thought, he was not being disobedient. It wasn't that he "wouldn't," but that he "couldn't."

There's also the rider who is looking for the quick fix—the magic formula. You probably know the type. She jumps from instructor to instructor and from clinic to clinic looking for the "key." Sometimes she thinks the "key" might be a special exercise. Sometimes it's a different bit, bigger spurs, or some sort of training gadget. Or perhaps the answer is to longe her horse for an hour until he's so exhausted that he's tractable.

This instant gratification approach to training is unrealistic and always leads to frustration. This rider needs to follow a systematic program and be content with a little bit of progress each day. She'll actually be better off and will enjoy the process a whole lot more by thinking of

4.34 Reprogram your "mental computer." Replace your negative thoughts with positive ones.

training in terms of months and years rather than days and weeks.

Most distressing to me is the rider who vents her emotional problems on her horse. Years ago at a clinic I taught a woman who was riding an extremely sensitive ex-racehorse. This mare was very tense and the rider was using this as an excuse to abuse and bully her. I tried to appeal to this rider with logic, saying that since the mare was so nervous to begin with, any strong punishment would only make her worse. To that she replied, "....but it makes me feel better." I have to say it's the one and only time I gave up on a student. My comment was, "Then I can't help you," and I left.

Most riders, on the other hand, fall into the category of true horsemen—they are compassionate riders who really love their animals. A good example of the right attitude is the following story about Marcia Kulak, a three-day event rider. Marcia had grown up dreaming of one day being able to represent her country in international competition, and she had worked diligently for a lifetime to make her dream a reality.

Just prior to the 1992 Olympics in Barcelona, Marcia and her horse Chagall were short-listed for the United States team. The final selection of the team members was to be made at the Savernake Forest Horse Trials in England. Earlier in the week before the competition, Marcia noticed that Chagall's left front leg was slightly filled. Although he was sound and would have most probably passed the veterinary inspection before competition, she decided to withdraw. She wouldn't let ambition color her judgment when it came to her horse's health. She might have achieved her personal goal of riding in the Olympics, but there was no way she'd even consider doing that if there were a risk that she'd return home without her best friend intact.

We also have my friend, dressage team member Sue Blinks, whose love and concern for the welfare of her horses precedes all else. I've always said if I died and were reincarnated as a horse, I'd want to be in Sue's barn. Sue, like Marcia, is also very competitive, with high goals, and is very protective of her animals. She never lets ego or ambition affect her training decisions.

Sue found her young horse, Flim Flam, in Germany as a three-year-old. Flim is a real talent and as they have progressed through the dressage levels, they often have been seen in the winner's circle with record-breaking high scores. Because of Flim's incredible talent and athleticism,

ambitious trainers have often tried to persuade Sue to push his training along at a faster rate.

Despite substantial outside pressure and the lure of gold medals, Sue sticks to her conviction that dressage is a process and takes time. She believes that it's both physically and mentally detrimental to demand more of a horse than he's been prepared for systematically, and she just won't sacrifice her animals. As I'm sure you can imagine, her horses adore her and turn themselves inside out to please her.

ATTITUDE TOWARD TRAINING

By the way, how do you stack up as a trainer? Patient, creative trainers often see schooling as a big jigsaw puzzle. They first look on the cover of the puzzle box to see what the final picture should look like. And then they content themselves with filling in the blanks one piece at a time. In the beginning the final picture isn't even recognizable. But piece by piece it begins to take shape (fig. 4.35).

For instance, let's say you get a thoroughbred off the track to reschool as a potential combined training horse. Thoroughbreds are born to gallop and this particular horse is very bold. So the training for the cross-country and stadium jumping phases comes easily to him and progresses relatively smoothly.

His performance in the dressage phase of a combined training event, however, is sadly lacking. Because of his background as a racehorse, his body is tense and his back is stiff. One of the consequences is that the quality of his trot

4.35 Patient, creative trainers often see schooling as a big jigsaw puzzle. They fill in the blanks one piece at a time.

suffers by becoming ground bound. He hurries along, lifting one diagonal pair of legs and putting them back down on the ground before lifting the other diagonal pair. Consequently, there is little, if any, period of suspension. And it's the period of suspension that makes a trot expressive and pretty to watch.

So you need to work on this one piece of the puzzle before tackling anything else. In chapter 13 on troubleshooting, I'll explain how to do this in depth. But for now, in a nutshell, the process of improving his trot, which can take anywhere from several weeks to several months, looks something like this:

1. Slow the speed of the trot to reduce tension.

2. Relax your horse's body by asking him to stretch his head and neck forward and down.

3. Add energy back into the trot with the goal of longer rather than faster steps.

4. If tension builds or the strides get quick, slow down again.

How long does it take to complete the puzzle? It all depends on your horse. Horses hardly ever progress according to human timetables. They develop at their own rate and will excel at some movements but need more time for others.

The whole jigsaw puzzle process should be fun and rewarding. Since you've made a conscious decision to be patient, there's less anxiety than if you felt pressured to fix everything in one day. Training progresses more or less smoothly because you are allowing yourself the luxury of time to develop your horse's understanding of a movement as well as his strength so he can perform it easily.

Remember that no matter how hard you try to get everything right, you're going to make mistakes. Rather than berating yourself, think of these mistakes as opportunities to develop your abilities as a rider and trainer. If everything always went smoothly, you'd never have a chance to refine your skills. So rather than getting frustrated when your horse keeps picking up the wrong canter lead, think how lucky you are that his mistakes give you the chance to learn how to prepare him better for the transitions.

In addition, you have a built-in instructor. Your horse gives you direct and immediate feedback on your progress as a trainer. His resistance decreases proportionately as your skill develops.

Enjoy the process of figuring out how to explain to your horse that you'd like him to do things differently. See your stumbling blocks as stepping stones and you'll have fun with all phases of his development. Each small change in your horse's behavior is proof that you're progressing with him both mentally and physically. You experience not only greater communication and cooperation but also improved strength and athletic ability.

KEY POINTS

- In order to effectively communicate with your horse, you need a balanced, independent seat.

- Riding on the longe line is the best way to develop an independent seat.

- Your attitude toward yourself and your horse will determine not only how far you go but how much you enjoy the journey.

- Mental training exercises can have a tremendous impact on your riding skillset.

- No one will ever care about your horse's welfare as much as you do. He depends on you to make the right choices for his well-being.

- You'll never be discouraged or bored if you see training as an intriguing puzzle and yourself as the problem solver.

STAGE ONE

DRESSAGE 101

Now that you have started your horse on the longe line, it's time to address his basic education under saddle. I'm assuming your horse is either young, green, or uneducated in dressage, but that he's at least able to be ridden quietly in the walk, trot and canter. The material that follows is not for the totally green horse, although many of these things do apply to him.

In Stage One: Dressage 101, (chapters 5, 6, and 7), I'll be explaining the work that is the foundation for everything you do with your horse. This includes the concepts of **Forward, Straight, and Rhythm (the Basics), the Paces and Gaits,** as well as **Contact**. As you progress to later stages of training, you'll discover that if you're having difficulty with a particular movement or exercise, the cause of the problem is almost always found as a fault in the Basics. So that is where you need to search for the answers to your training dilemmas.

Once you've mastered the Basics plus the movements in Stage Two: Nuts and Bolts (chapters 8, 9, 10, 11 and 12), you'll have an obedient horse who is fun to ride. You might decide that Stages One and Two are all you need. But if you do decide to go on to Stage Three: The Professionals' Secret and Stage Four: Fancy Stuff, it will be an easy progression because you already will have laid the proper groundwork for more advanced schooling.

5

The ABCs of Dressage
FORWARD and STRAIGHT

No matter what style of riding you prefer, your horse needs to move in a **forward** and **straight** manner. These two basic rules, together with **rhythm,** are the foundation for all correct work in every riding discipline. (I'll discuss rhythm at length, in chapter 6.).

All riders need to be concerned with straightness. When a horse isn't moving straight, one hind leg continually carries a greater share of the weight. As a result he can become sore. This soreness can be expressed in a variety of ways including a painful back, lameness, resistance such as throwing his head up in the air, or even behavior problems like bucking and rearing.

You should place just as high a priority on teaching your horse to go forward as you do on making him straight. In this chapter I'm going to discuss two aspects of "forward riding." The first is that your horse *physically* goes forward over the ground and the second is that he *mentally* goes forward in response to refined driving aids.

This is where your horse's education must begin.

> *"One of the most fundamental rules of equitation is: straighten your horse and ride him forward."*
>
> **Alois Podhajsky, former Director of the Spanish Riding School in Vienna, in his book *The Complete Training of Horse and Rider***

• • • • •

FORWARD

In dressage the word "forward" refers to the direction the horse moves over the ground. In other words, your horse moves forward as opposed to moving sideways. Forward designates where the horse goes, not how he gets there. Expressions such as "needs energy," "needs a livelier tempo," "needs longer strides," and "needs to cover more ground" explain how the horse should proceed in a forward direction.

Although physically moving forward over the ground is part of going forward, I also want you to consider the mental aspect of going forward.

Specifically, it is equally important that your horse *thinks* forward. If your horse is "thinking forward," he will react immediately to the lightest of leg aids. In "rider speak" we call it "hot off" or "in front of" your leg.

Keep in mind that a horse can actually go forward over the ground quite well and still not be thinking forward. I've ridden many Thoroughbreds who appear to an observer to be going forward with energy but are, in fact, rather dull to the driving aids.

To check to see if your horse is thinking forward, lightly close your legs. If he reacts immediately and enthusiastically to a feather-light squeeze, you're in business. If he doesn't, don't adjust your aid by repeating it or making it stronger to get a response. Instead, go through the process described in the next few pages of putting him in front of your leg.

Maybe you're skeptical that your horse will ever be hot off your leg. After all, you've had him a long time, and he's a pretty lazy fellow. You've always had to work hard to get him going. But

believe me, it is not only possible, but it is also essential that you train him to do this. To prove to yourself that you can train your horse to respond to light leg aids, just watch what he does on a summer's day when the flies are out.

At the mere touch of a bug on your horse's side, he flicks it off with his tail. Now, if your "thick-skinned" friend is sensitive enough to feel a fly on his side, then he ought to be able to feel subtle leg aids if you take the time to school him to react to them (fig. 5.1).

PUTTING YOUR HORSE IN FRONT OF YOUR LEG

To put the horse in front of your leg, follow this simple guide. If you give a light leg aid and your horse eagerly responds by going forward, reward him. The reward encourages him to react the same way the next time you give a leg aid. On the other hand, if you give a leg aid and your horse doesn't answer at all, or responds in a sluggish way, punish him. (I'll discuss how in a moment.)

5.1 Your equine partner is sensitive enough to feel a fly on his side, so he ought to be able to feel subtle leg aids.

The punishment will motivate him to change his response the next time you give an aid.

First, ask your horse to go forward in a transition from walk to trot by closing both of your legs *very* lightly on his sides. If he doesn't respond (and he probably won't if you're used to giving strong leg aids), punish him by sharply sending him forward. Don't worry if your horse breaks into the canter when you punish him. The point is that he must go *forward* even if he overreacts.

Before you actually punish your horse, take a moment to consider his temperament. The easygoing fellow might need a few taps with the whip or several sharp kicks to send him forward, but you should modify the severity of the punishment for the sensitive soul. The point is not to terrorize the animal but to get a clearly forward, hot-off-the-leg reaction.

Also, if your horse is the type that bucks when you use the whip, it's better to kick him instead. First of all, you don't want to get bucked off. And secondly, if he's bucking, he's obviously not going forward and he's missed the point of the punishment.

Once you've chased him forward, it's vital that you go back to what you were doing and retest with a light leg aid. If he responds electrically by immediately going forward into an energetic trot when you retest, praise generously. At this point it's still okay if he breaks into the canter when you do the retest—later on you can refine the aid and explain to him that you want him just to trot. But for the moment *any* forward reaction is desirable. If his reaction to your legs is "better," but not a hundred percent wholeheartedly

5.2 What I want you to do is whisper with your aids and have your horse shout his answer—not the other way around.

forward, repeat the whole process from the beginning until he does it right.

I can't emphasize enough that if you forget to do the retest, he'll only become more dull to the aids than he already is because you will have taught him to go forward only when he feels the whip or a good kick, rather than when he feels a light aid.

MAINTAINING HIS ENERGY BY HIMSELF

Make sure you don't fall into the trap of "helping" your horse to go forward by using your legs every stride. Unless you're giving a specific aid, your legs should lie quietly on the horse's sides. If you use your legs constantly, you dull the horse's reaction to your legs. You end up doing all the work, and your horse pays little attention to your efforts. What I want you to do is *whisper* with your aids and have your horse *shout* his answer rather than the other way around (fig. 5.2).

5.3 Constant leg aids are annoying to your horse. He will either become cranky or tune you out altogether.

Many riders are not even aware how much they "help" their horses to go forward. Others erroneously think that it's their job to keep their horses active. In the walk, these riders use alternate leg aids. In the posting trot, they squeeze each time they sit. And in the canter, they squeeze once during each stride. This is wrong. Your horse needs to maintain the momentum and liveliness of his gait all by himself.

Using your legs a lot really backfires on you. As I said earlier, if you use your legs repetitively to keep your horse going, you use yourself up and have no strength left to give other signals to your horse. Plus, constant leg aids are annoying to your horse, and he either becomes cranky or tunes you out altogether (fig. 5.3).

Here's a simple test you can do to see if you're "helping" your horse too much. First, ask your horse to walk forward energetically. Then, take your legs completely away from his sides so you don't accidentally "cheat" and give a little nudge with your legs here and there. Now notice how long it takes before your horse starts to slow down. And how long does it take before he stops completely? The length of time it takes for either of these things to happen gives you a pretty good idea of just how hard you're working to keep him going.

Make up your mind that your horse must maintain his activity in each gait on his own. Then do the following to explain the new rules to him.

After asking your horse to go forward in the walk, don't use your legs at all. The moment your horse slows down, chase him forward by kicking or tapping him with the whip as you did when you were putting him in front of your leg earlier. Re-establish the walk, and repeat the whole process. As long as your horse continues to march forward energetically on his own, praise him with your voice enthusiastically while he's walking. As soon as he slows down even a fraction, chase him forward again.

Go through the exact same procedure in the trot and in the canter.

I realize that the punishment might seem severe both in this exercise and when you're putting your horse in front of your leg. But the bottom line is that eventually you will have a happier horse. It's a lot more pleasant for both of you when you can use your legs lightly to give signals rather than grinding, pushing and squeezing every stride.

STRAIGHTNESS

Straightness refers to both the position of the horse's legs and the alignment of his spine. When a horse's legs are straight (I'll refer to this as **leg-straightness**), his hind feet follow in the exact same tracks as those made by the front feet. This is true whether he's on a straight line or a curved line.

When his spine is straight (I'll refer to this as **axis-straightness**), it overlaps his line of travel. His spine corresponds to whatever line he's on, whether it's straight or curving. Axis-straightness on lines such as the long side of an arena, the trail, or the approach to a jump means that the horse's shoulders are directly in front of his hindquarters, while axis-straightness on circles, corners, and curved lines means the horse's spine is bent accordingly (fig. 5.4).

If you look at a straight horse coming toward you while you're on the ground, you see only the two front legs, the base of his neck is centered in the middle of level shoulders, and his nose is in the middle of his chest. If you look at the same horse going away from you, you see only the two hind legs and the top of his tail in the middle of his hips. In either case, if you see more than two legs, the horse is crooked (fig. 5.5).

Some people believe that a horse's inherent crookedness is a result of his position in the womb. Others feel that carrying the rider's weight causes a horse to struggle with his balance and become crooked. And there's always the issue of an asymmetrical rider contributing to crookedness.

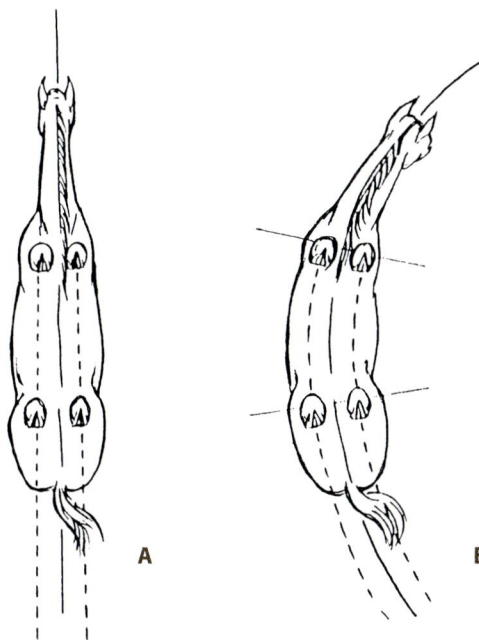

5.4 A & B Straightness: The horse's hind feet follow in the tracks of the forelegs on a straight line (A) and on a curve, which requires bending (B).

5.5 A & B Axis straight and leg straight, front view (A) and rear view (B).

5.6 Sitting in balance: a vertical line can be drawn through the rider's head, hip, and foot, and the pelvis vertical.

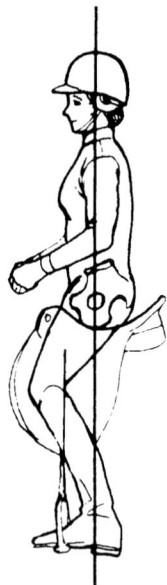

5.7 A & B Draw an imaginary line down the midline of your saddle from the pommel in the front to the cantle at the back. Is your body equally on both sides of the line? A straight and even rider has hips even, shoulders level, and head balanced (A). A crooked rider has her hips one way and shoulders the other (B).

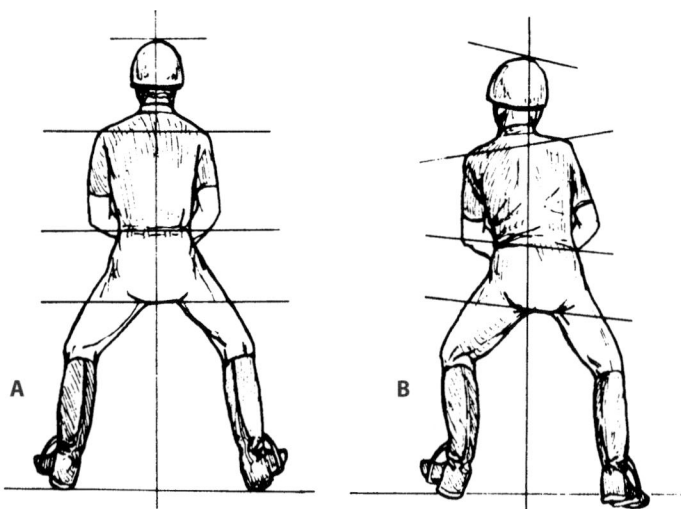

A

B

Whatever the reason for the crookedness, you will have to work on making your horse straight every single day in training. This holds true regardless of whether you're just starting out or whether your horse has reached the highest levels of dressage schooling. Striving for straightness is a continuous, on-going process. Your horse will always want to become crooked and you'll constantly need to take measures to keep him straight, or correct him when he does become crooked.

Making and keeping your horse straight is a priority. Your horse needs to use both of his hind legs equally so the energy that starts in his hindquarters can be transmitted over his back to his forehand—this is the **connection** our experts spoke about in Chapter Two. When your horse is straight and connected, the energy is automatically recycled back to his hind legs. It ends up being self-perpetuating, like a flywheel turning by itself. However, if your horse is crooked, the energy leaks out, and you constantly have to work at keeping the "rpms" up.

The fact that we as riders are not symmetrical either complicates the task of making our horses straight. Most of us have one hand that is stronger than the other. If you ask your horse to halt and you use your right hand more strongly than your left hand, you'll make his hindquarters move over to the left and he'll become crooked.

We also don't always sit absolutely straight and centered over the middle of a horse's back (fig. 5.6). To check if you're sitting straight and centered, draw an imaginary line down the midline of your saddle from the pommel in the front to the cantle at the back. Is half of your body on either side of the line? If you lean to the right, let's say, your horse will feel this and try to compensate for your crookedness by stepping in that direction with his right hind leg (fig. 5.7).

RIDER-CREATED CROOKEDNESS

Often, riders make horses crooked by bending the animals' necks too much to the inside or the outside of the line they're following. The photos on the next page illustrate the differences between straight and crooked on both lines and circles.

In the first photo (fig. 5.8), Bekki is bending Maeve's neck too much to the **inside** (right) while riding on a straight line. The horse's neck is bent too much to the inside because Bekki is using too much inside rein without supporting enough with the outside rein.

The result is that the horse's spine doesn't correspond to the line she's on—her shoulders are falling out toward the rail, her haunches are drifting in toward the center of the ring, and her hind feet can't follow the tracks of her front feet.

Photo 5.9 shows Bekki bending Maeve's neck too much to the **outside** (left) while on a straight

5.8 Maeve is not axis-straight because her spine does not overlap her line of travel. Her neck is bent too much toward the inside of the ring because Bekki is using too much inside rein without an equally supporting outside rein.

5.9 Once again Maeve's spine isn't overlapping the track. But this time Bekki has used too much *outside* rein without a complementary influence of the inside rein.

line. As a result, the mare's shoulders fall in toward the center of the ring and her hindquarters drift out toward the rail. Once again, the horse's spine doesn't correspond to the line she's on and her hind feet don't follow the tracks of her front feet.

In the next photos, 5.10 and 5.11, the rider is keeping her horse straight by having an equal and complementary influence of the two reins. To correct the mistake in photo 5.8, which shows too much bend in the horse's neck to the inside, she takes a firmer feel on the outside rein and softens the contact on the inside rein.

To correct the mistake in photo 5.9, which shows too much bend in the neck to the outside, Bekki relaxes the outside rein and gives some soft squeezes on the inside rein to reposition the horse's head so that it is in the middle of her chest.

Photo 5.12 shows the same fault as photo 5.8, but here the mare is going left on a circle. Her neck is bent too much to the inside (left) of the circle because the rider is not coordinating her reins correctly. Consequently, the horse's spine doesn't correspond to the arc of the circle—her shoulders and front feet fall to the right. Because

5.10 Maeve's entire spine from poll to tail is absolutely straight, and her neck is lined up directly in front of the rest of her spine.

5.11 Maeve is straight in every sense of the word! She is leg-straight, as well as axis-straight.

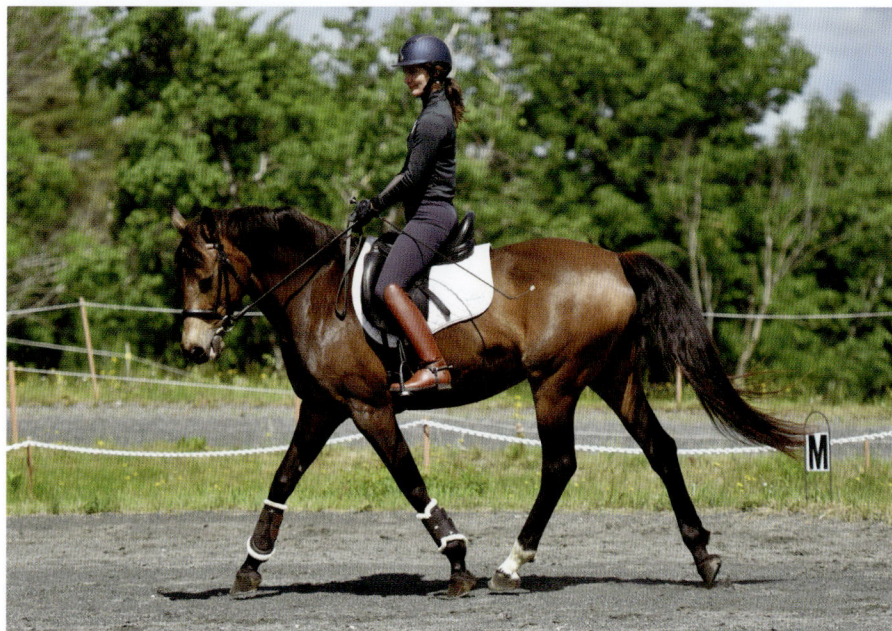

5.12 Maeve's spine doesn't overlap and correspond to the arc of the circle to the left because Bekki is bending the horse's neck too much to the inside.

5.13 She's crooked here as well because her neck is bent to the outside of the arc of the circle. Bekki is using her outside rein, but she has let her inside hand go forward so it has lost its influence.

the horse's hindquarters remain on the original track of the circle, her hind feet cannot possibly follow the tracks made by her front feet: she's no longer "straight."

Photo 5.13 shows the same fault as photo 5.9, but now we see it on a circle. The neck is bent too much to the outside (right); the shoulders fall in toward the center of the circle. As a result the hind feet can't follow the tracks made by the front feet and the horse is not straight.

In photo 5.14 we see the horse being ridden "straight" on a circle. Bekki is asking Maeve to look to the inside (left) by vibrating the inside

(left) rein, while supporting with the outside (right) rein so the mare doesn't bend too much to the inside (left). She bends her horse in her rib cage by placing her inside (left) leg on the girth and her outside (right) leg behind the girth. Positioning her outside leg behind the girth not only helps bend the horse around her inside (left) leg, but also prevents her hindquarters from swinging out and off the line of the circle.

To maintain straightness, you need to ride with both legs and both hands. Depending on what you're doing, some of your aids will be active and some will be passive. On the circle

5.14 On a circle, "straight" means "bent"! Maeve is straight here because her body is evenly curved from poll to tail so that it overlaps the arc of the circle to the left exactly.

that I just described, the inside aids are active and the outside aids are passive. There should always be a marriage of inside and outside aids—don't use one set of aids and abandon the horse by not using the other set of aids.

Perhaps your horse doesn't want to stay straight between your legs and hands. He feels very "wormy" as he bounces from side to side, becoming crooked by falling in and out from the line or curve with his shoulders, hindquarters, or both. Rather than correcting these losses of balance each time they occur, try instead to maintain the straightness. Make a corridor with

your legs and reins, and let your horse bounce against the aids like a ping-pong ball until he finally stays straight.

CROOKEDNESS—HINDQUARTERS TO THE INSIDE

Earlier I said that when a horse is leg-straight, his hind feet are lined up directly behind his front feet. The rider must keep in mind, however, that the hips of the horse are wider than the shoulders. If you ride along a fence line and place the forehand too close to the rail, the horse will have no option but to drift inward with his hindquarters, because he doesn't have room for them. In this case the rider is causing the crookedness.

Another reason that a horse drifts inward with his hindquarters is to avoid bearing weight on his inside hind leg. In order to cope with the demands of curves in good balance, this hind leg has to bend more and do more work than the outside hind leg (fig. 5.15).

In both cases, do not push the hindquarters back out. Straighten the horse by placing the forehand in front of the haunches. You should straighten the horse in this way because even though the hindquarters are deviating to the inside, you want to use your inside leg on the girth to send your horse *forward*, not to push him sideways.

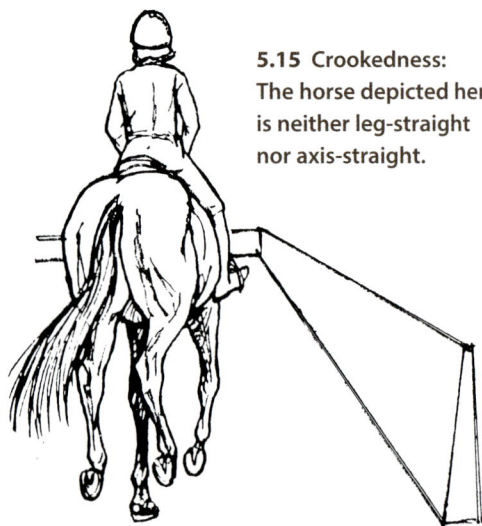

5.15 Crookedness: The horse depicted here is neither leg-straight nor axis-straight.

Riding in the shoulder-fore position is also an excellent exercise to make your horse straight. I explain this in great detail in chapter 9.

KEY POINTS

FORWARD

■ Riding your horse forward and straight is the foundation from which all correct training starts.

■ Think of the word "forward" not only as moving over the ground in a forward direction, but also as your horse "thinking forward." That is, when you use the lightest of driving aids, your horse reacts immediately and enthusiastically.

■ You're traveling down the wrong (and exhausting) road if you're from the "more leg, stronger leg" school of thought. Instead, teach your horse to be in front of your leg so you can do less and he can do more.

STRAIGHTNESS

■ By nature all horses are crooked. It is our responsibility to make them straight so they can develop evenly.

■ When a horse is straight, his spine overlaps the line he's traveling on and his hind feet follow in the tracks of his front feet. Therefore, a "straight" horse is straight on lines and bent when on the arc of a circle or corner.

6

SHALL WE DANCE?

Paces, Gaits, and Rhythm

A primary aim for all riders interested in improving their horses through dressage training is the development of their horses' basic paces. All the movements and exercises that I'll be discussing shortly are not an end in themselves. They are a means to an end. They're designed to make the horse more athletic so he can move with grace and beauty. In common usage, you'll often hear the words **"paces"** and **"gaits"** used randomly and interchangeably. And the fact is that the various organizations that define and describe them are not always in agreement as to which word to use in certain cases. I don't want you to be confused by the inconsistent use of these words. So for the sake of clarity and consistency, in this book I'll call the walk, trot, and canter, when discussing them generically, the paces. I'll refer to the "gears," or variations of length of stride and balance within each pace, as the gaits—specifically: the working, collected, medium, and extended gaits of all three paces.

To reap the benefits of classical training, your horse does not necessarily have to be blessed with lofty, expressive paces. Dressage can take the most common animal as well as the truly gifted athlete and help both of them to move more expressively.

When training is correct, the basic paces always improve. When the training is incorrect for whatever reason—harsh gadgets, "front to back" riding that focuses on the position of the horse's head and neck and ignores the hind-quarters, shortcuts—the quality of the paces degenerates (fig. 6.1).

6.1 A–C Examples of good and bad balance: a well-balanced Western horse whose gait appears to show the results of dressage training (A), a poorly balanced turn (B), a light-in-hand saddle seat horse—a nice, balanced picture (C).

In this chapter, I'll look at the halt, the medium walk, the working trot, and the working canter, because that is what you'll be concerned with at this stage of your horse's education. From chapter 16 on, I'll discuss the collected and the extended gaits that will be used when you and your horse are more advanced.

6.2 A halt in good balance.

THE HALT

In a good halt, your horse should stand absolutely motionless, yet he should be alert and attentive enough to move off instantly from the lightest of aids. To be immobile, he must be in good balance. Good balance in the halt means that your horse's body is straight and his weight is evenly distributed over his four legs. This is what we call having "a leg in each corner." His front legs are side by side and so are his hind legs. He should maintain a soft contact with your hands, and he can chomp quietly on the bit (fig. 6.2).

THE AIDS FOR THE HALT

When stepping into the halt, your horse should always look like he's closing himself up from the back to the front. This means you'll use your driving aids first and send him forward up to restraining hands. Never drag your horse into the halt by pulling on the reins.

This results in a poorly balanced halt where the hind legs are left trailing out behind his body. In that position they can't support his weight. When this happens your horse has no option but to fall on his forehand and lean on your hands for support. Then, with his hind legs out behind his body in the halt, he's not in a "ready" position to react immediately to your light leg aids for an upward transition. So what you may perceive as a disobedience—a feeling that he is "behind the leg"—in reality might be that he is physically unable to respond to your command to go forward (figs. 6.3 to 6.5).

The aids for the halt are as follows:

Legs: close both calves to drive the hind legs under your horse's body.

Hands: close both hands in fists to resist the driving aids. Relax your hands as soon as your horse stops.

Seat: stretch up and brace your back by tightening your stomach muscles. "Still" your seat so that your hips no longer follow the motion of your horse's body.

6.3–6.5 Trot to Halt Transition: Preparing to halt from an energetic working trot at the spot marked by the letter B. A few strides before B, Lexie Evans drives Cuz I Can's (CC's) hind legs farther underneath her body by closing both of her legs and pushing with her seat. Note the lowering of the horse's hindquarters as they are driven under her body. Lexie captures and contains this energy by closing her hands in fists. As CC steps into a balanced halt, Lexie relaxes all her aids without taking them off. Instead, she maintains a soft contact with her legs on CC's barrel and her hands with her horse's mouth.

In the first stages of training, school the halt as an obedience exercise. Later on, you'll use the halt to increase the engagement of the hind legs so you can improve your horse's balance.

IMMOBILITY—THE BEGINNING OF DISCIPLINE

The first time you ask your horse to submit obediently to your requests is when you teach him to stand still while being mounted. Too often, I see riders neglect this very basic opportunity to establish the ground rules about who makes the decisions in this partnership. Riders will be "mid-mount" and their horses walk forward. Or they manage to get completely aboard, and then the horses decide to walk off on their own.

> ### "It's important for you to think about the transitions in and out of the halt."
>
> • • • • •

Your horse should stand absolutely immobile while you mount, and he should wait until he receives a specific aid from your legs before he moves off. If you let your horse take over simply because you haven't paid enough attention to this aspect of obedience, you might find him starting to make his own decisions in other areas.

Insisting that your horse stand still while being mounted is your first chance to establish your role in the relationship. You must firmly, but quietly, establish your authority. What I do

with horses that don't stand still is, as I begin to mount, I say the word, "whoa." My horse already knows what "whoa" means from our work on the longe line. If he takes even one step forward as I start to get on, I immediately get off, make him stand, and say "whoa" again. I might have to do this several times. But, as soon as he stands absolutely still, both while I'm mounting and while I'm sitting in the saddle, I make a big fuss over him. I'll pat him and tell him he's good or even reach over and give him some sugar. Then, when I'm ready, I'll close my legs in a definite signal for him to walk forward. I'll praise him again for waiting and then for reacting attentively to the aid to move off.

TRANSITIONS TO AND FROM THE HALT

It's important for you to think about the transitions in and out of the halt. The downward transition to the halt should be crisp but not abrupt. By crisp, I mean that your horse shouldn't do any "dribbly" trot or walk steps that get progressively shorter and shorter until he finally stalls out and stops. His last step of trot or walk before the halt should look just as active as the strides that he takes when he's motoring along with lots of energy.

If the downward transition looks abrupt, it's a good indication that you used your hands too much or too sharply, or, that you suddenly and harshly applied all of the aids.

In an upward transition, your horse should respond immediately to your aids with a deliberate step from the hind legs. In other words, your horse shouldn't shuffle with short, lazy steps until he finally accelerates into his first full stride of the walk, the trot, or the canter. If he does this because he's "behind your leg," you need to put him "in front of your leg" as I described on page 50. If he shuffles off because his hind legs are out behind his body, you need to pay more attention to getting his hind legs underneath him during the next downward transition to the halt. Make sure that you use your driving aids and "close him up" from back to front so that he's in a better balance to do whatever comes next.

EVALUATING THE BASIC PACES

At this stage in your horse's career you will be concerned with the medium walk, the working trot and the working canter if you compete at the lower levels of dressage or are riding in another discipline and cross-training your horse with dressage. Even more advanced dressage horses being schooled in the collected, medium, and extended gaits are still ridden in the working trot and canter during their warm-up and cool-down phases of a training session.

As you ride the walk, trot, and canter, some excellent images to hold in your mind are that the walk marches, the trot swings, and the canter springs. But every horse's paces are unique to him. If you get frequent instruction, your teacher may say, "There. That's a good working trot." or "He needs to be more energetic for working canter."

For those of you whose lessons are few and far between, I'll give you three specific criteria to help you identify high quality paces on your own. Then, I'll also delve into them more fully under the individual headings of Walk, Trot, and Canter that follow.

The three criteria are:

- Rhythm
- Energy
- Hind Leg Placement

RHYTHM

In order to lay a solid foundation for training in any riding discipline, maintenance of a regular **rhythm** in all paces should always be a priority. Each horse's rhythm is individual to him, but a good rhythm is steady and regular with equal spacing between the steps of each stride of each pace.

The **tempo,** on the other hand, is the rate of repetition of the rhythm. To further understand the difference between rhythm and tempo, think of a dance like a waltz. The rhythm is always the same in a waltz—it's always done in a three-beat time. But the tempo can change, depending on whether the waltz is played faster or slower.

Your seat is the primary aid for influencing rhythm and tempo. You can steady rhythm, and slow tempo, by **"stilling" your seat**. When you "still" your seat, you stretch up, tighten your stomach muscles, and stop following the motion of the horse. (For more on this, see page 115). Alternatively, you can use a **"driving" seat** to quicken the rhythm and speed up the tempo. To "drive" with your seat, you also sit up tall, but you push with your seat as if you're trying to move the back of the saddle toward the front of the saddle.

I will discuss how you can tell if your horse's rhythm is regular in the description of each pace that follows.

ENERGY

The second criterion for high quality paces is energy. Energy refers to vigor, activity, and liveliness—especially from the haunches. In dressage we often use the word **impulsion** when we speak of power in the trot and the canter. (We use the word "activity" when discussing the walk.) Impulsion refers to the "thrust" coming from the hindquarters. When moving with impulsion, the horse gives the impression of a desire to carry

6.6 *Impulsion* refers to the "thrust" coming from the horse's hindquarters, giving power and energy to the horse's trot or canter.

himself forward and spring off the ground (fig. 6.6).

A good working gait always has some degree of energy. But how can you tell if your horse has enough energy? Simple. Ask for any upward transition—such as going from the trot into the canter or from a working trot into a lengthening of that trot. If you have to add energy in order to do the transition, there isn't enough activity in the gait to begin with. For instance, you should be able to do the trot to canter transition without first revving your horse up. All the energy you need for the transition to the canter should already be in the trot you are doing.

HIND LEG PLACEMENT

The third characteristic to look at when evaluating the basic paces is where the horse puts his hind feet in relation to his front feet.

Although you can lean over while riding and look at the footfalls in the walk, you'll have to ask someone to give you feedback on where the horse is stepping in the trot and the canter. Alternatively, have someone take a video of you riding. While being videotaped, adjust your working gait by slowing down and then speeding up the tempo or by adding energy, and announce what you're doing loud enough to be heard on camera. Make a verbal note on the tape of what you're doing as well as what you're feeling. Then when you study the tape later, you can easily compare what you felt when you were riding with what you see on the tape.

THE WALK

Four different types of walk are recognized by the governing body of dressage. The two that you'll be concerned with for the time being are the **medium walk** and the **free walk**. In Stage Four we'll look at the other two—the collected and the extended walks, which are more advanced movements (fig. 6.7).

As the primary gait in the walk, the *medium* walk used to be called the *working* walk—corresponding to the working trot and the working canter. However, the new description, medium walk, is preferred over working walk because it has a connotation of marching more freely forward. Previously, in an effort to ride what they considered to be a *working* walk, riders ended up shortening their horses too much and restricting them with the reins. This can be disastrous because it's very easy to ruin a horse's natural walk if he feels confined. When he feels restricted, his rhythm can degenerate and become **lateral**—a rhythm fault that I'll describe shortly.

To avoid this hazard, we now work young or uneducated horses in what is called the medium walk. This walk is a free, regular and unconstrained walk of moderate lengthening. The horse walks energetically but calmly with even and determined steps, the hind feet touching the ground in front of the hoof prints of the forefeet (fig. 6.8).

6.7 A–D Types of walk: free walk (A), medium walk (B), extended walk (C), collected walk (D).

6.8 The medium walk "marches." It is an active, ground-covering walk. The inside hind leg is just coming to the ground as Tricreek Lock Corrib (Corey) finishes the third step of a walk with four clear beats. Note that her inside hind leg "overtracks"—it comes to the ground beyond the point where her inside front foot left the ground.

6.9 The free walk is a gait of relaxation. Here, Lakewin allows Jax complete freedom to lower and stretch out his head and neck.

The free walk is a pace of relaxation in which the horse is allowed complete freedom to lower and stretch out his head and neck (fig. 6.9). The reins are totally loose so that the walk can be as unencumbered as possible. You'll do a free walk with your horse at the beginning and end of your ride as well as any time you give your horse a break.

RHYTHM IN THE WALK

Let's begin by looking at the sequence of legs and rhythm of the walk (fig. 6.10).

Starting with the outside hind leg, the sequence of legs in one walk stride is: outside hind, outside fore, inside hind, inside

fore. Assess the rhythm of your horse's walk by counting with each leg movement. Start counting the rhythm out loud when the outside hind leg strikes the ground. You should develop a feel for this in all three paces, so beginning at the walk is a good idea since you'll have more time to think. Close your eyes so you can really feel when that outside hind foot is on the ground bearing weight. When the outside hind leg is on the ground, the horse's outside hip is higher, so you should also feel your outside seat bone or hip being raised slightly or pushed forward.

Each time you feel this, say "One." You'll say "One...one...one...one..." each time the outside hind leg is on the ground. Then add in the other

6.10 A–D The sequence of legs in one walk stride: The first beat is outside hind (A); the second beat is outside fore (B); the third beat is inside hind (C); the fourth beat is inside fore (D).

6.11 A lateral (or "pacey") walk.

legs as they move. The sequence of your counting should sound like an even "One, two, three, four; one, two, three, four; one, two, three, four." This is a regular four-beat walk.

If you hear something like "One, two, …three, four" instead, your horse's rhythm is not regular. When the legs on the same side move too close together like this, we say the walk is becoming **lateral** (fig. 6.11). If the rhythm degenerates further and the legs on the same side move together completely so that you count only two beats, the horse is pacing, not walking.

Both a "lateral walk" and a "pacing walk" are caused by tension and stiffness, especially in the back and neck. Neither is correct for basic training in dressage, so make sure that the purity of the walk—the regular four-beat rhythm—is always a priority.

There are different reasons that horses lose regularity in the walk. Some horses are born with walks that aren't one hundred percent "pure," or "regular." Other horses are born with pure walks, but they can momentarily lose their regular

rhythm if they are tense in their backs or feel restricted by the rider's hands.

The following are some suggestions to help you make and keep the walk rhythm regular. You should experiment and do whatever it takes to maintain regularity. It's a requirement for all correct gaits and imperative if you want to correctly develop your horse.

If your horse's walk loses regularity, try either slowing him down or speeding him up. For most horses, slowing down encourages them to become more even in their steps, so that they have a four-beat walk. Some horses, however, are helped by riding them in a faster tempo than they are inclined to go. (For an additional tip to help the rhythm in the walk, see the shoulder-fore exercise in chapter 9).

Many horses have a regular rhythm in the walk when ridden on a loose rein. But as soon as the rider picks up a contact, the rhythm changes. Usually this irregularity is rider-created because the horse feels restricted by the reins. The rider's contact with the horse's mouth must be gentle and elastic so that the horse doesn't feel "claustrophobic."

A good practice exercise for horse and rider is to do many transitions from a free walk on a loose rein to taking up a contact for the medium walk. As you pick up the reins to establish contact, visualize your horse's legs continuing to move with the same long, full, regular steps of the free walk. Your goal is to keep the rhythm exactly the same by giving the horse the same feeling of freedom, whether he's on contact or on a loose rein.

ENERGY IN THE WALK

Now let's go on to our second criterion for a correct basic gait—energy. In a good medium walk your horse should march with active, determined steps. Check that your horse has enough energy in the walk by asking him to step into the trot. Ask for the trot by lightly closing both of your calves on his sides. Does he eagerly step into the trot or does he shuffle lazily through the transition? If he has enough energy in the walk, the transition is crisp and distinct.

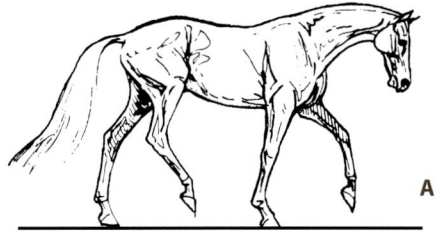

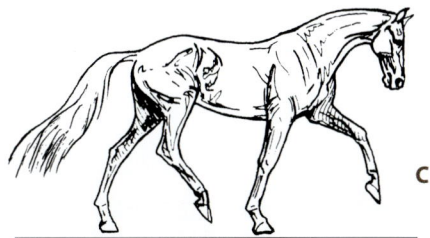

HIND LEG PLACEMENT IN THE WALK

The third criterion for evaluating the walk is where the horse puts his hind feet. In the medium walk, your horse should overtrack to some degree—that is, his hind feet should step in front of the hoof prints made by the forefeet. The amount of overtrack depends on many factors, including conformation and breed. I like a moderate overtrack of four to six inches. I find that when horses have huge overstrides, you can sometimes run into difficulties later in schooling when you go to collect or shorten the gait, because it tends to become lateral rather than remaining a pure, regular, four-beat walk.

THE WORKING TROT

The **working trot** is the trot in which the young or uneducated horse presents himself in the best balance. One of your primary aims when

6.12 A–D Types of trot: working trot (A), collected trot (B), medium trot (C), and extended trot (D).

schooling your inexperienced horse in dressage is to maintain the quality of the working gaits during all the exercises and movements.

Four different trots are recognized, but for the time being you should be concerned only with the working trot. Later on, if you decide to take

6.13 The trot swings. In the working trot, Corey's legs move together in diagonal pairs. The horse clearly "tracks up" as her hind foot steps into the spot where her front foot leaves the ground.

6.14 A–C The sequence of legs in one trot stride: the first beat is *inside hind* and *outside fore* (A), followed by suspension (B), and then the second beat—*outside hind* and *inside fore* (C).

your horse to more advanced levels, you will be schooling him in the collected, medium and extended trots (fig. 6.12).

In the working trot, the horse goes forward in balance with even, powerful, elastic steps. He should show good hock action (bending of the hock joints), which is only possible when he moves with impulsion (fig. 6.13).

Now let's look at the sequence of legs and rhythm of the trot (fig. 6.14).

RHYTHM IN THE TROT

In one stride of the trot, the sequence of legs is: one diagonal pair of inside hind and outside fore, followed by a period of suspension during which all four legs are off the ground, then the diagonal pair of outside hind and inside fore.

You should hear yourself counting an evenly-spaced, "One…two… one…two…one…two. . . ."

If you're in posting trot and you're on the correct diagonal, you'll be rising out of the saddle at the same time that you see the horse's outside front leg coming off the ground and going forward. Therefore, since the horse's legs move in diagonal pairs in the trot, you are in the air when the outside hind leg is on the ground and you are sitting in the saddle when the inside hind leg is on the ground (fig. 6.15).

In fact, this is one of the reasons that we have posting diagonals. It's easier to use your leg and,

6.15 A & B Posting on the correct diagonal: The rider rises when the horse's *outside foreleg* and *inside hind leg* are in the air.

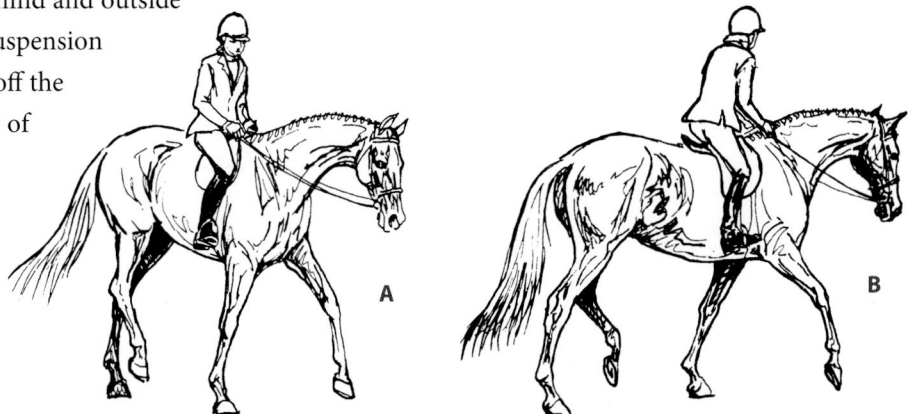

therefore, influence a hind leg when you're sitting in the saddle rather than rising in the air. Since your horse's inside hind leg is the leg you want to energize on circles and turns, you'll feel more coordinated about activating that leg when you're sitting rather than posting.

I don't mean to give you the impression that you use your inside leg every time you sit. Doing that would make your horse dull to your aids very quickly. Unless you're specifically giving an aid to ask your horse for more activity, your legs rest quietly on your horse's sides.

If you're in sitting trot, you can do the same exercise that you did in the walk. Decide when

the outside hind leg is on the ground by closing your eyes and feeling the moment your outside seat bone is raised slightly or pushed forward. Count "One…one…one…one…," each time you feel this. This is the moment that the diagonal pair of outside hind and inside fore are on the ground. Then add in the second beat. Do your "One…" and "Two…" sound evenly spaced?

If the trot rhythm is not regular, you first need to be sure that the horse isn't uneven because he's lame. Check with your veterinarian to eliminate this possibility.

FAULTS IN THE TROT

A common fault in the trot is when the horse hurries his steps so that the foreleg comes to the ground before the diagonal hind leg does, so that two separate hoof beats are heard instead of one (fig. 6.16 A). This horse is carrying most of his weight and that of his rider on his shoulders. The solution is to shift the horse's center of gravity back toward the hind legs so that his shoulders can be lighter and freer. Transitions going from the trot to the halt and back to the trot are particularly useful in this situation. (You can also do a shoulder-fore exercise. More on this under the section on shoulder-fore in chapter 9).

Another common fault is when the hind leg is put down before the diagonal foreleg. Again two hoof beats will be heard (fig. 6.16 B). This occurs when the horse is lazy with his hind legs and drags his feet along the ground. To help activate his hind legs try the following frequent transitions:

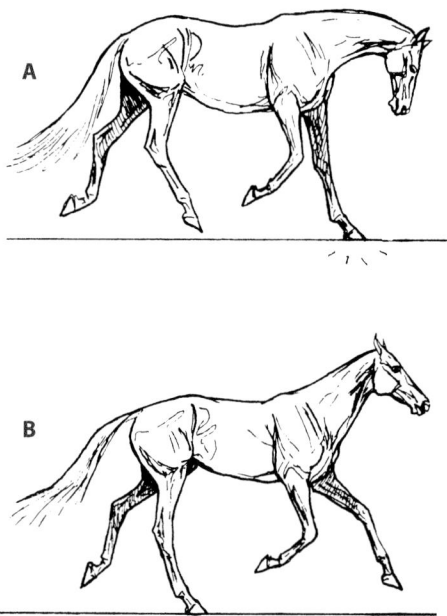

6.16 Faulty trots: irregular, diagonal breaking up, *foreleg* first, and on the forehand (A), and irregular, diagonal breaking up, *hind leg* first, and "running" (B).

1. Alternate lengthening and shortening the stride. To adjust the length of stride, close both of your legs and ask your horse to cover more ground for several strides. Then steady him back to the shorter strides for a few moments by stilling your seat and using your outside rein. Repeat this several times to freshen the trot.

2. Quickly go from trot to walk or canter. First go forward in the trot, do a transition to the walk or the canter for only three or four strides, then go right back into the trot again. (In chapter 8 I'll discuss the aids for all of these transitions more thoroughly.)

The trot also becomes irregular when one hind leg doesn't reach as far under the body as the other, so that the steps look uneven. You may be able to feel this yourself because there will be an emphasis on one of the beats of the trot, and you will find yourself counting, "One, *two*, one, *two*." It's a good idea to ask an observer to watch the hind legs and visually check that each one steps equally under your horse's body.

STRENGTHENING EXERCISES TO IMPROVE THE TROT

Some horses will take a shorter stride with one hind leg because they're either lazy, or weak behind. If your horse's left hind leg is lazy, close your left leg to ask the left hind leg to step more under the body. Do some exercises in the trot such as those described below to strengthen

the weak hind leg and encourage it to take long strides and carry weight.

Ride to the right (clockwise) around your arena. This will put your horse's left hind leg on the outside of the ring, next to the rail. Position your horse's head to the left so that it is towards the rail. Then use your left leg a couple of inches behind the girth to push his hindquarters to the right for a few strides. As you push his quarters to the right, you'll be driving his left hind leg deeper under his body. Then straighten the horse and close both of your legs to ask him to go more forward with longer steps for a few strides. As you settle back to the working trot, repeat the exercise by sending his left hind leg sideways under his body again.

> *"Your goal is to put your horse's left hind leg under his body so that it must always carry both his weight and your weight."*

• • • • •

Another strengthening exercise is to move the horse's hindquarters an inch or two sideways and keep them there as you ride all the way around the ring. Push his hindquarters slightly to the right no matter which direction you're riding. Your goal is to put your horse's left hind leg under his body so that it must always carry both his weight and your weight. As with all "weight-lifting," the muscles doing the work eventually get stronger. As the muscles get stronger, both hind legs can step under the horse's body with equal power.

ENERGY IN THE TROT

Once you know you have a regular rhythm, go on to the second criterion and check the energy level of the trot. Remember that the ease with which you can do a crisp transition will give you information about energy. In the walk example I asked you to do a transition from walk to trot. For variety's sake, check your energy level in the trot by doing a different kind of transition—a lengthening in the trot. Close both of your calves on your horse's sides and see if he reacts immediately by covering ground with longer strides. If he has lots of energy in the working trot, the transition will be dramatic.

HOOF PLACEMENT IN THE TROT

Ask someone to watch where your horse's hind feet land. In the working trot the horse should "track-up"—his hind feet stepping into the hoof prints of his forefeet. (See fig. 6.13 on page 72.)

THE WORKING CANTER

Like the working trot, the working canter is the canter in which the young or uneducated horse presents himself in the best balance.

Four different canters are recognized in dressage, but for your purposes the working canter is the gait you will be riding. Later, I'll introduce the collected, medium, and extended canters (fig. 6.17).

RHYTHM IN THE CANTER

Now let's look at the sequence of legs and rhythm of the canter. The canter has three beats. In one canter stride, the sequence of legs is: first the outside hind, next the diagonal pair of inside hind and outside fore, and finally the inside fore followed by a period of suspension during which all of the legs are off the ground (fig. 6.18).

Your horse has two leads in the canter. When he's cantering on the correct lead, he moves with

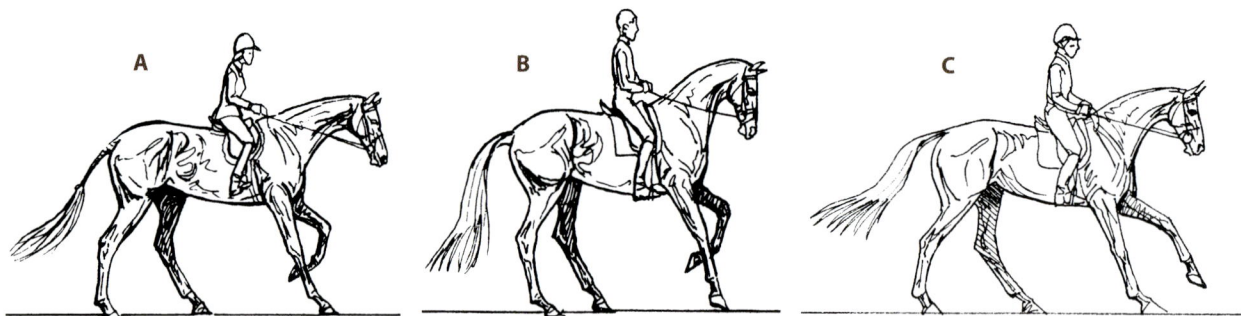

6.17 A–C Types of canter: working canter (A), collected canter (B), and extended canter (C).

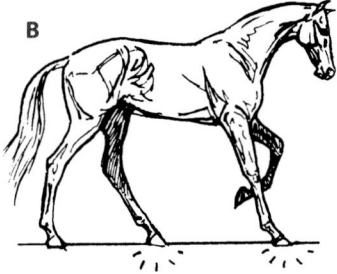

6.18 A–E The sequence of one canter stride with the horse on the left lead: the first beat is the outside (in this case, right) hind (A); the second beat is the diagonal pair—inside hind and outside fore (B); the third beat is the inside fore or leading foreleg (C); then pushing off that foreleg (D); followed by suspension (E).

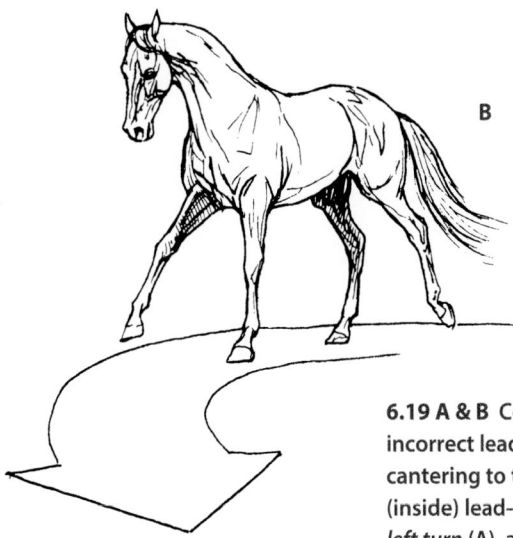

6.19 A & B Correct and incorrect lead when cantering to the left: correct (inside) lead—*left lead* on *left turn* (A), and incorrect (outside) lead—*right lead* on *left turn* (B).

6.20 A–C Faulty canters: irregular, four-beat canter, diagonal breaking up, *foreleg* first, and on the forehand (A); irregular, four-beat canter, diagonal breaking up, *hind leg* first (B); lateral, four-beat canter, approaching a pace (C).

his inside foreleg leading. In other words, when going to the left (counterclockwise), he strikes off first with his right hind leg, then comes the diagonal pair of the left hind leg and the right foreleg, and lastly his left foreleg "leads" or steps out further in front of his body than the right

foreleg (fig. 6.19 A). When going to the right (clockwise), he should canter on the right lead. He starts with the left hind leg, then comes the diagonal pair of the right hind leg and left foreleg, and finally the right foreleg reaches in front of his body.

You should be able to hear yourself count an even rhythm "One…two…three…one…two…three…" During the second beat of the canter, your seat moves from the back of the saddle toward the front of the saddle. You can also check that you're counting correctly by looking at your horse's mane. You'll see that his mane lifts up on the second beat while you're saying "two."

Rhythm faults occur when the canter becomes four-beat and the horse moves along awkwardly rather than covering the ground in a series of graceful bounds. There are three ways the rhythm can become irregular so that the canter degenerates into four beats.

First, when the horse canters too much on the forehand, the diagonal pair of legs can split and the foreleg comes to the ground before the opposite hind leg (fig. 6.20 A).

Second, when a horse is crammed together and forced to go with a shorter stride than he can manage for his degree of training, it's possible that the diagonal pair will split and the hind leg will come to the ground before the opposite front leg (fig. 6.20 B).

Lastly, when a horse is very stiff in his neck and back, the rhythm of the canter can become almost "lateral." It will appear that the left fore and hind legs and the right fore and hind legs move almost together (fig. 6.20 C).

6.21 The canter "springs." In this active, bounding, working canter, note how Corey's inside hind leg reaches well underneath her body.

Often a horse's canter becomes faulty when there's a lack of energy. To freshen a canter that is losing regularity, ask your horse to canter more forward over the ground with brisk, energetic strides.

Check for a good working canter by closing both calves and asking for a transition to a lengthening in the canter. Is it easy? Or do you have to wake your horse up first before he'll give you more effort?

HIND LEG PLACEMENT IN THE CANTER

For the third criterion of working canter, have someone watch your horse's inside hind leg. In a good working canter, it reaches well under the body. To check this, have your person on the ground look from the side at the distance between your horse's hind legs during that second beat of the canter. In a good working canter, the inside hind steps well under the horse's body: your ground person will see a wide space between his hind legs (fig. 6.21).

KEY POINTS

■ When training methods are correct, the horse's paces always improve.

■ Your goal is to teach a horse under saddle to move as gracefully and expressively as he does when he's at liberty.

■ Initially, you'll school the halt as an obedience exercise. Later on, you'll use transitions in and out of the halt to improve your horse's balance.

■ Three elements of high-quality paces are regularity of rhythm, good energy, and hind legs that step well under the body.

  1. Regular rhythm refers to the even spacing between each of the steps within a stride.

  2. When a horse has sufficient energy in his paces, he finds it easy to do transitions either within the pace or from one pace to another.

  3. In the walk, the horse's hind feet should step in front of the tracks made by his front feet. In the trot, the hind feet should step into the tracks of the front feet. In the canter, the horse's inside hind leg should step well underneath his body.

7

CONTACT
Your Communication Center

No matter which riding discipline you prefer, all of you reading this book will benefit from learning how to establish a sympathetic **contact** with your horse's mouth. Your reins serve as transmitters from your brain, through your hands, to your horse's mouth. Establishing this contact with his mouth allows you to communicate with his hindquarters—his engine. Even those of you who just want an obedient, well-schooled partner need to know about contact so you can stop and steer.

For those of you who decide to go on to Stages Three and Four you'll see that contact is essential to establishing a **connection** from your horse's hindquarters to the bit. In order for the energy that originates in the hindquarters to be fully used, it must travel over your horse's back, through his neck, and be received by your hands. When this occurs, your horse will be connected, also known as **"on the bit."** We'll explore this in chapter 14.

In this chapter I am going to describe five properties that are necessary in order for you to establish an inviting contact with your horse's mouth. The late Colonel Bengt Ljungquist,

"If God had given us conformation for riding, our forearms would reach from elbow to bit."

Charles de Kunffy, in *Training Strategies for Dressage Riders*

• • • • •

former coach of the United States Dressage Team, described this contact as follows: "If you take a flat piece of wood, close your fingers around it and put it in a running stream of water, you will feel a gentle and steady tug on your hand from the current. That is the feel you should strive to have when you ride: a live but comfortable link with the horse's mouth and the sensation that he wants to take you forward while staying in constant communication." (See fig. 7.1.)

Later, I will also explain some of the basic ways to use the reins to communicate with, and influence, your horse. These subtle variations of the use of the reins are called the **rein effects.**

7.1 Take a flat piece of wood and hold it in a stream. This sensation is like the gentle tug you should feel when you have a comfortable link to your horse's mouth.

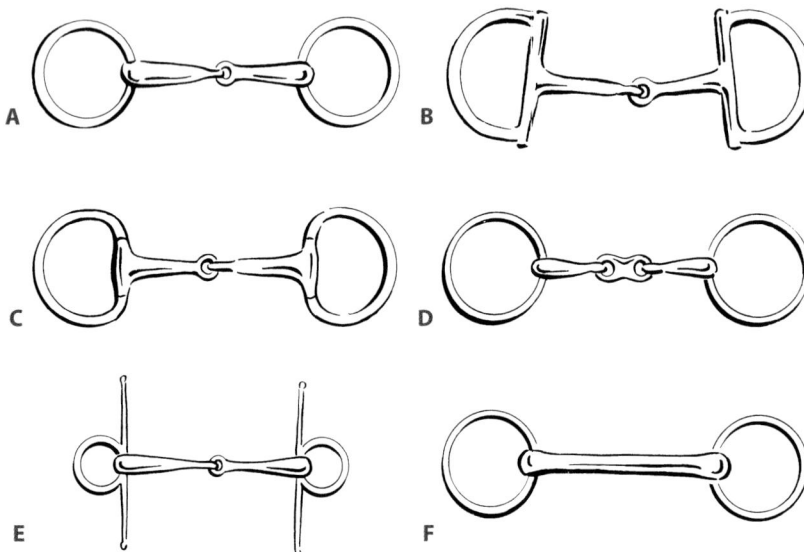

7.2 A–F Appropriate snaffle bits: hollow-mouth loose ring (A), eggbutt (B), full-cheek or Fulmer (C), dee ring (D), French link (E), straight bar (F).

I want to mention here that when you work on establishing a good contact, I'd like you to use a snaffle bit. There are many different styles of snaffles (fig. 7.2). Of these, generally, the thicker the bit, the more gentle the action. But, depending on the shape of your horse's mouth and the thickness of his tongue, thicker is not always better. You need to find the bit that is most comfortable for your horse. He'll most likely show you when he's uncomfortable by opening his mouth, twisting or tossing his head, or showing a reluctance to be bridled. If you are not sure if your bit is appropriate, it's best to ask a professional to advise you.

QUALITIES OF CONTACT

The five qualities of contact that make an inviting link are:

- Straight line from bit to hand to elbow
- Firmness
- Consistency
- Elasticity
- Symmetrical hands

STRAIGHT LINE

Always maintain a straight line contact from the bit through your hands to the elbows so that your arms seem like they are simply an extension of the reins (figs. 7.3 and 7.4). When you pick up contact, imagine that your arms no longer belong to you—they are part of the reins and they belong to the horse.

The straight line allows the action of the reins to pass through your hands, shoulders, and back so that it can influence the horse's back. If your hands are carried too low or too high, that straight line will be broken and the action of the reins will stop at your hands. Any time there is an angle at the point where the reins meet your hands, the signals you try to transmit to your horse will be interrupted as though they were being sent on a cut telephone line (fig. 7.5).

7.3 A classical straight line contact from the bit through Bekki's hand to her elbow in the walk. It's hard to tell where the rein leaves off and her arm begins.

7.4 In the rising trot, the rein looks like an extension of Bekki's forearm.

7.5 A–C Bit and rein angles and their effects: With a straight line from bit to elbow, the bit acts neutrally (A); when the line is broken upward, the bit acts upward in corners of the horse's lips (B); when the line is broken downward, the bit acts downward against the bars of the mouth (C).

FIRMNESS

Although your hands should always be quiet and sensitive, in the initial stages of training contact should also be firm. Provided that you're using a snaffle bit, take a good solid one or two pounds in each hand. If the contact is too light, there's no connection from the hind legs into the hands. If your horse doesn't seek the contact from you, take it from him. But do this only by riding him forward from your legs into a firm contact (figs 7.6 and 7.7).

A lot of riders don't feel comfortable with the idea of having one or two pounds of weight in their hands. They think that contact should always be feather light. The lightness they want is the result of a horse being in self-carriage. But, in the beginning stages of training which are what we are concerned with now, self-carriage isn't relevant.

Self-carriage becomes an issue when I begin to discuss **collection** (the shifting of the horse's center of gravity toward the hind legs) during Stage Four starting on page 233. Prior to collection, a contact that is too light merely indicates a lack of connection. At this stage, if the contact is too light, it is probably because the rider is either leaving a loop in the reins and allowing the horse to go along with his nose poked forward (fig. 7.8), or because she is riding the horse behind the bit (see fig. 12.11).

So, don't be afraid of firm contact. It's a necessary but temporary stage. The horse must first be taking a solid contact with your hands before he becomes light in the correct way.

7.6 Jax avoids taking a contact with Lakewin's hand by dropping "behind the bit."

7.7 Lakewin rides him actively forward from her legs to make the contact more firm. As a result, she's created a solid connection from his hind legs into her hands.

7.8 Contact firm and too light: A correct contact is firm and consistent (A); when the contact is too light, the horse may go above bit (B).

7.9 If you tend to hold your horse's mouth in a "death grip," visualize your reins as fragile threads that can easily break.

On the other hand, it isn't desirable to have a "death grip" on the horse's mouth. If you know you are the type of rider who tends to hang on with too strong a contact, try this image to help you become more sensitive. Visualize that the reins are delicate threads and you'll break them unless you maintain a really delicate contact with your horse's mouth (fig. 7.9).

CONSISTENCY

Consistent contact means that you don't allow the reins to go slack and then tight and then slack again, and so on. This inconsistent contact punishes the horse in the mouth with every step he takes. A steady contact, even if it's a bit too firm, is preferable to the contact that repeatedly touches the horse's mouth and then gets loose.

ELASTICITY

Elastic contact refers to the action of your elbows. In all three paces, your elbows should move. However, the action of the arms is different in walk and canter than it is in the posting trot.

In the walk and canter the horse uses his head and neck in a forward and back motion, so your elastic elbows should open and close forward and back as well. Your hands go toward the horse's mouth during each stride, maintaining the exact same contact all the time. It may help you to think of starting with your arms bent at right angles and your elbows at your sides. Let's call this "home" position. During each walk or canter stride, extend your arms forward toward

7.10 "Home position" for the elbows in the walk and canter. Ally Tessie's elbows are softly bent.

your horse's mouth while maintaining a consistent contact, and then let your elbows return to "home" position (figs. 7.10 to 7.13).

To help you understand how important this elastic contact is to your horse, follow the motion of his head and neck with elastic elbows for several strides, and then lock your elbows at your sides. If you're in the walk, your horse will slow down or stop altogether. If you're cantering, eventually your horse will break to the trot.

7.11 Ally is following forward with her arms so Northern Illusion (Rowen) can use the full range of motion of his neck.

7.12 Ally starts to bend the elbows again in order to stay in contact with Rowen's mouth as he shortens his neck.

7.13 "Home position" again. Ally is ready to start another sequence of following forward and back.

I see many people who have ridden with locked elbows for some time—even years. The horses they ride usually have shortened strides because they feel that they can't move their heads and necks for balance. If you have this tendency to lock your arms, exaggerate following the motion of your horse's head, even at the expense of temporarily losing the contact. Once he develops some confidence that he's not going to run into stiff arms, you'll find that he starts to stretch his neck and his strides become longer.

In the trot the horse's neck stays still. So when you sit to the trot, your arms don't move either. But when you post up and down, your elbows need to allow for your movement so that the contact can remain consistent. The opening and closing of the elbows is comparable to the amount you open and close your knees in posting trot. If your elbows are locked, your hands go up and down and the contact is disturbed because there's a jerky motion on the horse's mouth (figs. 7.14 to 7.17).

Sally Swift, creator of *Centered Riding,* explains how she demonstrates to riders that a rigid contact is distracting and uncomfortable for the horse. "While standing still, I offer the rider one finger just above the withers where the hands would normally hold the reins. I then ask the rider to hold onto my finger and rise up and down as if posting to the trot. As the rider rises up and pulls on my finger, I immediately say, "Ouch!" The student invariably looks surprised, not having noticed that as he rose, he tried to take his hand up too. Because he was holding on

7.14 In the two photos on this page, you can see that Lexie has locked her elbows in posting trot. As a result, her hands go up and down as she goes up and down.

7.15 Because Lexie's arms feel rigid to her horse, CC stiffens her neck and braces against her rider's hands.

7.16 In these photos, the contact is more inviting. When Lexie sits in the saddle, her elbows are softly bent by her sides.

7.17 As she rises, her elbows open like a hinge. Notice that they open to the same degree as her knees do. Because Lexie's arms feel elastic, CC willingly accepts the contact with her rider's hands by relaxing her neck and softening her jaw.

to me, he couldn't bring his hand up, so he balanced himself on my finger."

To get the idea of elastic elbows in the posting trot, place your hands on the horse's withers and keep them there as you go up and down. You'll feel the elbows flex and extend as the hands stay steady. If you find it difficult to get the timing, try it at the halt. Keep your hands on the withers and notice how your elbows open as you stand and bend as you sit. Once you have some muscle memory, try again at the trot.

It's easy to experience the difference between elastic and locked elbows in the posting trot. Make your elbows elastic and notice how your hands stay still. Then lock your elbows and note how they move up and down.

Keeping Elastic Elbows While Doing Transitions

Practice elastic elbows in each pace. Then ride transitions from one pace to another and concentrate on maintaining elasticity during the strides right before and immediately after the transitions. These are critical moments when most riders tend to lock their elbows. If you stiffen your elbows during a transition, your horse might do one of several things. He might stop coming forward with his hind legs during the transition; he might protest by throwing his head up; or perhaps he'll evade the contact altogether by overbending his neck and ducking behind it instead of seeking the contact.

Your horse isn't being disobedient if he does any of these things. He is simply finding it

7.18 Because the rider depicted here is stiffening his elbows through this canter-to-trot transition, the horse protests against the "rude" contact by throwing his head up and tensing his back.

impossible to go forward through a blocking and non-allowing contact during those transitions (fig. 7.18).

I had an auditor at a clinic tell me that she knew her mare very well, and if she took a firm contact as I suggested, the horse would rear. I told her I agreed with her if she took a firm contact with rigid elbows. But I believed that the mare wouldn't even object to a very heavy contact as long as the connection remained elastic.

The auditor was still pretty skeptical when she left the clinic, but two weeks later I received a note from her. Not only did her mare accept the firm, elastic contact, but she was happily working in a much **rounder** frame (see page 10 for my description of "round") than she ever had before.

SYMMETRICAL HANDS

The last quality of contact that we are going to look at is evenness in the rein. This means that you should feel equal weight in each hand, and should not allow your horse to hang on either rein. You need to offer an inviting, symmetrical contact with your hands softly closed around the reins, thumbs the highest point of your hands, and one hand the mirror image of the other.

The contact is not symmetrical and, therefore, not inviting if:

1. One hand is higher than the other (fig. 7.19).

2. The hands aren't equidistant from the rider's body (fig. 7.20).

7.19 This rider won't be able to offer her horse an even contact because one hand is higher than the other.

7.20 When one hand is drawn closer to the saddle, it blocks the activity of the horse's hind leg on the same side.

7.21 Here the thumb is no longer the highest point of the rider's right hand. The position of one hand should always be the mirror image of the other.

3. The position of one hand looks different than the other (fig. 7.21).

Do this exercise to give yourself the correct feeling of symmetrical contact. First, you need to have your hands close together so you'll be able to tell if they look identical. Then, keeping the reins the same length, put both of them in one hand for a few strides and follow with an elastic elbow. With the reins in one hand, your only option is to offer your horse the same feeling on both sides of his mouth. Now put the reins back in both hands. Try to give your horse the same feeling in his mouth as you did when the reins were in one hand. See how close together and symmetrical your hands are? Once you feel comfortable with this hand position and it becomes automatic, challenge yourself by maintaining it during changes of direction and transitions.

THE REIN EFFECTS

The different signals and the way that you use the reins to communicate with your horse are called the "**rein effects**." There are actually five rein effects, and they include the *opening rein,* the *indirect rein,* the *direct rein of opposition,* the *indirect rein of opposition in front of the withers,* and the *indirect rein of opposition passing behind the withers.*

If you wish to learn more about these rein effects than I am including here, they are described very well in Anthony Crossley's book entitled, *Training the Young Horse.* I'll only be

7.22 The rein effects: The direct rein (A), the indirect rein (B),and the opening rein (C).

7.23 The indirect rein: Turn your fingernails up toward your face so your "pinky" finger, rather than your thumb, points toward your hip. To feel this, imagine you are turning a key to unlock a door.

referring to three rein effects in this book. That's all you'll need for the moment to get the job done (fig. 7.22). The common denominator with all of these actions of the reins is that your arms never move backward toward your body. To do so would have a negative, stopping effect on your horse's hind legs.

Our three rein effects include:

1. The *direct rein* follows an imaginary line drawn from your hand to your hip on the same side. For example, your left hand is directed toward your left hip.

You can use your direct rein in a variety of ways, such as closing it in a fist, bending your wrist so that your fingernails come closer to your body, or vibrating the rein by squeezing and releasing it as if you're wringing water out of a sponge.

2. The *indirect rein* follows an imaginary line drawn from your hand to your opposite hip. That is, your left hand is directed toward your right hip. You also want to turn your fingernails

up toward your face so that your "pinky" finger rather than your thumb points toward your hip. Imagine that you have a key in a door and you're turning the key to unlock the door (fig. 7.23).

Your hands still stay side by side. This is a momentary adjustment. After you've given the aid, your hands should go back to the symmetrical position.

When you use the indirect rein, it's essential to remember two things. First, always use your driving aids at the same time that you use your rein. Many instructors are reluctant to teach the indirect rein, and rightly so, because they find that students start using it to replace their legs. If you always use it in conjunction with your leg, you'll be fine.

Next, it's important to keep in mind that although your hand comes as close to your horse's withers as possible, it never crosses over to the other side of his neck. Each hand must work independently on each side of his body.

3. The *opening rein* or "leading" rein, as it is sometimes called, involves moving your hand laterally, away from your horse's neck. So, for an opening left rein, your left hand moves to the left.

KEY POINTS

- Your reins serve as transmitters from your brain, through your hands to your horse's mouth, allowing you to affect his hindquarters.

- Your goal is to establish a sympathetic and inviting link with your horse's mouth so that he wants to step into, and accept, a contact with your hands.

- The five qualities that make up correct contact are
  1. A straight line from the bit to your hand to your elbow.

  2. Firmness

  3. Consistency

  4. Elasticity

  5. Symmetrical hands

- The variations in the ways that you can use the reins are called the "rein effects." In this book, I focus on three of them—the direct rein, the indirect rein, and the opening rein.

STAGE TWO
NUTS & BOLTS

In the next two chapters I'll look at basic flat-work—or the "nuts and bolts" of classical training that most horses in any discipline will be capable of doing. The chapters are divided into work on a **single track** (going straight forward) and **two-track** lateral movements (forward and sideways at the same time). I'll examine the movements and exercises technically in terms of description, purpose and aids. Then I'll incorporate imaging to enhance skill development.

You'll see that the movements aren't necessarily an end in themselves. Sometimes exercises can be done to lay a foundation for more advanced work or to break through current mental or physical blocks. For example, if your horse habitually runs with short, quick, sewing machine-like strides when you ask him to lengthen, you can use leg-yielding to loosen, supple, and stretch his muscles. The leg-yields will develop a greater range of motion sideways and, in turn, when you send him straight forward again, he'll be able to cover more ground with each stride.

Or, let's say your horse always gets crooked in a canter depart by swinging his haunches to the inside. You can ride shoulder-fore—one of the easier lateral movements which I describe in chapter 9—before the transition to give him the idea of staying **engaged** and keeping that inside hind leg stepping under his body.

Start thinking like this and you'll wonder why you ever thought flatwork was boring. Plus, you won't feel stymied by a problem. Just figure out what your horse already knows how to do, and use it to overcome obstacles.

If you don't have a regulation dressage arena (see appendix for details), mark out a rectangle in a field or in your ring. The short sides should not be any shorter than 60 feet. The long sides can be two to three times longer (120-180 feet) than the short sides. Place four markers directly across from each other in the middle of each side of your arena. A and C are placed in the middle of the short sides, and B and E are in the middle of the long sides. (See a diagram of an arena like this on page 145, fig. 9.20.)

You'll notice that each new movement I describe has a section called "Aids." You use **aids** to communicate with your horse non-verbally. Basically, you have two seat bones, two legs, and two hands with which you can give aids. It is the way that you combine these six aids as well as the various actions of seat, leg, and hand that allow you to be very subtle and specific with your requests. When the lines differentiating the movements are precise, "disobediences" that are really miscommunications are rare. This is because one combination of aids means one, and only one, thing. When you want to ask for something different, you have a different set of aids. As a result, your horse doesn't have to play multiple choice. The language is very clear.

Although I will describe the aids for each new movement and exercise, I want you to remember that once you've given the aids to start a movement, your horse should continue doing it on his own until you give him the aids for a different movement. Now, that's the ideal! But the reality is that you'll probably have to remind him to continue from time to time. However, you don't want to fall into the trap of bugging him with your aids every stride. Find moments where you can just relax and ride in harmony. Constant nagging with the aids will not only wear you out but it'll backfire because your horse will eventually tune you out.

For many of the movements and exercises, I'll talk about inside and outside—both in reference to the aids and to the horse's body. Some of you might think that when you're in an arena, the "inside" is always the side closest to the center of the ring, and the "outside" is the side closest to the rail. This isn't always the case. The horse's inside and outside is always determined by the **flexion** and bend. Specifically, the inside is the

direction toward which the horse is flexed (also known as "positioned at the poll") and bent through his body.

In order to make your aids clear to your horse, it will be helpful for you to think that he *always* has an inside and an outside. So even when you're out riding straight along the trail, imagine you are on an enormous circle. Flex and bend your horse ever so slightly in one direction so that you can establish one side as the inside of his body and the other, his outside.

Once you have learned the aids for each movement you can use your imagination to go beyond the mechanics and produce a beautiful picture. Your subconscious mind consists, in part, of a goal-striving mechanism that seeks to accomplish the pictures that exist in your mind. What's more, your subconscious can't tell the difference between what's real and what's vividly imagined. So *perfect* practice...makes perfect. In your imagination you never miss. You're an Olympic rider on an Olympic caliber horse that can do anything, or you've just won the Super Horse title at the World Quarter Horse Show.

Create the perfect picture in your imagination, and you and your horse will soon reach that ideal. Whatever you repeatedly see in your mind's eye in great detail eventually becomes reality. So pretend you're a champion! See your skills as already in existence and your subconscious has no option but to make it so. For more on this process, read about the theory of **psychocybernetics** in my book *That Winning Feeling! Program Your Mind for Peak Performance.*

CHAPTER EIGHT

Straightforward

FLATWORK

In this chapter, we'll look at all the movements and exercises that you can do with your horse while riding straight forward on a single track—that is, with your horse's hind feet following directly behind the hoof prints made by his front feet. These movements include circles and corners, upward and downward transitions, backing up, lengthenings in trot and canter, and counter-canter. Once your horse has been introduced to these gymnastic exercises, he'll be ready to start work on **two tracks** covered in chapter 9.

CIRCLES AND CORNERS

DESCRIPTION

No matter what your riding discipline, at some point you're going to have to ride a corner or a turn. From a practical standpoint alone, you can hardly keep going straight forever! But there is another reason to ride circles and turns. And that reason is **bend**.

Bend is the common denominator for all varieties of curved lines. And correct bending

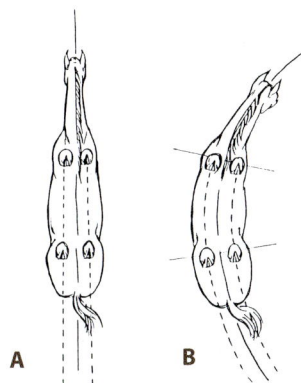

8.1 A–C Straightness and spinal alignment review: The horse's hind feet should follow in the tracks of the forelegs on a straight line (A) and on a curve, requiring the horse to bend (B). A stiff horse cannot track correctly through a curve (C).

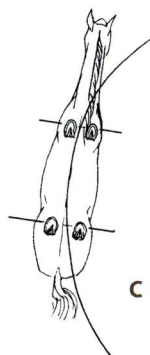

is essential because (confusing as it may sound) it's a requirement for a *straight* horse.

In chapter 5 I explained that in order to be straight, a horse must be straight on straight lines and bent on curved lines. In both cases the horse's spine corresponds to, and overlaps, whatever line he's on. As a result, his hind feet follow the same tracks as those made by the front feet (fig. 8.1).

In order to improve your horse's ability to bend so that he can be *straight,* incorporate circles and other patterns that involve bending, such as figure-eights, shallow loops, and serpentines, into your work.

As a general rule, when you make large circles or gentle loops in the trot, you have the option of posting or sitting. Smaller circles, however, are usually done in the sitting trot.

Even if you ride an accurate circle with the perfect size and shape, you won't develop your horse's flexibility if he doesn't bend properly.

One issue you face in your quest for correct bend is the fact that horses bend more easily in

THE AIDS FOR BENDING

The marriage of inside and outside aids creates a horse that bends while turning along a prescribed line. Your inside rein asks your horse to look in the direction he's going and your inside leg asks him to bend through his side. Your outside rein supports and limits the amount of bend in your horse's neck. Your outside leg prevents his hindquarters from swinging out and, therefore, helps bend his body around your inside leg.

To remind yourself to use a complementary influence of the aids, think of how a farrier shapes and bends a shoe. He puts the shoe against the anvil and hits it with the hammer. He cannot bend the shoe with just the anvil or the hammer. He needs both. So, your outside aids are the anvil, and the inside aids are the hammer, and the horse is the shoe (fig. 8.2).

As you ride circles and turns, be sure to look directly between your horse's ears. Riders often have the tendency to turn their heads and look too much to the inside of the line they're on. If this has become a habit, retrain yourself by overcompensating for a while and look at your horse's outside ear on circles and turns.

The aids for a circle or turn to the left (counterclockwise) are as follows:

Seat: weight is on the left seat bone.

Left leg: on the girth as a pole for the horse to bend around and to maintain the activity of the inside hind leg (fig. 8.3).

Right leg: behind the girth to help bend the body around the inside leg and prevent the quarters from swinging out. The degree that the outside leg is back depends on the size of the figure. For a large circle or loop it only comes back an inch or two. On a very small circle, the outside leg might be a few inches behind the inside leg (fig. 8.4).

Left rein: vibrates for flexion at the poll to the inside. The rider should just barely be able to see the inside eye or inside nostril of her horse.

Right rein: steady and supporting to limit the degree of bend in the neck. It also functions as the turning rein as it brings the horse's shoulders around the circle or corner.

8.2 For bending, think of your outside aids as the anvil, your inside aids as the hammer, and your horse as the shoe.

8.3 The inside aids on a large circle to the left. Ally's left leg is on the girth so Rowen can bend around it. Note that the stirrup leather is perpendicular to the ground. The inside hand is active while the outside hand is steady. Even though the action of the two reins is different, both hands remain side by side.

8.4 It's easier to see that Ally has her weight correctly on her left (inside) seat bone by looking at her seat from the outside of the circle. Note that on a large circle, her outside leg is only slightly behind the girth. You can tell it's back because the stirrup leather is a bit behind a perpendicular line drawn to the ground, and you can see a little more of the horse's barrel between the girth and her leg.

8.5 The rider is bending the horse's neck only; the horse is not evenly bent through the body.

the neck than in the rest of the spine (fig. 8.5). It's vital to maintain a uniform bend from poll to tail.

Another issue is that, like people, horses are stronger on one side and weaker on the other. With a horse, the strong side is known as the **stiff side**; it is more difficult for him to bend on this side. This is partly due to the muscles on the other side of the body, which are short and tight due to lack of suppleness. These shortened muscles need to be gently stretched and elongated so they allow the horse to bend more easily around the leg on his stiff side.

The weak side is the **soft side**. A horse finds it easier to bend on this side. Riders often describe the soft side as the "good" side because it feels better, or more comfortable, to ride in this direction. However, the soft side is not necessarily the "good" side. This is because the horse is often not using his hind leg on the soft side as actively as he does the hind leg on his stiff side. As a result, the hind leg on the soft side becomes weaker.

Dressage riders usually call the horse's soft side his **hollow** side. However, I'm going to call

it the soft side because I don't want to confuse you with a second usage of the word "hollow" that refers to a horse who is not connected over his back. But don't worry too much about this for now. We'll get into that in depth when I discuss putting your horse "on the bit" in chapter 13.

Your job is to make your horse bend equally on both sides. You really have your work cut out for you because if you look at your horse when he's just standing in his stall, he probably has his body curved more in one direction than the other. There is a theory that this curve in the horse's spine is related to the position of the horse in the womb. However, whatever the reason, you only have an hour or so each day to undo what your horse does with his muscles naturally. (I will give you some exercises to help you with your horse's stiff and soft side later in this chapter, on page 104.)

THE NEED TO INCREASE INFLUENCE OF THE BENDING AIDS

If the horse is bending and turning easily, the inside aids are slightly active and the outside aids stay fairly passive, as I've discussed. When one part of the horse's body is not bending correctly, the appropriate aids become more active. In the following exercises, I'm still referring to a circle (counterclockwise) to the left, as I explain how to increase the aids. As you circle to the left, your inside is the left side and your outside is the right side:

8

1. If your horse leans on your left leg and doesn't give in his rib cage, or is lazy with his left hind leg, make your left leg active by squeezing and releasing at the girth. You might have to use more active inside aids when you're riding your horse on a circle and his stiff side is on the inside. Here's an image that might help you with this. Think of your left leg pushing your horse's barrel way over to the right to encourage him to bend (fig. 8.6).

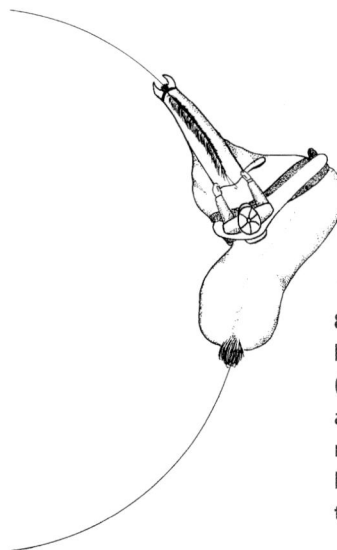

2. If your horse's hindquarters swing to the right and are outside the arc of the circle, his hind feet are not following the tracks of his front feet. In this case, press a bit more strongly with your right leg behind the girth. Here's an image that should give you some incentive to use your supporting right leg: pretend you're riding on the edge of a cliff. If you don't keep the hindquarters in line, they'll fall off the edge (fig. 8.7)!

3. If your horse doesn't want to look in the direction he's turning, flex him to the left by activating the left rein. First, gently squeeze and release the rein. If your horse still ignores you and positions his head to the outside of the turn, you can give several small indirect rein aids (fig. 8.8).

4. If your horse bends his neck too much to the left and his shoulder falls out to the right, take a firmer hold on the right rein. Remember that horses are more flexible in the neck than elsewhere in the spine, so be sure to limit and control the amount of bend in the neck by supporting with the outside rein (fig. 8.9).

8.6 If your horse is leaning on your inside (in this example, left) leg and doesn't "give" in his ribcage, visualize your left leg pushing his barrel to the right—all the way!

8.7 If you need an incentive to encourage you to use your supporting outside (in this example, right) leg, pretend you're riding on the edge of a cliff. If you don't keep the horse's hindquarters in line, they'll fall off the edge!

8.8 The horse depicted here isn't looking in the direction he's turning. He's circling to the left and looking to the right.

8.9 A & B To prevent your horse from bending his neck too much to the left and "popping" his shoulder out to the right (A), take a firmer hold on the right rein and soften your left hand (B).

Imagine that your right rein together with your arm act like the side reins you use when longeing. A correctly-adjusted outside side rein prevents the horse from bending his neck too much to the inside and stops his shoulder from falling out sideways. As a result the horse can be **axis-straight** (see p. 53).

MARRY YOUR INSIDE AND OUTSIDE AIDS!

Have you ever had a situation while riding on a circle, where your horse just leaves the circle and runs off to the other end of the ring? For instance, you're circling to the left and your horse runs off to the right. If you had an instructor there she might yell, "Outside rein!" which is your right rein. But every fiber in your being tells you to pull on the left or inside rein to get back to your circle.

The problem here is that if you only use the inside or left rein to direct your horse back to

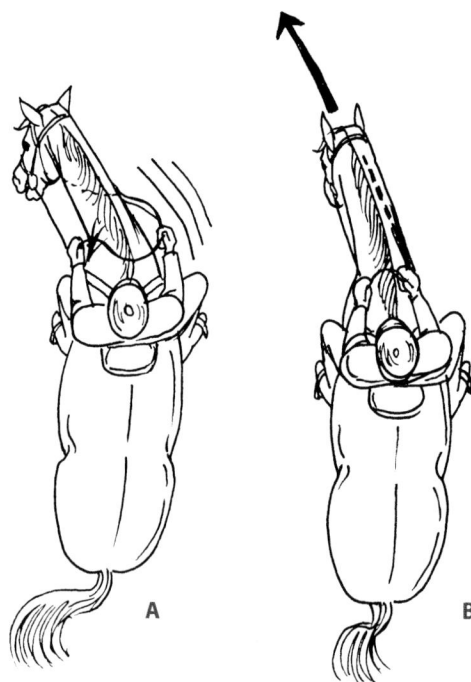

the circle and you don't also support with the outside or right rein at the same time and to the same degree, you'll only pull your horse's head and neck around and his body can continue going where he wants.

Remember the marriage of the inside and outside aids! When you're increasing your inside rein to bring your horse back to the circle, you must also increase the outside aids for support so you can limit the amount of bend in the neck and control the outside shoulder.

These same dynamics exist when you ride a circle that isn't quite the right shape. I frequently see circles that aren't truly round because the horse's shoulders are escaping and drifting to the

8.10 Correct and incorrect lateral flexion: Correct lateral flexion at the poll (A), incorrect with a tilted head (B), and incorrect in the neck (C).

outside of the arc of the curve in much the same way (though to a lesser degree) as the above example where the horse is running off. If you want round circles—and who doesn't—make sure you have a complementary influence of inside and outside aids.

LOOSENING THE POLL ON THE STIFF SIDE

The first step in riding a circle or corner is to have the horse looking in the direction he's going. To do this, the horse must flex at the poll. The poll is actually the top of the horse's skull, (the first vertebra located just behind the ears) but in common dressage usage, "flexion at the poll" refers to the closing of the two joints immediately behind the poll. When I talk about "lateral flexion" or "position to the inside" on a curved line, I'm specifically referring to flexion of the second cervical (neck) joint (fig. 8.10).

Sometimes flexing a horse at the poll is difficult because he feels "locked" there. Usually it's harder to flex him laterally on his stiff side. However, occasionally a horse is simply locked

in the poll and it's difficult to flex him either left or right. To loosen your horse in the poll, give several small indirect rein aids on the locked side; as I mentioned earlier in the section on rein effects (p. 98), turn your wrist as if you're unlocking a door, or scooping a spoonful of sugar out of a bowl. Your hands should stay side by side while your fingernails face upward and your baby finger points toward your opposite hip (fig. 8.11). Never draw your inside hand across the horse's withers.

8.11 To flex your horse at the poll, use an indirect rein. For the left indirect rein, as an example, the left hand rotates and angles toward your right hip (see also p. 000).

8.12 If your horse is stiff on the left side of his body, and soft on his right, ride to the right and go through corners as if you were on a straight line—without bending aids—to correct his tendency to overbend in this direction.

8.13 To help soften the horse with a stiff left side, first ride a small circle to the left. Then go onto a large circle but keep the bending aids on as they were when you were asking your horse to curve his body along the arc of the smaller circle

EXERCISES TO HELP STIFF AND SOFT SIDES

The following are some exercises to help you with a horse that shows a marked stiffness on one side of his body.

1. The first exercise is to compensate for this one-sidedness by bending your horse too much on the stiff side and not at all on the soft side until he becomes more even. Do this while riding both on straight lines as well as on curved lines.

For instance, let's say your horse is stiff on the left side of his body and soft on the right. When you go right (clockwise) around an arena, a field or a circle, don't use your bending aids. Ride as if you're on a straight line (fig. 8.12). Riding a corner without any bending aids will prevent the horse from "collapsing" or "curling" on his soft right side.

Alternatively, when you go left around an arena to his stiff side, use bending aids as if you're on a curve even when you're on the straight lines. By doing so, you get more practice time stretching the shortened muscles on the soft side—the outside of your horse's body.

2. Here's another bending exercise to help soften the stiff side. Ride a large circle and then a smaller circle inside and touching it (fig. 8.13). Adjust your bending aids for the smaller circle and stay on it until your horse bends easily. Then, keeping your aids on as if you're still on this small circle, go back to the larger circle. Visualize the outside of your horse's body—his soft side where the muscles are shortened—stretching and lengthening to allow him to bend around your inside leg. Even if you can only do this in the walk for a while, the exercise helps your horse to bend on his stiff side. When he becomes more flexible, you can do it in the trot and then in the canter.

RIDING CORNERS AND CIRCLES CORRECTLY

Many riders just cruise through corners and turns without thought. When correctly ridden, each corner gives you a chance to develop your horse's ability to bend. Every corner in an oblong arena should be ridden as if it's one-quarter of a circle.

A circle is the first gymnastic exercise that we teach a horse on the longe line. By making a round circle, he learns to bend laterally through his side and to bend the joints of his inside hind leg. So every correctly ridden corner presents an opportunity to do the same thing. In a rectangular area, you're given this chance to "gymnasticize" your horse four times as you go once around the ring!

A good rule of thumb is to go into the corner only to a depth that your horse can handle without losing his rhythm and balance. However, once he can easily negotiate a shallow corner, challenge him by going into the corners a bit more "deeply." By "deeply," I mean rather than getting lured into following the well-worn track while riding around the corner, make a new path by riding slightly outside the old track and a bit closer to the fence.

Sloppy corners and circles begin with the rider, but eventually develop as a way for the horse to physically escape the demands of bending and, therefore, be subtly disobedient. If you allow your horse to do as he chooses because you're being careless, he'll begin to make more decisions—a situation you wisely want to avoid.

TRANSITIONS

DESCRIPTION

Generally the word **transition** applies to any sort of change. In training, a horse can show the following kinds of transitions:

1. Transitions from one pace to another, such as going from walk to trot or from trot to canter.

2. Transitions within a pace, such as from a working gait to a lengthening of that working gait.

3. Transitions from movement to movement, such as from a leg-yield into a lengthening.

All transitions should be made quickly, yet must be fluid and smooth. The regular rhythm of the pace as well as the tempo is maintained right up to the moment when the pace is changed or the horse is asked to halt.

This next section deals specifically with the transitions from one pace to another. I'll discuss both upward transitions, in which the horse is asked to go from the halt or from a slower pace into a faster one, as well as downward transitions, in which the horse is asked to go from a faster pace to a slower one, or to the halt.

To practice this, sit on your horse in the halt and focus on the immobility of your seat. Then, when you want to do a downward transition, mimic the stillness that your seat had when you were in the halt. Pick a particular point in the ring or on the trail and as you pass that spot, make your body immobile (figs. 8.14 and 8.15).

After you learn how to "still" your seat, you need to educate your horse so you can use your seat as the primary aid for downward transitions. To do this, combine your stilled seat with your voice. Your horse already knows simple voice commands from work on the longe line. If you want to go from canter to trot, tighten your stomach muscles to brace your lower back, "still" your seat, and say "Terrot" in the same way you do while longeing.

If your horse doesn't listen to your voice and back, take advantage of the walls of an indoor arena or a high rail outside. Let's say you want to

THE AIDS FOR UPWARD TRANSITIONS

The following is a list of general aids for all upward transitions, although later in this chapter I address some of the problems connected specifically with transitions to the canter under the section called Helpful Hints For Canter Departs.

1. Halt to walk; walk to trot:

Seat: use a "driving" seat, where you give a little push with your seat as if you're trying to move the back of the saddle toward the front of the saddle.

Legs: close both legs equally on the horse's sides.

Hands: maintain a soft, equal contact with the horse's mouth.

2. Canter depart from walk or trot (left lead):

Seat: weight on left seat bone.

Left leg: squeeze on the girth to promote "forward."

Right leg: swing behind the girth once in a windshield wiper action to signal the outside hind leg to begin the first beat of the canter.

Left rein: vibrate to position the horse's head just enough to the inside so you can see the inside eye. This positioning is called flexion. (Flexion is discussed in detail on page 136.)

Right rein: hold it steady to support and limit bend in the neck to the left, as well as to keep the horse from going faster in the walk or trot.

As far as upward transitions are concerned, you shouldn't have to push or drive your horse into the next pace. You should be able to give a signal with light aids. If you feel like nothing is happening and you want to squeeze harder, you need to go back to the Basics and put him "in front of your leg" again, as I described earlier on page 50.

8.14 The rider is in a "ready" position to use her back. She is stretching upward with her shoulders directly above her hips, and there is a gentle curve in the small of her back.

8.15 Here, the rider has "stilled" her seat for a downward transition. She tightens her stomach muscles as if she is doing a situp. As a result, the curve in her back has lessened. Note that her shoulders remain over her hips—it's important not to lean back when you "still" your seat.

THE AIDS FOR DOWNWARD TRANSITIONS

Canter to trot; trot to walk; walk to halt:

Legs: first close both legs as you did for upward transitions. You do this to keep the hind legs active and stepping well under the horse's body.

Reins: momentarily close both hands into fists to contain that energy and stop the horse from going faster.

Be sure not to use the reins for downward transitions without using your legs at the same time: any use of the reins without equal use of your legs will discourage the horse's hind legs from coming under his body. The flow and balance will be interrupted and the horse's frame will change. The problem with this is that you usually get some of the result you're looking for. Therefore, you continue to do the same thing and it becomes a habit. You know the cycle! The goal: to get from trot to walk. The method: pull on the reins. The payoff: you're walking. Now you're trained (and the horse too) to pull on the reins for downward transitions.

Seat: use a **"stilled seat"**—that is, sit with equal weight on both of your seat bones and use your back in a stopping, non-following, or retarding way; think about stretching tall and tightening your stomach muscles the way you would when doing a sit-up. This will cause you to brace your lower back. Keep your back braced while you stop your hips from following the motion of the horse.

8.16 When you're saying, "Whoa," and your horse continues to creep along, instead of resorting to the reins, turn him toward the arena wall or rail. He'll stop—I guarantee it!

go from walk to halt. You're "stilling" your seat, saying "Whoa," and he continues to creep along, not halting. Instead of resorting to the reins at this point, turn him toward the wall. When he meets the wall or rail, he'll stop and you can then praise him and try again without the wall (fig. 8.16).

Sometimes I find that riders get overly concerned that they aren't using their backs "correctly." There's no need to worry. We all have different bodies that move in different ways. As long as you use your back the same way each time, somehow get the response by combining the use of the back with a voice command that the horse knows, and then praise the result, your horse will learn to respond to your back—believe me!

What is necessary for your back to work for you is that you must be sitting in the correct position with an independent seat so you have a "ready" back. Regardless of the style of riding you do, you want to be centered and in balance. As a Western, saddle seat, or dressage rider with longer stirrups, you need to sit vertically so that a plumb line attached to your ear will pass through

the tip of your shoulder, hip joint, and ankle, straight through your center. Stretch up tall so there's a gentle curve in the small of your back. If you ride hunters, jumpers, or combined training horses with shorter stirrups for jumping, you need to bring your upper body forward in order to be in balance. A plumb line dropped through your center would also pass through your feet. Your hips stay behind the plumb line to offset the weight of your forward-reaching head and shoulders.

When you tighten your stomach from this balanced and "ready" position, and stop your seat from following the movement, the horse will do the downward transition.

✳ HELPFUL HINTS FOR ALL TRANSITIONS

Both upward and downward transitions should be clear and distinct but not abrupt. They should be done in a fluid manner. The horse should go directly from working gait to working gait. While teaching, I often see a rider allow her horse to take steps that are lazy, little, or in a different rhythm. Many times the horse even rushes off into the new gait. Remember, there shouldn't have to be any adjustment to build energy back up or steady the horse's tempo back down to a good working gait. For the most part I've found that simply making a rider aware that she needs to put her full attention into maintaining the quality of the working gait—before and after the transition—is enough to fix the problem.

Sometimes this extra awareness isn't enough, and you'll find it necessary to do an exercise to give both you and your horse the feeling of maintaining energy as you start the next gait. Ride a few transitions from medium walk into a lengthened trot, or from working canter to a lengthening in the trot, in order to make the trot after the transition more energetic. Then, when you do an upward or a downward transition, pretend you're going to do a lengthening rather than the normal working trot, and you should end up with good energy at the working trot. You can do this for the walk and canter, as well.

☀ HELPFUL HINTS FOR DOWNWARD TRANSITIONS

Some horses tend to rush off after a downward transition—particularly when going from the canter to the trot. If your horse does this, immediately halt. Praise him by patting or using your voice by saying, ("Good boy!") to explain to him that he's done the right thing by stopping. Although the halt should be done fairly sharply, your goal is not to punish but to educate. So the

reward is essential! Do this several times until you feel that your horse chooses to do the downward transition into a controlled and balanced working trot.

Later in this book (chapter 12) I'll show you how you can also use backing up, small circles, and leg-yielding to explain to your horse that he's not to rush off after a downward transition.

☀ HELPFUL HINTS FOR CANTER DEPARTS

Frequently, I see horses who don't do a distinct upward transition from the walk or the trot into the canter. The horse hobbles through the first canter stride in almost a four-beat rhythm.

The problem here is usually a lack of energy. To make the transition more distinct, change the emphasis of your aids. You'll still give the signal for the strike-off by swinging your outside leg behind the girth, but now focus more on your inside leg, which is on the girth. Give a sharper squeeze with this leg than you did before, to remind him to go energetically forward.

There's another common situation that you might run into during a walk-to-canter or trot-to-canter transition that we will deal with in the next chapter. There are times when a horse will swing his haunches toward the inside of the ring to avoid the engagement of his inside hind leg. You can help the horse avoid this tendency by riding him in a shoulder-fore position, which I describe in chapter 9.

Another canter problem you will run into with a young or uneducated horse is picking

8.17 To teach yourself not to pull on the inside rein during a canter depart, exaggerate softening your inside hand by putting it forward as your horse steps into the canter.

up the wrong lead. Often this happens in one direction more frequently than in the other. Keep in mind that the horse will pick up whatever lead he's bent and positioned toward at the moment of departure. Sometimes, the rider has the horse nicely bent around the inside leg, but in the moment of the depart, the horse counter-bends and ends up picking up the wrong lead. The solution is to maintain active bending aids—vibrate your inside rein and squeeze with your inside leg—*right through the moment of the transition.*

If you need help maintaining the correct bend to the inside, first spiral in to make the circle smaller. Then, increase the size of the circle by pushing the horse back out to the larger circle with your inside leg which is on the girth. This is an example of leg-yielding—a lateral movement which I'll describe in detail in the next chapter. Keep your inside leg on the girth and feel the horse give in his rib cage and bend around your inside leg while he's stepping sideways. Do this several times until he's softly bending correctly. Then, when you've enlarged the circle almost back to its original size and while you're still leg-yielding, ask for the canter depart.

The previous helpful hints have been directed toward correctly preparing *the horse* for transitions to the canter. The next two hints are for you, *the rider.*

If you pull on the inside rein during a canter depart, you interrupt the horse's flow and balance, and he can't go forward through the transition. He feels blocked by your hand and takes a short step into the canter. If you tend to do this, you should exaggerate when correcting this riding problem until it's resolved. While asking for the depart, put slack in your inside rein by placing your inside hand several inches toward the horse's mouth. When this becomes your new habit, don't actually loosen the rein, but just think about softening your hand forward (fig. 8.17).

Here's another hint for you to keep in mind when you ask for a transition into the canter. The signal for the canter depart is to swing the outside leg behind the girth in a windshield wiper-like action. But because horses are often dull to the aids, a rider often gets into the habit of bringing that outside leg back and holding it there for a few seconds until the horse finally answers. This sets a bad precedent, because horses should be trained to respond immediately to any aid.

If this has happened to you, you need to put your horse in front of your leg again. Swing your outside leg back and forth once. If your horse does not immediately strike off into the canter, give him a sharp kick or tap him with your stick to chase him forward. Then retest his reaction to your leg by once again swinging your leg back to signal the transition to the canter. You might have to do this several times until you "retrain" your horse to react more quickly to the aid.

BACKING UP (THE REIN BACK)

DESCRIPTION

No matter what type of riding you do, at the very least you need to be able to tell your horse to stop, go, turn left, turn right, and back up. Your horse needs to be able to understand and do those things in order to be an enjoyable and obedient riding mount.

In dressage, backing up is called the **rein back**. It's a movement which is shown in competition and judged by some very specific criteria. We can use some of these criteria as guidelines for improving how your horse backs up.

In the rein back the horse steps straight backward by raising and setting his feet down almost simultaneously in diagonal pairs. To the naked eye it appears that the legs move in diagonal pairs, and in classical training it's considered a fault if the horse goes back in a four-beat rhythm. The fact is, however, that each front foot is raised and set down an instant before the diagonal hind foot, so that on hard ground sometimes four separate beats are heard. But you shouldn't be able to see this.

During the rein back, the horse must be active and energetic and should pick up and set down his legs clearly and deliberately without dragging or stepping wide with his hind legs. In your mind's eye, picture your horse stepping up over ground poles as he goes backward (fig. 8.18).

8.18 If your horse tends to drag his feet when he backs up, imagine that he is stepping up over poles on the ground.

8.19 In the rein-back, lighten your seat and point your seat bones toward the back of the saddle, as if pushing a stool out from underneath you.

※ HELPFUL HINTS

INTRODUCING THE REIN BACK FROM THE GROUND

While teaching the rein back, I've seen a lot of uneducated horses who absolutely refuse to back up. They don't necessarily rear or fuss, but they remain rooted to the ground. In desperation, the riders start yanking on the reins. Not a pretty sight!

When I have a horse like this, I go through several stages. I start teaching the rein back from the ground, and say the word "Back" as I place my hand on his chest and gently push. When he steps back, I praise with treats or a pat. (It's a good idea, by the way, to take advantage of every opportunity you have when handling your horse in the barn to teach him the word "Back.")

THE AIDS FOR BACKING UP

Seat: lighten your seat by tipping forward slightly and pointing your seat bones toward the back of the saddle as if pushing a stool out from underneath you (fig. 8.19).

Legs: close both legs slightly behind the girth.

Hands: close in fists, then when the horse begins to step back, soften them. If the horse resists the reins, you can softly vibrate them.

Then, transfer this idea to your mounted work. Start with an assistant who can press on his chest just as you did with your ground work while you give the aids and say the word "Back." The assistant can gradually move a bit further away from the horse and just stand there while you ask the horse to back up. If your horse doesn't move, she can walk up to him and press on his chest again. Eventually you'll be able to back up without help but still using the voice command combined with your aids. Finally, back up simply from the aids alone without the use of your voice (fig. 8.20 and 8.21).

INTRODUCING THE REIN BACK FROM THE SADDLE

Making Your Horse Wait

Sometimes the difficulty with a horse that's just learning to back up is that he begins to anticipate and back up every time you halt. For this eager horse who tries too hard to do what he thinks you want, do a lot of transitions to the halt without asking him to back up. When he doesn't take the initiative anymore, do the occasional rein back.

This problem may be caused by the rider, so always make your horse wait several seconds after halting before giving the command to back up.

Along the same lines as the horse that anticipates backing up is the horse that rushes backward. One of my students, Ruth, had a lovely well-schooled Hanoverian gelding that she was showing in upper-level dressage competitions. All of his work was of a very high quality

8.20 Use an assistant who can press gently on your horse's chest to give him the idea of stepping backward.

8.21 Gradually wean your horse away from needing help from the ground by having the assistant stand farther away. If the horse refuses to move back, the assistant can take a step or two toward him to remind him of what he's supposed to do.

8.22 Before backing up, come to a balanced halt. Rowen is square and in pretty good balance here.

8.23 To start backing up, Ally tips her upper body slightly forward, brings both legs a bit behind the girth, and closes the fingers of both hands in fists.

except for the rein back. He was absolutely panicked by it and would rush backward when asked to perform it. We weren't sure why he did this. Maybe there were some "skeletons in his closet" from an earlier bad experience. Whatever the reason, we had to explain to him that he didn't have to run backward frantically.

To overcome his tension, Ruth used tactful aids and asked him to go back only one or two steps before stopping and praising a lot. While stepping back, she quietly said, "Whoa, whoa." She would intersperse these short rein backs here and there throughout a schooling session until it became part of his daily routine, and it was no big deal anymore. To help keep him calm, Ruth imagined him taking deliberate, methodical steps in slow motion while he carefully picked his feet up out of deep mud and placed them back down again (figs. 8.22 to 8.26).

Backing Up Straight

Sometimes horses don't back up in a straight line. This is often because one hind leg is weaker than the other and the horse avoids placing the weaker hind leg underneath his body. I once spent an entire competitive season compensating for this weakness in a young horse by riding the rein back with my left leg placed further back than the right. Sometimes I could just leave it there passively to guard against him swinging his haunches to the left, but sometimes I actually had to press with it in order to get him to back up straight.

When I was at home I often worked on correcting this problem by schooling him in an indoor arena. I tracked right so that his left side was next to the wall when I asked him to back up. Eventually he understood, and as his hindquarters became stronger, it was easy for him to

8.24 With each step backward, the diagonal pairs of legs appear to move together.

8.25 You can see that Rowen reaches nicely into Ally's hand because there's a solid straight line of contact from her elbow to his mouth, and his face is slightly in front of the vertical.

8.26 If Rowen's steps were a bit longer, this rein-back would be even better.

keep his left hind leg underneath his body, so I was able to return to positioning my legs side by side.

If you find that your horse consistently doesn't back up straight, make sure the rein pressure is even. If you have a stronger feel on the right rein, for instance, he will step to the left.

Having said that, there are times when you will purposely ask your horse to go sideways while backing up. It's helpful to do this with the horse that backs up a step or two but then stalls out and refuses to go back anymore. For this type of horse, push him sideways by placing one of your legs further back than the other and pressing with it. Pushing him sideways helps to keep him in motion as you back up. When he has finally learned to step back for as many steps as you ask—crooked or otherwise—you can then start backing up on a straight line again.

Teaching Your Horse To Take Better Steps

I often see horses that back up by taking very short steps. Because the steps are short, the horse's back drops, and he sticks his head and neck up in the air. This is uncomfortable for both horse and rider.

If your horse does this, I suggest that you continue backing quietly until your horse takes his first longer step. Even if you can't feel the longer step or the subsequent raising of the back, you'll see your horse's head and neck begin to lower. His lowered head and neck mean that the steps are getting longer. As soon as this happens, stop and praise him. Walk forward for a few strides and start the process again, always stopping and rewarding him when he takes some long steps. While doing this, picture his hind legs staying well under the body as if he's stepping forward toward your hand, even though you're going backward. Soon your horse will learn to back up with long strides.

Sometimes you'll find that your horse takes long steps when you ask him to back up but he drags his feet. Ride some brisk trot-to-halt transitions. These transitions will engage his hind legs underneath his body so that the backward steps are crisp and active. Make sure you apply your driving aids as the horse steps into halt, so that the hind legs are well underneath the body, and he has a better chance of moving the legs back in diagonal pairs.

LENGTHENINGS

DESCRIPTION

The horse that is working at the basic levels in dressage should be able to show two "gears" in his trot and canter—a working trot and canter, and a **lengthening** of both paces.

In a correct lengthening of the working trot and canter, two things visibly change. While maintaining the same rhythm and tempo (the rate of repetition of the rhythm) of whichever gait he's working in, the horse elongates both his stride and the frame of his body to the utmost that he is capable of doing at this stage of his development. All horses should learn how to lengthen their strides and bodies because it's a great way to promote suppleness.

A lengthening can be developed from the working trot and the working canter. During the lengthening of a gait it's of the utmost importance for your horse to maintain both the same regular rhythm and the same tempo that was established when he was in the working gait. The sound of his footfalls should not change. What does change is the length of his stride and his frame so that he's covering more ground with each stride (figs. 8.27 to 8.30).

For the sake of clarity and for some of you readers who know a bit about dressage, I'd like to mention here that there is a difference between a *lengthening* in trot and canter and what is called in dressage vernacular a *medium* or an *extended* gait. Riders often incorrectly use these terms interchangeably. That's probably because they

8.27 An active, lively working trot, clearly showing the horse stepping up into the tracks of his forefeet.

8.28 When Rowen lengthens his working trot, he covers more ground with each stride, the goal being that his hind foot touches the ground in front of the place that his front foot left the ground.

8.29 Bekki and Maeve showing a well-balanced working canter.

8.30 A lengthening of the working canter. Notice how active the mare's inside hind leg is and how far it reaches under her body. The balance is well maintained rather than shifting to the forehand as so often happens when you ask a horse to lengthen.

8.31 In an extended trot (rather than a lengthened trot) the horse's center of gravity is more toward the hindquarters. As a result, his balance seems to be going uphill, like an airplane taking off.

THE AIDS FOR LENGTHENINGS

When you're ready to ask for an upward transition to a lengthening, the aids applied simultaneously are as follows:

Seat: use a driving seat, as though you're pushing the back of the saddle toward the front of the saddle.

Legs: press lightly with both legs to signal your horse to express his energy forward over the ground in longer strides.

Reins: soften your hands a bit forward, but keep a contact with your horse's mouth and a bend in your elbows. Do not "throw the reins away."

do share some similarities, specifically that the horse's strides and frame of his body elongate while the rhythm and tempo of the gait stay the same. However, there is a major difference: in a medium or extended gait, the horse's balance and center of gravity are in quite a different place than when he just performs a lengthening.

A lengthening is developed from a working gait. In a working gait the horse's balance and center of gravity are somewhat on his forehand, so it's reasonable to assume that the horse's balance in a lengthening is also somewhat toward his forehand.

A medium or extended gait, on the other hand, can only be developed from a *collected gait*. In a collected gait, the horse's hindquarters are lower than in a working gait, and they support a greater proportion of his weight than his front legs. The horse's center of gravity, therefore, is more toward the hind legs. (This is the aim of **collection** or **self-carriage.**) During a medium or an extended gait, the horse's center of gravity remains more toward the hindquarters, just as it was in the collected gait. As a result, his balance and silhouette seem to be going uphill, like an airplane taking off (fig. 8.31).

For now I'll only be dealing with lengthenings which are developed from the working gaits. Starting in chapter 16, I'll discuss collected, medium and extended gaits more fully.

8.32 To help you understand the type of suppleness you need when doing lengthenings, think of your horse's body as a rubber band that can easily stretch and contract.

Lengthenings can be done on both straight lines and circles. But keep in mind that because of the bend and the demands being made on the inside hind leg when you're on a curved line, lengthenings on a circle are physically harder than those ridden on a straight line.

I suggest you add lengthenings to your horse's education once he is fairly steady and balanced in his working gaits. Some people delay starting lengthenings with their horses for several years, and I believe this is a mistake. Think of how a gymnast needs to stretch and elongate her muscles when she's young. If she doesn't develop her suppleness early on, it will be very difficult to find that elasticity later.

Your horse's working gaits should already contain sufficient energy for him to be able to do lengthenings easily in trot and canter. If they don't, you need to first make your horse more active so he has enough power to lengthen. You can do this by checking that he is forward—both

forward over the ground as well as "hot off your leg," which I discussed earlier in the book (see pp. 50-51).

❋ HELPFUL HINTS FOR LENGTHENINGS

Here's an image that will help you understand the type of suppleness you're developing when you practice lengthenings. Think of your horse's body as a rubber band that can easily stretch and contract. Not only will this quality make him more athletic, but it's also extremely useful for all disciplines of riding (fig. 8.32). Take show jumping, for instance. Just think how many jumping faults could be avoided if your horse's stride were easily adjustable like this!

MAINTAINING THE TEMPO OF THE WORKING TROT

As with most new work, when you begin to incorporate lengthenings into your training, you start in the trot. It's a bonus if you have a horse that can naturally lengthen his trot. Many Warmbloods and Arabians have this ability, but I've worked with a lot of Thoroughbreds, Connemaras, Morgans, and Quarter Horses who really need help developing their lengthenings in the trot.

If you ask your horse to lengthen in the way I've described and the tempo gets quicker because he runs with short, fast steps, you need to systematically develop his lengthenings. Part

8.33 When asking for a lengthening, I picture my horse floating, with his feet never touching the ground.

of his difficulty may be purely physical. He may lack the suppleness and strength that he will gain in time by basic dressage training. But part of the problem may be that the horse just doesn't understand that he is to take longer strides in the same tempo. He actually thinks he's being obedient when he rushes off because he feels you close your legs, and he responds eagerly by immediately going forward.

I often find that I can help him understand that he is to lengthen his strides without speeding up, by asking for the lengthenings while going up hills. Once he gets the idea, I go back into the ring and see if he can transfer this concept of lengthening in the same tempo on the level footing.

Sometimes I do something a bit unusual with the horse that tends to quicken his trot tempo when asked to lengthen. Since it takes time to develop the lengthening, I go out in a big field

or I go all the way around the ring and round off the corners so that I don't have to slow down for them. First, I take up a heavier contact than normal. In this way, I can temporarily act as the horse's "fifth" leg and purposely support him so he doesn't lose his balance. Then I ask for a lengthening in posting trot. While posting to the trot, I rise very high and stay in the air a fraction of a second longer than normal. I pretend that I can hold the horse in the air with my body. And, in my mind's eye, I picture him floating over the ground with his feet never touching the ground (fig. 8.33).

I ask my horse to give me a greater and greater effort and eventually one of two things will happen. The first is that he realizes that his legs can't go any faster, and he "shifts into over-drive" and takes some longer, slower steps. At this point I immediately stop, praise him, and let him walk on a loose rein.

In my experience I've found that the first time, I might have to go all the way around a ring once or twice before I get a couple of longer, slower steps. But after the reward, the next effort yields results much sooner. And the same for the next attempt.

The other thing that might happen is that he loses his balance and falls into the canter. This isn't the disaster it seems to be. If my horse hadn't lost his balance and cantered, his next trot step probably would have been a bit longer. So I reestablish the trot and immediately ask for a lengthening. It's in that moment that I'm most apt to get a longer stride in a better tempo. And once again if I get even one or two better steps, I stop and praise him. The reward helps the horse to understand that by doing something different, even if initially he doesn't understand what it is, he'll be praised.

Once I can get two or three better steps as soon as I ask for the lengthening, I leave them for another day. During each session the horse builds his understanding of what's being asked, and over time he physically gets strong enough to lengthen in a good tempo for a greater number of steps.

HEAR THE TEMPO

Use some good auditory images to help you while you're teaching your horse to lengthen in the same tempo as his working gait. Pretend you're standing by a paved road and your eyes are closed. Because the tempo stays exactly the same, you can't tell from the sound of the foot-falls whether your horse is in the working gait, lengthening, or doing the transition in between.

Here's another auditory image to help you teach your horse to lengthen the trot in the same tempo as his working trot. Pretend you hear a metronome ticking. The tempo stays exactly the same both when you're in the working trot and when you're in the lengthening (fig. 8.34). (Even though I'm discussing trot lengthenings at the moment, you can use the same type of auditory image if your horse quickens his tempo in a canter lengthening. "Hear" the tempo as if your horse is moving over the ground with big, ground-covering bounds in slow motion.)

If your horse still tends to quicken his tempo when you ask him to lengthen, overcompensate

8.34 Pretend you hear a metronome ticking. The tempo of the lengthened trot should not change at all from the "ticking" you heard in your horse's working trot.

by imagining that you "hear" the tempo get slower. Pretend that the tempo gets slower because your horse stays suspended in the air for a long time. If you're doing a posting trot, try rising and sitting more slowly to see if you can be the one to set the pace rather than automatically posting at the speed that your horse chooses.

USE FIRMER CONTACT FOR SUPPORT

Don't be surprised if the contact with your horse's mouth during lengthenings becomes somewhat heavy. Remember that lengthenings are developed out of a working gait and the weight in your hands is somewhat firm to begin with. (I discussed contact in chapter 7.) In addition, while your horse is learning how to balance himself during lengthenings, his center of gravity might shift even a bit further to his forehand. Don't be alarmed by this. It's a stage of his

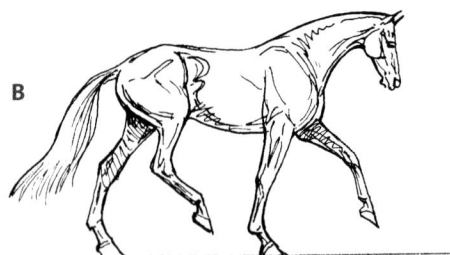

8.35 A & B The activity of the hind legs directly affects the horse's balance. Look at the difference between a horse trotting with his hind legs trailing out behind his body (A), and a horse trotting with his hind legs under him (B).

training, and it's fine to temporarily support him by maintaining a firmer contact. Later on, if you decide to go on to more advanced work, you'll develop "uphill" extensions out of collected gaits. Because the horse will be in self-carriage when he's in a collected gait, the contact will be lighter.

However, there's a fine line between a solid, supporting contact and one in which your horse is leaning so heavily on your hands that your arms ache. Here are some things you can try to improve a contact that is too heavy. Before you even begin to ask for a lengthening, make sure you drive the horse's hind legs more under his body by closing both of your legs. In order to carry himself, your horse needs to have his hind legs underneath him. If his hind legs are trailing out behind his body, he can't support himself in the lengthening, and he has no option but to lean on your hands (fig. 8.35 A).

You can also ride some quick transitions: from trot to halt and back to the trot again or from the canter to the walk and back to the canter again. This will help to rebalance your horse and make the weight in your hands more comfortable.

Another reason the contact can get too heavy is that you may be asking for too many

8.36 A & B The position of the horse's head and neck affects the quality of the lengthening. In a correct lengthening, the toe of forefoot points toward the spot where it will touch down (A). The foreleg cannot touch down in front of an imaginary line drawn down from an extension of the horse's profile to the ground. In an incorrect lengthening, the horse's toe flips up, his back is tense, and his front foot has no option but to retract before he can place it on the ground (B).

8.37 Ally is cranking Rowen's neck in, making it hard for him to lengthen his stride in the trot. Note how the toe of his extended front leg flips up in front—a sure sign that his rider is restricting him with the reins.

lengthened strides at one time before your horse is ready. Doing well-balanced lengthenings with his hind legs underneath his body for only a few strides at a time is much more valuable for your horse than lengthening for many strides with his hind legs pushing out behind his body.

Remember that when you do the downward transition back to the working gait, be sure that you close your legs to send his hind legs under his body. It might feel natural to ask for the downward transition from the lengthening to the working gait by just using the reins. But, as you know by now, if your goal is to rebalance your horse and improve the contact, you need to *add* hind legs while doing the downward transition (see Aids for Downward Transitions, p. 107).

ALLOW THE FRAME TO ELONGATE IN LENGTHENINGS

In trot lengthenings, the front feet should touch the ground on the spot toward which they are pointing when each leg is at its maximum extension. When a horse has to draw his front legs

back toward his body before placing them on the ground, or his toes flip up in front, it usually indicates that he hasn't been allowed to lengthen his frame (fig. 8.36).

Sometimes a rider makes it difficult for the horse to lengthen to his utmost. Although I said earlier that you shouldn't be concerned if the contact is a bit too firm, you want to be sure that you're not making it heavy because you're cranking his neck in. If you keep your horse's neck short by restricting him with strong or non-allowing hands, he has to draw his foreleg back before putting it down (fig. 8.37). Allow your horse to lengthen his neck and point the tip of his nose more or less forward. To help you to do this, think about "opening the front door" by

8.38 Allow your horse to lengthen his neck by "opening the front door." Soften your hands toward his mouth, and cock your wrists upward to allow your little fingers to go more forward.

softening your hands a bit toward your horse's mouth and by cocking your wrists upward in a way that allows your little fingers to go more forward (fig. 8.38).

SIT UPRIGHT

When you use your driving seat to ask for the transition into the lengthening, don't try to "help" your horse to lengthen by leaning back. Even though you might feel that you can drive him forward this way (and I see many dressage riders doing this in lengthenings and extensions), you'll just end up driving his back down and making it hollow. Stay vertical at all times.

I learned this lesson the hard way while trying to qualify for the Olympic Festival with Jolicoeur at a competition that was being held at Knoll Farm in Brentwood, New York, back in 1987. One of the finest international judges in

the world, the late Mr. Jaap Pot, was there. He was a stickler when it came to the correctness of the rider's seat. I remember Jo and I doing huge extended trots for him. I thought we had done really well until my score sheet came back with extremely low marks for the extensions and the simple comment—rider leaning behind the vertical. Believe me, it made an impression.

COUNTER-CANTER

DESCRIPTION

Counter-canter—also known as "false canter"—is an obedience and suppling exercise. Up until the point that you introduce it, all of your horse's education has been to canter with the inside foreleg leading—the "correct" lead. This is known as "true" canter.

In counter-canter you ask your horse to canter on what is considered the wrong lead. For instance, while riding to the left, ask your horse to stay on the right lead. This is contrary to everything he's been taught about the canter to this point. He might initially become confused and think he's doing the wrong thing by cantering with his outside foreleg leading. He might also feel a bit awkward and uncomfortable until he develops the strength and balance to negotiate this movement (figs. 8.39 and 8.40).

To avoid confusion, understand that when you hear the words "inside" and "outside" in relation to counter-canter, they refer to the lead you're on rather than to the direction you're

8.39 Ally canters Rowen across the diagonal in true canter on his right lead.

THE AIDS FOR COUNTER-CANTER

For counter-canter on the right lead while going to the left (counterclockwise): the aids are those used for right lead canter:

Seat: weight on right seat bone.

Right leg: on the girth.

Left leg: slightly behind the girth.

Right rein: vibrates for flexion.

Left rein: supports to prevent the neck from bending too much to the right.

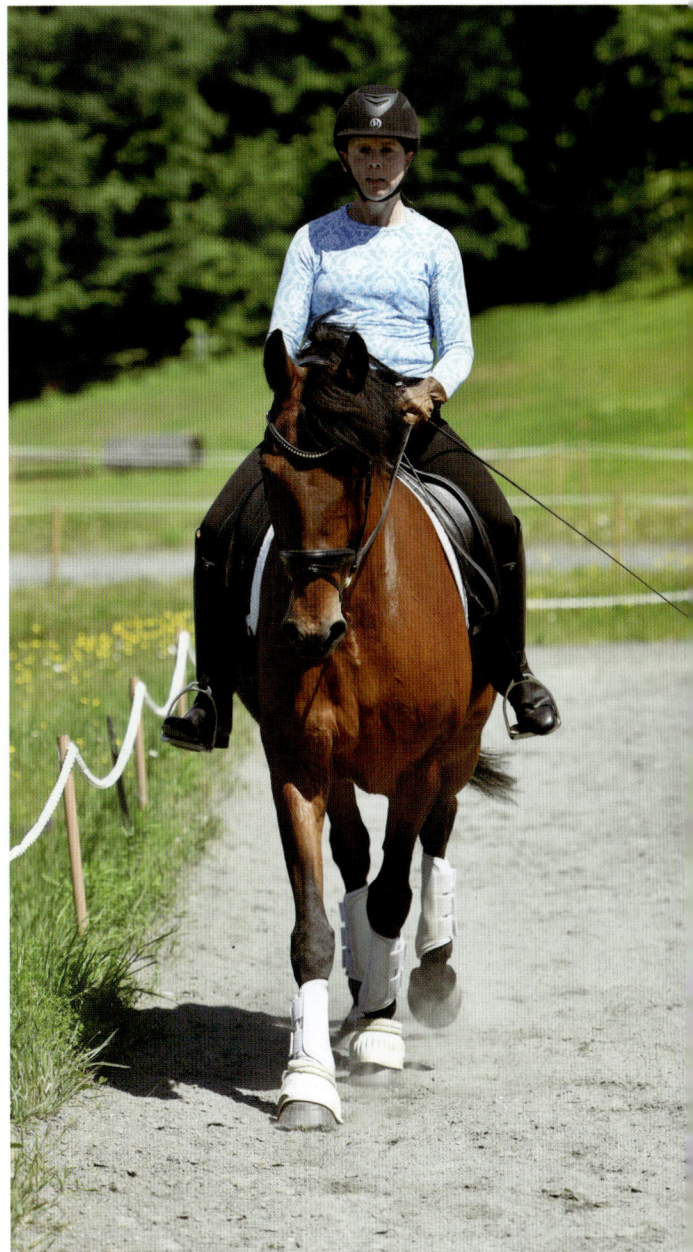

8.40 Ally keeps Rowen on the right lead after she reaches the long side (she's now in counter-canter) by keeping her weight on her right seat bone, her right leg on the girth, and her left leg slightly behind the girth.

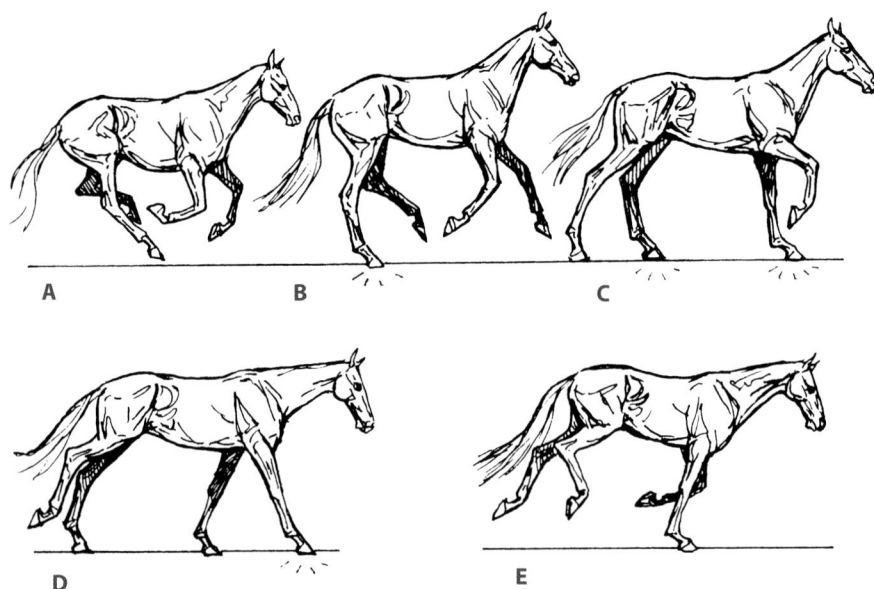

8.41 A–E A faulty, disunited or cross-canter sequence with the horse going to the right: suspension (A), first beat with the right hind (B), second beat with the lateral pair of left hind and left fore (C), third beat with the right fore (D), and pushing off with the horse on the left lead behind and right lead in front (E).

going. The leading leg is always on the inside. So, when you are riding to the left in counter-canter on the right lead, the right side of the horse's body is the inside even though it's the side closest to the fence.

TEACHING COUNTER-CANTER

Introduce counter-canter gradually. It's best to start on a straight line or a very gentle curve, rather than on a circle or in tight turns or corners. By following a systematic plan, you can minimize problems such as stiffening, breaking to the trot, switching leads, or cross-cantering (also known as a "disunited canter"). A horse cross-canters when he canters on one lead with his front legs and the other lead with his hind legs (fig. 8. 41). For instance, when you are trying to canter correctly on the right lead and your horse cross-canters instead, the sequence of his

legs becomes right hind, then the lateral pair of left hind and left fore together, and finally the right fore. Essentially, he's on the left lead behind and on the right lead in front. When a horse cross-canters, he looks and feels awkward and out of balance. (See the drawings on p. 81 for a correct canter.)

The following are counter-canter exercises starting with the simplest and progressively increasing in difficulty. Don't attempt a more difficult pattern until your horse can negotiate the earlier one confidently.

1. Start by going to the left (counterclockwise) while in left lead canter—a true canter. After coming through the second corner of the short side of the ring, arc gently off the track (fig. 8.42). Canter three or four strides toward the middle of the ring and then turn back toward the track before the next corner. In this exercise you'll

8.42 Counter-Canter Exercise 1:
Ride to the left in true canter. Arc gently away from the track on the long side, and then back to it again. You are doing counter-canter for the few strides when you head back to the long side.

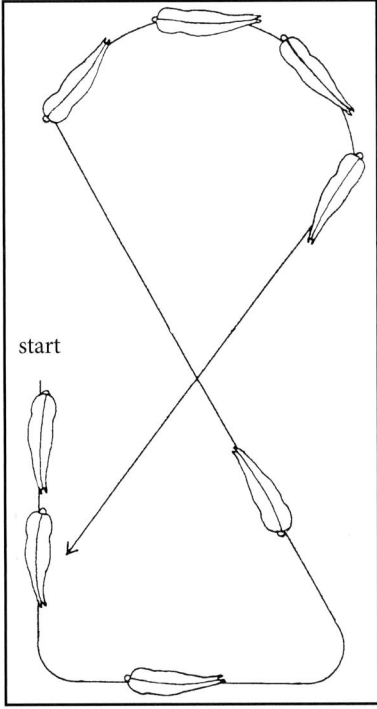

8.43 Counter-Canter Exercise 2: Ride to the left in true canter. Go across the diagonal but don't change your canter lead as you do normally. Stay on the left lead around the short side, and then go back across the opposite diagonal.

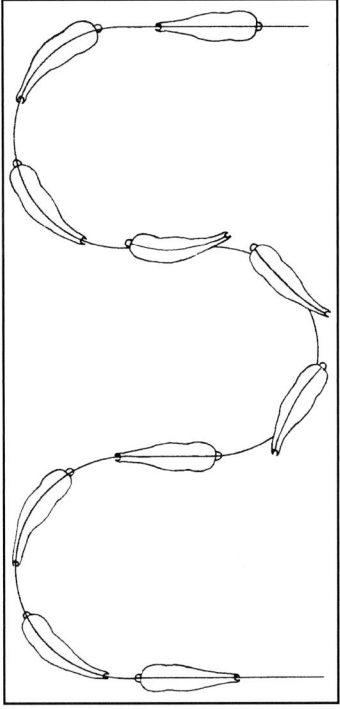

8.44 Counter-Canter Exercise 3: Ride a series of three large loops—a serpentine—on the same canter lead.

only be doing counter-canter for a few strides—the strides during which you're changing direction and beginning to head back toward the long side that you were on originally.

2. Once again, start by riding to the left (counterclockwise) in true canter. Go across the diagonal of the ring, but don't change your canter lead as you do normally. Instead, stay on the left lead through the short side and go back across the next diagonal (fig. 8.43). This exercise is somewhat more demanding than the previous

one because you're asking your horse to stay in counter-canter throughout the entire short side. However, be sure not to go into the corners too deeply because that will greatly increase the degree of difficulty, and your horse is apt to lose his balance at this stage.

3. Ride all the way around the ring in counter-canter, making sure not to go into the corners too deeply.

8.45 If you have a mental block about picking up the counter-canter lead while going left on the long side of your ring (for example), pretend you're going to pick up true canter and circle your horse right out through the rail.

4. Do a large circle in counter-canter (at least 20 meters or 66 feet in diameter).

5. Ride a series of three large loops (a serpentine), staying on the same lead (fig. 8.44).

6. Increase the number of loops on the serpentine.

Once your horse understands counter-canter, as an obedience exercise try picking up the counter-canter lead while you're on the long side of your arena. Some horses and riders find it difficult to pick up the counter-canter lead while close to the rail because it makes them feel claustrophobic. So, if either you or your horse has this psychological block to picking up the counter-canter lead on the track around your arena, try working a few feet away from it. Then, when you're going to the left and you go to pick up counter-canter on the right lead, think of it as a true canter and that you are going to turn toward the rail on your right, canter right through it and out of the arena! (See fig. 8.45.)

HELPFUL HINTS FOR COUNTER-CANTER •

In the following examples you'll be in counter-canter on the right lead while you're riding to the left (counterclockwise). Your horse maintains his natural flexion at the poll to the right and he is also slightly bent to the right toward the side of his leading leg. Most of these hints will help you stay out of your horse's way.

First, consider your reins. If you hang on the inside (right) rein, you'll block your horse's inside hind leg and he'll probably break to the trot. Think about softening your inside hand forward and, if necessary, use an active inside leg to maintain the canter. Keep your arms elastic and your elbows moving so you can push your hands forward toward your horse's mouth on the third beat of the canter.

Next, think about how your upper body normally rocks back and forth with the motion of the canter. Ideally, you want to rock behind the vertical with each stride because if you come in front of the vertical, you'll be putting more weight on your horse's forehand. "See" yourself rocking backward with each stride so you can think about cantering your horse "up" in front of your body rather than letting his hind legs escape out behind your seat and his body. Be sure to stop the motion of your body when you're on the vertical. Don't allow your shoulders to come even slightly in front of the vertical. If you do, you'll give your horse an escape route that allows him to lose his balance and fall on his forehand.

Here's an image that might help you with this concept of leaning back so you can help your horse lower his hindquarters and "sit down behind" so that he's "up" in front. Pretend that you're sitting on a see-saw and each time you lean back and push your end down, the other end goes up (fig. 8.46).

Finally, feel the same roundness and impulsion in each counter-canter bound as you have felt in true canter. Experience the same ease, balance, and comfort in counter-canter that you have in true canter. Stay loose by convincing yourself that you're really riding true canter and the arena wall or rail just happens to be on the other side. Remember to breathe deeply and rhythmically. If you get tight and hold your breath, so will your partner.

8.46 Lean back when riding counter-canter to help your horse lower his hindquarters—"sit down behind"—so that he is "up" in front. Pretend you are sitting on a seesaw and that each time you lean back and push your end down, the other end goes up.

COMMON PROBLEMS

The most common mistake that I see when a rider starts counter-canter is that she bends her horse's neck too much toward the side of his leading leg (the "inside" leg) so that his shoulders fall to the outside of the line they're on (fig. 8.47).

In other words, when the horse is going left in counter-canter on the right lead and the neck is overly bent to the right (inside), he ends up leaning on the left (outside) rein and falling sideways on his left shoulder. In this position he is no longer **axis-straight.** In order to be in

8.47 Here Ally has made Rowen crooked in counter-canter by bending his neck too much toward the leading leg (the right leg). As a result, the horse's shoulders fall to his left and his hindquarters drift to the right.

good balance, he needs to have his shoulders straight between the reins.

In counter-canter on the right lead, the right hand vibrates for flexion but the left hand must support to limit how much the horse bends his neck to the right. Keep in mind that the balance and position in counter-canter should be identical to that of true canter.

Sometimes I'll help my students understand this feeling of keeping the shoulders between the reins rather than letting the horse fall sideways onto his outside shoulder by doing the following exercise. While in the counter-canter, I have them counter-flex their horses at the poll. For example, while riding left in counter-canter on the right lead, they'll vibrate the left rein to position their horses so they can just see the left eye. By doing this, the horse's shoulders slide back to the right, and they end up between the two reins. In this way, both horse and rider learn the feeling of being straight in counter-canter.

Frequently, when learning counter-canter, a rider allows her horse to pick up speed. If your horse goes too fast, his hind legs will sprawl out behind him. Once again he'll lose his balance by either running onto his forehand or breaking to the trot. Do several transitions from the counter-canter to the walk and back to the counter-canter again to help him keep his hind legs underneath him. The transitions will help rebalance him. In chapter 13 you'll learn how to use half-halts to control the speed and maintain balance.

The rhythm of the horse's canter should stay exactly the same in counter-canter as it is in true canter. Sometimes, however, the rhythm of the canter gets labored and degenerates into four beats. This often happens because the rider is too restrictive with the reins or because the horse's body gets long and strung out so that his hind legs are no longer well underneath him. When this happens, freshen and restore the rhythm by riding more forward into a lengthening and then make an effort to maintain this crisp rhythm while in counter-canter.

KEY POINTS

- This chapter has contained movements and exercises that most horses, being ridden in any discipline, will be able to do.

- The movements are useful not just as an end in themselves to make your horse more athletic, but they can also be used to lay a foundation for more advanced work or to work through a problem.

- Transitions are a good indicator of a horse's suppleness. They should be prompt, fluid, and smooth without either any rushing or any decrease of power.

- Correct bending on circles, turns, and corners improves your horse's ability to be straight.

- A horse's one-sidedness causes him to bend more easily in one direction. The goal is equal bending on both sides of his body.

- The marriage of inside and outside aids enables a horse to bend while he's turning along a prescribed line.

- An obedient riding horse needs to be able to back up as readily as he goes forward.

- In a lengthening, the horse elongates his stride and his frame while maintaining the same rhythm and tempo he had in the working gait.

- If a working gait is powerful and energetic, it already contains sufficient activity to do a lengthening.

- Counter-canter is used as an obedience and suppling exercise.

9

Going Sideways
LATERAL MOVEMENTS

With the information you've acquired to this point, you and your horse are laying the groundwork to excel in any riding discipline. You now have a horse who moves forward obediently in all three paces. He does fluid transitions from one pace to another. And his increasingly supple body allows him to lengthen and shorten his frame and stride within each pace like a rubber band, as well as bend equally through his side to the left and to the right.

So, what's the next step in your horse's education? Well, it's time to start teaching him to go sideways (fig. 9.1). In dressage jargon all of the sideways movements are called "lateral work," or work on **two tracks**, and it is this phrase that compels me to digress for a few moments here and discuss the word "tracks" (fig. 9.2).

TRACKS

We use "tracks" in so many different contexts. So, in the interests of clarifying this word, I'm going to describe all the different ways we use it.

First of all, you know the path that you make

9.1 "How many tracks? Which way? Help me!"

in the dirt as you go 'round and 'round your arena? Sure you do. That's the dip you have to rake by hand to fill it in when it gets too deep. That's a "track."

In chapter 6 you learned about the working trot. In the working trot, your horse should "track up." In other words, if you looked on the ground, you should see that the hoof print made by the hind foot steps directly into the track of the hoof print made by the front foot.

Then again you can be traveling around your ring with either your left or your right leg on the inside. In this case we refer to the way you're going as "tracking to the left" or "tracking to the right."

So far, those usages of the word "tracks" are pretty clear-cut. But when I introduce

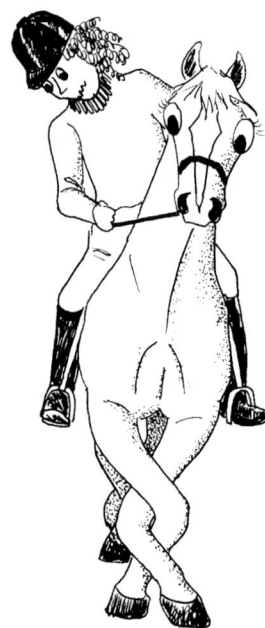

9.2 Track to the right, on two tracks, in the track!

leg-yielding and shoulder-fore later in this chapter, I get into the more complicated uses—fun stuff known as lateral work.

To begin, let's consider the concept of *direction*. When you're just riding on a straight line you're working on a **single track**. In this case the "single track" refers to the fact that you're only going in one direction—forward.

When you do any type of lateral work, you'll be working on **two tracks**. The phrase "two tracks" refers to the fact that you're going in *two directions* at once—forward *and* sideways.

Not only can you use the words "single track" and "two tracks" to describe how many *directions* you're going, you can also use the word "tracks" to describe how many legs you see coming toward you if you are standing directly in front of a horse.

For example, both the **leg-yield** along the track (see fig. 9.28), and **shoulder-fore** (fig. 9.3), both *two-track* lateral movements, are done on "four tracks." They are called this because if you stand in front of the horse and watch his legs, you see all four of them—unlike the situation

where the horse is being ridden on a *single track* and you just see his two front legs (his hind legs being hidden from your view).

With the more advanced two-track movements that I describe later in this book (**shoulder-in, shoulder-out, haunches-in**, and **haunches-out**), the horse is described as being on "three tracks" because you can only see three of his legs coming toward you. For example, in a shoulder-in counterclockwise to the left, you would see the right hind, the right fore, and the left fore. You would not see the left hind because it's hidden behind the right foreleg (fig. 9.4).

Now that I've thoroughly confused you about "tracks" I'll try to sum up:

- Single-track movements: you see two legs coming toward you when standing directly in front of the horse.
- Two-track movements: you see either three or four legs coming toward you.

Lateral work will greatly enrich your training program. To begin with, it enables you to expand your horse's understanding of, and obedience to, the leg. Up until this point, you've only used your leg to ask your horse to go forward. Now,

9.3 During *shoulder-fore*, the horse is on *four* tracks. Each one of his four legs can be clearly seen traveling on its own track.

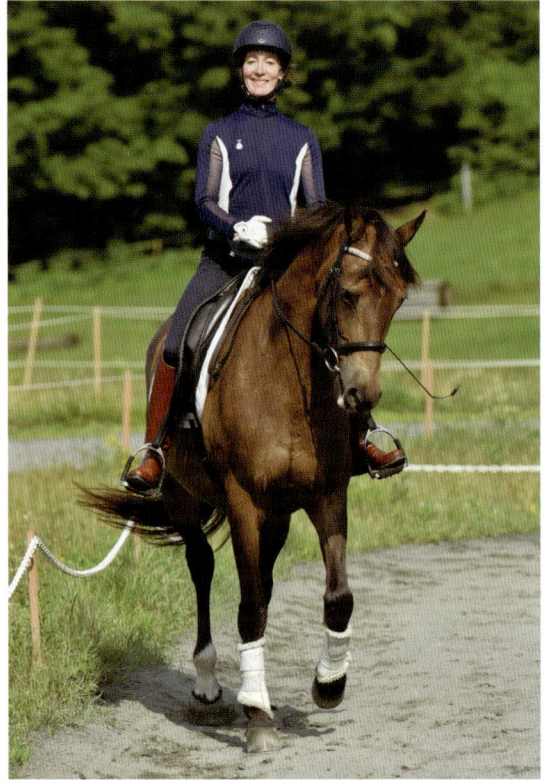

9.4 During *shoulder-in*, the horse is on three tracks. Only three legs can be clearly seen because the inside hind leg is directly behind the outside foreleg.

he'll learn that with a slightly different placement of your leg, you will be telling him to do something else—go sideways as well.

I use lateral work for everything from loosening and stretching my horse's muscles during a warm-up to strengthening a weak hind leg. The important point to remember is that lateral work is not an end in itself. In other words, you don't decide to go sideways because you're bored going straight forward and want to do something different. Lateral movements are a means to an end. Depending on what your horse needs, you'll pick the relevant and appropriate lateral movement to solve a problem or develop a particular quality, such as strength or straightness.

I've seen many riders who become obsessed with going sideways when they start lateral work, forgetting they *must* still go forward! Never go sideways at the expense of the quality of the horse's paces. Always strive to maintain "forward" movement over the ground with energy, and in a regular rhythm. If you lose any of these qualities, stop trying to go sideways. Instead, ride straight ahead and re-establish whatever you lost before resuming the lateral movement.

Lateral movements can be subdivided into two groups. They are differentiated by whether the horse is "straight" with no bend but just flexed at the poll, or asked to bend all through his body.

9.5 A & B A horse with his hindquarters engaged (A) and the joints of the hindquarters involved in engagement (B):

1. Lumbosacral joint
2. Hip joint
3. Stifle joint
4. Tarsal (hock joint)
5. Fetlock (ankle) joint
6. Pastern joint
7. Coffin joint

The first category of lateral movements, where the horse's body remains straight with no bend, includes the **turn on the forehand** and **leg-yielding**. These two movements are the easiest to perform because the horse is ridden without bend, and there are not a lot of physical demands made on his hind legs.

I will describe turn on the forehand and leg-yielding in this chapter, along with shoulder-fore. Shoulder-fore is one of the movements from the second group, the group which includes the lateral movements with bend. Even though shoulder-fore has a greater degree of difficulty than a turn on the forehand or a leg-yield, it can be done in a working gait. At this stage of your horse's training, he should be ready to start it.

The second category of lateral movements are all exercises where the horse is asked to go sideways *with* bend through his body. They include shoulder-fore, shoulder-in, haunches-in (also known as **travers**), haunches-out (also known as **renvers**), half-pass, walk pirouettes,

and canter pirouettes. But, as I said earlier, the only one in this category that you need to deal with at this stage of your horse's training is the shoulder-fore.

All these lateral movements with bend are more difficult for the horse to perform than a leg-yield. This is because you're asking your horse to bend through his body at the same time as you are asking him to go sideways. This requires him to bend the joints of his hind legs more than he's ever had to do before.

This increased bending of the joints of his hind legs is referred to as **engagement**. When the horse "engages" his hind legs, he **flexes** the joints of the hind legs and of the lumbosacral area and lowers his hindquarters (fig. 9.5). I know this might sound a little complicated for you right now, but I wanted to mention it. This way you can file it away in your mental computer and by the time you get to learn about **self-carriage** (in chapter 15), the information will be easy for you to retrieve from your memory bank.

9.6 A & B Balance in turns: The joints of the inside hind leg engaging as the horse bends along the arc of a circle (A), and the joints of the inside hind leg engaging in a turn at speed (B).

With that to look forward to, all you need to know for now is that the more the horse engages his hind legs, the more he changes his balance and can carry himself through whatever movements you ask of him (fig. 9.6). In the meantime I am including shoulder-fore in this chapter because I want you to use it now, not so much as a way to change your horse's balance, but as a way to make your horse **straight**.

FLEXING AND FLEXION

The Closing of Joints

I also need to take a moment here to discuss and broaden our usage of **flexion** (another word that can be confusing). Generally speaking, "flexion"

refers to the closing of a joint so that the angle between the bones is decreased.

You first heard this word in chapter 8 where I discussed riding circles and corners to explain inside positioning at the horse's poll. That is, a horse is flexed or looks in the direction he's going (for example, he looks left while going counterclockwise to the left) on curved lines. The rider should just be able to see the horse's left eye or left nostril. This type of flexion refers to the closing of the second cervical (neck) joint and is specifically called "lateral flexion." This is the "flexion" that you'll be most concerned with at this stage of your horse's education.

Another use of the word involves the closing of the joints of the horse's *hindquarters*, thus lowering them. This promotes the "engagement" I discuss above.

Later, I'll also be talking about a slightly different kind of flexion at the poll. You'll see that when a horse flexes "in" (rather than left and right, as above), he closes the joint between his head and neck. This is specifically called "longitudinal flexion." So when I get to talk about giving a **half-halt** and putting your horse **on the bit**, you'll see that part of the **round** frame achieved by working on the bit includes flexion "in" at the jaw and poll. (Another part of your education to look forward to!)

How Lateral Flexion Relates To "Inside" And "Outside" of the Horse

It's important, before I give the details about riding turns on the forehand, leg-yields, and shoulder-fore, that I review the use of the terms "inside" and "outside" as they relate to the horse. We use the horse's flexion and bend to determine which side of the horse's body is referred to as his inside and which is his outside. The inside is always the direction toward which the horse is flexed or bent. Some of you might still be under the impression that the inside rein, leg, or side of the horse always refers to the side toward the center of a circle and that the outside rein, leg, or side of the horse's body is either furthest from the center of a circle or is the side closest to the rail. So far, in this book, this has been the case. However, with lateral work, what we call inside and outside may change.

For example, as you begin to ride leg-yields in various patterns, you'll see that the inside and the outside of the horse often changes. You don't have to be confused by this. Just remember that even though the horse's body doesn't bend in leg-yielding, he is asked to *flex* at the poll. So, the inside is always the side toward which he is flexed, even if it's not the side closest to the inside of the ring (fig. 9.7).

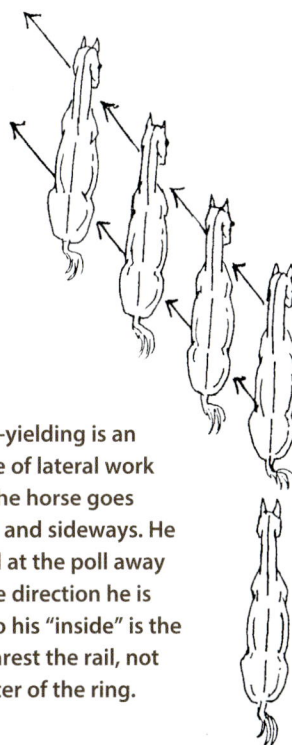

9.7 Leg-yielding is an example of lateral work where the horse goes forward and sideways. He is flexed at the poll away from the direction he is going so his "inside" is the side nearest the rail, not the center of the ring.

TURN ON THE FOREHAND

DESCRIPTION

If your horse has never done any lateral work, you might like to introduce the concept of going sideways by teaching him how to do a turn on the forehand. I say "might like" because there are disadvantages as well as advantages to having your horse learn this movement, which I'll discuss in a moment. In a turn on the forehand, the horse learns to yield away from the rider's leg when he is at a standstill. His front legs remain more or less on the same spot, while his hindquarters make a 180-degree turn around his forehand so that he ends up facing the opposite direction (fig. 9.8).

The advantages of learning this movement include introducing the uneducated horse to the sideways-pushing aids. The turn on the forehand also has a practical use when you're out hacking and you want to open and close a gate without getting off your horse.

However, once a horse understands the idea of yielding sideways to the leg, most riders hardly ever use the turn on the forehand again.

9.8 Starting the turn on the forehand.

THE AIDS FOR THE TURN ON THE FOREHAND

For turn on the forehand to the left (figs. 9.9 to 9.14):

Seat: sit squarely and balanced over the middle of your horse.

Right leg: a couple of inches behind the girth for sideways movement.

Left leg: on the girth for support and to prevent the horse from turning sideways too quickly.

Right rein: vibrate for flexion at the poll.

Left rein: steady and supporting to keep the neck straight.

9.9 Start the turn on the forehand from the halt. Kleary's Extraordinaire (Claire) is standing with "a leg in each corner." Rider Eliza Haun will ask Claire to do a 180-degree turn to change direction by pivoting around Claire's left front leg.

9.10 Eliza begins by asking Claire to flex her poll to the left as she takes the first step.

9.11 Note that Eliza is using her right rein quite firmly to prevent her horse from bending her neck to the left.

9.12 Stay centered over the middle of the horse's back, as Eliza is here.

9.13 A good angle from which to see how wide the hind legs are stepping.

9.14 Note how the left hind leg steps *over* and *in front of* the right hind leg. Claire responds obediently to her rider's aids.

This is because of the disadvantages of riding this movement. With every other lateral movement that you teach your horse, you'll ask him to go forward as well as sideways. But with the turn on the forehand, the horse doesn't go forward—he starts and finishes the movement in the halt. Some people think that the absence of forward movement is sufficient reason to avoid teaching the turn on the forehand.

An even greater drawback is what the movement does to your horse's balance. Think about the name of the exercise: *turn on the forehand.* Because the hindquarters are mobilized around a stationary forehand, the horse's center of gravity gets shifted more toward his front legs. But what we're striving for in dressage is to get horses *off* of their forehands!

So consider using the turn on the forehand only in the very beginning stages of teaching your horse to go sideways. Once he understands how to move away from your legs, don't use it for training anymore.

✳ HELPFUL HINTS •

If you ask your horse to do a turn on the forehand and he just refuses to move away from your leg, start to teach him from the ground. Stand by his head, facing backward toward his hindquarters. Hold the rein closest to you with the hand that's nearest to the horse. You can position his head so that his neck is slightly bent toward you.

Place your other hand on his barrel a couple of inches behind the girth area, where your sideways pushing leg will be when you're mounted.

Push with this hand. When your horse moves sideways in response to the pressure of your hand, praise him.

LEG-YIELDING

DESCRIPTION

Leg-yielding is the lateral movement in which the horse's *inside front* leg and *inside hind* leg pass, and cross in front of, his *outside* legs. His spine is straight, and he is flexed at his poll in the opposite direction from the way he is moving. For instance, if you ask your horse to move sideways to the left, you want him to flex or "look" to the right.

Because there's no bend through the whole body, only flexion at the poll, leg-yielding doesn't increase self-carriage like the exercises in the second group of lateral movements mentioned on page 133. However, it is a good loosening, stretching, "toe-touching," warm-up exercise for the horse that is doing any discipline and any level of

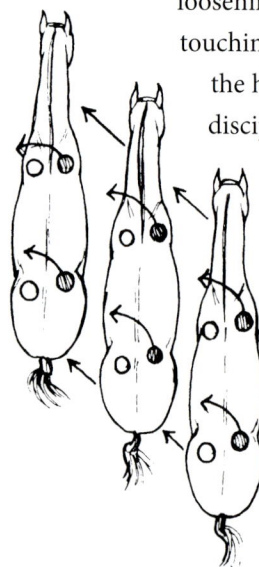

9.15 Leg-yielding with the correct angle to the rail. A horse needs to travel in this position when leg-yielding on a diagonal line.

9.16 A & B Leg-yielding faults: too steep an angle—the horse needs to go more forward (A) and too shallow an angle—the horse needs to go more sideways (B).

A

B

dressage. In addition, it teaches the horse to obey the rider's leg when asked for sideways movement. Finally, it gives the rider an opportunity to learn coordination of aids for lateral movements (figs. 9.15 and 9.16).

I've already mentioned, on page 110, how you can use leg-yielding to help your horse pick up the correct canter lead. And in chapter 12 I'll show you ways to incorporate leg-yielding into your program to help solve many different training problems. Leg-yielding as an exercise is extremely beneficial because of the way it affects the horse's hind legs. The bottom line in riding is the saying "He who controls the hind legs, controls the horse." The hind legs are the horse's engine, and all work should be directed to them. The more the hind legs are active, engaged, and underneath your horse's body, the easier it will be for him to balance himself and do what you ask of him.

Leg-yielding can be done at the walk, the posting trot, and the sitting trot. Depending on a horse's personality, you might decide to introduce the leg-yield at one pace rather than another. Sometimes a tense horse benefits from this exercise being explained in the walk because it's quieter, and he has more time to understand. You can use mental images to help this type of

horse relax, by picturing his eye remaining calm and his back staying relaxed. On the other hand, another horse might build tension in the walk so the trot would be a better choice to start leg-yielding. The trot is also preferable for a lazy horse because there's more natural impulsion in this pace.

As with every other movement you do with your horse, all of your aids have a role to play. Some aids are active, and some are passive, but they're all important. They all need to be coordinated in order to do a good leg-yield.

Remember that leg-yields are a blending of forward and sideways movement. If the horse leg-yields easily, the rider's legs stay quietly placed on his sides. The leg on the girth indicates forward movement while the leg behind the girth asks for sideways movement. If either quality is lacking, make the appropriate leg more active by squeezing and releasing with it on the horse's side.

The aids described above should be given in the following sequence: take a moment to

For a leg-yield over to the right (figs. 9.17 to 9.19):

Seat: sit squarely and balanced over the middle of your horse (fig. 9.20).

Right leg: on the girth for forward movement.

Left leg: behind the girth for sideways movement. Both legs are passive unless the horse needs to be sent either more forward or more sideways. In that case, the appropriate leg squeezes and releases.

Left rein: vibrates for flexion at the poll.

Right rein: steady and supporting to keep the neck straight.

9.17 A very nice start to a leg-yield to the left on a diagonal line in the walk. Bekki flexes her horse, Maeve, at the poll to the right while keeping the rest of the mare's spine straight.

center yourself so you're sitting in the middle of the saddle. Ask for flexion at the poll to the left. Then bring your left leg slightly behind the girth to initiate sideways movement. Those are the active aids. While you go sideways, continue to think about supporting with the passive aids—the right rein and right leg.

Shortly, I'll discuss all the places and patterns that you can leg-yield. But before I do, I want to make a point about the alignment of your horse's body when you leg-yield on a diagonal line or increase the size of a circle. For the most part, your horse's body is parallel to whatever line you're leg-yielding

9.18 Here, you can clearly see the difference in the position of Bekki's legs. The left one is at the girth to ensure forward movement, and the right one is behind the girth to ask the horse to step sideways.

9.19 Maeve has tipped her head and Bekki has collapsed slightly on the right side of her waist, causing her shoulder to drop.

toward. However, his forehand should be just slightly ahead of his hindquarters, so it meets the track or final arc of the circle first. (The reason for teaching this positioning of the horse's body in the leg-yield is to make it easy and familiar when you go on to teach the half-pass, which is introduced on page 281.)

9.20 When leg-yielding, sit squarely and balanced over the middle of your horse (A). If you lean and twist your body, you'll make it difficult for your horse to go sideways (B).

9.21 The finish of a good leg-yield to the right on a diagonal line in the trot. Although the horse's body is basically parallel to the rail, we can clearly see that the forehand will reach the track ever so slightly ahead of the hindquarters.

It's often the rider's tendency, or the horse's desire, to lead with the hindquarters so they reach the destination before the forehand. Be aware that this often happens in one direction more than the other, so make the necessary adjustment to align your horse's body correctly.

A good way to think of this is to pretend someone is going to take a photograph of you at several points during your leg-yield. When the horse's body is aligned correctly, every single picture should show the forehand slightly in advance of the hindquarters (fig. 9.22).

PLACES AND PATTERNS FOR LEG-YIELDING

You should aim to become adept at leg-yielding in many different places in the arena. It can be done on diagonal lines, straight lines or circles. Mix and match leg-yielding for variety and fun.

Leg-Yielding on a Diagonal Line

Leg-yield from the middle of the ring over to a specific point on the rail or from the rail toward the center of the ring. The pattern you make on the ground is a diagonal line, since you're going both sideways and forward (fig. 9.23). While leg-yielding on a diagonal line, remember that the horse's body is almost parallel to the rail, with the forehand slightly more toward the rail than the hindquarters.

Leg-Yielding Along the Track

You can leg-yield along the track in two different ways—in the **head-to-the-wall** position, and the

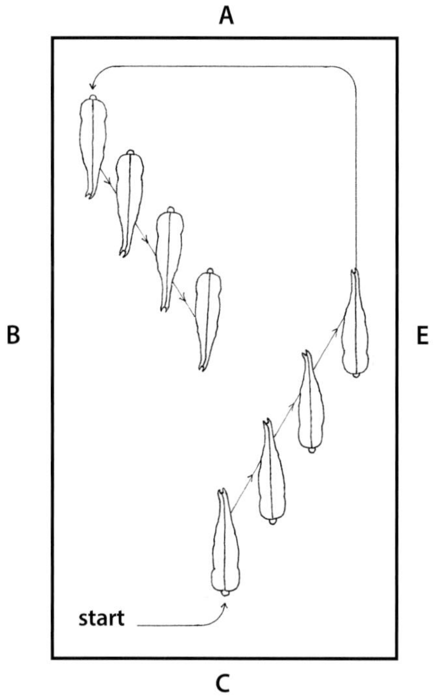

A

B

C

start

9.22 Leg-yield on a diagonal line from the middle of the ring over to a specific point on the rail, or from the rail toward the center of the ring.

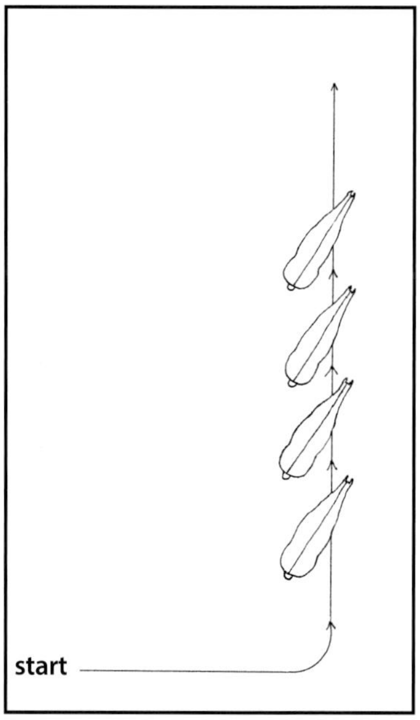

E

start

9.23 Leg-yielding along the track in the "head-to-the-wall" position.

start

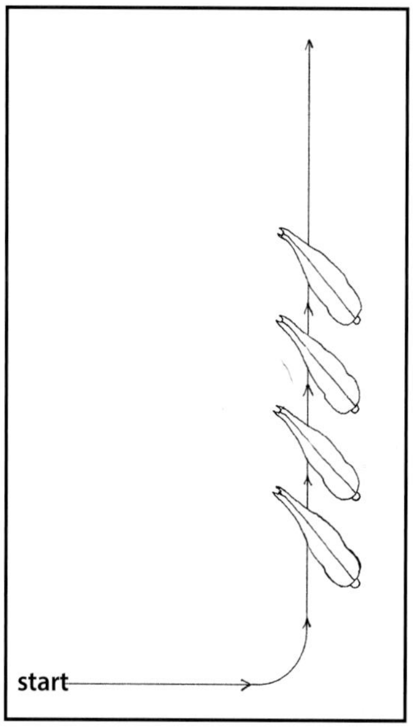

9.24 Leg-yielding along the track in the "tail-to-the-wall" position.

tail-to-the-wall position (figs. 9.24 and 9.25). In both cases the angle of displacement of the hindquarters is about 35 degrees. At a 35-degree angle, the horse's body forms almost half of a right angle to the rail.

1. Walk your horse forward with his forelegs on the track and move his hind legs away from the rail. This is known as leg-yielding in the head-to-the-wall position (figs 9.26 to 9.28).

When you do this in posting trot, switch your posting diagonal. You want to be sitting in the saddle when the inside hind leg is on the ground. Remember our discussion of "inside" being determined by the horse's flexion? If you

are riding to the left (counterclockwise), you flex your horse to the right and move his hind-quarters away from your right leg. Since your horse is flexed to the right, this now becomes his "inside," even though this is the side closest to the rail. So, to be on the correct diagonal for influencing his right hind leg, you should be sitting in the saddle when the diagonal pair of right hind leg and left foreleg is on the ground, and posting in the air when that same diagonal pair is also in the air.

2. You can also ride a leg-yield with the horse's tail to the wall (fig. 9.29). If you're in a ring that has a rail or fence, first bring the horse's forelegs

9.25 Bekki leg-yields Aluinn Dixie Gold (Nieve) along the track in the head-to-the-wall position.

9.26 Note how Nieve is slightly flexed at the poll to the left, but her spine remains straight.

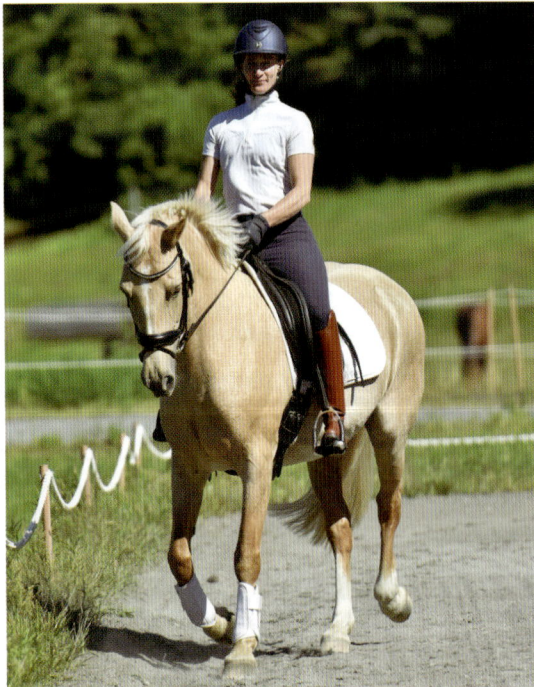

9.27 A different view of the leg-yield in the head-to-the-wall position. Bekki is nicely centered over her horse's back, but Nieve could show more clear flexion to the right.

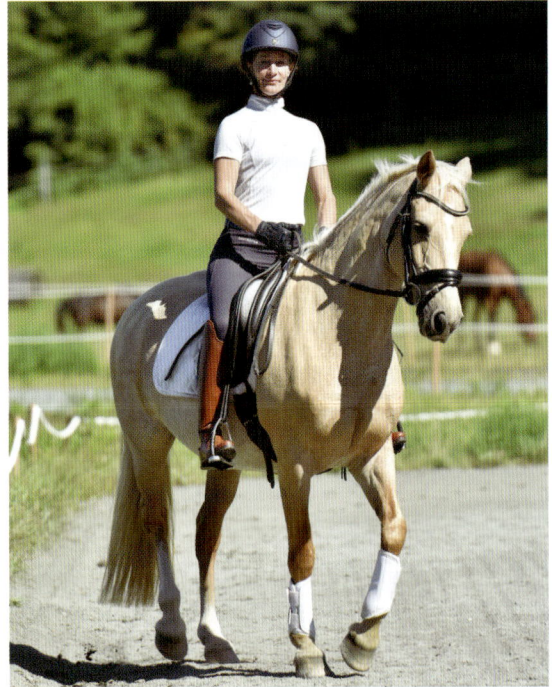

9.28 Leg-yielding along the track in the tail-to-the-wall position. Nieve's spine is nicely straight.

slightly to the inside of the track so that he has room to move his hindquarters over toward the rail without hitting it. Then displace his hindquarters toward the fence at about a 35-degree angle.

When you ride this pattern in posting trot, stay on the normal diagonal. This is because the inside and the outside of the horse don't change in the tail-to-the-wall position as they do in the head-to-the-wall position. When riding to the left, the horse remains flexed to the inside (left) and his hindquarters are moved sideways to the right.

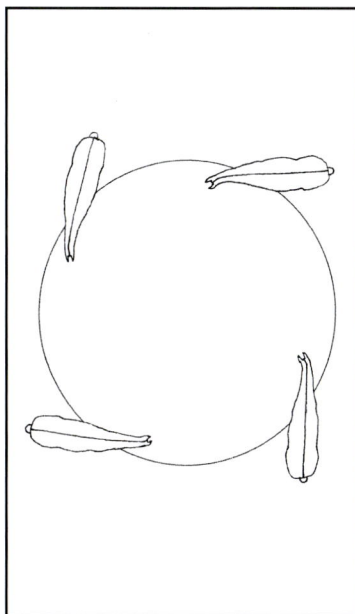

9.29 Leg-yielding with the hindquarters out on a circle.

9.30 Leg-yielding with the hindquarters in on a circle.

Leg-Yielding Along the Arc of a Circle

Leg-yielding can also be done along the arc of a circle. This pattern significantly increases the difficulty level of the movement, so make sure your horse is comfortable leg-yielding along a diagonal line, or the track, before you try this. In all of the examples below, your horse is circling to the left (counterclockwise).

1. Put the horse's front legs on the track of the circle and move his hindquarters out at a 35-degree angle to the circle. Your horse remains flexed to the left and his hindquarters are displaced to the right. His front legs stay on the original track of the circle and his hindquarters describe a larger circle (fig. 9.30).

2. Put the front legs on the track of the circle and move the hindquarters *in* at a 35-degree angle. Change your horse's flexion so that he looks to the right and move his hindquarters to the left toward the center of the circle. His front legs stay on the original circle and his hindquarters describe a smaller circle (fig. 9.31). If you do this exercise in posting trot, change your diagonal for the reason given under "Leg-Yielding Along the Track," on page 144.

Increasing The Size of the Circle

When increasing the size of a circle in leg-yielding, your aids are slightly different from the ones described for all of the previous leg-yields. In the following examples, rather than bringing your leg behind the girth to ask your horse to go sideways, keep that leg on the girth because in this exercise, that leg has two functions: asking the horse to move sideways, *and* asking the horse to bend around the leg as he goes sideways. Remember, your horse needs to *bend* on a circle in order to be *straight*: a *straight* horse is straight on lines and bent along the arc of curves (see chapter 5).

So, it's still true that you want to keep your horse straight during all leg-yields. But to be straight as he increases the size of a circle, your horse must be bent!

You might wonder how your horse can distinguish between the inside leg that tells him to bend but stay on the circle, and the inside leg

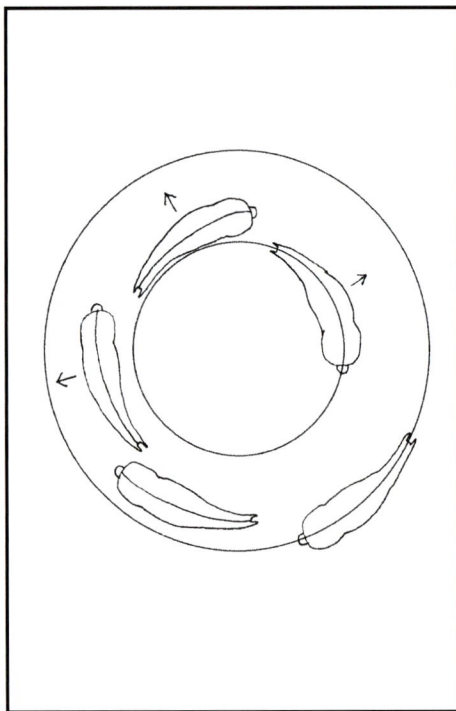

9.31 Leg-yielding to increase the size of a circle.

that tells him to bend but increase the size of the circle. The answer is actually a combination of several things: telling him to go sideways by the amount you use that leg; sitting in the direction of movement by stepping down into the outside stirrup; looking where you want him to go; and guiding him with your mind. If you find yourself feeling skeptical that these subtle signals will work, try it—you'll like the result.

Remember, also, to maintain the correct alignment of your horse's body to the line of the circle in the same way that you do when leg-yielding on a diagonal line. The forehand and the hindquarters basically stay parallel to the arc of the circle, but the forehand leads slightly and reaches the final circle just before the hindquarters do.

To increase the size of the circle in leg-yielding, apply your aids as follows: if you're circling to the left, your horse remains flexed to the left and his entire body moves to the right, away from your left leg that stays on the girth (fig. 9.32 and see photo 12.8).

✳ HELPFUL HINTS FOR THE RIDER

USE LIGHT LEG AIDS

Be sure not to use strong leg aids when introducing the leg-yield to your horse. The well-trained horse moves sideways from the *placement* of your leg, rather than the *pressure* of your leg. If this isn't the case, you must get the horse to listen to your leg. First, place your leg back. If he doesn't move sideways eagerly, either take the leg off and kick vigorously enough to get a reaction, or use the whip. Support enough with your other aids so that the kicking or tapping sends him sideways rather than forward. Then retest by moving the leg back again. If he moves away immediately, praise him. If he reacts sluggishly or if you're tempted to squeeze hard, chase him sideways again and then test again. You shouldn't have to force your horse sideways with strength. Through training, he should learn to move sideways easily from the position of your leg.

Sit Square and Centered

There is another reason you don't want to use a strong pushing leg: the importance of sitting squarely. If you push hard with your right leg, your body has the tendency to lean to the right, and this makes it even harder for your horse to move sideways to the left.

Some people lean because they get left behind the movement: if you have this tendency, use some exaggerated images to help you counteract it. As you leg-yield to the left, imagine you have three-quarters of your body weight on the left side of the horse's spine (fig. 9.33). Or think about putting your right seat bone in the middle of the saddle—this will help you end up in the middle.

✳ HELPFUL HINTS FOR THE HORSE

INCREASE THE CROSSING OF THE LEGS

Your horse may try one of several evasions so that he can avoid crossing his legs. Prevent his escape by checking the following four criteria.

9.32 If you tend to lean to the right when you leg-yield to the left, imagine you have three-quarters of your body weight on the left side of your horse's spine, so you end up sitting squarely.

You'll notice that the first three of these are part of the foundation for all training. They are:

1. Forward: maintain energy and forward motion over the ground.

2. Straight: keep the horse's neck straight.

3. Rhythm: maintain regular rhythm and consistent tempo.

4. Achieve Sufficient Angle: it should be 35 degrees when you leg-yield along the track or along the arc of a circle.

It's only when all four of these qualities are present and correct that the horse will be crossing his legs sufficiently for the leg-yield to be of benefit as a loosening and suppling exercise (fig. 9.34).

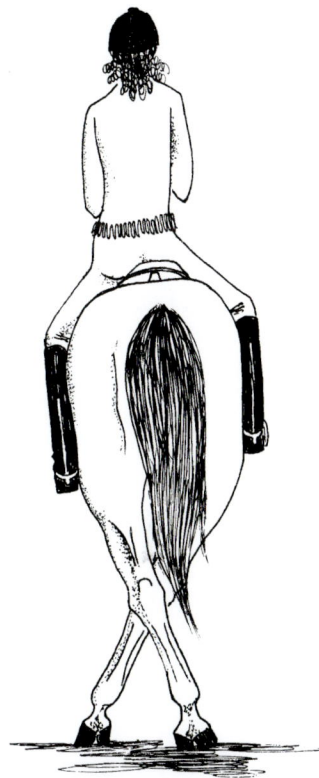

9.33 This leg-yield shows good form. Nieve is crossing her hind legs up by her hocks.

9.34 Her front legs cross up by her knees.

INCREASING FORWARD MOTION AND ENERGY

As I said earlier, good lateral work is a blending of forward and sideways movement. Sometimes a horse loses his forward momentum because he's not quite physically ready to do a lot of lateral work. Other times the rider causes the loss of forward motion by asking the horse to go sideways at too steep an angle, restricting the horse with her hands, or doing too much lateral work without interspersing work on straight lines to renew the horse's desire to go forward. Whatever the reason, going sideways should never be done at the expense of going forward with energy.

The following are some ideas to help you if your horse needs to be encouraged to go more energetically forward while leg-yielding.

1. If lack of agility is causing your horse to lose his forward motion, introduce leg-yields by asking for less than the normal 35-degree angle. Maintaining forward movement is more important than going sideways, so ask for less angle. As your horse becomes more agile, gradually ask for more angle in stages. At each stage, check that your horse is still easily going forward before increasing the angle any further. Eventually you need good energy and forward movement at a 35-degree angle for the leg-yield to be beneficial. But it might take several weeks or more to get to that point.

2. If lack of strength is the issue, try riding fewer sideways steps until your horse gets strong enough to maintain his energy. Leg-yield for a few steps at a time only; then go straight forward and ask for a lengthening to relax his muscles and renew his desire to go forward, then go sideways again for a few steps.

3. Try leg-yielding in a "staircase" pattern. Start a diagonal-line leg-yield for a few steps, then ride straight forward parallel to the rail. Repeat the pattern until you run out of room in your ring (fig. 9.35). This is also a good exercise to check your horse's responsiveness to your legs. The leg that's on the girth says "Go forward" and the leg that's behind the girth says "Go sideways." Your horse should respond immediately and appropriately to whichever leg becomes active.

If you are doing your leg-yield in the sitting trot and losing energy, overcompensate for this loss of activity by leg-yielding while lengthening in the posting trot. Post very high while you're leg-yielding, to encourage your horse to take long strides. When you eventually go back to sitting the trot, pretend that the exercise you're doing is really leg-yielding in the lengthened trot rather than leg-yielding in the working trot.

KEEPING THE HORSE'S NECK STRAIGHT

The most common mistake that I see in leg-yields is a bend in the neck to the inside rather than just flexion at the poll. Remember, in a leg-yield to the left, the right (inside) rein asks for flexion *only* at the poll while the left (outside)

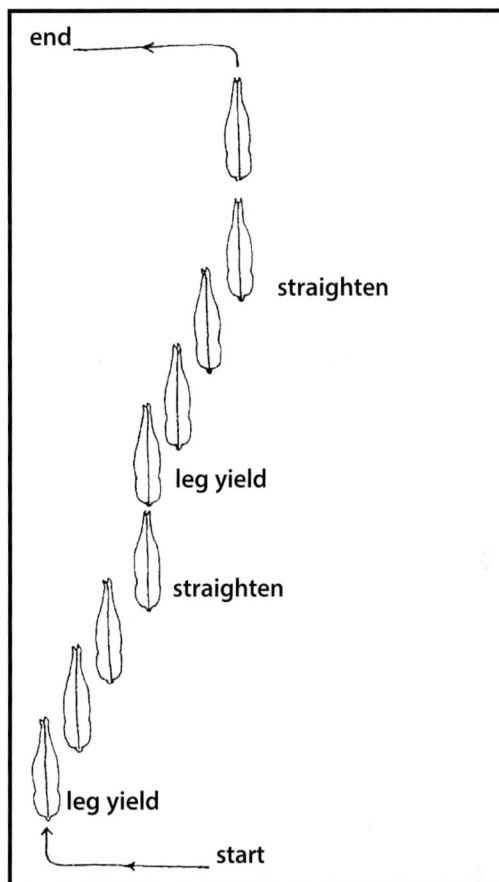

9.35 To help your horse move more energetically forward, leg-yield in a staircase pattern. Start a diagonal-line leg-yield for a few steps, then ride straight forward parallel to the rail to freshen the trot. Repeat the pattern until you run out of room.

rein supports to keep the neck straight. If the influence of the two reins isn't correct and there's too much emphasis on the right (inside) rein, the horse will bend his neck to the inside rather than only flexing at the poll. This overuse of the right (inside) rein without a supporting left (outside) rein makes it impossible to keep the horse **axis-straight**. In other words, his neck

9.36 Ally has Rowen nicely positioned as they start a leg-yield to the left. Rowen's body is straight and he is ever-so-slightly flexed away from the direction toward which he is moving. (He is flexed to the right while moving to the left.)

9.37 However, because Rowen is soft on the right side of his body, he bends his neck too much to the right. His shoulders pop to the left, and he is no longer straight and parallel to the rail.

bends too much and his shoulders don't stay lined up directly in front of his hindquarters. The more the horse's shoulders pop out to the left, the more his hindquarters trail to the right (figs. 9.36 and 9.37).

If the neck is bent and the horse is not axis-straight, the legs don't cross well and the purpose of the exercise is lost. Because it's difficult for the horse to respond to the rider's sideways pushing leg when his body is in this contorted position, the desperate rider usually resorts to "rein yielding." She "rein-yields" by using an indirect rein to try to move the horse

sideways, when she should be keeping the horse's neck straight and insisting that the horse move away from her leg.

If you see your horse's neck bending, relax the inside (right) rein toward his mouth and support more with the outside (left) rein. Feel the heaviness of this supporting outside (left) rein and imagine that this rein is a side rein keeping your horse's neck straight and providing a physical barrier to prevent his shoulder from falling out.

Here's something else to consider when keeping your horse's neck straight. Often when you leg-yield away from a horse's soft side, he bends his neck even if you are trying to use equal influence of the two reins. As a correction, ride the leg-yield in that direction either with no flexion at all or with a little flexion toward the direction you're going. For example, if your horse is stiff on the left side of his body and soft on the right side and you want to leg-yield over to the left, don't flex him to the right at all (fig. 9.38).

MAINTAINING RHYTHM AND TEMPO

Sometimes you have to deal with a horse wanting to change his tempo by speeding up when you start to leg-yield. It's important that the speed and the regular rhythm of the working gait stay the same as you change from moving straight ahead into the leg-yield.

If the horse speeds up either because of tension, confusion, or to avoid the difficulty of the exercise, here are a couple of things you can do in the head-to-the-wall position to slow him down.

First, you can momentarily increase the angle to greater than 35 degrees until it becomes too difficult for your horse to run. As soon as your horse slows down, praise him and decrease the angle back to 35 degrees.

Or, you can do transitions from trot to walk and back to trot again while still leg-yielding, until he anticipates slowing down rather than running.

Another advantage of doing head-to-the-wall leg-yields in an indoor ring or facing a high rail is that you can ask the hind legs to

9.38 During the next leg-yield, Ally corrects Rowen's tendency to bend too much in the neck by flexing him at the poll to the *left*, instead of the right. Changing the flexion helps keep Rowen's body straight.

cross over more, and you don't have to deal with your horse going faster when you use your leg. In the head-to-the-wall position, the wall or rail slows him down. When doing leg-yields in other patterns and the horse runs forward, a rider often resorts to pulling on the reins. This stops the hind legs from coming forward and you're worse off than if you hadn't done a leg-yield at all, because it's difficult for the horse to be in good balance if his hind legs aren't stepping well underneath him.

Here are some images and ideas to help you maintain the rhythm and the tempo of the working gait while leg-yielding. Support your aids by "hearing" the rhythm of the footfalls remaining regular and even—every step the same before, during, and after the exercise. Imagine the horse's frame (his **outline** or **silhouette**) staying the same or improving as you change from moving straight ahead to going sideways. Repeat to yourself words like "free," "flow," or "loose" to capture the feeling of the movement.

ACHIEVING SUFFICIENT ANGLE

Even if you think you're correctly coordinating the reins, sometimes it's difficult to know if the horse's legs are crossing enough. As I said earlier, there's little value in doing a leg-yield if the inside legs aren't crossing (or are barely stepping) in front of the outside legs. This point applies particularly to the hind legs as you'll see later when I give you leg-yielding exercises directed specifically to influencing the horse's hindquarters—his engine.

Most people introduce their horses to leg-yielding by doing it on a diagonal line such as from the middle of the ring over to the track. Often it's difficult to feel if the horse is crossing enough when the leg-yielding is done in this pattern. You feel like you're accomplishing your purpose because you manage to get from point A to point B, but that doesn't necessarily mean your horse is crossing his legs sufficiently.

What you need to do is develop a "feel" for how much your horse is crossing his legs. You can do this by changing from the diagonal-line pattern and instead leg-yield with your horse's head to the rail along the track. First, ride around the ring to the left and establish good energy and rhythm in your working gait. Next, flex your horse right, toward the rail, and displace the hindquarters to the left, toward the center of the ring so that they are at a 35-degree angle to the rail (slightly less than half of a right angle). Then, make sure you keep your horse's neck straight by supporting with the left rein.

When all three elements are present—the rhythm and energy correct, hindquarters at a 35-degree angle to the wall, and the neck is straight—then there's usually good crossing of the legs. Once you get a feeling for what your horse does when he's crossing sufficiently, go back to the leg-yield on the diagonal line. See if you can make that leg-yield "feel" the same as the good leg-yield that you did in the head-to-the-wall position.

If you're in the head-to-the-wall position going to the left and you still can't get enough angle, use a quick, opening, inside (right) rein.

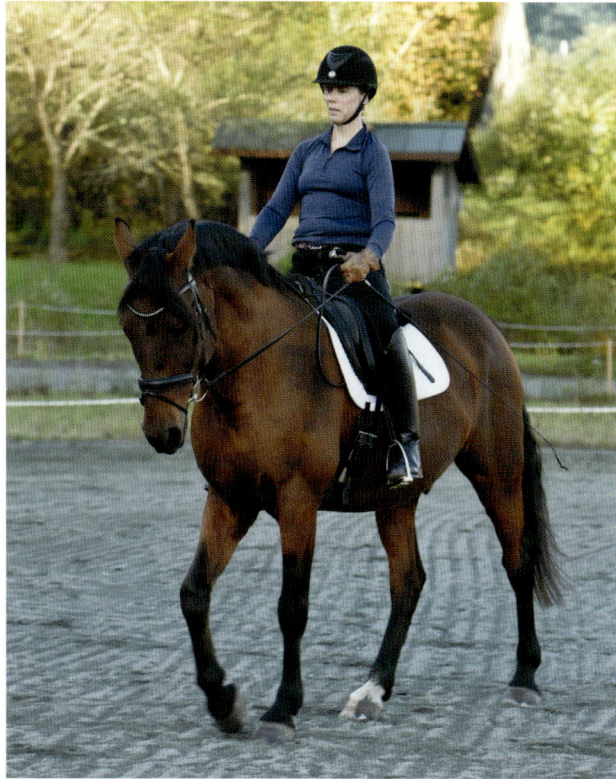

9.39 Use a quick opening rein aid to increase the horse's angle to the rail sideways. Ally brings her left hand directly to the left for one stride without pulling backward on it. At the same time, she keeps the horse's body straight by supporting firmly with the right rein.

Move your hand laterally (your right hand moves directly to the right) for one stride and then immediately place it back in riding position. Then if you need to, you can open it again (fig. 9.39). Keep in mind that the opening rein won't have the desired effect unless the outside (left) hand is low and supporting so that the shoulder doesn't pop out to the left. If the two reins are properly coordinated, the action of the rein will go to the inside (right) hind leg, and this leg will be sent sideways to the left.

USING BOTH HIND LEGS EQUALLY

Many horses and riders have better sideways or forward motion in one direction than the other. It's important that you ride the leg-yields the same in both directions, so that you're sure that your horse is using his hind legs equally. If your leg-yields don't look the same to the left as they do to the right, there is an exercise you can do that will make them more equal.

In your arena marked with letters as I described at the beginning of Stage Two (p. 102) turn down the centerline at A, and leg-yield to E. Then, change direction across the diagonal and turn down the centerline at A again, but this time leg-yield to B (fig. 9.40). You can do many variations on this theme.

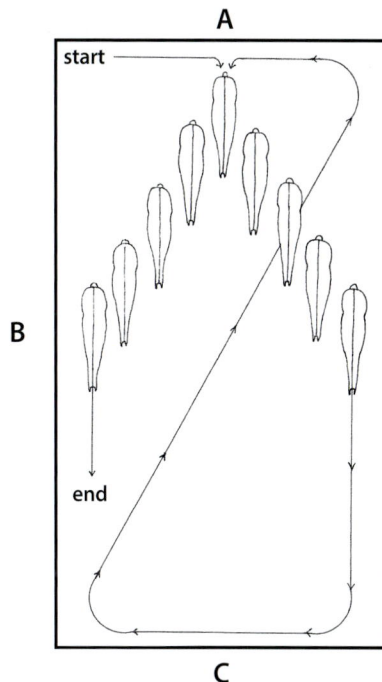

9.40 To encourage your horse to use both hind legs equally, try this exercise: Ride to the right, turn at A, and leg-yield left to E. Change direction across the diagonal, turn left at A, and leg-yield right to B.

In one direction your horse might want to go too much sideways and you get to the side of the ring before the E marker. In the other direction, it may be more difficult to go sideways, and you end up beyond your mark for B. Riding leg-yields accurately to specific points ensures that your horse uses both hind legs equally.

It's also possible that if you're having difficulty going sideways in one direction and not the other, it may be you, the rider, causing the problem. Maybe you're getting left behind the movement—the horse is going sideways to the left and your upper body leans to the right—making it hard for your horse to move over. If this is happening, here's an image that may help. Visualize stepping down into the outside (left) stirrup or falling off the outside of the horse (see fig. 9.32).

9.41 Note the difference in bend and angle required for the *shoulder-fore* (A) compared to the *shoulder-in* (B). As mentioned previously in this book, in shoulder-fore, the horse is on *four* tracks, and in shoulder-in, on *three* tracks.

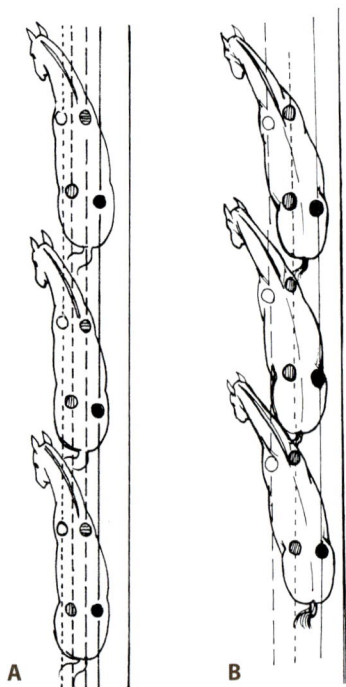

A   B

SHOULDER-FORE

Now that you've learned how to ride a leg-yield—a lateral exercise *without bend*—I'm going to discuss an exercise from the second category of lateral movements, the ones *with bend*. This exercise is called **shoulder-fore**. Please be aware that I'm discussing shoulder-fore here, not shoulder-in, which is a more advanced lateral movement that I'll introduce on page 260 (fig. 9.41).

I know I told you earlier in this chapter that because lateral movements *with bend* help a horse develop self-carriage, they are usually done with an animal that is more advanced in his schooling. But it's important for you to know how to ride shoulder-fore now, not as an exercise to promote self-carriage, but as a way to make your horse *straight*—an issue you deal with every day.

Besides, the amount of bend required in shoulder-fore is so slight that your horse should be able to cope with it. The bend is actually no greater than the arc of a large, 20-meter (about 60 feet) circle. If you look at a nine-foot segment of this circle—the approximate length of your horse's body—you'll see that the curve is barely noticeable (see fig. 9.41).

In chapter 5 on *forward* and *straight*, I emphasized that straightening your horse is one of the most fundamental rules of all kinds of riding. Dealing with weight on his back and the confines of a ring often increases your horse's struggle with his balance and he can become even more crooked than he is in freedom. Most often, your horse expresses this crookedness by carrying his hindquarters to the inside of the ring and leaning out with his shoulders toward the rail, so that his hind feet don't follow directly in the tracks of the front feet (fig. 9.42).

DESCRIPTION

In shoulder-fore, the horse is slightly bent around the rider's inside leg, which is the one closest to the center of the ring. The rider brings the horse's forehand a small amount in off the track so that his inside hind leg steps between his front legs. If you were to watch a horse coming straight toward you in the shoulder-fore position, you would be able to see all four of his legs (see fig. 9.43).

Riders often mistakenly feel that they have to make a huge adjustment to position their horses in shoulder-fore. It's actually a very small displacement of the forehand. To make this point, I tell my students to look at the distance between their horse's front feet. Then I ask them to tell me how many inches they'll have to move their horse's shoulders over to cover half that distance. The answer is usually only about four inches—a very small amount, indeed! So, don't be intimidated by the idea of doing an "advanced dressage" movement. The challenge is more about making the adjustment subtle enough, rather than how to do it at all.

During shoulder-fore the horse looks in the opposite direction from the way he's moving. In

9.43 A good shoulder-fore with the horse clearly on four tracks. Ally is looking straight ahead and keeping her inside leg forward on the girth rather than drawing it up and back.

9.42 Most often, a horse expresses his crookedness by carrying his hindquarters to the inside of the ring and leaning out, with his shoulders toward the rail. His hind feet don't follow directly in the tracks of his front feet.

9.44 Three common evasions to the shoulder-fore, as compared to the correct position (A): head and neck in (B), shoulders falling out (C), and haunches drifting out (D).

other words, if you are riding to the left, your horse is flexed and looks to the left, but his legs and body move to the right. This movement can be ridden in all three paces—you can easily ride shoulder-fore in medium walk, working trot, and working canter.

Shoulder-fore can be done on both straight and curved lines. Keep in mind when you introduce any new movement that you must always increase the degree of difficulty systematically and gradually. In other words, it's easiest for your horse to start shoulder-fore in the walk on

a straight line. When he can do this willingly, ask for it in the trot on a straight line. Then, place him in shoulder-fore in the canter on a straight line.

Once your horse can easily cope with the demands of shoulder-fore in walk, trot and canter on a straight line, ask him on a circle starting from the walk and gradually advancing to the trot and canter. After that, you ask him to hold this position during transitions from one pace to another—once again starting on straight lines and progressing to doing the transitions on a circle.

✳ HELPFUL HINTS

When you first attempt to straighten a horse who is used to carrying his hindquarters to the inside, I guarantee you that he's going to look for an escape route. This is because it's a lot easier for your horse to let his hindquarters drift to the inside of the line he's traveling on than it is to bend the joints of his inside hind leg and step toward his center.

There are three common ways that horses try to evade the difficulty of the shoulder-fore. In the following examples, we're still traveling to the left (fig. 9.44).

Your horse's first escape route will probably be to try to bring only his head and his neck to the inside (left in these diagrams). When he does this, his shoulders are able to fall out to the right toward the rail and his hindquarters might actually drift even more to the inside of the ring than they were before you tried to straighten him. So he ends up being even more crooked than when you started!

Here's how you can block off this escape route and at the same time learn the feeling of moving his shoulders to the inside rather than just his head and his neck. First, counter-flex him at the poll: vibrate the right rein and see his right eye. Then, bring both of your arms laterally to the left to move his shoulders to the left. Counter-flexing your horse will make it more difficult for him to escape by popping his shoulders out toward the rail. Once you learn the feeling of controlling his entire forehand, go back to flexing him correctly—to the inside. While you have him correctly flexed, check that the shifting of his forehand to the inside feels the same as it did when he was counter-flexed.

Once you are able to move your horse's forehand to the inside, he'll probably look for his second escape route by stepping to the inside of the ring with his entire body. You'll know this is happening when you end up on a different track than the one you started on. For example, if you started on the track near the rail, after ten or fifteen steps you might end up further from the rail than where you started. Or, suppose you started on a large circle and after several strides you find yourself on a smaller circle.

The correction here is to use a strong inside leg at the girth to drive your horse's inside hind leg toward his center. Make sure you don't try to hold him over on the track or out on the larger circle by bringing both of your arms to the outside. If you do, you'll end up with your horse in the same "head and neck-in with shoulder falling out" position that he was in during the previous example.

If you manage to block off both of the previous escape routes, your horse's third and final effort to avoid the difficulty of the exercise will probably be to lose energy and slow down. In that case use your driving aids actively. Give some sharp squeezes with your inside leg and push with your seat as if you're trying to move the back of the saddle towards the front of the saddle. Also, imagine that you're riding shoulder-fore in a lengthening of whatever pace you're in. This will get both you and your horse *thinking forward*.

ADDITIONAL USES FOR SHOULDER-FORE

Straightening your horse is my primary purpose for introducing the shoulder-fore at this point. However, there are other benefits to learning how to ride this movement now.

Riding your horse in the shoulder-fore position will not only straighten him but will also strengthen and increase the carrying, rather than the pushing, power of the inside hind leg. This is because in shoulder-fore the horse's inside hind leg is asked to step further under his body, move more in the direction of his center of gravity, and carry weight. Therefore, if you choose to continue with his dressage education beyond the basics, you'll be laying a foundation for more advanced work such as shoulder-in.

Shoulder-fore is also very useful as an exercise to improve the regularity of rhythm with a horse who has a "lateral" walk (see p. 70). Ask him to go sideways in shoulder-fore until the rhythm becomes regular. Then, straighten him for only as many steps as the rhythm remains regular and four-beat. As soon as the rhythm starts to degenerate into a lateral walk, immediately place him in the shoulder-fore position again. In this way, you explain to your horse that his only option is to walk in an evenly spaced four beats. He never gets the chance to do a lateral walk because as soon as the rhythm changes, you keep it regular by going sideways.

In the trot a common fault occurs when a horse hurries so much that his foreleg comes to the ground before his diagonal hind leg. Two separate hoof beats can be heard instead of the one together. This is because the horse is carrying most of his weight and that of his rider on his shoulders. You need to shift this horse's center of gravity back toward his hind legs. Riding shoulder-fore will help this situation.

Finally, shoulder-fore is useful when a horse swings his haunches in toward the inside of the ring to avoid engaging his inside hind during the canter depart. You can correct this by riding shoulder-fore in walk or trot just prior to asking for the canter as well as during the canter depart itself. Use an active, inside leg and a firm, outside rein to keep your horse in the shoulder-fore position through the transition. If you don't hold him in shoulder-fore during the depart, he'll become crooked to make the job easier for himself.

KEY POINTS

- In lateral movements, the horse moves forward and sideways at the same time.

- There are two groups of lateral movements. The first group includes turns on the forehand and leg-yielding. The horse is not bent during these movements. The second group includes shoulder-fore, shoulder-in, haunches-in, haunches-out, halfpass, walk pirouettes and canter pirouettes. These movements are more difficult because the horse is asked to bend as he goes sideways.

- Flexion refers to the closing of a joint so that the angle between the bones is decreased. A horse can flex at the poll left, right, and "in." Flexing the joints of the hind legs and lumbosacral area is called "engagement."

- Turn on the forehand is the only lateral movement done from a halt. It is a useful exercise to teach a green horse the idea of moving away from the leg.

- Leg-yielding is a good warm-up exercise because it loosens, stretches, and relaxes the horse's muscles.

- Shoulder-fore is the main exercise used to straighten a crooked horse.

10

Suppling for
BALANCE AND HARMONY

In a perfect world, all horses are relaxed, supple, athletic, and obedient. The reality is, however, that few of us ride horses that show all of these qualities all of the time (or even some of the time!).

In chapter 13 I'll teach you how to give a half-halt, to help you deal with the less-than-perfect horse. This is the most valuable tool I can give you to control and communicate with your horse. With this half-halt you'll be able to cope with any number of situations that arise during training. It can help you reduce your horse's tension, loosen his stiffness, teach a resistant horse acceptance of the rein, connect your horse from back to front, bend him on his stiff side, as well as ask him to pay attention to you when he's distracted.

As a preliminary exercise to the half-halt, I'm going to teach you a simple exercise that I call **suppling**. Please take a moment to look at figs. 10.2 to 10.6 starting on page 164, so you'll have an idea what suppling looks like before I explain further. Done correctly, suppling can help you deal with all the training issues that I mentioned above. But I want to emphasize that using suppling to deal with training problems

is a temporary stage. Once you and your horse have learned about half-halts, they will be all you will need to improve his balance, attention, and harmony.

The advantages to suppling are that it's easy to learn to do and enormously effective for loosening very stiff or resistant horses in a short period of time. There is a disadvantage, too. Unlike the half-halt, which is an invisible aid, suppling is very obvious to an onlooker. It's quite apparent that you are bending and straightening your horse's neck. Not only do we always strive to ride with the most discreet aids possible in training, but from a practical point of view, suppling is too visible to be done in most competitive events.

Suppling is easy for anyone to do and that's one reason why I'm explaining it before we get to the half-halt. The other reason is that I see countless *distorted* versions of suppling being done by riders in all disciplines. For example, a rider will bend her horse's neck to such an extreme degree that rather than loosening him, she knocks him off balance. Or, she'll waggle her horse's head back and forth dramatically and repetitively.

The worst-case scenario, however, is when it is used as a way to punish a horse. Unfortunately, I've seen advanced riders as well as novices guilty of doing this. Suppling a horse in an abusive way is never acceptable. Because of the widespread confusion about how to supple as well as misuse of suppling, I feel compelled to include a section about it in this book.

To get started I'll show you how you can supple a horse to make him less stiff, both laterally (through his side) and longitudinally (over his back). In the next chapter, I'll show you how you can use suppling to do all sorts of problem solving.

First, let's consider the dilemma of the uneducated horse when he's asked to cope with a rider's weight on his back. This horse finds it simple to be in good balance when he's in freedom. But, when a rider sits on him, he naturally contracts his back muscles and drops his back to hollow it away from that weight. When the rider picks up the contact, he stiffens his neck and pokes his nose forward (fig. 10.1B). In this posture he uses his neck as a balancing rod in much the same way as you hold on to a banister for balance when you go down a flight of stairs.

As long as your horse moves over the ground in this position, his body feels stiff as he shuffles along with short, tight steps. His back seems frozen and the only thing that appears to move are his legs. I call this being a "leg-mover" and, in this case, your goal with suppling is to unlock

THE AIDS FOR SUPPLING

When you supple your horse, you'll actively use the leg and rein aids on one side of your horse. However, it is essential that you place equal emphasis on the passive supporting aids that are on the other side. The goal is to supple the horse between the active and passive aids, not just away from the active aids (figs. 10.2 to 10.6).

The other thing to remember is that even though the visible part of suppling is the bending and straightening of your horse's neck, you should never just work a "part" of your horse (the neck in this case). Always ride the whole horse from back to front by using your leg each time you bend his neck with the rein. To check that my students are thinking along the right lines, each time they supple their horses, I'll have them say out loud, "My leg sends my horse's hind leg forward towards my hand." This reminds them to work their horses from their leg forward into their hand.

Suppling can be done in all three paces and either to the inside or the outside of the ring. For clarity of aids, however, right now I'll assume we're riding to the left and you're going to supple your horse to the left, which is the inside.

and loosen this horse so he can move gracefully through his whole body.

As you use your inside rein, bend your horse's head around to a degree that would be between 10 and 11 o'clock if you were looking at a clock with 12 o'clock straight ahead. If you bend his neck more than that, you'll knock him off balance, causing him to stiffen even more to save himself.

Be sure to maintain a consistent contact with his mouth before, during, and after you bend him. Often riders drop the contact and put slack in the rein as they straighten their horses' necks

10.1 A & B When a horse's back is supple, loose, and round, he can move freely and gracefully (A). When his back is stiff and hollow, his movement will be choppy and unathletic (B).

Aids for Suppling to the Left

Active aids:

Inside rein: use as an indirect rein. The action of the rein is toward your opposite hip. Your left hand comes as close to the withers as possible without crossing over. Turn your knuckles up toward your face so that your pinkie finger points toward your right hip (fig. 10.7).

Inside leg: each time you bend your horse's neck to the left, close your left leg on his side. This way you'll be sending his left hind leg forward into your left hand. I'm assuming, of course, that your horse is "in front of your leg." If he isn't, as far as he's concerned, you're just riding him with your hands and you need to go back and review how to put your horse in front of your leg (p. 56).

Passive Aids:

Outside rein: the outside right rein is steady and supporting at all times. Many riders mistakenly feel that they must let this hand go forward toward their horse's mouth when they bend the horse with their inside hand. Keep your hands side by side at all times.

Outside leg: steady and supporting to prevent the horse from swinging his quarters to the outside. It's placed on the girth if you're on a straight line and behind the girth if you're on a curve.

10.2 Look at how Claire carries herself before suppling. Her steps are short, her back is low, her neck and head are short and high, and she is resisting Eliza's hand. Notice how similar her body is to the horse in fig. 10.1 B.

10.3 Eliza begins suppling her horse by closing her inside leg as she bends Claire's neck to the inside.

10.4 As soon as Eliza has bent her horse's neck, she immediately straightens it with the other rein. She is careful to maintain the contact with Claire's mouth on the inside rein as she straightens her with the outside rein.

10.5 As Eliza continues to straighten the neck, Claire begins to lengthen and lower it.

10.6 The result of effective suppling. The horse's hind leg reaches farther underneath her body, the whole topline is longer, and Claire has a willing and pleasant expression.

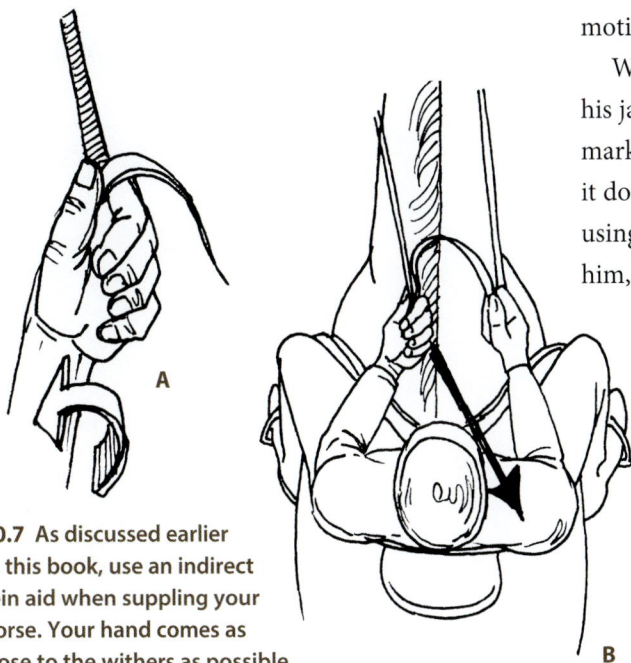

10.7 As discussed earlier in this book, use an indirect rein aid when suppling your horse. Your hand comes as close to the withers as possible without crossing over it. Turn your knuckles up toward your face so that your pinkie finger points toward your right hip.

(figs. 10.8 and 10.9). Your horse won't object when the rein is slack, but you'll be jerking him in the mouth when you establish contact again. Stay connected to him. Imagine having a dance partner holding on to you firmly but gently as he guides you around the dance floor. It's a solid, secure feeling, and the last thing you want your partner to do is let go of you as he lowers you into a dip!

The timing of the act of bending and straightening should be fairly quick, but very smooth. It does not have to be in the rhythm of the gait. Bend your horse's neck around in a two- or three-second span of time and then immediately straighten him with the other rein. Pretend that you're giving him a massage. Pleasantly manipulate his neck in a smooth, continuous motion—not too fast or too slow.

When you meet resistance and the horse locks his jaw, don't hang on to the rein. If you feel a marked stiffness or resistance in the beginning, it doesn't matter. You must straighten him by using the outside rein as soon as you've bent him, whether he resists or not. Otherwise, the relief that you get from the stiffness comes from just flexing him in the jaw. And remember that we always want to work the horse's entire body from back to front, not just his jaw.

If your horse is so stiff that he resists by stopping, jigging, or swinging his hindquarters sideways, ease your way into suppling by bending his neck less. Once he's loose enough that you can "take his neck

10.8 This is a good start to suppling.

10.9 But here Bekki drops contact with the inside rein as she straightens her horse's neck with the outside rein. She needs to maintain the straight line from her elbow through the rein to the bit.

away" a little, try to bend it to between 10 and 11 o'clock again.

Supple your horse three times and then relax for at least seven or eight strides before you start another series of three "supples." Don't just supple continuously. Give the horse's body a chance to react, and then evaluate whether or not he feels looser.

TESTS OF SUPPLENESS

After you've done several series of three "supples," you'll find that your horse will begin to relax his back, lower his head and neck and take longer, more fluid strides. This is what you're looking for. But you might ask how long you need to continue suppling, and if it's okay to only supple one side of the horse's body regardless of the direction you're going. To answer those questions, I'll give you three ways to determine when your horse has become supple.

1. Before you start to supple your horse, take a moment to evaluate how much weight you have in your hands when your horse's neck is straight. Then ask yourself how much power it takes you to bend his neck around to between 10 and 11 o'clock. You might find the weight increases from two pounds to five, or even fifteen, pounds. When your horse is supple, you should be able to bend his neck around without using any strength. This doesn't happen overnight. But if you initially had to use fifteen pounds of power and now you only need thirteen pounds, you know your horse is becoming somewhat more

supple. Little by little, the strength you need to bend him will decrease from thirteen pounds to ten to eight to five until eventually the weight of the rein stays the same before, during, and after the "supple."

This usually happens on one side of his body before the other. So concentrate on suppling the side that's crying for attention. You might end up suppling your horse 80% of the time to the left and 20% of the time to the right. Or perhaps you'll always need to supple him to the right regardless of which direction you're going. Listen to what your horse tells you and do what he needs.

2. It's a good sign that you're successfully loosening your horse when he lowers his neck after you've suppled him three times. But ideally you want to see him lower his neck *while* you're bending him (see photo 10.5 in earlier suppling sequence). If he lengthens and lowers his neck and stretches toward your hand each time you bend him, he's showing marked suppleness.

3. When you do this exercise with a supple horse, his neck is the only thing that deviates from the line you're on. As you bend his neck, his body continues to overlap the line of travel even if you do not support him with strong outside aids. You know your horse is stiff when you use the inside rein and the action of the rein ricochets through his body so that his hindquarters swing to the outside.

10.10 Suppling the poll to the inside. Note that the rest of the horse's body stays straight and overlaps the line she is on.

10.11 Suppling the poll to the outside. The only thing that has changed is the direction toward which Maeve is looking. The mare's body is still straight and on her line of travel.

SUPPLING THE POLL

You can also do a more subtle version of suppling in order to loosen your horse just in his poll rather than his whole neck. You can use this when you have trouble flexing your horse on a circle, he's locked against your hand, or he's tipping his head. You'll know you need to do this exercise if you find it difficult to flex him to the inside when you're circling, turning, or leg-yielding (figs. 10.10 and 10.11).

Go on either a circle or a straight line in the walk and ask your horse to flex to the outside and then to the inside for a few strides each. Do this by turning your wrist a couple of times as if you had a key in a door and you were unlocking the door. (It's the same movement with your wrist that you need to do for an indirect rein aid, which I explained earlier on page 93.) When your horse is supple in his poll, he will keep looking in whichever direction you flex him all by himself, even when your wrist is back in its normal position. Once you've flexed him, he should keep looking in the direction you've indicated until you specifically ask him to look straight ahead or flex the other way. You shouldn't have to hold him in flexion with your hand. Once you can do this in the walk, try it in the trot and the canter.

When you supple the poll, remember to use a passive supporting rein on the other side. Otherwise your horse will bend further down his neck (which is the suppling I described earlier in this chapter) and the value of this particular exercise is lost because you won't be isolating and loosening his poll. When your horse is flexed either left or right, the position of his neck should look exactly the same—straight on lines and bent along curves. You should merely see his inside or outside eye.

Here's an image for you to think of when you do this poll suppling exercise. Imagine that your horse is so loose in his poll that his head is attached to his neck with a spring like those little dashboard toys that people sometimes put in their cars—their heads loosely bouncing around! (See fig. 10.12.)

10.12 When suppling the poll, imagine that this joint is so loose that your horse's head is attached to his neck like a dashboard bobblehead!

KEY POINTS

■ Suppling can be used to relax, loosen, and connect your horse, as well as teach him to accept your hand.

■ Always supple by actively using your leg at the same time that you bend your horse's neck. For example, think of your left leg sending your horse's left hind leg forward into your left hand.

■ Make sure that you support with the passive aids so that you supple the horse between the active and passive aids.

■ Time your suppling so that it is done fairly quickly but very smoothly.

■ When he's supple, a horse meets the following requirements:

   1. You don't need to use strength to bend his neck.

   2. His neck gets longer and lower as you supple him.

   3. His legs stay on the line of travel.

11

Putting it All Together

SAMPLE SCHOOLING SESSION

You now have a lot of information about the Basics and the various exercises you can do with your horse as you begin your dressage program, but you might be wondering how to put it all together in a logical sequence. I know from experience that you're not alone with this quandary because at clinics I'll often see versions of the following three scenarios.

A rider leads her horse from the stable to the ring and mounts. She shortens the reins right away, walks around for a minute or two, and then warms up by doing transitions back and forth from the walk to the trot.

A rider will warm up her horse by walking, trotting, and cantering around for five minutes on a totally loose rein. Her horse trucks along with his head stuck straight up in the air, and his back muscles rigid and contracted.

Then there's the rider who takes a 45-minute lesson with me and because she wants to "practice," takes her horse into another ring afterwards and drills him for another hour!

Because these hypothetical schooling sessions are, in fact, quite common, I'd like to give you some guidelines about how to put the information that you've learned to this point together in a way that makes sense and is in your horse's best interest.

TIME FRAME

First, let's talk about a sensible weekly program and then decide how to organize your daily work. As far as a weekly program is concerned, even those who specialize in dressage don't spend every single day working in the ring. A normal week for a dressage specialist includes five days of work, one day off, and one "play" day. Playing can be anything from hacking, to jumping low fences, to galloping on the track that we're fortunate to have available. The play day is normally scheduled sometime in the middle of the work week so that our horses don't work in the ring five days in a row. This plan keeps the horses mentally fresh and enthusiastic about their work. Plus, since muscles get stronger when they're at rest, doing something totally different from the "weight lifting" that is required by dressage horses allows these muscles time to rest, repair, and get stronger. So, you see, play is just as important as work.

My combined training riders have a built-in variety to their weekly program. They usually devote two or three days each week to their flatwork. The other days they warm up as they would if they were going to work on the flat, and then they do whatever is on their schedule—stadium jumping, a cross-country school, a gallop for wind, or a conditioning hack.

As far as daily work goes, if I'm going to concentrate totally on flatwork, my sessions usually last somewhere between forty-five minutes to an hour. This time includes walking, both at the beginning and the end of the ride. With a very young horse, like a three-year-old, my sessions are often as brief as twenty minutes and definitely no longer than half an hour.

When I work with students who are planning

11.1 Warming up: For the first five or ten minutes after you get on, give your horse a chance to walk around on a loose rein.

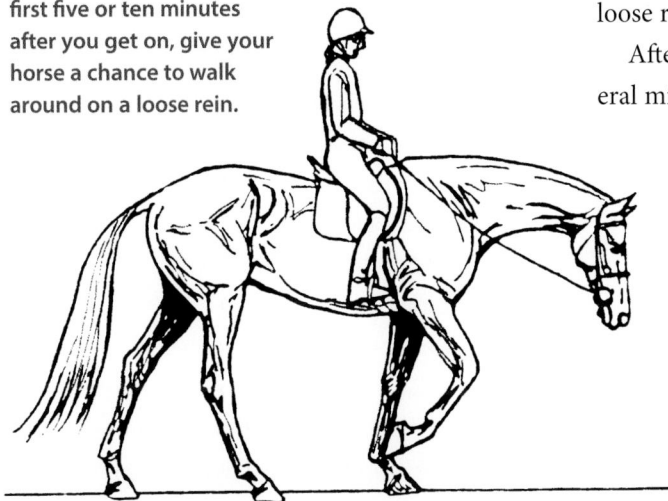

to jump or condition during their ride that day, we'll spend perhaps fifteen minutes doing a warm-up which I'll describe shortly, and then they'll go on to the rest of their program. You'll need to modify both your daily and your weekly routine depending on your particular specialty. Always keep in mind that your horse is an athlete; in order to work productively and reduce the risk of injury, most athletes divide their training sessions into three stages—warming up, work, and cooling down.

WARMING UP

In their natural state, horses mosey around, graze, and rest. They do this pretty much continuously over the course of a day. Nowadays, however, these normally roaming creatures live in stables for the most part. It's unfair to take a horse who has been standing around in a stall and expect him to go directly to work. So, for the first five or ten minutes after you get on, give your horse a chance to just walk around on a loose rein (fig. 11.1).

After walking around "on the buckle" for several minutes, pick up a contact so you can begin your warm-up.

When I think of warming up, the key word that sticks in my mind is *relaxation*. As far as I'm concerned, any work done in tension is pretty much a waste of time. So I spend as little or as much time as necessary relaxing my horse both physically and mentally before I go on to the work

11.2 I think of the warm-up as the loosening, stretching, "toe-touching" part of my horse's schooling session.

phase of my ride. I'm sure you can imagine that with certain horses on particular days, my entire ride consists only of the warm-up!

As I mentioned in the chapter on suppling, it's easier to relax a horse physically first. Once his body is relaxed, his mind usually follows suit. So after I pick up a contact with a young horse, I'll go directly to the posting trot. I do this because it's easy to ruin the quality of the walk by working a young horse on contact in the walk (see chapter 6, p. 73 on paces, gaits, and rhythm). Then I'll begin to loosen my horse's body by suppling him. If my horse is further along in his education, I'll start suppling in the walk. Then, when he's relaxed in the walk, I'll go on to the posting trot. I'll supple him while trotting both to the left and to the right, and once he's relaxed in both directions, I'll do the same thing in the canter.

I like to think of the warm-up as the "toe-touching" part of my schooling session (fig. 11.2). After each series of three "supples," I'll let a few inches of rein slip through my fingers so that my horse can stretch his head and neck forward and down toward the ground (fig. 11.4).

Remember that the length of your reins determines the length of your horse's neck. So the longer your reins, the more he can stretch. However, it's important to maintain the contact with his mouth when you do this. So, don't just drop the reins in an effort to get your horse to stretch. Instead, open your fingers slightly and allow your horse to choose how much rein he'll take as he seeks the contact forward and down. You'll often hear people refer to this position as "long and low" (figs. 11.3 to 11.5).

I was giving a lecture once during which I was describing this long and low frame, and a woman raised her hand to ask a question. She said, "When I pick up the contact with my horse's mouth, he immediately dives way down with his head and neck and sucks dirt. Is this good?"

My response to her question was, "Well... there's good 'dirt-sucking' and there's bad 'dirt-sucking.' If his hind legs are still stepping well underneath his body, that's good 'dirt-sucking.' If his hind legs are trailing out behind his body, that's bad 'dirt-sucking.'"

The point that I'm making here is that not all "long and low" is created equal. The important thing is where your horse's hind legs are when you allow him to stretch forward and down to the ground. That determines just how much rein you give him and just how far you let him out.

11.3 Supple your horse in the usual way by bending his neck as you drive him forward with your inside leg.

11.4 Encourage him to stretch and lower his neck and head by opening your fingers and letting him "chew" the reins out of your hands, but don't give him so much extra rein that the reins become loose and you lose contact with his mouth.

11.5 The longer you let the reins go, the more your horse can stretch.

THE WORK PHASE

After you've warmed up "long and low" (for however long it takes!) and your horse is relaxed, give him a break and let him walk on a loose rein for a few minutes. When you pick up contact again, shorten the reins to a more normal working length for you.

Then you can begin to incorporate all the movements you've learned in the preceding Nuts and Bolts chapters—circles, transitions, lengthenings, backing up, leg-yields, shoulder-fore,

and counter-canter. Spend a couple of minutes reviewing and refining each exercise. Then "listen" to your horse. He'll tell you what he needs to practice.

In other words, whatever you find difficult to do, that is the work that's crying for attention. Focus on the "needy" movement or exercise until it gets a *little bit better*. This is all you need to do each day to make progress happily and with a minimum of resistance. A "little bit better" and a "little bit better" eventually add up to a "whole lot better." If you expect perfection every day, both you and your horse will end up frustrated.

I'd like to make two other points about your attitude toward training. First, take frequent breaks by walking on a loose rein in between each of your exercises. Not only will this reward your horse, but it actually expedites the training process. You'd be surprised how giving your horse a break when you think he just isn't "getting it," can help him relax and figure things out. Somehow, when you start again, more often than not, he miraculously does a whole lot better.

The other point is to be very generous with your reward. I've seen riders struggle with their horses over a particular movement and when the horse finally improves, they nod their heads as if their horses owed it to them. Well, your horse doesn't owe you anything, and he certainly doesn't know that you're nodding your head. Let him know that he's good by patting, verbally praising or by giving him a brief rest by walking on a loose rein. Telling him he's a "star" becomes a self-fulfilling prophecy. (So is telling him he's

a pig!) He'll revel in your appreciation of him and he'll try even harder. Remember, as far as your horse is concerned, *absence of reward is the same as punishment.* So make the following your motto: Ask often, expect little, and praise lavishly.

COOLING DOWN

In order to avoid stiff, sore muscles the next day, every good athlete's training session includes a period of cooling down. Your cool-down is simply a shortened version of your warm-up. Most of my riders do a "long and low" posting trot in each direction until they feel any residual physical or mental tension dissipate. Then they walk on a loose rein for another five minutes or go for a short hack. They dismount before they return to the stable. They loosen the girths and lead their horses the rest of the way back to the barn. (And if you were a fly on the wall in the barn, you'd overhear them telling their horses just how brilliant and perfect they were that day!)

KEY POINTS

- Schedule variety into your program to refresh your horse's mind and to allow his muscles to repair and get stronger.

- Every schooling session should include a warm-up, work, and a cooling down period.

- As far as work goes, always reward him and be satisfied when your horse does a movement or exercise "a little bit better."

12

Troubleshooting with
BASIC FLATWORK

Now that you're familiar with the nuts and bolts of basic flatwork, I'll show you how you can use that knowledge to troubleshoot some common problems.

In this chapter you'll find that we can solve all sorts of resistances and disobediences by using the information that you've learned to this point. (Later in this book, I'll again deal with training issues, using more advanced dressage movements to solve problems).

TENSION

No matter what your riding discipline, in order to do productive and rewarding work you want a relaxed, calm horse. Relaxation should be a priority because for the most part, attempting to train a tense horse is a waste of time and not very pleasant for either one of you.

The first thing to keep in mind is that, like yourself, a horse has both a mind and a body, and it's impossible to separate them. In my experience, I've found that although it can be somewhat effective to calm a tense horse's mind

by speaking to him in soothing tones, it's much more effective to first relax the body because then the mind, in turn, becomes more quiet.

With physical relaxation as my goal, I supple my horse as I described in chapter 10. As my horse's body begins to loosen and relax, inevitably I find that his mental stress diminishes. Another thing to remember is that speed and tension are closely related; often I'll relax a tense horse by working him in a very slow trot.

In chapter 6, I said that *energy* is one of the criteria of high-quality paces. However, when my primary goal is to reduce tension, I do not want energy yet. This is because I think of the word energy as meaning "more." If I ask for energy, I'm going to get *more* of whatever I have. So if I have a tight horse who moves with short, quick steps, asking for "more" will give me a tighter horse who moves with even shorter, quicker steps. So, before I ask for energy, I make sure that I like the qualities I have because that's what I'm going to get more of when I put the energy back in.

Once my horse begins to relax, I carefully add energy. If I find I've asked for too much and the tension creeps back in, I turn the level down a notch. Little by little my horse learns to stay relaxed as I add activity by increments in order to bring his trot back up to a normal, energetic, working gait.

RUSHING AND RUNNING AWAY

If your horse tends to rush around out of control and he won't listen to your back and outside rein when you ask him to slow down, turn him onto a small circle. Circles tend to take speed away from a horse so you can slow him down. Remember you never want to pull on the reins, because doing so stops the hind legs. Once you stop the hind legs, your horse's back goes down and his head and neck come up. Pulling on the reins causes a loss of connection from the back to the front.

Here's an exercise for the horse that rushes. Work on a large circle, and as soon as your horse runs, arc onto a smaller circle within that circle. Stay on the smaller figure until he slows down, then melt back onto the larger circle. The moment he speeds up again, whether it's one stride or twenty strides later, turn back onto the smaller circle (see fig. 8.13).

Once you can moderate and control the speed on a circle, challenge the horse by going on a straight line where he might tend to run even more. As soon as he rushes, do a small circle until he slows down. Then, go straight again.

Sometimes it's only in our minds that we think we can't slow down a rushing horse. If this has become a mental block for you, let's look at the situation logically. You know that when you're finished riding, you'll be able to stop your horse in order to get off. Well, if you can come to a complete stop in order to get off, you can certainly give a fraction of the aid that you use to stop, and instead slow your horse down.

So, let's say your horse is racing around in the trot. Apply your aids as if you're going to stop and dismount. Bring your horse almost to the halt and then just before he stops, soften your hands and allow him to trot forward again at a more civilized speed. Do this as often as you need to until he chooses to maintain a steady, controlled pace.

Perhaps you have an off-the-track Thoroughbred who doesn't come forward with his hind legs. Instead he walks and trots with short, quick, tense steps and, as a result, he rushes over the ground at a pretty fast, uncontrolled-feeling clip. Since you know that taking longer strides will slow him down, you close your legs to ask his hind legs to step further under his body. However, his reaction to your aids is just to go faster.

To decrease this horse's speed, ask him to leg-yield. The leg-yield forces him to slow down because his hind legs must take longer strides. As soon as you feel a reduction in his tempo, reward and straighten him. When he begins to accelerate again, push him sideways until he learns to step with long strides whether he's going sideways or straight ahead.

If you have an indoor ring, do the leg-yield in the head-to-the-wall position. Having the wall in front of him will back him off so that you won't have to resort to pulling on the reins.

You can also remind your horse not to rush by backing him up. Remember that one of the reasons that a horse rushes is because his hind legs are too far out behind his body. So, if your horse gets rolling along too fast, halt, back up, and then resume whatever pace you were doing.

Not only will backing up physically get your horse's hind legs further underneath him, but mentally, he'll be anticipating stopping and backing up rather than barreling along.

Another rushing problem is presented by the horse who is confused about changing his canter lead. Let's say you'd like to ride a change of lead

12.1 To help prevent your horse from rushing through a lead change, go across the diagonal in right lead canter, trot in the middle, and immediately step into left shoulder-fore. Straighten your horse before the corner, then ask for left lead canter.

through the trot, but as soon as you trot, your horse rushes off or, when he canters again, picks up the same lead as before. (For a change of lead through the trot, you switch from one canter lead to the other by trotting for three or four steps in between each canter.)

Try this exercise (fig. 12.1). Pick up right lead canter. Go across a line that divides your ring diagonally. Trot in the middle and immediately step into left shoulder-fore. In the left shoulder-fore, the hind legs stay on the diagonal line, and you guide the shoulders slightly to the left of that line by bringing both of your hands to the left. Be sure to maintain a firm left leg *on* the girth so your horse doesn't drift to the left of the diagonal. Ride left shoulder-fore in trot for the rest of the diagonal, then straighten before the corner and pick up left lead canter.

Do the same thing on the next diagonal. Riding shoulder-fore prevents your horse from rushing off in trot because the movement engages his inside hind leg and keeps it underneath him. Also, the slight bend of the shoulder-fore helps position him to pick up the correct lead.

THE LAZY HORSE WHO NEEDS A LOT OF LEG

There's practically nothing worse than a horse that doesn't listen to your legs. You use your legs, your horse reacts a little, so you squeeze harder, and he temporarily responds to the aid. Then he gets dull to the stronger aid, and you have to do even more. Pretty soon you're exhausted and you have to take a break. This means that your horse has successfully trained you to let him do less work.

If you've ever been lured into this cycle, the first thing you need to do is resensitize the horse to light leg aids. (This is described in detail in chapter 5.)

I remember giving a clinic on the Basics—forward, straight, and rhythm. Shortly after, I received a nice note from one of the participants in which she exclaimed, "I can hardly believe it! This is the first time in three years that I've brought my horse back to the barn and he's breathing harder than I am!" That's the way it should be!

Once you've resensitized your horse to your leg, you can use the movements from chapters 8 and 9 to ask your horse: "Are you paying attention? Are you listening to refined aids?" It's not necessary to do each exercise very long. It's your horse's initial reaction to your leg that gives you the answer to these questions.

TRANSITIONS

If your horse seems a little dull, ride frequent transitions from pace to pace to put him mentally on the aids. He should feel "hot" off your leg for the upward transition and quick to respond to your back and outside rein for the downward transition. Don't stay in any pace for more than a few strides. It's the frequency of the transitions that makes him more alert. For the lazy horse, pretend you're doing the transition from

a working gait into a lengthening of the next gait—from working trot to lengthened canter, for instance—so that you inspire him to go more forward.

By the same token, you can check that your horse is paying attention by doing transitions within a pace. Do several lengthenings and shortenings. You don't have to do a lot of steps. Just ask the right questions. Will you go more forward as soon as I ask? Will you listen to a light aid to come back from a lengthening?

LEG-YIELDING

You can also use leg-yielding to ask obedience-to-the-leg questions. A submissive horse moves sideways just from the position of the leg behind the girth rather than from strong pressure. You don't make a 1200 lb. animal go sideways. (Or do anything else, for that matter!) You ask him to do so with a signal, and when the training is correct, he responds. The process of making the horse responsive to a leg that is behind the girth is described in chapter 9.

The following obedience-to-the-leg exercises can be done for a few strides each. Once again, you simply want to ask the questions and evaluate your horse's initial response.

1. Walk or trot on a straight line along a track or the rail. Position your horse's head toward the rail, by squeezing and releasing with the fingers of the hand that's on the same side as the rail, just enough so that you can see his eye. Then slide your leg near the rail back a few inches.

12.2 To help your horse react to your request for a leg-yield, imagine that your leg that is positioned behind the girth is a red-hot poker. As soon as you move this leg back, your horse should move away from it immediately and eagerly.

Your horse should immediately swing his hindquarters to the inside of the ring while his forehand stays on the track. If he doesn't, kick him or tap him with the whip and ask again. Imagine that the leg that's behind the girth is an electric cattle-prod or a red-hot poker. As soon as you bring your leg back, your horse should move away from it eagerly (fig. 12.2). As soon as he does, slide your leg back to the on-the-girth position and go straight forward. Then, ask for the leg-yield again. Do four or five of these transitions on the long side of your ring.

2. Go on a circle in the walk or the trot and alternate a leg-yield where you move the hindquarters away from your left leg, with straightening for a few strides. Then, move the hindquarters away from your right leg. In all cases, the horse's front legs stay on the original track of the circle and the hindquarters are displaced left and right (fig. 12.3).

3. Leg-yield along a diagonal line and make a "staircase" by moving your horse's whole body sideways away from the long side for a few steps. Then ride him straight forward for a few strides. Then leg-yield again. Your horse should respond immediately to the frequent changes in leg position, from behind-the-girth which asks him to go sideways, to on-the-girth which asks him to go forward (fig. 12.4).

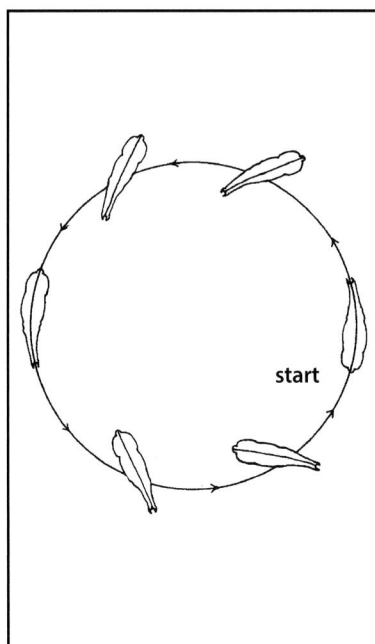

12.3 On a circle, leg-yield away from your left leg, straighten, then leg-yield away from your right leg.

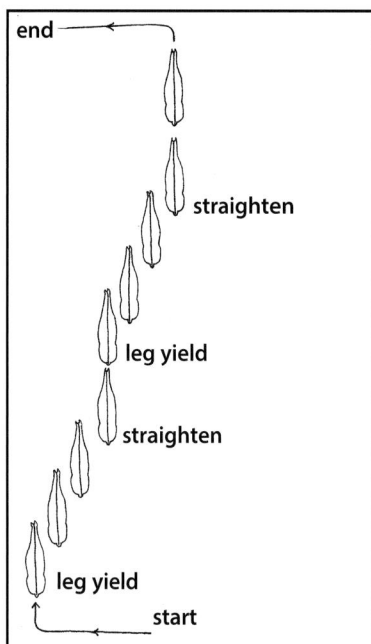

12.4 Leg-yield along a diagonal line and make a "staircase." Your horse should respond immediately to your frequent changes of leg position.

12.5 Support your leg-yielding aids by visualizing your horse's legs crossing with wide, long strides.

12.6 Check your horse's desire to go forward by going backward. Put your "gear shift" in reverse for four steps, drive forward for four steps, then go back to reverse. This should be a continuous motion.

Support your leg-yielding aids by picturing in your mind's eye that the hind legs continually are crossing and spreading with very wide, long strides (fig. 12.5).

BACKING UP

You can ask "forward-thinking" questions even when your horse is going backward. Here are three exercises to do to check his desire to go forward.

1. Back up a few steps and then immediately go forward into trot without any hesitation. As soon as your legs change position from behind-the-girth to on-the-girth, the horse should react by trotting forward keenly.

2. Back up a few steps and while still going backward, start to position your horse for a left lead canter depart. Flex him to the left until you just see his eye, put your weight on your left seat bone, and close your right hand in a fist. As soon as your right leg comes behind the girth, your horse should step forward into the left lead canter.

3. Do a "rocker" where your horse takes four steps backward, four steps forward, and four steps backward again. This should be a continuous motion with no halting in between each series of four steps. In your mind's eye, support your aids by "seeing" the automatic gear shift in a car. Put it on "R(everse)"—the horse goes back; move it to "D(rive)," and he goes immediately forward; then shift back to R, and he smoothly steps backward again (fig. 12.6).

SPEEDING UP AND SLOWING DOWN

You can help the horse that goes in fits and starts to maintain a constant tempo if you understand what horses do normally. They generally speed up when leaving a circle or corner, starting across a diagonal, or approaching wide open spaces. And they tend to slow down as they begin circles and turns.

So, anticipate these reactions and train in what I call a benignly antagonistic way by doing the opposite of what your erratically "tempo-ed" horse chooses to do.

For instance, as you start a circle, ask for a few strides of a lengthening. Then as you leave the circle and head into an open stretch, halt. By staying one step ahead of your horse and doing the opposite of what he wants to do, pretty soon he'll begin to wait for your signals rather than making his own decisions about his tempo.

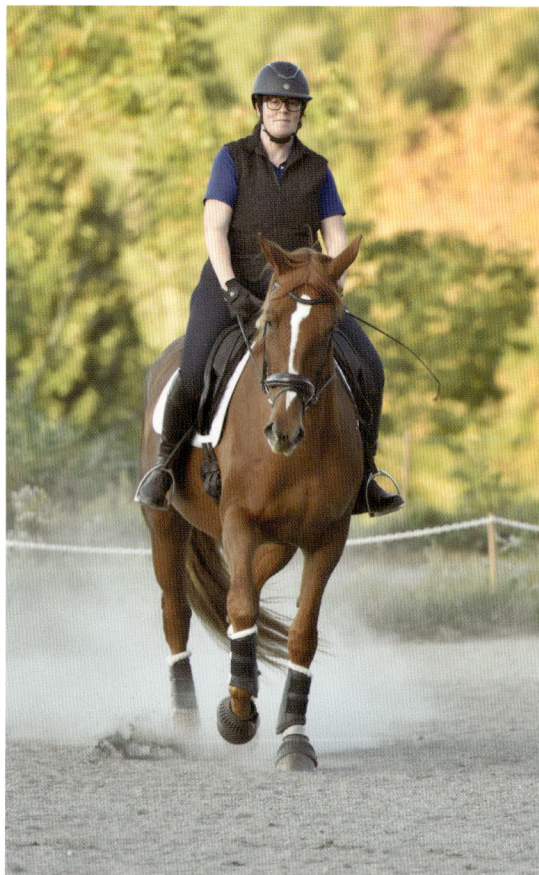

12.7 Eliza is preparing to pick up the left lead canter from the trot, but Claire is leaning on her inside (left) leg. Because Claire is flexed to the right and her rib cage is bulging slightly against Eliza's left leg, it is possible Claire will pick up the wrong lead.

PICKS UP WRONG LEAD

Part of being obedient to the leg includes a willingness to respond immediately and correctly to the aid for the canter. Set the horse up for the canter by vibrating the inside rein for flexion, supporting with the outside rein to keep the neck straight, and putting weight on your inside seat bone. Then your inside leg, which is at the girth, asks for forward movement while your outside leg swings behind the girth in a windshield wiper-like action to signal the outside hind leg to strike off.

Sometimes your aids will be right, but your horse will still make mistakes. Here's how you can use some of the movements you've learned to help him canter on the correct lead.

Maybe your horse is picking up the wrong lead because he's leaning on your inside leg. To remedy this, trot on a large circle. Decrease the size of the circle by spiraling in, and then increase the size of the circle by leg-yielding back

12.8 To help set Claire up for the left lead canter, Eliza changes her horse's flexion and bend by leg-yielding Claire away from her left leg as if she is increasing the size of a circle. Eliza needs to stay centered over Claire's back with her left leg on the girth and her right leg behind the girth.

out (figs. 12.7 and 12.8). Do this several times. When your horse feels softly bent around your inside leg, ask for the canter at the moment you are back on the larger circle (fig. 12.9).

Sometimes the problem is a lack of what I call **"throughness."** If that's the case, improve his "throughness" or **connection** by suppling him (see chapter 10). Repeat the spiraling in and leg-yielding out exercise that you just did. But this time while you're leg-yielding back out to the larger circle, "supple" him toward the inside of the circle three times. Give your signal for the canter depart right after the third "supple." This way you can take advantage of the connection or "throughness" you've created from suppling.

Or, perhaps he picks up the wrong lead because he's lazy with the outside hind leg (the strike-off leg). Trot on a large circle and activate the outside hind leg by leg-yielding his hindquarters in toward the center of the circle for a few strides and then straightening. Do this several times to drive his outside hind leg under his body as well as to make him think about this leg. Then be sure you take the time to re-bend him along the arc of the circle before you ask for the depart.

12.9 If your horse is picking up the wrong canter lead, it may be because he is leaning on your inside leg. Trot on a large circle. Decrease the size of the circle by spiraling in, and increase the size of the circle again by leg-yielding back out. Do this several times. When your horse feels softly bent, ask for a canter depart the moment you are back on the larger circle.

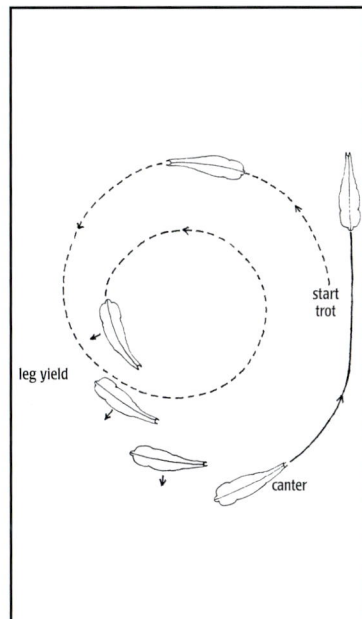

start trot

leg yield

canter

HORSE DOESN'T ACCEPT CONTACT

Horses can show non-acceptance of contact in a variety of ways, such as carrying their heads too high, fighting the bit, reacting incorrectly when the reins are used, and ducking behind the contact so that there is slack in your reins. Before looking for a training solution, check that your horse's bit fits him properly and isn't too harsh, and that his teeth are in good shape with no sharp edges, in case these are the reasons for his actions.

I'm going to discuss the first three of these resistances together. When a horse holds his head and neck up in the air, it's called "coming above the bit" (fig. 12.10). This is somewhat uncomfortable for both horse and rider but not as unpleasant as the second resistance, when the horse fights the bit by yanking and pulling on the reins.

12.10 This horse is not accepting contact—he is coming above the bit.

The third resistance, a more subtle expression of non-acceptance of the bit, is when the horse allows you to establish a pleasant, elastic contact with his mouth, but as soon as you use the reins to give an aid, he resists by pulling, putting his head up or shortening his neck. It's that unpleasant sensation of feeling like, "I don't dare touch the reins. I can sit up here and look pretty, but I feel like I'm walking on eggs because even the slightest movement will disturb everything." Well, even though you may have been taught to have "good," quiet hands, your reins are part of your aids and you need to be able to use them.

"Suppling" can help you deal with all of these contact issues. When you supple the horse who is above the bit, he lowers his head and neck. When you supple the horse who is yanking at the bit, you take the bit away from him. And as you supple the horse who reacts incorrectly when you use the reins, he learns to lower and lengthen his neck and go toward the bit as you touch his mouth. Therefore, you teach him two things—not only can you use the reins but using them helps him to move better!

For the time being, use suppling for all of these resistances. Later on, you'll use a more subtle aid, the half-halt, to resolve all of these problems of non-acceptance of the bit.

The fourth contact issue is the horse that ducks behind the bit (fig. 12.11). This horse needs to learn to go forward from your legs and step into your hand. Give him the idea by closing both legs and sending him forward over the ground in a lengthening. Do this several times; once he responds to your legs immediately,

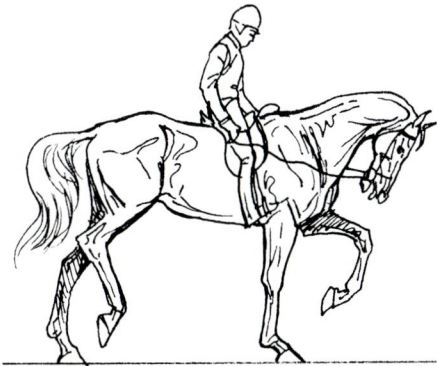

12.11 Another example of not accepting contact: ducking behind the bit.

30 feet

30 feet

12.12 When your horse is not accepting the bit, do the leg-yielding on a figure eight exercise, going back and forth between circles, as described in the text. Each time you use an opening inside rein, your horse should willingly take longer strides sideways.

close your legs *as if* you want a lengthening but don't actually let him cover more ground. Rather than asking him to go more forward over the ground this time, you're now asking him to go forward through his body. If you're successful, you'll see him raise his head, and you'll begin to feel some weight in your hands. When he does this, praise him lavishly. You're teaching him a very important concept here and he needs to be encouraged for the slightest effort to seek a contact with your hands (see figs. 7.6 and 7.7, p. 89).

You can also use a leg-yielding exercise to help your horse accept the reins. At the same time it will enable the action of the reins to go to the hind legs and affect them in a positive way, rather than stopping them and causing the horse's back to stiffen and become hollow as occurs when he resists contact.

Begin this exercise on a small figure-eight in the walk. Put your horse's front legs on the perimeter of each circle of the figure-eight and push his hindquarters to the outside so that they end up making a larger circle (fig. 12.12). Each time you give a little squeeze with your inside

leg (the one closest to the center of the circle) behind the girth, use an opening inside rein as described in the leg-yielding section (fig. 9.36, p. 165). Go back and forth from one circle to the other. Each time you open a rein and squeeze with your leg, your horse should take a bigger step sideways. In other words, when you bring your left hand to the left and close your left leg, his hindquarters should swing to the right. In this way he learns that you can use your reins positively to help him; his hind legs end up taking longer strides rather than being blocked by the use of your hand.

STIFFNESS

One of the best ways to loosen a stiff horse is by suppling as I've described in chapter 10. Not only is a supple horse more comfortable to ride, but he can be more obedient simply because his body allows him to respond to your requests more easily.

You can also use some of the movements and exercises from Nuts and Bolts in chapters 8 and 9 to unlock the stiff horse and make him more supple. The key to developing suppleness through those movements is transitions. Any transition—any change—whether it's from one pace to another, going from a straight line into a leg-yield or from bending in one direction to the other such as on a serpentine, will help you promote suppleness.

> **"Picture smooth transitions that are as soft as a butterfly coming to rest on a leaf."**

● ● ● ● ●

TRANSITIONS

When a horse is supple, he can smoothly do transitions from pace to pace or within a pace like lengthenings and shortenings. Your horse's suppleness is directly related to the ease and fluidity with which the transitions are done. If there's no change in rhythm, tempo, balance or frame, your horse is showing marked suppleness. So, ride many transitions until he's very adjustable.

While lengthening and shortening, remember to imagine that your horse's body is like a rubber band. It can easily stretch and contract. Pretend you're on pavement and you can hear the tempo of the steps of each pace staying

exactly the same whether he's doing longer or shorter strides. Support the process by picturing smooth transitions that are as soft as a butterfly coming to rest on a leaf.

This reminds me of the time I was in the warm-up area at a big show in Virginia. I was riding Jolicoeur and we were coming up behind Pam Goodrich, noted dressage trainer and member of the United States Equestrian Team at the World Championships in 1986, and her horse, Semper Bene. I did a transition from the trot to the halt, and without turning around Pam said, "That was too abrupt, Jane." Now, I already had great admiration for Pam's talent, but I didn't realize that having eyes in the back of her head was another one of her many assets! When I questioned her about it later, she explained that she could hear that the transition was hard instead of soft.

LEG-YIELDING

Suppose you ask your horse to lengthen, and because he's feeling tight, he runs with quick, short steps. Use leg-yielding to help him. Do several steep leg-yields that have an angle greater than the standard 35 degrees (perhaps in the walk) to stretch his muscles and increase his range of motion. Then go back to the trot lengthening and see if he feels freer.

You can also develop suppleness by riding a zig-zag in leg-yielding while in rising trot (fig. 12.13). To do one zig-zag, come through the corner, change your posting diagonal so that you're on the wrong diagonal, and leg-yield away from the rail. Just before you're across from the midpoint of the long side, straighten, change the flexion, change your diagonal, and leg-yield back to a point just before the corner.

You can also do two zig-zags, finishing the first one just before the middle of the long side. In this case, don't come too far off the track. The point of this exercise isn't to go sideways for a great distance, but to develop suppleness through the frequent transitions. It's important to do the exercise symmetrically by covering the same amount of ground when you yield to the left as when you yield to the right. This is a way to be sure that there's equal effort from each hind leg.

This is also a very good coordination exercise for the rider. Your posting diagonal is changed because you want to be sitting in the saddle when the inside hind leg is on the ground. At this moment it's easier for you to use your leg, and it's the best time to influence you horse's hind leg.

HARD TO STEER

MOBILIZING THE SHOULDERS

If you're circling to the left and your horse ducks out to the right, your instinct usually is to pull on the left (inside) rein to bring him back on the circle. The problem here is that the more you pull

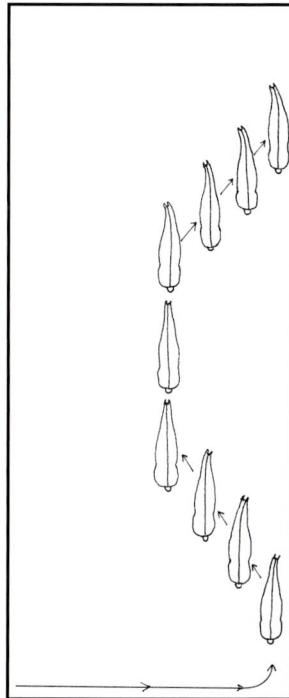

12.13 You can develop suppleness by riding a zigzag with leg-yields at the posting trot.

his face to the inside, the more his body can fall in the opposite direction. If you turn your horse's shoulders, the rest of his body will follow. But in order to execute this, your horse has to have supple shoulders (i.e. they must be able to move easily in the direction you want to turn).

Often when a horse feels hard to steer it's because he's not very maneuverable with his shoulders. To increase the mobility of the shoulders and make them more supple, do several transitions from shoulder-fore to straight ahead and back to shoulder-fore on each long side of the arena. When the shoulders are mobile, you can easily move them in without an increase in the weight of the reins. If you try to do this exercise and you find it practically impossible to move your horse's shoulders, then his shoulders aren't supple at all, and he needs some loosening exercises directed to that part of his body.

Recently I had a jumper rider bring her horse to me for some help. She explained that her horse was bold and athletic and could even "jump a house," but she couldn't turn him well enough to negotiate the courses. After watching him work a bit, it was obvious that he didn't have very supple shoulders.

12.14 To supple Round Robin's Alpen Glow's (Alpen's) shoulders, Bekki makes a square with four 90-degree corners. To prepare, she rides Alpen on a line that is parallel to the long side of the arena, but a little away from it, and flexes him a bit toward the rail to the right.

12.15 Bekki brings both her hands a little to the left for a moment to slide Alpen's shoulders around the turn.

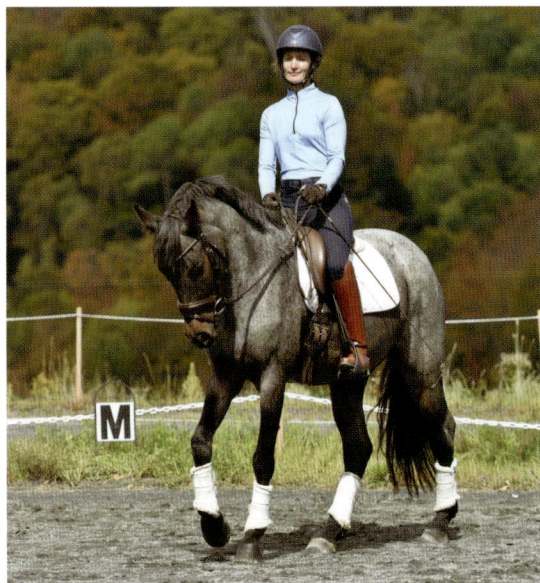

12.16 After she "knocks" the shoulders over, Bekki relaxes the contact for a moment before asking the shoulders to move over again.

We did a series of "shoulder mobilization" exercises to improve his ability to slide his shoulders left and right. We knew we were gaining in the suppleness department when she could move his shoulders around and there was no increase in the weight of the reins.

Following are three shoulder suppling exercises, listed in order from the simplest to the most demanding. They can be done in all three paces. First, make sure that flexion, which is created by vibrating the rein, is opposite the direction you want the shoulders to move. In other words, if you're going to slide the shoulders to the left, you'll want to first flex the horse to the right.

1. Go to the left and make a square that doesn't quite touch the rail on any side (figs. 12.14 to 12.17). In each of the four corners of your square, ask for outside flexion (counter-flexion toward the rail) and then move the shoulders to the inside of the turn by bringing both of your arms in that direction. The hand that is closest to the inside of the square (left hand) is used as an opening rein while the right hand gives an indirect rein aid. During the indirect rein aid, this hand comes as close to the withers as possible without ever actually crossing over them. For a horse whose shoulders are really stuck, you'll need a little leverage, so think of "knocking," "spinning," or "sliding" your horse's shoulders around the turn. As you work your way around the turn, "knock" the shoulders over with a quick but smooth action, then soften the contact for a second. Then "knock" again and soften again. It

12.17 They've finished their 90-degree turn and are continuing along the next side of the square. Bekki keeps Alpen flexed a bit toward the rail so that it's easy for her to move the horse's shoulders around the upcoming corner.

feels a little like "shoulder-reining" rather than neck reining.

2. On your square, alternate between a turn like the one described above for one corner and a small circle in the next corner—both done in counter-flexion. You'll continue to knock the shoulders in and then soften several times until you work your way all the way around the circle. When you've finished the circle, proceed to the next corner of your square.

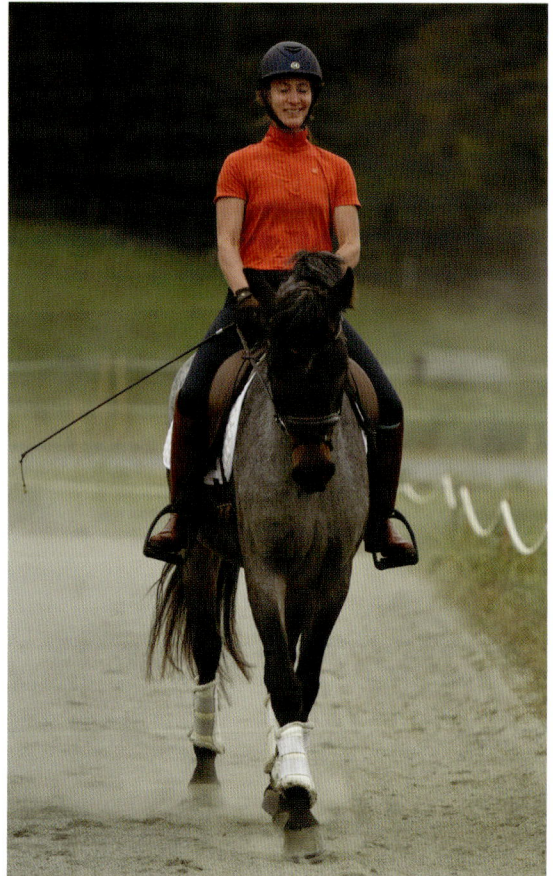

12.18 Bekki has flexed Alpen to the outside of the ring and has brought Alpen's shoulders slightly to the inside. She has moved the gelding's shoulders by bringing both her hands in the direction she wanted the shoulders to go.

12.19 Now Bekki has changed the flexion to the inside and moved Alpen's shoulders back toward the rail. Compare the position of Alpen's body to the pictures of Maeve when Bekki suppled Maeve's poll (figs. 10.10 and 10.11). During poll suppling, Maeve's shoulders stayed parallel to the chain and only the position of her head changed. In this exercise, Alpen's *shoulders* are moved left and right.

3. Ride straight down the long side of your ring or on the trail and ever so slightly slide your horse's shoulders in and out. Flex him to the left and move his shoulders to the right. Then straighten him for a few strides. Then flex him to the right and move the shoulders back to the left. As your horse becomes more athletic in his ability to slide his shoulders left and right, the weight in your reins will stay the same rather than increase. The shoulders only need to move a couple of inches in each direction. If you displace them too far, you'll get the hind legs involved rather than just isolating the shoulders. It's a very subtle exercise (figs. 12.18 and 12.19).

THE WIGGLY HORSE

Do you ever feel like you're wrestling an alligator or trying to hold onto a greased pig instead of schooling a horse? That's what riding the wiggly horse feels like. It's wonderful that he's so supple, but your four-legged friend feels like a centipede (fig. 12.20). Not only is this horse difficult to turn because he's all over the place, but it's just as hard to keep him going forward on a straight line.

I ran into one of these wormy guys recently at a clinic. His rider was trying to correct him by closing her appropriate hand or leg depending on where he was escaping. But as soon as she corrected him, he bounced off her aids and fell out somewhere else. She had fallen into a cycle of correcting her correction and then having to correct her next correction. The two of them looked like they had indulged in "one-too-many!"

I suggested that she make a solid, narrow corridor of her legs and hands and let her horse bounce from side to side between her steady, enveloping aids until he finally was able to go straight forward. To help her with this concept, she visualized standing in a hallway and throwing a ping pong ball forcefully against one wall. She "watched" the ball bounce from wall to wall until it finally rolled straight down the corridor.

We went through several stages. The first was to go all the way around the track, keeping him absolutely straight with no bend even when they were in a corner. When they could do that easily in all three paces, they did the same exercise three feet in from the rail with no track to help them. I told her to imagine she was on a

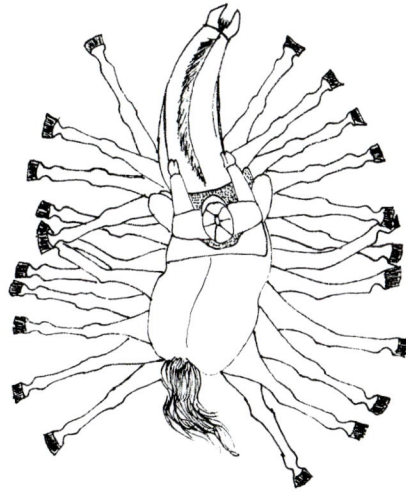

12.20 It's great to have a supple horse, but sometimes such a wiggly ride feels like a centipede moving in a hundred different directions at once.

12.21 Imagine you're on a balance beam that is placed exactly three feet away from the rail. If your horse's distance from the rail changes, you'll fall off the beam.

four-inch-wide balance beam such as gymnasts use (fig. 12.21). If he got any closer to, or further away from the rail, she'd fall off the beam.

Once they could do that with few "falls," they did several brief lengthenings of five or six strides each while staying on the beam, which was still three feet away from the rail. Eventually they added some circles, starting and finishing the same distance away from the rail and then continuing along the balance beam without getting drawn into the track. The final exercise was to turn onto the centerline, leg-yield over to within three feet from the rail, and then stop the sideways momentum with the outside aids so the horse could continue forward along a line parallel to but not quite in the track.

GOOD SIDE, BAD SIDE

Our goal for all horses is to help them become athletic enough so that they are equally strong and willing to carry weight with both hind legs. When both hind legs are equally strong, you won't feel like your horse has a "better" and a "worse" side. He'll be just as easy to ride to the left as he is to the right.

The catch is that the hind legs can become equally strong only if the horse is **straight**. Most horses aren't truly straight, just as most people are also either right- or left-handed. The solution for "one-sidedness," therefore, is to keep working on everything you've learned in this book, until your horse goes "forward, straight, and in rhythm"—then he will go equally well to each side.

Riders must also recognize that a horse's forehand is narrower than his hindquarters. If his shoulders are taken too close to the wall, he has no option but to become crooked by bringing his hindquarters to the inside to make room for them. This can be the result of "pilot error," or sometimes a young horse will put his shoulders toward the wall in an effort to support himself and maintain his balance.

STIFF VS. SOFT SIDES

This right- or left-handedness leads to the development of what we call stiff and soft sides. The stiff side may feel more difficult to bend, but generally the horse carries the inside hind leg under the body and will bear weight on that side. The soft side feels easier to bend, but the inside hind leg tends to drift to the inside of the ring, and avoids carrying weight. That might explain why a shoulder-fore on the stiff side, where the horse steps into the rein, is easier to do than on the soft side where the horse tends to bring his head and neck in and his shoulders fall out toward the fence.

We can compensate for this tendency by doing the opposite of what the crooked horse wants to do. In other words, ride the stiff side more bent and work the soft side absolutely straight. Let's say your horse is stiff to the right (figs. 12.24 and 12.25). While going to the right, bend him to the right even if you're on a straight line. While riding a large circle to the right, overbend the body as if you're on the arc of a smaller circle.

When riding this horse to the left, keep the soft side absolutely straight. Don't bend your horse at all on either curved or straight lines. When you turn him, pretend his body is as stiff and straight as a bus (figs. 12.22 and 12.23).

You can also use **suppling** to help loosen your horse's stiff side. If he's stiff to the left, always supple him on his left side regardless of the direction you're going (figs. 12.26 and 12.27).

12.22 Alpen's soft side is his left side. It's easy to bend him, but his inside hind leg drifts to the inside of the turn to avoid carrying weight.

SHOULDER-FORE

Use shoulder-fore to straighten your horse and make his hind legs equally strong. Always straighten your horse by bringing his forehand in front of the hindquarters rather than by pushing his haunches out.

To get comfortable placing the forehand in front of the hindquarters, practice riding around the ring in shoulder-fore, through corners, through transitions, and through school figures,

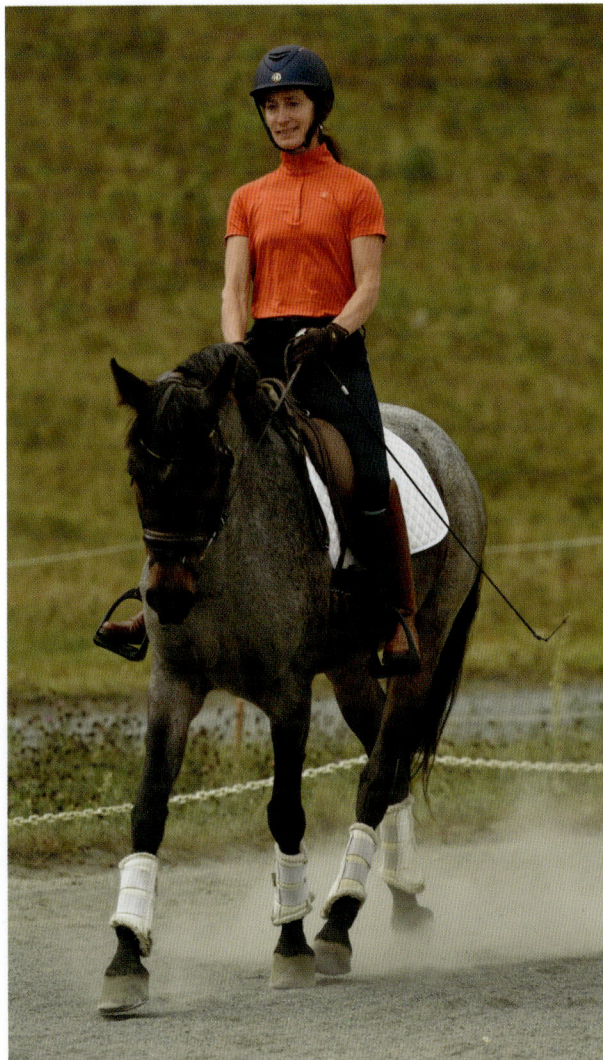

12.23 Bekki is correcting Alpen by doing the opposite of what the gelding wants to do with his body. Rather than letting him bend too much when he travels on curved lines to the left, Bekki keeps the horse's body absolutely straight—no flexion or bend. Note how riding Alpen straight is helping encourage his inside hind leg to step well underneath his body so it has to bear weight and get stronger.

12.24 It's harder to bend Nieve on her stiff side—the right. She doesn't flex to the right and her barrel leans against Bekki's inside leg.

12.25 To make her horse more athletic, Bekki bends Nieve slightly to the right all the time—both on straight and curved lines. She's careful to bend Nieve equally from poll to tail rather than letting her "cheat" by just bending her neck. Note her inside hind leg stepping farther under her body here.

12.26 Sometimes, a horse is stiff on the left side and finds it difficult to bend in that direction. While trotting on a circle to the left, Bekki supples Nieve toward the inside of the circle. Note how she keeps her horse moving forward energetically as she bends her neck to the left.

12.27 When Bekki changes direction and circles to the right, she continues to work on softening the left side of Nieve's body by suppling her toward the outside of the circle. Notice that Bekki firmly supports Nieve with the right rein as she supples the mare to the left. That way Nieve's front legs stay on the circle rather than moving to the left and coming off the original arc. Only her neck should move off the line of the circle.

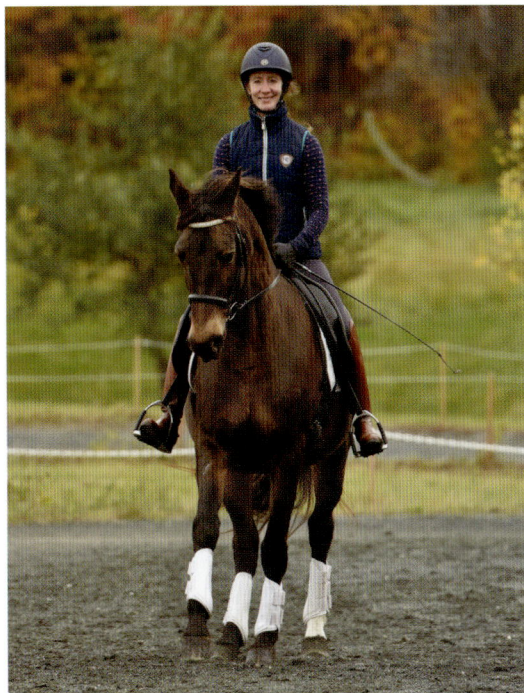

12.28 To help straighten a crooked horse, ride the horse in shoulder-fore position. Here, we see right shoulder-fore in counter-canter—the right hind leg is driven between the front legs as the forehand is brought toward the chain.

until it becomes automatic and easy for the horse to keep his inside hind leg under his body (fig. 12.28).

You can also ride shoulder-fore as a strengthening exercise for the hind leg that likes to drift to the inside and is more reluctant to bear weight. Use makes the muscle, and the weaker hind leg will get stronger as it's placed under the horse's body (12.29).

Increase the strengthening benefits of the exercise by staying in shoulder-fore throughout transitions. For example, go down the long side in sitting trot and ride several trot-walk-trot transitions while maintaining the shoulder-fore throughout. Be very aware that the horse doesn't

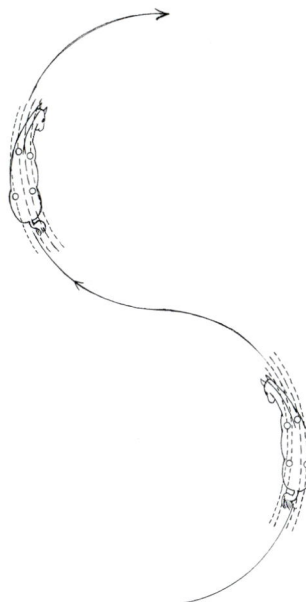

12.29 Use shoulder-fore to straighten your horse and make his hind legs equally strong. Always straighten him by bringing his forehand in front of his hindquarters, not by pushing the hindquarters sideways. Practice on figures and transitions until he's happy to carry weight on his inside hind leg.

drift to the inside (the responsibility of your inside leg), swing the hindquarters out (the responsibility of your outside leg) or decrease the angle (the responsibility of your two hands) at the moment that he steps into the new pace. That's the critical point when the horse will try to escape the difficulty of the movement. The same exercise can be done during canter-trot-canter transitions.

TRIPPING

If your horse trips a lot, the first thing you need to do is check that he's shod correctly and that his feet aren't too long.

If his feet are in good shape, make him more attentive and get his balance off his forehand and onto his hind legs by doing frequent transitions from one pace to another. Or, increase his energy level and freshen his working gaits by doing frequent transitions to and from lengthenings.

KEY POINTS

This chapter has shown you how to use the movements and exercises that your horse has learned to solve some common training problems. For example, you can:

- Relax a tense horse by suppling him.

- Relax a tense horse by reducing the energy of the pace.

- Control a horse that rushes by doing small circles or leg-yielding.

- Wake up a lazy horse by putting him in front of your leg and then keep him sharp by asking for frequent transitions and leg-yielding.

- Help a horse pick up the correct canter lead by increasing his "throughness" with suppling.

- Teach a horse to accept the bit by suppling and leg-yielding.

- Loosen a stiff horse by suppling, doing frequent transitions from pace to pace as well as within the pace, and leg-yielding.

- Make a horse easier to steer by doing "shoulder mobilization" exercises.

- Organize a wiggly horse's body by working on the "balance beam."

- Help a horse go equally well in both directions by working his stiff side with too much bend and his soft side absolutely straight.

- Straighten a horse and strengthen a weak hind leg with shoulderfore.

STAGE THREE

THE PROFESSIONALS' SECRET

D o you ever wonder why you struggle with movements and transitions that professional riders seem to do effortlessly? Are you puzzled by the fact that your trainer's horse can be persuaded to march by large rocks, farm equipment, umbrellas, and all manner of scary objects, while your horse is overwhelmed by his flight instinct?

Well, here in Stage Three, you're about to discover the secret of professional trainers. This is an exciting point in the education of both you and your horse. In fact, if I were told that I could only teach you one concept to help you train your horse successfully, I would choose the information you're about to learn in this stage.

Here's what professionals know that you don't. They know the formula for "putting their horses on the aids" (their horses react instantly and obediently to invisible signals); this secret is a versatile aid called the half-halt.

In chapter 13, I will dissect the half-halt into manageable pieces and put it back together for

The pure joy and expressive movement of a horse at play.

you in an understandable, user-friendly way. I'll even give you tips on what to do if your horse just doesn't seem to be getting it.

Then, in chapter 14, I'll show you how to use the half-halt to connect your horse—also known as putting him on the bit. You'll love this part, because when a horse is "on the bit," not only is he more comfortable to ride but it's also a lot easier for you to communicate with each other. This is the beginning of your being able to reach a whole new level of working together happily.

13

THE HALF-HALT

What, you may well ask, is a half-halt? How can I possibly do a half-halt? And why would I want to anyway? Well, like Robert Dover, I too feel that the half-halt is the most essential tool in riding. Learning how to give a half-halt not only allows you to take charge of your horse's body and mind whenever you need to, but it also enables you to proceed further in the development of your horse as an athlete.

The word "half-halt" itself often creates confusion. The term is something of a misnomer because the half-halt really has nothing to do with *halts* at all. In fact (as Olympic dressage rider Lendon Gray suggests), it might help you to call it a "half-go" since every half-halt should contain the feeling of *adding* power from the horse's hind legs up to your hand. But more about that later.

Think of the half-halt as an *aid*. You could call it a "bringing-to-attention" aid. It will help you rebalance your horse, mentally or physically, whenever you need to. Think of this aid in the same way that you use your outside leg behind the girth as an aid to signal your horse to canter, or you close both legs near the girth as an aid to

"The half-halt is the most important concept in all of riding, because it calls the horse to a perfect state of balance, harmony and attention."

Robert Dover, author of
The Gates to Brilliance

• • • • •

ask your horse to do a transition from the walk to the trot.

One major difference, however, is that you use the half-halt as an aid far more often. You use it every time your horse needs a reminder to pay attention to you, either because he's distracted by his surroundings or because you want to warn him that you are about to ask for a new movement. You give a half-halt to rebalance him every time he's heavy on the forehand, leaning the wrong way around corners, yanking at the reins, sticking his head up in the air, feeling stiff in his body, or is otherwise resistant and uncomfortable to ride.

13.1 Trying to train a horse to be more athletic without a half-halt is like trying to nail a board to a wall without a hammer. Impossible! You don't have all your tools.

As an instructor I often meet riders who blame themselves when they have a hard time controlling their horses. They think the fault is theirs because they're not properly coordinated or talented enough to ride and train as effectively as a professional does. Well, if they haven't learned how to give a half-halt, they're right!

After all, imagine someone giving you a board and some nails—but no hammer—and asking you to nail that board to a wall. It would be quite a task for you to put the board up. Well, trying to train a horse to be more athletic without the half-halt as an aid is like trying to nail a board to a wall without a hammer. It's pretty difficult because you don't have all your *tools* (fig. 13.1).

So I tell my students not to be so hard on themselves. I remind them, "You're not born knowing how to give a half-halt and your horse wasn't born knowing how to respond to one!" But with what you've been taught up to this point, you're ready to learn. I'll teach you in a clear-cut, step-by-step approach. Then it will be up to you to train your horse.

PREPARING TO GIVE A HALF-HALT

It's essential that you know how to give a half-halt because when you ride your horse you are always dealing with the issue of *balance.* Since your horse was not "designed" to carry weight on his back, he often loses his balance with a rider on top. The half-halt is the key—the *aid* that you use—to restore lost balance (fig. 13.2).

As we begin Stage Three, the half-halt is simply used to regain lost balance. Later on in Stage Four (chapter 15), I'll describe how more

13.2 Since a horse is not designed to carry weight on his back, he can easily lose his balance in a canter-to-trot transition.

advanced riders give half-halts to *maintain* balance, by using them while preparing for new movements and exercises.

Earlier in this book, I laid the groundwork for a half-halt; I told you about riding your horse forward and straight, in a regular rhythm, with an inviting contact. This groundwork must be established before you can give a successful half-halt. In other words, you can execute a half-halt only when you have the following prerequisites:

Horse

1. *Forward*—not only over the ground but also "thinking" forward.

2. *Straight*—with the hind feet following the tracks of the front feet and the spine overlapping the line of travel.

3. *Rhythm*—steady and regular.

Rider

Contact with the horse's mouth is inviting and sympathetic because it is firm, consistent, elastic, symmetrical and with a straight line from the bit to the hand to the elbow.

If you lose any of these qualities while giving the half-halt aid, stop what you're doing and re-establish whichever prerequisite is lacking. Only then can you try again to give the aid. For instance, if you give a half-halt and the horse stops *thinking* forward, you'll need to go through the process of putting him in front of the leg again before continuing to use half-halts to correct any of your horse's resistances.

For simplicity's sake, when first learning the half-halt, try it without the push from your seat. Just use your legs for the driving aids. Later, when you get comfortable with the timing and coordination of the half-halt, you can add the push with your seat toward the end of the three-second count as part of your driving aids.

You may have noticed that I said (when I laid out the aids above) that using the inside rein is optional. Since three seconds is a long time to keep your outside hand closed in a fist, some horses might bend their necks to the outside. (This usually happens going in one direction more than the other—when the horse's soft side is on the outside.) If this does happen, the horse obviously isn't straight anymore. He needs to be straight in order for your half-halt to be effective.

To prevent the horse from bending his neck to the outside, give a few soft squeezes on the inside rein at the same time that your outside hand is closed. Use of this inside rein is optional because its use depends on whether or not your horse bends to the outside.

If you're not sure how much inside rein to use or whether to use it at all, just apply a half-halt without it. Close your two legs and outside hand for three seconds and watch your horse's neck while you're doing it. If his neck stays straight, you don't need to use any inside rein when giving the half-halt. If the neck bends a bit to the outside, you need a little inside rein. If it bends a lot to the outside, you'll need even more inside rein during the next half-halt.

To sum up, the degree to which your horse's neck bends to the outside tells you how much inside rein to use in order to keep him straight (figs. 13.5 to 13.7).

If you find the previous explanation of the half-halt at all confusing, trying thinking about it this way instead. The half-halt is a marriage of the driving aids, the bending aids, and the outside rein. The outside rein is very important because it opposes too much speed from the driving aids, and too much bend from the bending aids.

In other words, if you applied the driving aids (seat and both legs) and bending aids (inside rein and both legs) to their extreme without adding the outside rein, your horse would run very fast on a very small circle. But the outside hand says, "You're not allowed to speed up or bend to a

THE AIDS FOR A HALF-HALT

Let's break down the half-halt—or if you prefer, the "half-go"—into its parts. The half-halt itself is the combination of the driving aids (both legs and seat), the outside rein, and the bending aids (both legs and the inside rein), maintained for about three seconds.

During those three seconds, close both legs and push with your seat as if asking for that 100% wholeheartedly forward response that you practiced when you put the horse in front of the leg (see chapter 5). This is the "go" part of your half-go. But, rather than allowing the horse to go more forward as you did then, receive and contain this energy almost immediately by closing your outside hand in a fist. This becomes the **rein of opposition**. Make sure you feel the energy surge forward into the rein just before you actually close this outside hand.

By using your driving aids a fraction of a second before you use your rein aids, you ride your horse from *back to front*. This is your goal no matter what type of riding you do, because it's the only way you can honestly **connect** your horse and make him more athletic and obedient. If you're preoccupied with creating an artificial "head-set" by fiddling with your hands, you'll be riding your horse from front to back, and you'll never truly be in charge. Remember, she who controls the hind legs—the "engine"—controls the horse. Always ride from *back to front* by directing the power from the hind legs forward into your hands.

To the naked eye, it will appear that you use all of these aids simultaneously. However, freeze-frame photography should show you using your driving aids first, then closing your outside hand, and finally, if necessary, vibrating your inside rein to keep the horse straight. (Remember, "straight" means straight on a line and bent along the arc on a curve.)

It is absolutely necessary for you to send your horse forward with your driving aids a fraction of a second before you close your outside hand. If you close your outside hand before you use your driving aids (or even exactly at the same time, for that matter), it's like picking up the telephone before it rings—no one is there!

13.3 When giving a half-halt, think about inflating a balloon. Your driving aids blow it up, and closing your outside hand in a fist puts the knot at the end. If you close your hand before you drive your horse forward, you'll tie the knot before you inflate the balloon. If you use your driving aids without closing your fist, you let the air whoosh out of the balloon. In both cases, your half-halt doesn't work.

To help you imagine this concept, think about a balloon. Your driving aids blow up the balloon, and closing your outside hand in a fist puts the knot at the end of it to keep it full of air. So, to give a good half-halt, use your seat and legs first, and then close your outside hand just as you'd inflate a balloon first and then tie the knot (fig. 13.3).

The Aids for a Half-Halt (on a circle to the left)

Seat: Stretch up and use your seat in a driving way as if pushing the back of the saddle toward the front of the saddle. Be sure to stay sitting in a vertical position when you push with your seat. Leaning behind the vertical can cause the horse to stiffen or hollow his back, and his head and neck will probably go up in the air as well.

Legs: close your legs steadily as if squeezing toothpaste out of a tube.

Outside rein (right rein): close your hand in a fist.

Inside rein (left rein): vibrate, if necessary, to keep the horse's neck straight.

The aids are applied almost simultaneously, but basically they should be thought of in this order:

Driving aids first to create energy;

Outside rein second to contain energy;

Inside rein third, if necessary, to keep the neck straight.

Apply these aids for about three seconds by increasing the pressure of your legs and reins so that it is slightly more than the maintenance pressure you have when your legs are softly draped around your horse's sides and your hands have a firm but gentle feel of his mouth (fig. 13.4). After you give the half-halt, *relax*. This relaxing—the finish of the aid—is as important as the aid itself because it is the horse's reward. When you relax, let your legs rest lightly on your horse's sides again, keep correct contact with his mouth, and continue riding your circle.

13.4 The half-halt timeline.

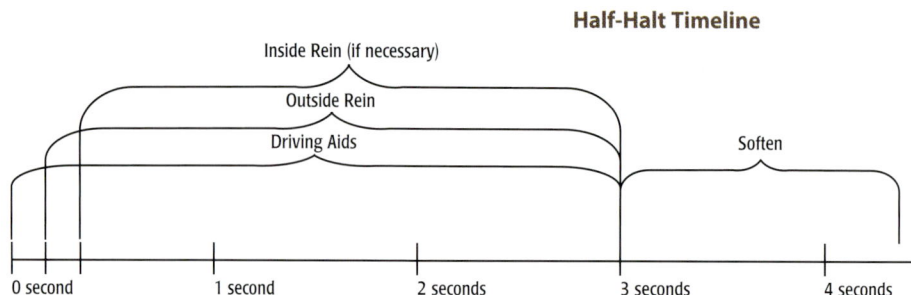

13.5 Bekki and Alpen are going to the left with Alpen's soft side (left) on the inside. Since Alpen's neck stays straight in front of his body as Bekki sends him forward through her outside hand during the half-halt, Bekki doesn't need to use any inside rein. Her driving aids and outside rein are doing the job perfectly.

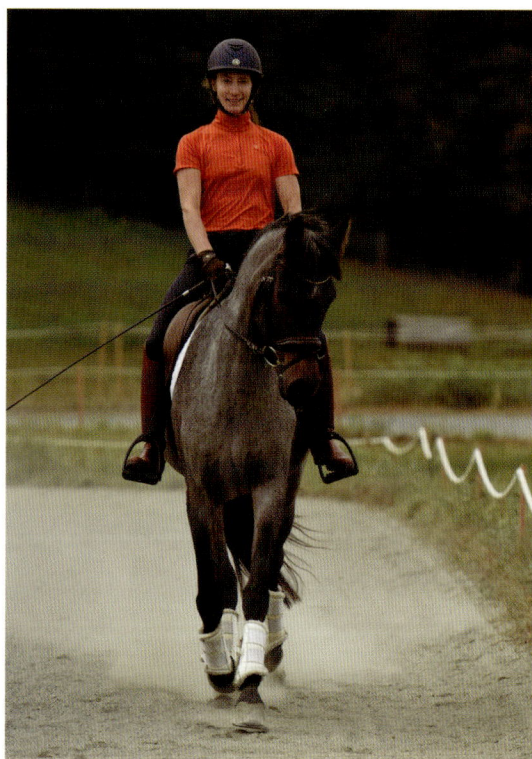

13.6 When Bekki combines her driving aids and outside rein during this half-halt going to the right with Alpen's stiff side on the inside, Alpen's neck bends to the outside. The bend in Alpen's neck tells Bekki she'll need to use a little inside rein next time she gives a half-halt in this direction in order to keep her horse's neck straight. This is what generally happens when the horse's soft side is on the outside.

13.7 In this case during the half-halt, Alpen's neck bends even more to the outside. During the next half-halt, Bekki needs to use an even greater influence of the inside rein to counteract the action of her closed outside hand.

chapter, you'll see that this change of balance and the resulting round frame is called **"connection"** or **"on the bit**." This is what you're looking for (figs. 13.9 to 13.12).

Robert Dover has a saying to help his students absorb the relationship between the driving and restraining aids during a half-halt. He says that if your horse slows down, you have too much "halt" (outside rein) and not enough "half" (driving aids). Alternatively, if your horse speeds

greater degree than you already have. Instead you must yield to the outside hand and because you're being driven, you'll bend your hind legs more."

When all three aids are correctly combined, the horse maintains his original speed and stays straight as he steps more forward under his body. He yields in front—flexing "in" (longitudinally as opposed to laterally) at the poll—to the closed outside hand, and he bends the joints of the hind legs to a greater degree. This changes his balance and **frame**, or silhouette, so that it looks more **round** (figs. 13.8 A & B). In the next

13.8 A & B Using a half-halt to improve balance: The horse in A is not in good balance. His hind legs are out behind his body and his weight is on his forehand. As his rider gives the half-halt as depicted in B, the horse bends the joints of the hind legs, steps more underneath his body, and yields in front so that he comes into a better balance.

13.9 This is the frame and balance that Rowen adopts on his own. His hind legs are out behind his body, lazily pushing him along. His back is hollow and low, his neck is raised and stiff, and he is not flexing in at the poll.

13.10 Ally starts to give a half-halt, and as she uses her driving aids to send Rowen through the outside rein, the shape of his topline begins to change.

13.11 Ally continues to drive Rowen through the outside rein. (The contact with Ally's outside hand is more firm than it is with her inside hand.) Rowen's hind legs are coming more underneath his body and they begin to carry rather than push.

up when you give a half-halt, you have too much "half," and not enough "halt."

Many riders are surprised when I tell them that the half-halt lasts for three seconds, because they have been taught that it only lasts for a moment. I tell you to do this for three seconds because I want you to use it to bend the joints of the hind legs for two to three steps.

I'm not saying that there won't be times when you give a shorter or a longer half-halt. In fact, once your horse has learned to respond correctly to the half-halt, you might apply the aid for only one second. On the other hand, if you're struggling to maintain a round frame during a transition, you can sustain it for four or five seconds. (I'll delve into variations of the half-halt at the end of this chapter.)

But it's helpful for you as you're learning to think of the half-halt as lasting for the amount of

time it takes to inhale and exhale—about three seconds for most people. When you breathe in, you tighten your stomach and the small of your back, and the breath is like a wave that travels up your stomach into your chest. As you breathe out, your shoulders go back and down and the wave goes down your back into your seat. At the same time, close your legs. As the horse begins to move forward, you'll feel this surge of energy come into the rein. At this moment, close your outside hand in a fist. Then you can relax all the aids and proceed forward in a new state of balance and attention.

Your first task will be to teach your horse the half-halt while riding in each of the three paces. Start on a circle, since the curve of the circle helps the horse step through that outside rein. Usually the horse begins to understand and change his balance and frame during the very first session, although it often takes several sessions before his response is more or less confirmed.

Once you can execute a half-halt in all three paces on a curved line, follow the track of the ring and do the same thing on a straight line. If you run into difficulties, go back to the circle and review the half-halt there.

In chapter 14, I'll explain other situations during which you can use this same half-halt to improve or maintain your horse's balance and frame. For now this is where you should start; teach your horse to respond to the half-halt during all three paces on circles and straight lines.

13.12 As Ally finishes the half-halt, Rowen looks like a more compact package from tail to poll. Ally will soften the aids now and follow up with another half-halt to improve his balance even further.

COMMON MISTAKES

Since most of us work without an instructor much of the time, it's helpful to be able to recognize our mistakes by evaluating the feedback we get from our horses. By noticing what the horse does when we give a half-halt, we can improve and refine the use of this aid.

The following are the most common mistakes riders make when learning how to coordinate the "parts" of the half-halt.

1. Too much bend of the neck to the inside during the half-halt. This happens when you've used too much inside rein or not enough outside rein (fig. 13.13).

2. Too much bend of the neck to the outside. In this case you need to vibrate your inside rein more (fig. 13.14).

3. Horse shortens his neck during the half-halt (fig. 13.15). He's telling you that you've brought your arms backward while you're giving the aid. Your arms must never be drawn backward while giving a half-halt, or doing anything else for that matter. To help you avoid bringing your arms back, picture your hands in the correct position and imagine that there's an invisible shield or wall directly behind them, making it impossible for you to bring your hands closer to your body. Instead of bringing your arms back, send your horse forward with your legs, and when he arrives at your outside hand, close it in a fist.

13.13 During this half-halt, Eliza has used too much inside rein, and has also allowed her outside hand to move forward. As a result, Claire bends her neck too much to the inside.

13.14 Here, Claire bends her neck to the outside of the circle because Eliza isn't using enough inside rein in order to keep the mare straight.

13.15 Because Eliza is pulling backward on the reins during this half-halt, her horse shortens and raises her neck. Never use your arms during a half-halt. Instead, keep your hands in correct riding position in front of your body and send your horse forward with your driving aids until he meets your hands.

4. Your horse becomes crooked by swinging his hindquarters in or out. You've probably either used unequal pressure from your legs, or your legs are not placed correctly on your horse's sides. Remember that when riding straight lines your legs should be side by side and when riding curved lines your inside leg is on the girth while your outside leg is behind the girth (fig. 13.16).

5. Your horse's tempo changes either faster or slower during the half halt. If you fail to "match" your driving aids with the closure of your outside hand in a fist, the horse's speed will change. By "match" I mean you should use these aids not only at the same time but to the same degree as well.

   a. If your horse goes faster, keep the same leg aids but close your outside hand more firmly.

13.16 Here's a different view of Eliza and Claire as they trot on a circle to the left. Because of the angle of the photo, you can see that during this half-halt, Claire has swung her hindquarters to the right and is no longer bent to the left along the arc of the circle. This can happen either because Eliza has pressed harder with her left leg than with her right leg or because her left leg is placed too far behind the girth, causing her horse to yield away from it.

b. If he slows down, you've probably used more influence of outside hand than driving aids. If you feel that you didn't use too much outside hand, then your horse might have fallen behind your leg. If this is the case, interrupt riding the half-halt and go through the process of putting him in front of your leg again. Once he is solidly going forward, you can resume giving the half-halt.

6. Forgetting to relax or soften after three seconds. This causes the horse to stiffen against the aids. Even if you feel that you're not getting the desired result from your half-halt because your horse is resisting, relax after three seconds. Wait for a few seconds, then try again.

✳ HELPFUL HINTS

USING LENGTHENINGS TO EXPLAIN THE HALF-HALT TO YOUR HORSE

If you're having trouble teaching the half-halt to your horse, first check your prerequisites for the half-halt (p. 216) and then go through the list of common rider mistakes (pp. 227 to 230). If that all seems fine to you but your horse still doesn't seem to understand what you're asking for, here are some additional ideas you can use to explain it to him.

First, let's talk about the uneducated horse and what he thinks he has to do when you give a half-halt. During the half-halt, your driving aids create energy and your outside rein contains that energy within the horse's body. The green horse says,

13.17 During a half-halt, your legs and seat create energy while your outside rein contains that energy within the horse. The green horse says "Now, wait a minute! How can you ask me to stop and go at the same time?" You need to teach him to go forward through your closed outside hand, and the instant he does, stop giving the aid and reward him.

"Now, wait a minute! How can you ask me to stop and go at the same time?" Since many horses tend to be lazy, if given this dilemma they opt to pay attention to the outside hand and stop or slow down rather than decide to go forward from your legs *through* that closed outside hand (fig. 13.17).

In this case I add extra "go" to my "half-go" by using the momentum of a lengthening to give the horse the idea that he must go forward "through" the closed outside hand. But before I tell you how to do this, let me take a moment to describe this sensation of stepping through the hand. When a horse isn't stepping through the hand, he feels as if he's jammed up against it. You feel the kind of resistance or blockage you'd feel if you were trying to drive your car with the emergency brake on. However, when he steps through the hand, the contact feels rubbery and soft; the energy feels like it can flow from the hind legs through the horse's body into your hand and back to the hind legs in an uninterrupted cycle, a bit like a flywheel that continues to turn by itself because it doesn't meet any resistance. Not only can you feel when your horse steps through your hand, but you can see it as well. As your horse steps through your hand, you'll notice that his neck changes shape. It gets longer, rounder, and often lower.

To use lengthenings as a way to explain to my horse how the driving aids and restraining aids can be combined, I start on a circle where I know my outside rein has to be more definite because of the bend. Then I ask for a lengthening, and when we're really "motoring" along, I close my outside hand in a fist for three seconds while maintaining the lengthening. While doing this, my inside rein is doing its usual job of keeping the horse straight—that is, I vibrate it just enough, together with my leg aids, to produce the bend needed on a circle.

If my horse doesn't become rounder, which I'm able to see by checking to see if he lowers and stretches his neck as well as rounding it, I soften my outside hand for a moment and ask again. When the power of the lengthening carries him forward through my closed outside fist and he becomes rounder, I immediately praise generously.

Once my horse understands, I alternate between closing my outside hand when I've got a good lengthening, and applying my driving aids and closing my outside hand (a normal half-halt) while in a normal working gait. In both cases my legs close in the same way to create energy. By riding my horse from back to front in this way, I explain that every half-halt contains the feeling of a lengthening.

USING LEG-YIELDING TO EXPLAIN THE HALF-HALT

You can also use a leg-yielding exercise to teach an uneducated horse the concept of going forward through a closed outside hand. Turn onto a line that divides your ring in half lengthwise, then leg-yield over to the track that goes around the outside of the ring. Start by asking your horse to do a leg-yield from the middle of the arena over to the left, away from your right leg. (Eventually you will be doing the exercise in both directions.)

As the horse crosses over with his right hind leg, that leg not only goes sideways, but it also goes more forward toward your outside (left) hand. At some point during this leg-yield, close your outside hand in a fist for about three seconds in the same way that you do during a half-halt. The sideways and forward action of the right hind leg as well as the momentum of the body traveling to the left will help drive the horse through that closed outside hand.

As soon as you see that the horse has stepped through your outside hand because he has lowered, lengthened, and rounded his neck, praise him. In this way he has a chance to feel how to carry his body and your weight in a new position. Once he understands the concept of going forward through your outside hand during the use of the leg-yield, go back to riding the half-halt while on a straight line. By alternating this leg-yielding exercise with the usual half-halt aid, you're explaining that in both cases you're asking him to do the same thing—step through the outside rein in order to change his balance and frame (figs. 13.18 to 13.20).

USING LEG-YIELDING TO IMPROVE THE HALF-HALT

I've used leg-yielding not only with green horses but also with stiff or tight horses who are taking short steps. I often tell my students that the neck is a barometer of what the hind legs are doing. You can read the neck to see if the hind legs are coming under the body if you think of the length of neck and stride as being proportional. If the neck is three feet long, the hind legs are taking a three-foot-long stride.

The other day I was helping a friend with her Grand Prix dressage horse. This horse has a lot of education, so when his rider picked up the reins, this fellow cooperatively raised and arched his neck. But the neck was very short, which told us that the hind legs weren't really coming forward. I told her to half-halt and push the hind

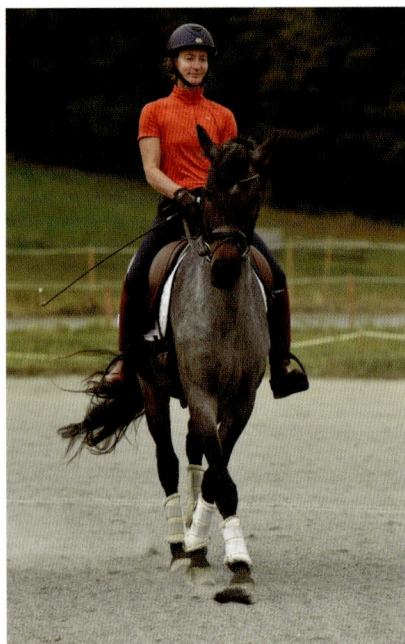

13.18 Bekki is leg-yielding Alpen from the center of the arena over to the long side. Even though Alpen's back isn't visible in this photo, you can assume that it is dropped and he is stiffening against Bekki's hand because his head and neck are up in the air.

13.19 As they leg-yield over toward the track and Alpen steps forward and sideways with his right hind leg into Bekki's left hand, the horse begins to relax and lower his neck.

13.20 Alpen has now stepped through Bekki's hand and softly yields to it as he lowers, lengthens, and rounds his neck and flexes in his poll and jaw.

legs further under, but the horse continued to take short, quick steps. As it turned out, he had been worked very hard two days before and then had been given a day off. His muscles were stiff and tight.

We used leg-yielding as a gentle stretching and loosening exercise. In human terms we asked him to touch his toes, but allowed him to reach them gradually by asking him to first touch his knees, and when that was easy, touch his calves, and when that was easy, touch his ankles. In equine terms, we first leg-yielded in the walk from the centerline to the long side. When that was easy, we asked for progressively steeper leg-yields. The next step was relatively gentle leg-yields from one corner of the ring to the opposite corner. When that was easy, we went from the corner to midway down the long side and back to the far corner that was on the same side as the one we started from. When that was also easy, we zig-zagged back and forth across the arena three times. All of this was done in the walk with long, slow, sweeping steps.

Finally, she straightened him and asked him to come on the bit with a half-halt. Thanks to the stretching of the muscles during the leg-yields, the range of motion of the hind legs was markedly increased, and it was easier for him to take longer strides. As the hind legs reached further under the body, the neck got proportionately longer. Unlike the young horse who didn't understand the concept of the half-halt asking him to come on the bit, this horse couldn't respond to the half-halt because of his short, tight muscles.

USING "INCREASING HALF-HALTS" FOR ACCEPTANCE OF THE OUTSIDE HAND

When you first introduce the half-halt to your horse, he may stiffen against your hand when he feels you use your outside rein. If this happens repeatedly, give an "increasing half-halt." Start with a light half-halt, but gradually increase the pressure of all the aids over the course of the three seconds. (If you need "more leg," you can tap your horse with a whip at the same time that you are using your legs and hands to the maximum.)

Now here's the important part: while you're doing this, watch your horse's neck very carefully. The moment it becomes even slightly longer, relax all of your aids. By lengthening his neck, your horse is telling you that he's starting to step through your outside hand. He should be instantly rewarded for this both by softening all of the aids and by praising him (figs. 13.21 and 13.22).

Then start again with a light half-halt, only increasing the pressure if necessary. Always start with a light half-halt rather than immediately going to a strong one, so that you give your horse the option to respond to a more subtle aid. You always want to ride using the most refined aids possible. It's not much fun for either you or your horse to ride from strength.

By way of explaining the half-halt to your horse, increasing its intensity says the following: "This is the half-halt, and it's not going away. In fact, it will become increasingly more insistent until you begin to step through my outside hand. However, the instant you begin to step through my hand, the aid will be finished and you'll be rewarded."

13.21 Bekki is cantering on a circle to the right here. Even after several half-halts, Alpen continues to stiffen against her outside rein rather than step through it. Alpen's neck is tense, short, and high. Notice how the muscles on the underside of his neck are bulging rather than soft and relaxed. Also, because he is coming against Bekki's hand rather than yielding to it, he tilts his head.

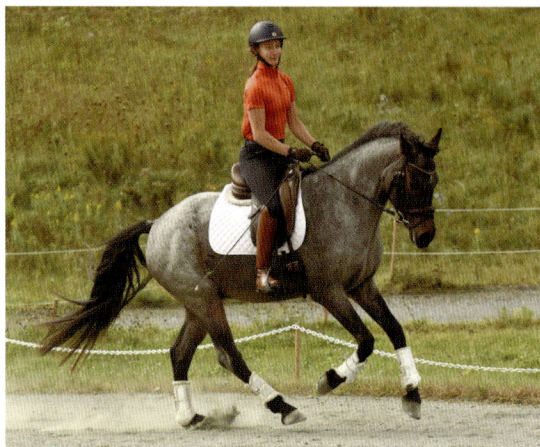

13.22 As Bekki uses an increasing half-halt, Alpen's shape is starting to change as the gelding's neck becomes slightly longer, lower, and rounder. The subtle changes Bekki sees and feels are her signal to immediately stop giving the half-halt and soften as Alpen's reward. Judging by the amount that Alpen's frame has changed with this increasing half-halt, Bekki will probably be able to give a normal half-halt next time to get Alpen to step completely through the rein.

In this way your horse learns that when he arrives at your closed outside hand, he should soften and yield to the action of the rein. He learns that he has other options besides jamming up against your hand. He needs to view the hand as a barrier, but it's a penetrable barrier. He can step through it and come into a different balance and rounder frame (fig. 13.23).

Remember, your horse doesn't know about the half-halt. It's your job to teach him. If you're having difficulties, take a moment to evaluate what could be going wrong. Ask yourself some questions. Is he forward, straight, and in a good working gait? Is my contact correct? Did I use too much inside rein? Did I need to have more influence of the inside rein? Did I remember to soften after three seconds?

Through patient repetition and rewarding any effort on his part, your horse will begin to understand the half-halt better. Then you will have an incredible tool that you can use to sort out all sorts of mental and physical "imbalances."

THE "DIFFERENT" HALF-HALTS

Do you remember when I said that the half-halt is the most essential tool in riding? Well, now we're going to take that statement to another level. At the more advanced stage of training, I want you to realize that everything you create in the horse is the result of subtle variations of the half-halt.

Over the course of the next few chapters, I'll describe several versions of this basic three-second half-halt that can be used to help you deal with all sorts of training issues. Since the half-halts are given in a slightly different way, I've assigned different names to each half-halt depending on its purpose. These are labels that I have created so that my students and I are sure we're talking about the same thing.

I know you'll be excited about this preview of coming attractions because you'll see how the half-halt will become the solution to many of your training woes.

In the next chapter, I discuss how the basic three-second half-halt you've just learned can be used to connect your horse or, as we say in the dressage world, put him "on the bit." I call it the **connecting half-halt**.

In chapter 16, you'll learn how to improve self-carriage with a **collecting half-halt**. This half-halt is of greater intensity and is done with shorter reins than the "connecting" half-halt. Also, once your horse reacts correctly to the aid, you'll find that it can be as brief as one second instead of the standard three seconds.

In chapter 21, you'll discover how **preparatory half-halts** can engage and ready your horse for a transition. These half-halts are applied more quickly than the basic three-second half-halt. They are done in the rhythm of the gait you're in and are timed so that they are given when the hind leg

13.23 As your horse goes forward through your outside hand (at last!), he becomes more beautiful as his balance improves, and his frame becomes more "round."

you want to engage is on the ground. Generally, this is the inside hind leg for a downward transition and the outside hind leg for a canter depart.

Also in chapter 21, I'll show you how you can apply a **reversed half-halt** to ask your horse to take an even contact with both of your hands. The elements of this half-halt are exactly the same as the "connecting" half-halt, but you simply switch the action of your inside and outside hands.

In that chapter, I'll also describe how you can blend the basic half-halt into the aids for all the transitions, movements, and exercises that you do with your horse so you can maintain good balance each time you start something new. In this case your half-halt might end up lasting as long as five or six seconds.

KEY POINTS

■ A half-halt enables you to restore your horse's physical and mental balance.

■ There is no "halt" in a half-halt. Think of it as a "half-go."

■ Before you give a half-halt, your horse must be forward, straight, moving in a regular rhythm, and you must offer him an inviting contact.

■ The half-halt is the marriage of the driving aids, the outside rein, and the bending aids, maintained for about three seconds.

14

CONNECTION

I n the last chapter I discussed the half-halt in a general way and taught you *how* to give this most useful aid. I also mentioned that you can use this tool to restore both *physical* and *mental* balance to your horse.

Now that you know how to do a half-halt I'm going to show you exactly how you can use the half-halt to improve one of the common physical "imbalances." The balance issue I'm going to discuss is the feeling that your horse is in two parts—the back and the front. The half-halt is used to create a bridge between these two. This is called **connection**, or, in "dressage speak," **putting your horse "on the bit**."

My first reason for teaching my own students to give a half-halt is so they can "connect" their horses. It's a priority, because I know how uncomfortable it is for me to ride a horse that's not connected, and I figure if it's uncomfortable for me, it can't be much fun for my horse. Often riders who normally bounce around in the trot and canter are surprised to discover how much easier it is to sit closely to their horses in these paces when their horses are connected.

In addition to pure comfort for both horse

"Going on the bit makes any horse move better, but it's particularly important for the endurance horse so he can move in the most efficient way possible."

**Becky Hart,
World Champion endurance rider**

• • • • •

and rider, it's advantageous to connect your horse because he becomes more graceful and more athletic as a result of carrying himself predominantly with his topline muscles. It's exciting to start with an animal that has average movement and make him more beautiful by developing his potential as an athlete.

"When training is correct the horse always becomes more beautiful... never less so," said Alois Podhajsky, late head of the Spanish Riding School in Vienna. When your horse is connected, his back serves as the bridge between his hind legs and his front legs. As I said earlier, your horse's power, his "engine," is in the hindquarters. He needs to be connected over his back so that the energy can travel from his hind legs over his back, through his neck, and be received by your hands (fig. 14.1).

In this book, I am going to limit my references to "**connection**" to the phrases, "**on the bit**" and "**round frame.**" Since there are lots of other terms that riders use to describe connection, I want to mention them here to avoid any confusion later. They include: "**throughness,**" "**through his neck,**" "**through the back,**" "**over the back,**" "**roundness,**" "**round outline, shape, or frame,**" "**packaged,**" or "**moving from the hind legs into the hands**." They can all be used synonymously with "connection," "on the bit" and "round frame." After all, a rose by any other name…!

WHAT DOES CONNECTION LOOK LIKE?

"Connection," "on the bit," "round frame": let's try to get a handle on what, to many novice dressage riders, is an elusive concept.

These terms have a physical as well as a mental connotation. Physically, when a horse is connected, his frame becomes round because his hind legs come more forward under his body with every stride as they step toward the rider's hand (fig. 14.2). This power from behind is received by the rider's hand and the result is a round shape. His back looks convex and his neck is arched. The round shape is desirable because

14.1 Your horse's engine is in his hindquarters, which is why you must ride him from back to front. His "horsepower" comes from behind.

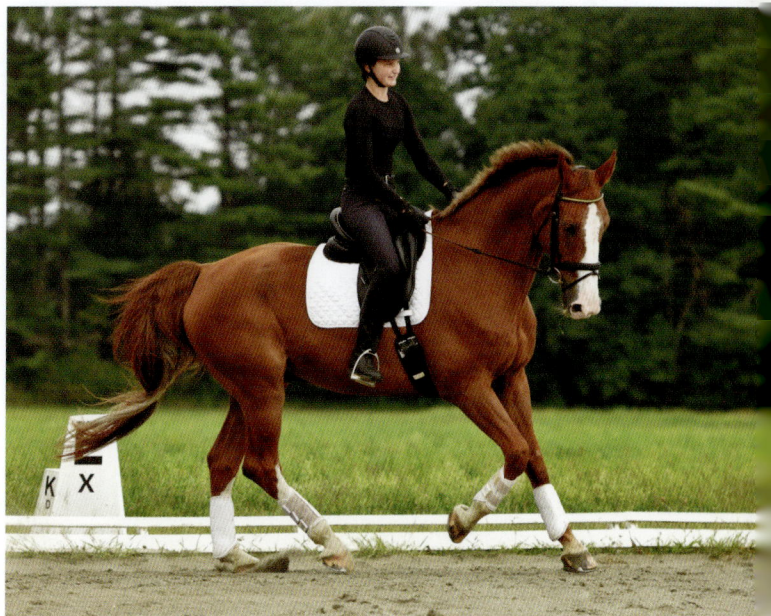

14.2 Adeline Tullar (Addie) and Rufian de Beaufour (Roo) show the "round" shape of a horse that is connected. Roo's convex back and arched neck are the result when his hind legs come well under his body and he steps toward Addie's hand.

14.3 When he is not "on the bit," Roo's hind legs don't step well underneath his body, his back looks braced, his neck is held stiffly out in front of him, and his nose is poked forward.

physically it makes him more comfortable to ride and more athletic.

Mentally, a connected horse becomes more submissive and obedient because his attention is on you, and his body is more balanced so he can react to your commands.

Keep in mind that when you're trying to decide if a horse is truly on the bit, it's not enough to just look at his neck. An arched neck can be deceiving to the uneducated onlooker. Always look at the whole horse—particularly the entire topline from the hindquarters to the poll—before you make up your mind about whether or not a horse is truly round. Here's what to look for:

First, for the sake of comparison let's look at a horse that's not on the bit (fig. 14.3). His hind legs aren't stepping well under his body, his back looks braced and tight rather than swinging elastically, his neck is stiffly held out in front of him for balance, and his nose is poked forward. This horse can't work on the bit, because his rigid or "frozen" back doesn't function as the bridge that enables energy to be transmitted between the hindquarters and the forehand. The power coming from the hindquarters hits a roadblock and dissipates. Horses that carry themselves like this can be very useful and still do lots of things, but they can't be truly athletic in this frame.

Second, look at a horse that is on the bit (fig.

14.4). This horse shows the desirable round shape of a connected horse. Starting from back to front, which we should always do in riding because the horse's power comes from the rear, this is what a connected horse looks like:

- His hind legs reach well underneath his body.
- His back muscles look relaxed so his back appears raised, round, and loose rather than dropped, concave, and rigid.
- His neck is long and gently arched as he stretches towards the bit.
- His poll is the highest point of his neck.
- His nose is slightly (about five degrees) in front of an imaginary vertical line drawn from his forehead to the ground.

This horse is also in "horizontal balance." If you look at the height of the horse's withers compared to the top of his croup, you'll notice that they are about the same—basically level. Also notice that a line drawn from the withers to the croup is parallel to the ground line. Hence the expression "horizontal balance."

This horizontal balance is what you'll be asking of your horse as you start out. When you go on to Stage Four, the roundness of the horse's body will stay the same as it is here, but his balance will change when you ask for self-carriage. When the balance changes, his croup lowers, and as a result, his withers are correspondingly higher. The line running from his croup to his withers ascends rather than being parallel to the ground as it is in horizontal balance (figs. 14.5 to 14.8 A & B).

14.4 This photo shows Roo connected and in horizontal balance. An imaginary line drawn from the top of his croup to his withers is basically parallel to the ground. He carries about 60 percent of his weight on his forehand and 40 percent of his weight on his hindquarters.

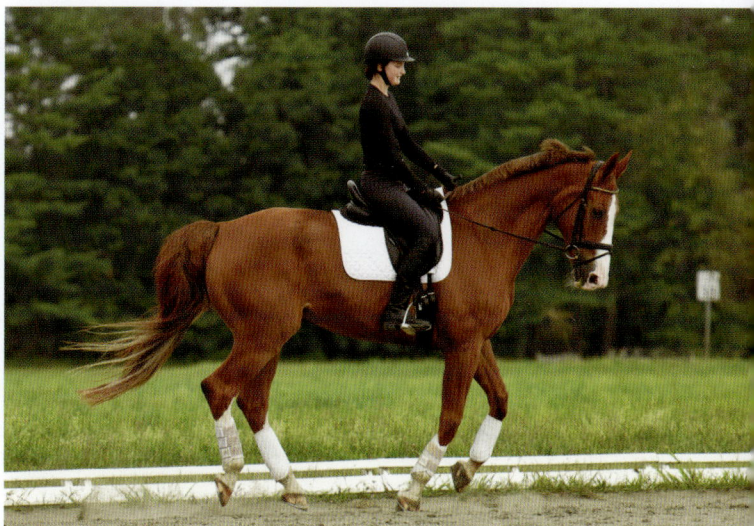

14.5 Roo is on the bit here, too, but his shape looks quite different from that of photo 14.4. This is because he is in a more advanced state of balance. Rather than traveling on the forehand in horizontal balance, he shows greater self-carriage. This means that he carries a larger portion of his weight on his hindquarters (maybe 10 percent more), and an imaginary line drawn from his croup to his withers ascends rather than looking like it's parallel to the ground.

14.6 Don't be fooled into thinking a horse is on the bit in a more advanced state of balance just because his head and neck are raised and arched. Be sure to look at the whole picture. When you compare Roo's shape to the way it is in photo 14.5, you can see that his back now looks low and concave, and his shoulders have dropped so that he no longer has an "uphill" look from croup to withers.

14.7 Even though Roo might look like he's in a round frame, he is not on the bit. He is "overbent" (or "overflexed"). His neck is short and his poll is low, his face is behind the vertical, and he has dropped the contact with the outside rein. In this frame, Addie has little control over her horse's engine—Roo's hind legs.

14.8 A & B Different stages of balance with horse on the bit: The horse in A is on the bit in horizontal balance. He engages his hind legs, raises his back, and flexes his hip joints, lumbosacral joint, and poll. The horse in B is also on the bit, but he's in self-carriage. He can hold his balance even when the rider surrenders the reins.

WHAT DOES CONNECTION FEEL LIKE?

It's often very difficult for riders to try to create something they haven't felt before. If you ride some leg-yields, you can get the feeling of what you're working toward with your half-halt. Close your outside hand in a fist while your horse is going sideways, and he should come into a rounder frame. This is the connection and feeling you're aiming toward—without having to go sideways to get it.

When he's connected, your horse should feel like he is compact, comfortable, and controllable rather than a jumble of disconnected parts!

WHO BENEFITS FROM CONNECTION?

An endurance rider from Nevada quickly put me in my place when I innocently asked if riders in her discipline had any interest in riding their horses on the bit. She spoke to me as if I were a child: "Jane, think about it. Isn't your horse less fatigued if he works for an hour in the ring 'on the bit' rather than in a hollow frame? Well, our horses need to go for miles and miles as efficiently as possible." I gave her an enlightened nod as I slunk off in embarrassment about my ignorance of her sport.

I was surprised again when I found out from hunter seat riders who were attending my dressage clinics that the requirements for them in competition have changed considerably. In the past it was acceptable for their horses to move with their backs down, their heads and necks up and their noses poked out. Now the judges have decreed that even hunters carry themselves in a round frame, and you need to ride in this way if you want to win.

Many pleasure riders—even those who just like to go out for a hack—have also joined the ranks of those who like to have their horses on the bit. It's certainly more comfortable to sit on a round, springy back that cushions you like a shock absorber than to be jarred by a hollow, stiff one. Plus, see that scary rock over there? The one that your horse is convinced is going to jump out and grab his leg any second? If your horse is "on the bit," it's going to be a lot easier to get him to go by it calmly and willingly.

A case in point is the story of Cellulosa. Cellulosa was a gift from a local sculptor who thought it might be amusing to place this very large, unique work of art at the entrance to the dressage area where I train in Florida. He appeared one day to stand sentry by our ring and his presence created quite a stir—particularly with the young horses.

The day Cellulosa arrived, a friend of mine was hacking Eastwood, my nine-year-old Dutch Warmblood. Woody didn't want any part of this strange creature (can you blame him?). He wheeled and spun away, obviously thinking it was much safer to head back to the barn. Fortunately, my friend had warned me about the trouble I might have, so the next day instead of just wandering by Cellulosa on a loose rein to do my warm up, I put Woody on the bit early on and kept him there until we were safely past without incident. While on the bit, Woody's attention was focused on me, and he marched right by.

How about jumpers and combined-training horses who go over fences? They need to be agile enough to cope with the tricky distances and turns created by clever course designers. The horse that's on the bit is ready to use his body like an accordion. He can compress and extend it, and turn handily as well. Your signals can travel to him without interruption. Because he's connected and his back is round, there's no broken circuit that stops the message from getting through.

The driving horse also benefits from being on the bit. When he moves in a round frame with a relaxed back and his head down, he is on the bit without leaning on it. He can only do this when his hind legs step well underneath his body (just as they need to do in riding), so that he doesn't use the bit as a "fifth leg." This balance is essential so that the driver can safely control both the horse and the carriage.

And, of course, working on the bit when schooling a horse in dressage techniques is essential. Consider the movements and exercises. They are not supposed to be an end in themselves, but are meant to be a means to an end—to develop one or more athletic qualities in your horse.

For instance, school figures such as circles and serpentines increase your horse's **flexibility**: his ability to smoothly bend left and right. Transitions create **suppleness**: his capacity to smoothly lengthen and shorten his body and stride. Lateral work promotes **self-carriage**: the shifting of the center of gravity toward his hind legs, which results in a lightening and freeing of his forehand. All these gymnastic exercises aren't effective as far as promoting your horse's athleticism unless they are done on the bit.

It's true that a horse can do all of these exercises either "off the bit" or not correctly on the bit. And you might actually seem to manage to get pretty far with his training. But, somewhere along the line, you're going to get stuck. And the only way to sort out the problems will be to go back to **the Basics** and then put your horse solidly on the bit. It's a hard lesson to learn, but shortcuts take more time in the long run. It's always better to build a good foundation from the beginning than to have to go back to the Basics later on and fill in the gaps.

HOW TO CONNECT YOUR HORSE (PUT HIM ON THE BIT)

At clinics, I'll often run into a rider who thinks that if she sits quietly and in harmony with her horse, the horse will become connected all by himself. Of course, it doesn't happen. What she needs to understand is that since a horse isn't "designed" to be ridden, it's normal for him to stiffen and drop his back when he feels weight on it. And when he feels contact with his mouth, he braces his neck and uses it as a balancing rod in much the same way as we use a bannister for balance when we go down a flight of stairs. Unless we show the horse that it'll be easier for him to carry a rider by putting him on the bit, it's probably not going to occur to him to adopt this round frame on his own.

You connect your horse (put him on the bit) with the same half-halt that you learned in the last chapter. But before you do a half-halt to connect your horse, take a moment to check your prerequisites for the half-halt. Is your horse going forward, straight, and in a good rhythm? Is your contact firm, consistent, elastic and symmetrical? Remember that at this point, we don't concern ourselves with whether or not he's round. While working on these four prerequisites, your horse can carry himself any way he

chooses, even if his back is hollow and his head and neck are up.

If you're primarily preoccupied with getting your horse's head down at all costs before you have your prerequisites solidly confirmed, you might end up "hand-riding"—most likely sawing left and right on his mouth. Or during a half-halt, you might vibrate the outside rein in the same way as you do on the inside rein, rather than just closing your outside hand in a fist.

You might then think that you've made your horse round because his neck is arched and his face is in. But if you were to see a photo or video, you'd notice that his neck is short and his face is on or behind the vertical rather than being slightly in front of it. If this is what you see, you've probably flexed him in the jaw rather than connecting him from back to front. This is a dead-end street. Your horse might look like he's in good balance, but if you hand-ride and focus on the jaw, you won't have much influence over the rest of his body. The roundness you have is a useless kind of round because you have no control over his hindquarters and his back can't comfortably cope with your weight. To make your horse truly round, you need to ride his *whole* body from back to front.

Once you've checked your prerequisites for the half-halt and they are all in order, give a half-halt to put your horse on the bit. As I described in the last chapter when you do a half-halt, you combine your driving aids, your bending aids, and your outside rein.

Apply the aids for three seconds and then relax them. The half-halt connects your horse because when your driving aids send his hind legs under his body and he steps "through" your outside rein, his back becomes round, much as a bow bends when it is tightly strung.

With each half-halt, be sure to reward him if his frame gets even slightly rounder. In this way, you'll encourage him to repeat and improve his response the next time. It's not going to be perfect in the beginning. But by rewarding each effort, you'll improve your horse's spirit of cooperation and his understanding of the use of the half-halt for connecting and putting him on the bit.

TESTING THE "CORRECTNESS" OF THE FRAME

Unless you work with a trainer on a regular basis, you can be quite easily misled into thinking your horse is on the bit when, in fact, this is not necessarily the case. As I mentioned above, a horse's body can mimic a correct round frame, but this round shape can just be in his neck rather than encompassing his entire body. Occasionally horses adopt this position on their own, although we usually see this when riders forget to use their driving aids and resort to "hand-riding" as I described earlier. Often, when a horse is hand-ridden, we also see some slack in the reins because the horse is *behind* the bit (rather than *on* it), and not seeking a contact from the rider's strong or overly busy hands.

Another subtlety you'll discover when attempting to work your horse on the bit is that connection is not necessarily an all or nothing thing. There are many stages and degrees of connection that fall along the spectrum from totally *off* the bit to completely *on* the bit.

On several occasions, a new student at a clinic I'm teaching will tell me that she doesn't have any problem riding her horse on the bit, but she's having a problem with a particular movement. I can take one look at the horse's muscling and know whether this is an animal that's been worked consistently on the bit or whether the rider has been fooled into thinking that her horse is on the bit. When a horse has been worked on the bit for an extended period of time the muscles of his topline (the muscles over the top of his croup, back, and crest of his neck) develop. In particular, the beginning of the crest in his neck is heavily muscled rather than looking weak and concave, with a dip right in front of the withers. If I get on a horse with a correctly muscled neck, his neck looks widest at the base by my hands and tapers up to the narrowest point just behind his ears. If the widest point of his neck is at his poll or somewhere in the middle of his neck, I know that this horse has not been properly ridden "through his neck" for any length of time (fig. 14.9 A & B).

I tell you this not to worry you, but so that you realize that it's easy to be misled, and it's essential to have some way to determine the correctness as well as the degree of connection. The following are some tests that will give you confidence that the round frame you've created is the result of riding the horse honestly from back to front. These tests can give you some peace of mind that you're on the right track.

Pick up the trot, close both legs, and ask for a

lengthening for a few strides. Feel the thrust of the horse coming from behind when you close your legs. Do this several times. Then give a half-halt and ask yourself the following question. If I hadn't closed my outside hand in a fist, would he have done as powerful a lengthening as the ones he has just been doing? If the answer is yes, you're riding your horse from back to front. If you don't feel the lengthening inside the half-halt, the round frame you think you've achieved might be the result of riding your horse from front to back—flexing him in the jaw and pulling his head in toward his chest.

The second test is to do a half-halt, then at the end of three seconds, open the fingers of both hands. Be sure not to straighten your arms to offer the reins to the horse, but let him take the reins from you only as much as he chooses. If he "chews" the reins from your hands by seeking the contact forward and down to the ground, your half-halt has connected him one hundred percent. If he stretches down somewhat, the half-halt has gone through a little. If he sticks his head straight up, he is not connected at all (figs. 14.10 to 14.14).

For the third test, give a three-second half-halt. After you think your horse has come into a round frame as the result of this half-halt, test by keeping your outside elbow bent by your side while putting slack in the inside rein by extending your inside hand forward toward your horse's mouth. (This is called a one-handed *über-streichen*.) If your horse stays straight in his neck for a couple of strides, he's stepping from behind into your outside rein and your half-halt has gone through one hundred percent. The amount

14.9 A & B Working on the bit develops a strong topline: good muscle developed from being ridden on the bit (A) and a weak, underdeveloped topline (B)—notice, in particular, the concave look of the muscles at the base of the neck, the back, and top of the croup.

14.10 Alpen's nice round shape indicates that he's given a good response to Bekki's connecting half-halt.

14.11 In order to check that Alpen is honestly on the bit, Bekki opens her fingers to see if the gelding will "chew" the reins out of her hands. Since there is an elastic connection from Alpen's hind legs stretching over his back into Bekki's hands, Alpen simply follows the natural progression of this connection as Bekki's reins get longer—and that is to go forward and down with his head and neck.

14.12 As Bekki allows the reins to get even longer, Alpen continues to seek the contact forward and down.

14.13 Bekki has given another half-halt, but when she slips the reins, Alpen only stretches a little. Alpen also looks flatter over his topline than in photo 14.12. This kind of response tells Bekki his half-halt was only partially successful and that she didn't have a truly solid connection from back to front.

14.14 When Bekki slips her reins after this half-halt, Alpen sticks his head and neck straight up in the air—a clear sign that Bekki's half-halt didn't do its job of connecting the horse at all.

his neck immediately bends to the outside, making that outside rein loose, is the degree that he's not connected (figs. 14.15 and 14.16).

Now you have not only learned how to give a half-halt, but you know how to use that half-halt to put your horse on the bit. This round shape is a prerequisite for the next logical step in your horse's training—self-carriage.

You'll discover in the next chapter that your horse must be correctly connected before he can be asked to carry himself, and that the same half-halt that you used to connect your horse in this chapter can now be used to promote self-carriage.

DEEP FRAME

Dressage riders often work their horses on the bit in a frame that is called "**deep.**" When a horse is deep, he has the shape of an upside-down triangle. The hind legs come under the body, the back is raised, the neck is long, the poll is low, and the

14.15 As Bekki canters down the long side, she gives a half-halt and then tests the connection through her outside rein by softening her inside hand forward. She knows she has a firm connection because Alpen's neck stays straight, even without the influence of her inside rein.

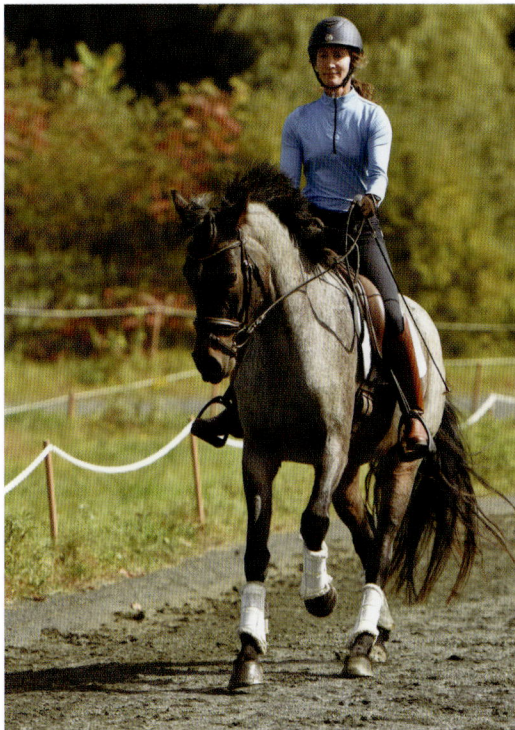

14.16 Here Bekki's half-halt has not solidly connected Alpen through the outside rein. As Bekki softens her inside hand forward, Alpen drops the connection and bends his neck toward the rail.

nose can be ever so slightly behind the vertical, but it must have the look and feel of seeking the bit.

This is a good frame to put your horse in at the beginning and end of your workout as a warm-up and cool-down. It allows the horse to stretch, loosen, and round the muscles of the topline. Working in a deep frame can relax a tense horse because as his muscles loosen he becomes more calm.

It's also a good frame to return to if you're having trouble maintaining a connection over your horse's back when teaching a new exercise. For example, if you start a leg-yield and your horse drops his back and comes above the bit, put him deep for your next effort. This position

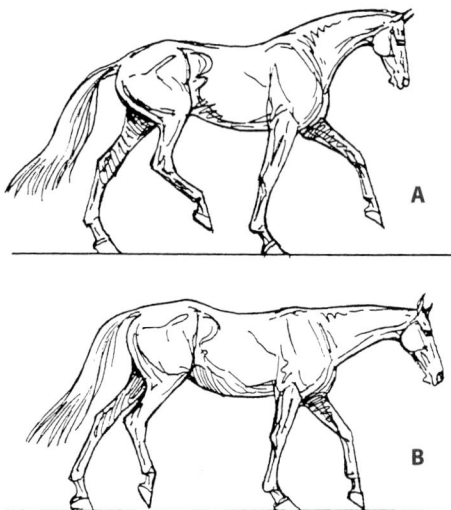

14.17 A & B Closed and open hind legs: Generally, it's beneficial to ride a horse "deep" if he's the type that moves with a "closed" hind leg that steps well under his body (A). If, by nature, he moves with an "open" hind leg that trails out behind his body, riding him deep won't improve his balance and "throughness" (B).

will teach him to do the movement using his whole body rather than dropping his back and shuffling along stiffly.

When riding your horse deep, it's important that you keep his hind legs coming forward under his body. It's not going to do him any good to stretch his neck long and low if his hind legs are trailing out behind and he feels like he's somersaulting forward, out of balance (fig. 14.17 A & B). If your horse tends to want to go with an "open" hind leg that trails out behind his body, you might not let him go as "deep" as the horse that tends to have a "closed" hind leg that steps well under his body (figs. 14.18 and 14.19).

It's just as important not to let your horse poke his nose too far forward and allow the reins to get loose. If you do, you'll lose the connection from the hind legs into your hands and his back will be flat instead of round (fig. 14.20).

Once you know how to give a half-halt, it's very simple to put your horse deep. Give a half-halt for three seconds and then open your fingers and allow your horse to "chew the reins out of your hands."

Remember that the length of the reins determines the length of your horse's neck. So, after you give the half-halt to connect your horse, open your fingers slightly and allow him to go forward and down with his head and neck. How deep he goes will depend on how much rein you let him have.

14.18 Addie is working Roo fairly "deep" in the trot. His hind leg steps well under his body, his back is raised, and his neck is long. Note that although his poll is low and his face is slightly behind the vertical, he definitely looks as though he's stretching toward the bit and seeking a contact with her hand.

14.19 Here Roo is being ridden slightly "deep" in the canter. This is a good example of a very round, convex-looking topline, from tail to poll.

14.20 If you ask your horse to go in a deep frame but then you drop the contact and let the reins get too loose as Amy Halley has done here, you'll lose the connection from the horse's hind legs into your hands. His back will be low and flat instead of round and convex.

"DEEP" IS NOT THE SAME AS "BEHIND THE BIT"

When a horse is in a deep frame, his poll is not the highest point and his nose may be slightly behind the vertical. This often confuses people because they see these two things and assume that the horse must be behind the bit.

Remember that it's *never* acceptable to ride a horse behind the bit because it indicates that the horse is being ridden from front to back. Being ridden from front to back means that the rider has forgotten to use her legs and is using her hands incorrectly. She does this either by using her hands too strongly or by sawing on the horse's mouth by alternately squeezing and releasing on the reins.

14.21 A & B At first glance, these two horses might look the same because both have a low poll and their noses are behind the vertical. But when you look at the whole picture, you can see that the shape of their toplines and the way they use their hind legs is totally different.

I tell people to be sure to look at the whole picture before they make a judgment about whether or not the horse is behind the bit. The horse that is deep and the horse that is behind the bit look similar because in both cases the poll is low and the nose is behind the vertical. The horse that is deep, however, has his hind legs coming under the body, a round back, a long neck, and takes a contact with the rider's hand. The horse that is behind the bit, on the other hand, doesn't come under his body with the hind legs, has a hollow back, a short neck, usually a dip in front of the withers, and avoids the contact with the rider's hand. It's a very serious fault to ride your horse behind the bit, but it's acceptable, even desirable, to ride a horse deep at times (fig. 14.21 A & B).

KEY POINTS

- Working a horse connected (on the bit) makes him more athletic in his movement and more comfortable to ride.

- The round shape of a horse that is on the bit must be created from back to front by driving the hind legs up to receiving hands.

- When on the bit, the horse's hind legs reach well forward under his body, his back is relaxed, his neck is long and gracefully arched, his poll is the highest point of his neck, and his nose is slightly in front of the vertical.

- The half-halt is the aid that you use to put your horse on the bit.

- Be sure to test the correctness of the round shape. Is it truly created from back to front or are you "hand-riding" your horse into an artificial "head-set"?.

- There is a world of difference between riding a horse deep and riding him behind the bit. Working a horse in a deep frame is correct and often desirable. Working behind the bit is never correct because there isn't any connection from back to front.

STAGE FOUR
FANCY STUFF!

Once you understand the half-halt and can use it to put your horse on the bit, you're ready for Stage Four. Fancy Stuff! includes all the aids, movements, and exercises that will help your horse "dance like Baryshnikov" rather than plodding along like an elephant! In this first chapter of Stage Four, I'll talk about the development of self-carriage—a quality of balance that benefits horses in many disciplines.

In chapters 16 and 19, I'll discuss how self-carriage enables your horse to work in this new and improved balance. Up until this point in his education, your horse has only been asked to show a working gait and a lengthening of that working gait. With the addition of self-carriage, you'll be able to produce three more

"gears" in each pace—the collected, medium, and extended gaits.

In chapters 17 and 18, I'll explain how the more advanced lateral movements are done and how they're used, not only as an end in themselves, but as a means to an end—self-carriage.

Once your horse is in self-carriage, you'll find that it's easy for him to learn flying changes in the canter: the process of introducing these changes is explained in chapter 20. In chapter 21, I'll show you how you can use the new tools in your bag of tricks to resolve some old training problems. And finally, in chapter 22, I'll give you some examples of how to organize your work so that you school your horse in a systematic, logical way.

15

Float Like a Butterfly

SELF-CARRIAGE

To one extent or another, most riders in all riding disciplines can benefit from having their horses in self-carriage—that is, lighter on the forehand, with their center of gravity further back toward their hind legs.

A trail horse isn't much fun when he's plowing along so much on his forehand that your arms ache at the finish of your ride, while a jumper needs to be rocked back onto his hind legs to successfully negotiate fences.

An endurance horse needs to push himself up hills with his hindquarters rather than pull himself up with his shoulders, and as he goes down hills he also needs to support himself with his hindquarters well underneath his body so that he doesn't pound his front end into the ground.

Reining and cutting horses require a lot of strength from their hindquarters and a light forehand in order to spin and accelerate.

In competitive dressage, with all other things being equal, the horse who shows more self-carriage wins. For instance, if two different horses both perform a half-pass with good quality—that is, the half-pass is done in a regular rhythm with good bend and correct alignment of the body—the horse whose center of gravity or balance is more toward the hind legs so that he carries himself, rather than being heavy on the forehand, will get the higher score.

The fact is, in any equestrian sport, the horse who is balanced further back toward his hindquarters has an advantage over the one traveling on his forehand, simply because he moves with greater athletic ability (figs. 15.1 and 15.2).

WHAT IS SELF-CARRIAGE?

You'll often hear various terms that imply or refer to self-carriage. They include: loading the hind legs, shifting the center of gravity toward the hind legs, lighter in your hands, elevating the forehand, "up" in front, gathered together, **packaged**, well-engaged behind, lowering and engaging the quarters, and **collection**.

But whatever it's called, let's try to clear up some of the confusion associated with the term. To many riders, it's merely a shortening of the horse's body with the head and neck raised and arched. To some extent this is true, but it's much more than that. In fact, you can shorten a horse

15.1 Piaffe: the ultimate display of self-carriage.

15.2 A Western horse working in self-carriage.

found it helpful when I describe self-carriage as a "loading of the hind legs." This loading occurs when the horse engages his hindquarters by bending the joints of his hind legs. Because the horse is engaging and lowering his hindquarters, his entire forehand raises and becomes lighter and freer.

The main tool that you use to change his balance in this way and produce self-carriage is a half-halt. (I told you the half-halt would be useful!) In addition, exercises such as doing small circles and transitions, as well as backing up, also help your horse learn to carry himself. I'll get into these in the next chapter. You can also do a variety of lateral exercises to create self-carriage, which I'll discuss in chapters 17 and 18.

The challenge in developing self-carriage stems from the fact that all horses are built with their center of gravity more toward their front legs. This is because horses are shaped like a table with a head and neck stuck onto one end. If your horse didn't have a head and neck, his weight

without having him in self-carriage at all. This can be done (but please don't do it!) by riding him from **front to back**—cranking his head and neck into a "head-set" without activating and engaging his hindquarters.

A more important component of self-carriage than the mere shortening of the frame is the position of the horse's center of gravity. This changes according to the stage of training and the degree that the horse can carry himself. That is, the more the horse is in self-carriage, the more the center of gravity has been shifted toward his hindquarters. My students have

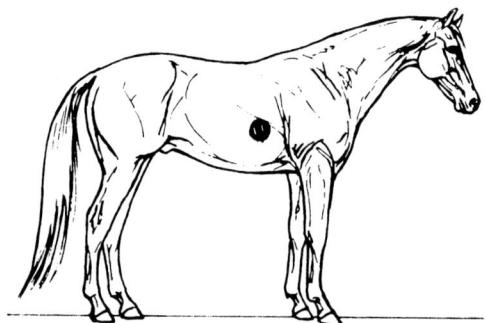

15.3 The location of a horse's center of gravity when he is standing still is more toward his front legs.

could be evenly distributed over the four legs of the table. But since his head and neck can weigh as much as 250 pounds, it's inevitable that his center of gravity is more toward his front legs (fig. 15.3).

No wonder your horse likes to "lie" in your hands! It's normal for him to have more weight on his forehand. Fortunately, he's born with the raw material that can be developed and strengthened so he can be trained to carry more weight on his hind legs and take the load off his front end.

To get the idea of loading the hind legs, pretend your horse is standing on two scales that can independently distinguish how much weight is on his front legs and how much is on his hind legs. In nature, the horse has about 60% of his weight on his front legs and 40% on his hind legs. As he begins the process of developing self-carriage, the weight proportion changes. Although initially he still has more weight on his front legs, it's less so than before. Then, as his training continues and he carries himself more, he will have equal weight on his front and hind legs. Eventually, when he's more advanced, he will show more weight on the rear scale than the front scale (fig. 15.4).

CONNECTION IS NOT SELF-CARRIAGE

Many riders confuse the idea of the horse being connected with being in self-carriage, or as it is often called, being "**collected**." For instance, I'll be teaching a clinic and a first-time participant walks her horse into the lesson on a loose rein

15.4 A horse starts off with approximately 60 percent of his weight on his forehand and 40 percent behind. Once he begins to carry himself, this becomes more equal, and eventually, when he is more advanced, he will carry more weight behind than he does in front.

and then asks me if she should "collect" her horse as she starts warming up at the trot. At this point I realize that this rider is using connection and collection synonymously.

Yes, I do want that horse *connected* as he starts to work, but the difference is that the connected horse's center of gravity can be very much toward the forehand because he's being worked long and low so he can stretch and warm-up his muscles correctly. It's not until he's properly warmed up that his rider should think about starting to shift his balance toward his hind legs and asking him to carry himself. Your horse can be connected without being in self-carriage, and this should be the case during a warm-up, anyway. However, he must always first be connected and properly warmed up before you ask him to carry himself and become *collected* (figs. 15.5 and 15.6).

15.5 & 15.6 These two photos show Hercules on the bit. His hind legs are active and stepping well under his body. His back is round, his neck is long and gracefully arched, and he takes a solid but pleasant contact with Carole Ann Tullar's (Pinky's) hand. The difference here is simply one of balance. In the first photo, Hercules is being warmed up in a deep frame and his balance or center of gravity is more toward the forehand. In the second photo, Pinky asks for more self-carriage by shifting her horse's balance or center of gravity more toward the hind legs.

WHAT DOES SELF-CARRIAGE LOOK LIKE?

As I've mentioned earlier, most horses in a natural state are in "horizontal balance," where the withers and croup are basically the same height, and the horse's topline is parallel to the ground. Most hunters or training-level dressage horses show this horizontal balance, and although these horses might be well balanced for their jobs, they are not collected (fig. 15.7). Depending on his level of training, a collected horse in self-carriage will *appear* shorter from poll to tail than a horse in a working gait, and the top of his withers will be relatively higher than the highest point of his croup. (See fig. 15.8). This elevation in front includes the entire forehand (not just the head and neck, but the withers, too) and it is the result of engagement—the bending of the joints of the hind legs and the subsequent lowering of the hindquarters (fig. 14.8 B.)

Don't be fooled into thinking a horse is in self-carriage just because his frame looks short. You can easily shorten a horse's neck by cranking him in with tight reins. But this is just the front-to-back riding I've talked about before, and merely simulates a collected frame while the horse is not being ridden from his hind legs forward into the bridle.

I've seen many riders who mistakenly think they're on the road to self-carriage because they've shortened their horse's frame in this way. Be sure to look at the whole picture. It's not enough that the horse's outline is short. If you're compressing him from front to back by cranking

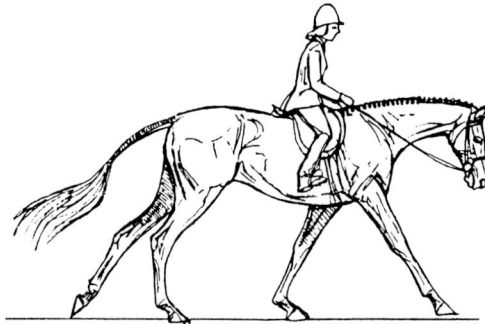

15.7 A horse in "horizontal balance" where withers and hindquarters are the same height, and the horse's topline is parallel to the ground.

15.8 Self-carriage: this horse "appears" shorter from poll to rail than in fig. 15.10.

him into a "head-set," you'll notice that he probably also has a low poll, short neck, low withers, hollow back, high croup and he looks tense and stiff. And if the frame, physique, and movement don't become more beautiful during training, then it's a sure sign you're not on the right road (fig. 15.9).

Looking at the horse's entire silhouette will ensure that you're also not deluded by seeing a high, arched neck. A rider can easily raise her horse's head and neck higher by lifting her hands in an attempt to elevate the forehand (please don't do this either!) But, when she does this,

15.9 When ridden from "front to back," the horse looks cranked into a stiff and constricted outline. Because he's being hand-ridden, he shows a low poll, short neck, hollow back, high croup, and his hind legs can't come under his body.

15.10 Note that Hercules' hind legs are stepping well under his body, his croup is low, and the elevation of his front end includes his entire forehand, not just his head and neck. He has the uphill look of an airplane taking off.

the horse's withers will remain low—the opposite of what happens with a collected horse. So always compare the height of a horse's withers to the height of his hindquarters before you decide whether he's really in self-carriage or just hauled in from front to back. When he's properly collected and in self-carriage, a horse has the uphill look of a speedboat in the water, or of an airplane taking off.

Another clue as to whether or not a horse has been correctly collected is to examine his way of going. Sometimes a rider thinks her horse is in self-carriage because his frame is shorter than normal and he covers less ground with each stride. However, if she's cranked him together by riding him from front to back, his movement has to suffer; he'll merely shuffle along stiffly. On the other hand, there's a lightness and gaiety in the paces of the horse in self-carriage. He looks animated and bounces over the ground expressively, much like the horse in freedom who gets the wind under his tail on a crisp autumn morning. Keep in mind that as you begin to ask for self-carriage, your horse may only be able to hold this new shape and balance for moments. It'll take time before he's strong enough to maintain it for long periods (figs. 15.10 to 15.14).

To sum up the qualities that you'll see with a horse in self-carriage: he has engaged hindquarters; a round back; withers that are higher than the top of his croup; a long, gracefully arched neck with the poll the highest point; his nose approaches the vertical; and he moves with buoyancy and expression.

15.11 Compare Hercules' balance in this picture to photo 15.10. If you were only to look at his arched neck, you might at first glance think he's in self-carriage. But here you can see that his hind legs are pushing backward and that his withers have sunk down so much that they are lower than the top of his croup.

15.12 & 15.13 In these two photos Pinky is pulling Hercules into a shortened frame. His neck might be raised and arched, but she is cranking it into this position. This can only have a paralyzing effect on her horse's movement. Photo 15.12 shows a short, tight stride in the trot, and photo 15.13 shows constricted movement in the canter.

15.14 The movement of a horse in self-carriage should resemble the lightness and gaiety of a horse at play.

WHAT DOES SELF-CARRIAGE FEEL LIKE?

The dilemma is the same here that it was when you were first starting to connect your horse or put him on the bit. Specifically, how do you create something you haven't felt before? Remember how I told you to learn the feeling of connection by doing leg-yields? Well, you can do the same sort of experimentation to learn the feeling of self-carriage. In this case, you'll have a chance to experience this new balance by doing some transitions.

For instance, to get the feeling of self-carriage in the trot, do several transitions from the trot to the halt and immediately back to the trot again. Make sure your horse does the transitions clearly and distinctly, without any dribbly walk steps in between. Each time you step into the halt, in your mind's eye picture him lowering his hind-quarters in the same way that a dog lowers his haunches to sit down.

After several transitions, just ride some sitting trot and see if his balance feels any different. Does your horse feel like he's carrying more weight on his hind legs and less on his front legs? Does he feel more "up" in front and lighter in your hands?

To get the feeling of self-carriage in the canter, go through the same process with several quick transitions from the canter to the walk and immediately back to the canter again. Then, just ride the canter and see if your horse's balance has changed.

One difference that you should feel after these transitions is that the contact with your horse's mouth will be much lighter. The transitions enable your horse to carry himself by creating a shift in the center of gravity more toward the hindquarters. As a result, he doesn't have to lean heavily on the reins for support.

A word of caution here, though. You should only work toward this lightness *when you're ready to start developing self-carriage.* Prior to that, when you're schooling your horse in the working gaits, the contact should be quite firm because you always want to feel the hind legs "stepping into your hands." (See chapter 13.) Lightness during early stages of training in dressage *would not* indicate self-carriage. It would only be the result of a lack of connection, or even contact. And remember, *connection is a prerequisite to self-carriage* (fig. 15.15). Please review chapters 13 and 14 if you have any questions about this.

When a horse is in self-carriage, he should feel like he's organized into a compact package, rather than strung out with his hind legs out behind his body, just pushing his mass along. With a horse that is in self-carriage in the collected gaits, any change of movement, speed, direction, or length of stride would be possible without further preparation from one step to the next.

For example, a horse that's in collected walk could be in collected canter or even piaffe in the very next stride (if he's been previously trained how to do that movement). As you get started you'll be working at collecting the trot, but you should still have the feeling that while in the

15.15 This hunter might feel light in the hand, but the "lightness" is from lack of contact, not because the horse is in any sort of self-carriage.

collected trot you could easily move to collected canter or to an extended trot or to a halt by the very next step. But I'm getting ahead of myself! More on this when I discuss the collected gaits in the next chapter. The point here is to give you a feeling for what self-carriage will feel like.

WHEN DO YOU ASK FOR SELF-CARRIAGE?

You might ask, "When is my horse ready to start developing self-carriage?" It's difficult to designate a particular time, because not every horse will react in the same way to the demands of carrying himself. But I don't want you to think of self-carriage as something that you suddenly ask for one day. Developing it is a continuous process.

Once your horse understands and becomes confirmed in all of the work in my Stages One through Three, you can begin asking your horse to carry himself. A good indication of when to start is if your horse has satisfied all the prerequisites to self-carriage discussed in the first three stages, with harmony and understanding:

In all three paces, he needs to move freely forward with regular steps and be straight (Stage One); do a good lengthening (Stage Two); and produce a reliable half-halt (Stage Three). If this is not the case, your horse isn't ready, and all your efforts will be doomed to failure. So, spend more time working on **the Basics** before you begin to ask for self-carriage.

If your horse has met all the prerequisites, you'll start to ask him to carry himself for short periods every working day. Bear in mind that asking for self-carriage is like asking your horse suddenly to do deep knee bends. Think of how difficult it would be for you to do five hundred deep knee bends! By the time you got to one hundred your muscles would be screaming and you'd insist that you couldn't possibly do one more. You would need to build your strength gradually and so does your horse. Be sure to give him frequent rest periods and be satisfied with asking for a little bit at a time (fig. 15.16).

If you're a competitive dressage rider, your horse is first asked to show self-carriage in the collected and medium gaits at the Second Level tests. However, remember that proceeding through the levels in dressage competition is a gradual, progressive development of self-carriage.

At the lowest level (Training Level) the horse's balance is **horizontal** and his center of gravity is toward the forehand.

At the next level (First Level) the horse's balance is somewhat shifted toward his hindquarters, and although he is still somewhat on the forehand, he's less on the forehand than the Training Level horse. Therefore, he's carrying himself more than he was at the previous level.

The Second Level tests ask for collected and medium gaits. So, the Second Level horse has his center of gravity even more toward his hindquarters, and he's less on the forehand than the First Level horse. Understand that this self-carriage at Second Level doesn't spring out of thin air. Your horse should be gradually and systematically working toward this goal throughout the prior levels.

15.16 Suddenly asking your horse for self-carriage is the same as expecting yourself to do five hundred squats without building up to it. By the time you get to one hundred, (or maybe just fifteen or twenty), your muscles feel like a quivering mass of jelly.

TIMETABLE

If you have a horse that isn't strong enough yet because he hasn't been in a program that systematically develops his strength over time, he might become bewildered or even angry when you ask him to carry himself.

15.17 This photo shows Alpen in a balance appropriate for a horse just starting out at my Stage Two. He is relaxed, moving forward with regularity, and accepting the contact, but his balance is toward the forehand. However, from these basic building blocks of relaxation, rhythm, and stretching toward the bit, he has a solid foundation from which he can learn to shift his balance toward his hindquarters.

15.18 In this picture Alpen is on the bit—appropriate for my Stage Three—and his balance is less on his forehand.

Or, you might have a horse that doesn't have the conformation to make it easy for him to carry himself. For example, a Thoroughbred with straight hind legs can find it difficult to bring them into position for self-carriage. Look at this type of horse while he's standing still and you'll notice that the angles made by the joints of his hind leg are more open (less acute) than, let's say, certain Warmblood breeds. As a result, it's more difficult for this Thoroughbred type to engage his hind legs and take more weight on his hindquarters.

Consider a Quarter Horse whose croup is usually higher than his withers. This conformation throws his center of gravity even more toward his forehand, and it will be harder for this fellow to shift his center of gravity toward his hind legs.

That's not to say that the horse who is built like one of these can't be taught to carry himself. However, the whole process will take more time than with a horse who is better built to do the job. You need to systematically develop an animal so that he is able to engage his hind legs. Then he can bear more weight behind and can produce the uphill balance of the horse in self-carriage.

Okay. You're a patient person. You're willing to take that time. But what's reasonable? *Don't think in terms of days or months.* Think in terms of years. If your horse has been started under saddle and you work on the schedule that I've outlined, I would expect it to take you two to three years to teach him to truly carry himself (figs. 15.17 to 15.19).

Remember that each horse is an individual. Horses that are bred specifically for dressage often are asked to carry themselves within a year or so after real training begins, but this is not going to be the case for most of the readers of this book! So, whether it takes two years or six years, the end result should be a more beautiful animal who goes with ease and grace and without any discomfort or confusion.

15.19 Here Alpen carries himself even more than he did in photo 15.18. Bekki asks for the balance of a more collected trot as discussed in my Stage Four by activating and energizing Alpen's hindquarters to a greater degree. This systematic development of self-carriage should take place gradually.

KEY POINTS

■ The center of gravity of a horse in self-carriage is more toward his hindquarters rather than toward his forehand as it is in his natural state. This change in balance allows him to move more athletically.

■ A horse must first be connected before he can be asked to carry himself.

■ When a horse is in self-carriage his hindquarters are lower and as a result, his entire forehand including the withers is raised.

■ When a horse is in self-carriage, it feels like any change in movement is possible from one step to the next.

■ Working in self-carriage takes a lot of the horse's strength—strength that needs to be developed gradually and systematically.

16

Coiling the Spring
THE COLLECTED GAITS

Now that you understand what self-carriage is, how it feels, and why it's desirable, we can begin developing the collected gaits. In order to help you understand what collected gaits are, I can't do better than quote the descriptions from the rule book of the U.S. Equestrian Federation (USEF):

THE COLLECTED WALK

"In the collected walk, the horse remains 'on the bit', moves resolutely forward, with his neck raised and arched, and showing clear self-carriage. The head approaches the vertical position and a light contact with the mouth is maintained. The hind legs are engaged with good hock action. The pace remains regular, marching and vigorous. Each step covers less ground and is higher and more active than the steps of the medium walk because all the joints bend more markedly" (figs. 16.1 and 16.2).

THE COLLECTED TROT

"In the collected trot, the horse remains 'on the bit.' He moves forward with his neck raised and arched and his nose approaching the vertical. The hocks are well-engaged, maintaining an energetic impulsion, thus enabling the shoulders to move with greater ease in any direction. The

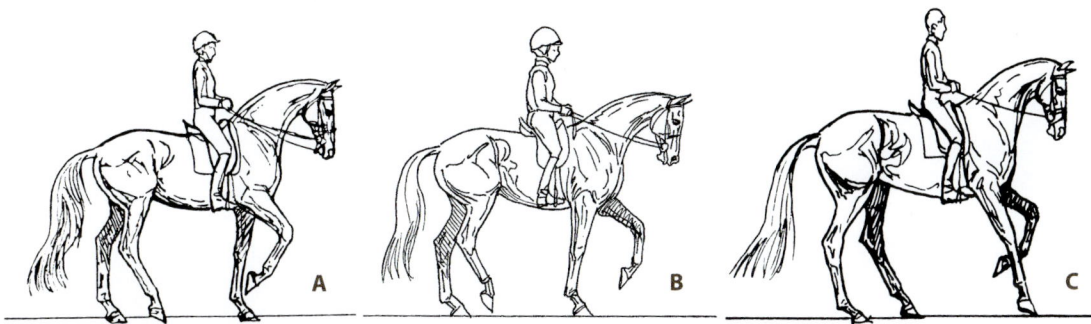

16.1 A–C Collected walk (A), collected trot (B), collected canter (C).

16.2 In collected walk, Hercules marches forward with his neck raised and arched, and showing clear self-carriage.

16.3 In collected trot, Hercules' steps are shorter than in any of the other trots, but the hocks are well-engaged so that he moves with greater lightness.

horse's steps are shorter than in any of the other trots, but he is lighter and more mobile" (figs. 16.1b and 16.3).

THE COLLECTED CANTER

"In the collected canter, the horse remains 'on the bit.' He moves forward with his neck raised and arched and his nose approaching the vertical. This canter is marked by the lightness of the forehand and the engagement of the hindquarters. Therefore, it is characterized by supple, free, and mobile shoulders and very active quarters. The horse's strides are shorter than at the other canters but he is lighter and more mobile" (figs. 16.1c and 16.4).

Notice in these descriptions that a common feature of the collected gaits is that the horse covers less ground with each step. However, even though the steps are shorter, the horse should still expend the same amount of energy (looking at it another way, he should use the same amount of calories per stride), or even more than he did in the working gaits to produce each stride. The shorter strides should feel like they are *bubbling over* with energy.

To do this, he'll have to lift each leg higher. By higher, I mean that if you're watching from the ground, you'll see that the legs make more of an up-and-down arc instead of taking long strides forward over the ground. If he only shortens the stride and the legs don't make a higher arc, he expends less energy. The result is a stride that is simply short—not collected. He'll just shuffle along over the ground with short, flat strides

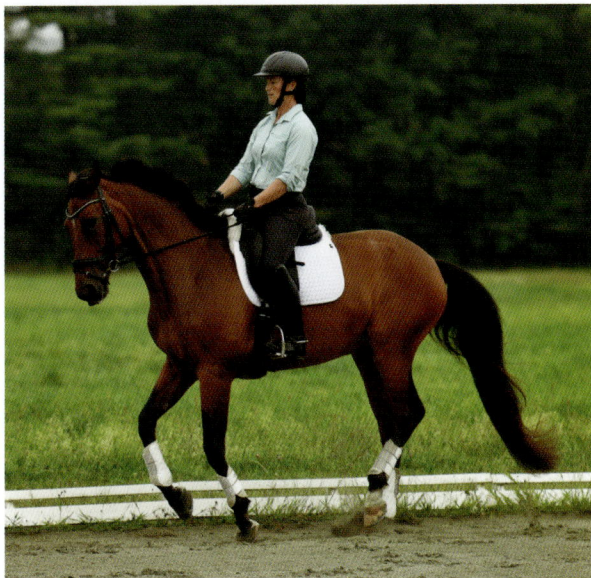

16.4 In collected canter, Hercules springs buoyantly over the ground. Because he's in self-carriage, he feels light and easily maneuverable to his rider.

rather than short, engaged strides (fig. 16.5).

In other words, if it normally takes a horse in his working gaits four strides to go completely through a corner, in the collected gaits, he might take six or seven shorter, higher, more engaged strides in the same tempo to make it through that same corner.

But before we get started, keep in mind that in order to collect your horse, he first must be relaxed, forward, straight, and regular in his rhythm (the prerequisites for the half-halt). You must then offer an inviting contact so that you can connect him with a half-halt.

Once again, it all comes down to the Basics. This is the foundation that all quality work is built upon. If you need to review how to connect your horse with a half-halt, refer back to chapter 14.

16.5 Roo's walk has been shortened, but it is not collected. He shuffles along with short, restricted steps rather than with shortened steps that make a higher arc off the ground. Also, his neck is short, and there is a big bulge underneath it—a sure sign that Addie is trying to pull him into collected walk rather than riding him from back to front by driving his hind legs forward into her hands.

In this chapter, we'll look at how the same half-halt that you used to connect your horse, plus the movements you already know, like transitions, school figures, and the rein back can now be used to collect the gaits.

Later on, in chapters 17 and 18, we'll look at some new lateral exercises, such as shoulder-in, haunches-in, half-pass, and turn on the haunches. You'll see that these movements aren't necessarily an end in themselves. They can be used as a means to an end, which is to develop the collected gaits.

USING THE HALF-HALT AS THE AID TO COLLECT THE GAITS

Now that you've *connected* your horse with a half-halt, let's use that very same half-halt to produce self-carriage so you can collect the gaits. This **collecting half-halt** also combines the driving aids, the bending aids and the outside rein, but its purpose is now different; it adjusts balance and shifts the center of gravity toward the hindquarters rather than simply connecting the "engine" to the front end. You'll find that all the elements of the **connecting half-halt** (driving aids, bending aids, closed outside hand) are present, but the emphasis changes in the *collecting* half-halt.

To review, the *connecting* half-halt is the marriage of three sets of aids: the seat and legs drive the horse forward, both legs and inside rein bend the horse, and the closed outside hand (**rein of opposition**) prevents him from going too much forward and from bending too much. Combining these aids should last about three seconds, and then you should relax by softening all of the aids. Later, as your horse becomes more highly schooled, you'll find that the half-halt can become more refined and often is as brief as a momentary closure of seat, legs, and hands.

But what, you might ask, is the difference between using the *connecting* half-halt to simply put your horse on the bit as we did in chapter 14 and giving a half-halt to *collect* the gaits? In one sense it's a "bigger" half-halt than you use to put your horse on the bit. When I say "bigger," however, I'm not necessarily referring to the strength of the aid. Rather, the horse's effort to **engage** should be "bigger." You ask for greater **engagement** with your *collecting* half-halt by driving the horse's hind legs further under his body so that he carries his own weight (and yours) completely, rather than using your hands as a fifth leg to help him out.

You'll also be influencing your horse differently with your outside rein. Before when you were simply putting your horse on the bit, you used your outside rein as the *connecting* rein. Now I want you to think of it as the *collecting* rein. When you use your outside rein, imagine it is shutting a door in front of your horse. When

16.6 In a collecting half-halt, your outside rein "shuts a door" in front of your horse. He has to bend the joints of his hind legs, lower his hindquarters, and "sit down" behind, thus carrying more weight with his hind legs.

your horse yields to the outside hand, which is closed in a fist, he bends the joints of his hind legs, lowers his hindquarters by "sitting down behind," and, therefore, changes his balance by carrying more weight on his hind legs (fig. 16.6).

Also, with each *collecting* half-halt, you'll need to shorten your reins a bit. This adjustment of rein length is important because the length of your reins determines how long your horse's frame is. When you apply a *collecting* half-halt, you'll be shifting your horse's center of gravity more toward his hind legs. However, if your reins remain the same length as they were prior to the half-halt, your horse's balance will slide back toward his forehand after the half-halt.

Understand that in an effort to go back down on his forehand, your horse will try to pull the reins through your fingers. Keep your hands firmly closed around the reins. Once your horse realizes that this route of escape from self-carriage is closed, he'll learn to find his balance between the new, shorter boundaries of your legs and hands.

16.7 This pleasantly round shape is the result of the connecting half-halt Pinky has given Hercules while in the working trot.

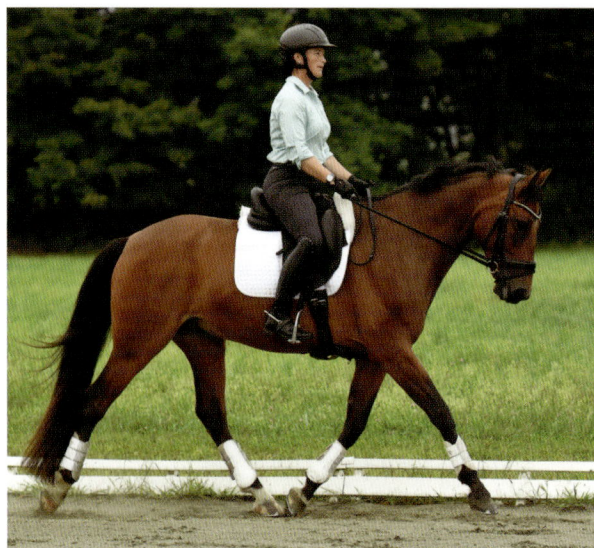

16.8 Pinky's goal is to collect the trot by shifting her horse's center of gravity more toward his hind legs. So to turn her connecting half-halt into a collecting half-halt, Pinky starts by asking for a lengthening in the trot.

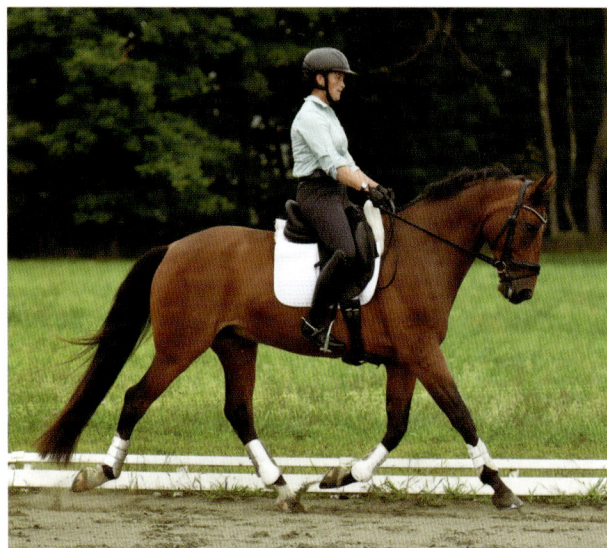

16.9 As Pinky begins to bring Hercules back from the lengthening, she keeps using her seat and legs as if she's still asking for the longer strides. She closes her legs, drives with her seat as if she's pushing the back of the saddle toward the front of the saddle, but she lets this power meet a more restraining hand so that the energy starts to stay within his body rather than being fed out in a lengthening.

16.10 As a result of the collecting half-halt, Hercules' balance is quite a bit different than it was in photo 16.7. He's a shorter and rounder "package," his hind legs are more active, and he carries considerably more weight on his hindquarters than he did before.

16.11 Here Pinky neglected to use her driving aids to send Hercules forward to meet her hand during the half-halt. Instead, she only used her hands. As a result, he has braced against them, stiffened his back, raised his head, and his hind legs are pushing out behind his body.

HOW TO RIDE THE COLLECTING HALF-HALT

Here's how to begin to turn your *connecting* half-halt into a *collecting* half-halt. Start off in the sitting trot. Ask your horse to do a lengthening so that when you close your legs, you both get a sense of thrust and power coming from his "engine." Then, when you bring your horse back from the lengthening to teach him a collected trot, do so with a *collecting* half-halt. This half-halt should have the same powerful feeling from behind *that the lengthening just did.*

You should always feel the vigor and thrust of lengthenings when asking for any half-halt and even more so for a *collecting* half-halt. When giving this *collecting* half-halt, apply the same

amount of legs and seat that you would to ask for a powerful lengthening. When the energy you create with your driving aids meets your closed outside hand, your horse should hold the energy within himself (rather than feeding it out in a lengthening) and the result is a more collected trot (figs. 16.7 to 16.10).

While maintaining your horse's rhythm and tempo, close your legs and at the same time, brace your back and drive with your seat so that you feel as if you're pushing the back of the saddle toward the front of the saddle. Use your seat by pushing it along in a sweeping motion (not straight down into the saddle) in order to drive your horse's hind legs further underneath his body, bend the joints of his hind legs, and create greater engagement.

With each transition from the lengthening back to the collected trot, ask within that half-halt for a greater degree of self-carriage. Do this by shortening your reins a couple of inches and then by applying your aids more strongly than you do just to put him on the bit. Depending on how he feels to you, this may mean making the whole half-halt stronger, or it may mean emphasizing the driving aids more than the outside rein.

Always be sure to use your driving aids. If you forget to do this, your closed outside hand just "subtracts" energy. As a result, your horse might brace against your hand, stiffen his back, and lose his hind legs out behind his body (fig. 16.11). Or, he might stop coming well forward with his hind legs and lose the rhythm and tempo he had in the lengthening. Always think of every *collecting* half-halt as the *addition* of impulsion and engagement, not merely the *subtraction* of forward motion.

MAINTAINING RHYTHM AND TEMPO DURING THE COLLECTING HALF-HALT

As I've mentioned before, because the term "half-halt" contains the word "halt," many people mistakenly think that a half-halt has something to do with stopping or slowing their horses down. Also, when you give a half-halt to collect the walk, trot or canter, the horse *seems* slower. This is because the steps are shorter, taking you more time to cover the same amount of ground that you covered with the longer strides of the working gait.

However, you should never slow down your horse's tempo or subtract the effort from his hind legs when you want to develop self-carriage and collect the gaits. If you do, you'll only get short steps without self-carriage. Using your hands too much results in short, unengaged steps. You need to drive your horse up to your hand so that he engages his hind legs and takes shorter, *higher,* more active steps. Think about *driving* him into a collected gait rather than *pulling* him into a slower one.

Keep in mind that the tendency of many horses is to slow down because at this stage they lack the physical strength to maintain their tempo (their rhythm may stay regular but the tempo slows down) when they're asked to show collected gaits. So always remember to maintain an even rhythm and a constant, unchanging tempo before, during, and after you give a half-halt. This rhythm and tempo must remain the same whether you're in the process of giving the half-halt or just riding the collected, medium, or extended gaits.

Remember the waltz that I described when we were discussing rhythm in the working gaits (chapter 6)? A waltz rhythm is always the same—a three-beat dance. But the tempo of the waltz can change depending on whether the music is played faster or slower. When giving a half-halt to create self-carriage and collect the paces, the "music" should always be played at the same speed.

More often than not when you're first teaching your horse to collect his trot, not only will he try to slow down but he might also lose the connection over his back. He does a disconnected trot, in dressage jargon, sometimes known as a "swimmy" or "passage-y" trot; his hind legs go backward, his front legs go forward, and his back sinks out from underneath you with every stride.

To correct this, keep in mind that horses almost always quicken their tempo when asked to lengthen, so if your horse wants to slow down when starting to learn to collect, you can use the lengthening to bring him back up to "normal" speed. Help him maintain his tempo by practicing some lengthenings to build thrust and energy. Keep this feeling of the quickness of a lengthening when you go to collect again. To check that the tempo stays the same, count out loud as you go from the lengthening to the collected gait.

USING SCHOOL FIGURES TO DEVELOP COLLECTED GAITS

On page 97, we looked at how to ride circles and turns. Now you can use these movements, also known as school figures, to develop the collected trot and canter. As long as they're done correctly, smaller circles produce greater engagement of the hind legs and, therefore, create a more marked shift of balance toward the hindquarters.

What I mean by "correctly" is that your horse doesn't evade the difficulty of the smaller figure by swinging his hindquarters out or pressing his barrel against your inside leg instead of softly bending around it. As long as your horse stays bent along the arc of the curve and his spine conforms exactly to the line he's on, tighter school figures demand that he carry himself and collect the gait he's in. So a 15-meter circle collects the trot and canter more than a 20-meter circle, and a 10-meter circle collects the gaits more than a 15-meter circle.

USING TRANSITIONS TO HELP COLLECTED GAITS

Doing frequent transitions from pace to pace also promotes self-carriage and the development of the collected gaits. Skipping a pace, such as doing a transition from the canter to the walk and back to the canter again (also known as a **simple change of lead**), or from the trot to the halt and back to the trot again, intensifies the collecting effect of a transition.

When you start to do these more advanced transitions that skip a pace, all sorts of things can go wrong. For example, when you try to go from the canter to the walk, your horse will probably fall on his forehand and end up doing the transition through a couple of steps of the trot. The same thing will most likely happen when you first attempt to go from the trot to the halt. Your horse will lose his balance and shuffle through

a few steps of walk. Keep in mind that in order for these transitions to be effective, they have to be done clearly and distinctly. Therefore, as you blend a half-halt into any downward transition, think about driving the hind legs further under your horse's body toward a more restraining hand (see Combining Aids to Improve Balance on page 350 for help in how to do this).

One other thing to think about when you do a transition from the canter to the walk is that in order for your horse to negotiate this transition in good balance, he needs to be covering ground in the canter no faster than the speed of the walk. If you ask for the transition from a normal canter during which your horse covers ground faster than he does at a walk, he has no option but to shift his balance onto his front legs.

To avoid this balance shift, think about cantering with shorter and shorter (but active) strides until your horse is covering ground in the canter at the same speed he'll be traveling when he walks. As you're cantering, half-halt and bring him more onto the spot for two or three strides before you actually "still" your seat and ask for the walk. This way he'll be able to softly step into the walk in the same balance he had during the last step of canter.

If you're still struggling with this canter-to-walk transition, pretend that you're actually asking for a transition to the halt. Then at the last moment soften your hands and allow your horse to walk on instead of coming to a complete stop. By the same token, if your horse walks into the halt during transitions from the trot to the halt, you can do the same sort of exercise: step into the halt and immediately back up without pausing. Do this several times and then just imagine that you're going to ask for a transition from the trot to the rein back, but allow your horse to halt instead.

Another thing that can go wrong when you start these more sophisticated transitions is that after doing the downward transition, your horse feels "**behind your leg**" for the subsequent upward transition. If you find yourself wanting to squeeze hard with your legs in order to do the upward transition, it means that you'll have to put your horse **in front of your leg** again as I described in chapter 5. (You see, even at the more advanced levels your work often boils down to going back to Basics!) Your horse must feel electric and "hot off your leg" in order for the upward transitions to contribute to the process of developing collected gaits.

Now let's get started using these more advanced transitions to increase self-carriage. First, ride around in the collected trot or canter and evaluate your horse's balance before the transitions. Where is his center of gravity? How much weight is on the forehand? How heavy is the contact in your hands?

Then do either trot-halt-trot transitions or canter-walk-canter transitions. Do only about five strides in each before you do the next transition.

After doing several transitions, take a moment to reevaluate your horse's balance. As you trot or canter around, ask yourself if your horse feels less on the forehand, is carrying more weight behind, and is lighter in your hands. If he does, the frequent transitions have done their job.

BACKING UP TO IMPROVE ENGAGEMENT

Backing up can also be used to promote the collected gaits by getting the horse's hind legs further underneath his body. I've seen students markedly improve their horses' self-carriage by doing a rein back and then asking for an immediate transition to the trot or the canter. Go forward for only a few strides so your horse can feel his new balance, and then halt before the self-carriage degenerates. Then repeat the whole exercise. Only trot or canter a few strides at a time so that your horse has a chance to feel his ability to shift his center of gravity toward his hind legs.

KEY POINTS

- In the collected gaits, a horse's steps are shorter, higher, and more active than they are in the working gaits.

- By modifying your *connecting* half-halt slightly, you can turn it into a *collecting* half-halt.

- Always think of *"driving"* your horse forward into a collected gait.

- When you give a *collecting* half-halt, the rhythm and tempo of the pace should stay the same as it was before the half-halt.

17

Going Sideways

LATERAL MOVEMENTS TO DEVELOP COLLECTION

I gave you an introduction to lateral movements—**work on two tracks**—in chapter 9, and I'd like to do a quick review here to refresh your memory.

All lateral work is not an end in itself. Instead, it is used as a means to an end: to warm up, loosen, and supple your horse's muscles as well as teach him to be obedient to your leg when it is placed behind the girth. In this chapter and the next, where I go into more advanced lateral movements, you'll see that the "end" also includes developing your horse's strength and his ability to carry himself more than would be possible if he were limited to **work on a single track**.

You don't decide to go sideways just because you're bored with going in a straight line and you'd like to do something different. Although, making your training fun and interesting is a side benefit that is as important for you as it is for your horse.

There are many mental as well as physical benefits gained by introducing lateral work. Besides keeping your work interesting, lateral movements increase your horse's obedience to the aids as he reponds to new combinations of your seat, legs, and hands. Physically, lateral work makes your horse more athletic in any number of ways.

For instance, in chapter 9, you learned how leg-yields, which are done in the working gaits, help to make a horse supple and loose so that he can move more freely. As a result, he can carry himself with more harmony and lightness. You also discovered that every horse is crooked to one degree or another; you learned how to use shoulder-fore to make your horse straight—one of the fundamental rules of classical training.

Now in this chapter and the next, you'll discover many additional benefits to doing lateral work. The more advanced lateral movements, which are ridden in the collected gaits, supple all parts of the horse's body and increase the elasticity of the "**bridge**" connecting his hindquarters through his back to his front end. They enable the horse to become more graceful in his movement as his gaits become more balanced, harmonious, and expressive. They increase the engagement of the hindquarters and, therefore, contribute even more to self-carriage, which you've already begun to develop in the collected gaits.

A lateral movement means that your horse goes forward and sideways at the same time. There are two categories of lateral movements, and the major difference between these two groups can be summed up in one word—bend.

The first category—lateral movements without bend—includes leg-yielding and turn on the forehand. I described these in detail in chapter 9. The turn on the forehand is an exercise in obedience to the leg. Leg-yielding is a useful warm-up exercise; it allows the horse to loosen, supple, and stretch his muscles.

The second group, the focus of this chapter and chapter 18, has exercises that require bend and are, consequently, more demanding. This second group includes shoulder-fore, shoulder-in, haunches-in, haunches-out, and half-pass. I discussed shoulder-fore in chapter 9, but I'll review it and deal with the rest of the lateral movements with bend here. I'm also going to introduce the turn on the haunches as part of your two-track education.

Since bending is a requirement of the second category of lateral movements, I want to take a moment to review the concepts of **"inside"** and **"outside."** In many riding situations, "inside" and "outside" refer to the placement of your horse's body in relation to the arena: the "inside" of your horse's body refers to his side that is closest to the center of the arena, and the "outside" refers to his side that is closest to the rail. This is not the case in dressage. Instead, "inside" and "outside" are always determined by the direction toward which the horse's body is bent or flexed: if your horse is looking to the right and

bent around your right leg, then his right side is his "inside," regardless of whether he's traveling around the arena to the right or to the left. (See fig. 9.5, p. 148, if this still sounds confusing. And don't worry—you'll get used to it!)

This second group of lateral movements is performed in the collected gaits, and when done correctly they actually improve self-carriage. Here's why: the fact that your horse is bent while he's going sideways necessitates that he engage his hind legs and shift his center of gravity toward his rear. Think of it as a formula: Bend + Sideways = Engagement.

Since bend is the essential ingredient in changing a lateral movement into an exercise that increases self-carriage, you can see why it's so important to work on correctly executed school figures. The more flexible and bendable your horse is, the better he can negotiate small circles and the more the lateral work can improve his balance in the collected gaits.

Remember that if your horse isn't bending well while you're doing lateral work, you'll need to momentarily abandon doing these more advanced lateral movements. After all, without bend, your lateral movement just becomes a leg-yield (figs. 17.1 and 17.2). So if you need to, go back to practicing bending exercises like circles and serpentines for a while. Then, as your horse becomes more flexible, you can resume going sideways. You'll find that as his bend improves, you'll be doing more productive lateral exercises.

For example, if your horse normally bends well but after a few steps of a lateral movement, he loses the bend, interrupt the lateral exercise

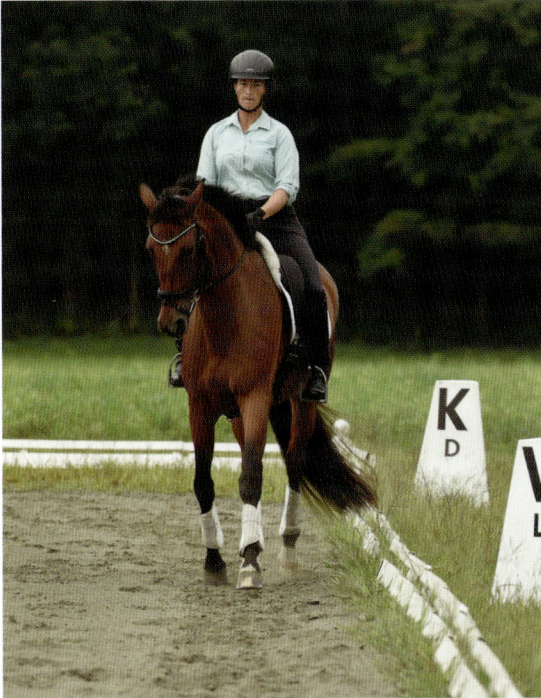

17.1 In this shoulder-in there is a gentle bend through the entire length of Hercules' body. His hindquarters are parallel to the rail and his hind feet travel straight down the track while his forehand is brought toward the middle of the ring at a 30-degree angle from the rail.

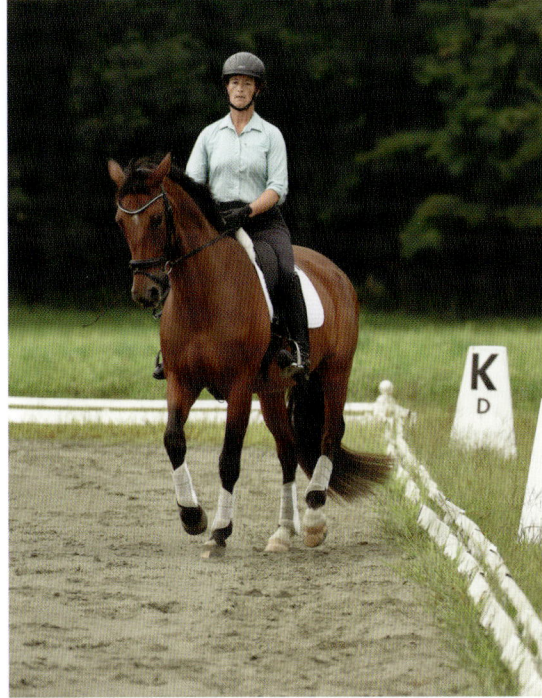

17.2 Here Hercules' body is no longer bent and a movement that began as a shoulder-in has degenerated into a leg-yield. It's easy to see that there's no bend because his hindquarters have swung out and they are no longer parallel to the rail.

and arc onto a circle instead. Once you've re-established the bend, continue with the lateral exercise. If you're doing a shoulder-in or a half-pass and your horse starts to lose his bend after a few strides, turn him onto a small circle immediately. Stay on that circle for as long as necessary to recreate the bend and then continue the movement (fig. 17.3).

When we get started shortly, you'll need to decide which pace you'll work in for your more advanced lateral movements. If you have a horse with a "safe" walk—meaning he has no tendency to lose the regular rhythm of his walk and he'll

stay in front of your leg—it's easiest to start in the walk because it is slower and you'll have more time to get organized and coordinate your aids. If you're concerned about the quality of the walk degenerating or your horse getting behind your leg, you'll need to start in the trot. This might be a little more difficult for you because it's faster, but preserving the quality of the walk is always the priority. Plus, the greater impulsion in the trot will help you maintain the "forward" aspect of these "forward and sideways" movements.

I'm also going to strongly recommend that if you haven't already marked off an arena with

17.3 If you are doing a shoulder-in and your horse starts to lose his bend, turn him onto a small circle and stay on it for as long as needed to recreate the bend before continuing the shoulder-in.

shoulder-in, with bend

circle to restore bend

bend lost

shoulder-in

Shortly, I'll get into the first new lateral movement that you do with your horse—the shoulder-in. However, before I get started, I need to digress for a moment and review the use of the word "tracks" as it relates to lateral work (material I covered in chapter 9, but bears repeating).

TRACKS

We use the word "tracks" in so many different contexts. In the interests of clarifying the word, I'll describe all the different ways we use it in training.

First of all, the path that you make in the dirt as you go around your ring is a track.

Next, think of a working trot. In the working trot, your horse should "track up." In other words, if you looked on the ground, you'd see that the hoofprint made by each hind foot steps directly into the track of the hoofprint made by the front foot.

Then again, you ride around your ring with either your left or your right leg closest to the center of the arena. This determines whether you are "tracking to the left" or "tracking to the right." It might seem odd, but in order to "track to the right," for example, you'd have to enter the ring and turn to your left!

So far these usages of the word "tracks" are pretty clear-cut. But now we get to the fun stuff—lateral work.

To begin, let's consider the concept of *direction*. When you're just riding on a straight line, you're working on a "**single track**." In this case, the "single track" refers to the fact that you're only going in one direction—*forward*.

letters, you do so before starting these lateral exercises. This will make it easier for you to have reference points so that you can ride accurately. Precision is essential so that your horse doesn't "cheat" and use his stronger hind leg more than his weaker one; sometimes his evasions can be so subtle that you won't realize it. Riding toward designated markers will give you confidence that your horse is making an equal effort with both hind legs. (See chapter 22 for arena diagrams.)

When you do any type of lateral work, you are working on "**two tracks**." The words "two tracks" refers to the fact that you're going in *two directions* at once—forward *and* sideways.

We also use the word "tracks" to describe how many legs we see coming toward us when standing directly in front of a horse. In each of the following examples, the horse will be going to the left and I'll start with the leg that is closest to the rail.

Leg-yields are done on "four tracks" because you can see all four legs coming towards you. If you are doing a leg-yield with your horse's head to the rail you see the right foreleg, the left foreleg, the right hind leg, and the left hind leg, in that order (fig. 17.5).

Shoulder-fore is also on four tracks, but the legs are lined up differently. Starting from the rail, you see the right hind, the right fore, the left hind, and the left fore (fig. 17.4 B).

During shoulder-in, shoulder-out, haunches-in, and haunches-out, the horse is on three tracks because you can only see three of his legs coming toward you. For example, in left shoulder-in, you see the right hind, the right fore, and the left fore. You won't see the left hind because it's hidden behind the right fore (fig. 17.4 C).

To sum up: with single track movements you see two legs coming toward you; with two track movements you see either three or four legs coming toward you (figs. 17.4 to 17.7).

17.5 A good example of a leg-yield in the head-to-the-wall position. Maeve's spine is straight, she's clearly on four tracks, and the angle of her hindquarters from the track is about 35 degrees.

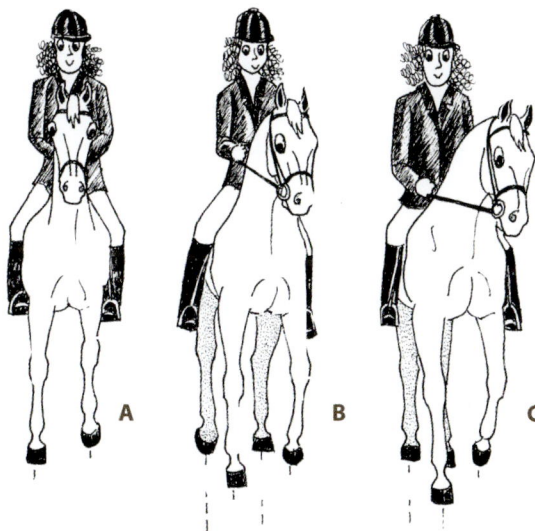

17.4 A–C *Straight,* with the horse moving on a single track, showing two tracks on the ground (A); *shoulder-fore,* a two-track exercise on four tracks (B); and *shoulder-in,* a two-track exercise on three tracks (C).

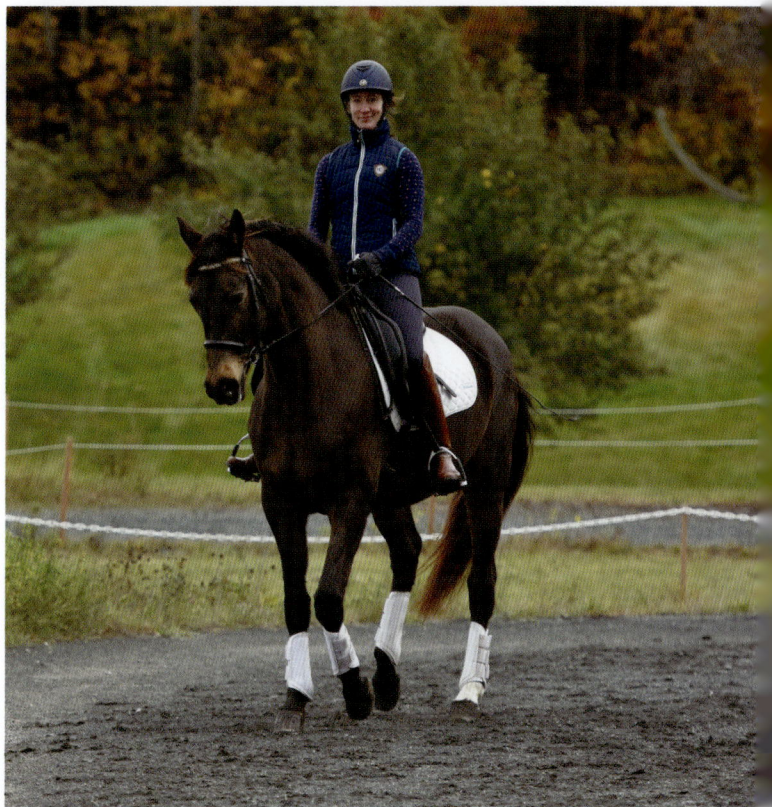

17.6 During shoulder-fore, Maeve is also on four tracks. Each of her four legs is visible and makes a separate track on the ground. But the angle is very slight compared to the angle created by the four tracks that you see in a leg-yield.

17.7 The haunches-in is one example of a two-track movement with bend being done on three tracks. Maeve's outside hind leg isn't visible because it's lined up directly behind her inside foreleg.

SHOULDER-IN

USES

The first of the more advanced lateral movements that you need to learn is the shoulder-in. Shoulder-in is a suppling, straightening, strengthening as well as an "increasing self-carriage" exercise (figs. 17.8 and 17.9).

It supples the horse because it stretches and loosens the muscles and ligaments of the inside shoulder and forearm where the horse passes his inside foreleg across and in front of his outside foreleg. This suppling effect increases the horse's ability to move his forearm gymnastically in other lateral movements.

It is a straightening exercise because it enables the rider to place her horse's forehand in front of his hindquarters.

It strengthens and improves self-carriage because with each step the horse moves his inside hind leg underneath his body and places it in front of his outside hind leg under his center of gravity. By doing so, his inside hind leg gets stronger because it has to carry additional weight. Also, in order to move his inside hind leg in this way, the horse must lower his inside hip. When this is done, it contributes to the development of self-carriage.

Learning shoulder-in should be a simple concept for you to absorb because you're already familiar with shoulder-fore, which can be thought of as an "introductory" shoulder-in. To remind you, in shoulder-fore the horse is very slightly bent to the inside along his whole body. He should be positioned so that the rider can just see his eye and nostril.

The angle that the horse's forehand is brought in off the rail in shoulder-fore is about 15 degrees. His forelegs are brought slightly to the inside of the ring so that when viewed from the front, you would see the inside hind leg stepping in between the front legs. Since you can see all of the horse's legs from this position, you could say that during shoulder-fore, the horse is doing a two-track exercise on four tracks!

Shoulder-in is similar to shoulder-fore, but differs in that the horse's bend and his angle to the rail are increased and the horse travels on

17.8 In shoulder-in, the horse's front legs are brought in off the track at about a 30-degree angle to the rail. Your horse's inside hind leg should be lined up directly behind his outside foreleg. He is on three tracks.

three distinct tracks rather than four—one for the outside hind leg, a second track for the inside hind leg which is lined up directly behind the outside foreleg, and a third track for the inside foreleg.

The exciting thing about learning shoulder-in is that once you master it, you'll have the main tool you need to do all of the other lateral movements.

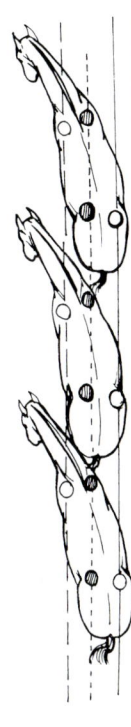

17.9 In this shoulder-in, Wilkinson (owned by Elise Ames) is evenly bent from poll to tail around Joy Congdon's inside leg. Wilkinson's forehand is brought in off the track at approximately a 30 degree angle. Because his inside hind leg is lined up directly behind his outside foreleg, three separate tracks on the ground are visible. Wilkinson is bent and traveling to the right, but his legs and body are moving to the left.

As you'll discover shortly, all these other lateral exercises are either near or distant cousins of shoulder-in.

DESCRIPTION

Shoulder-in is a lateral movement in which the horse is flexed to the inside and slightly bent around your inside leg (in this case the one closest to the inside of the ring) and both his front legs and forehand are brought in off the track at approximately a 30-degree angle. At this angle, your horse's inside hind leg will be lined up directly behind his outside foreleg and he's on three tracks.

During shoulder-in, your horse's inside foreleg passes and crosses in front of his outside foreleg and his inside hind leg is placed in front of his outside hind leg.

It differs from the rest of the lateral exercises with bend because the horse is flexed at the poll to the inside, and bent around the rider's inside leg, but moving in the opposite direction from the way he's bent. For example, if your horse is bent to the right and traveling around the ring to the right, the direction that his legs and body move in a shoulder-in is to the left.

Some people bring their horse's forehand in to a greater degree than the angle that produces the three tracks I just described. When this is done, all four legs are visible (fig. 17.10). The three-track versus the four-track debate isn't an issue as long as the horse's bend is maintained so the exercise doesn't become just a leg yield. (Remember, a leg-yield is ridden without bend—the horse is only

17.10 Joy has brought Wilkinson's forehand to the inside slightly more than before so that now he is on four tracks. However, he is still doing a good shoulder-in because Joy has maintained his bend around her inside leg. The wider angle to the rail is fine as long as Joy does the movement the same way when she goes in the other direction, so that both sides of the horse develop evenly.

flexed slightly at the poll, away from the direction he is going. It is not as beneficial an exercise as the shoulder-in.) What's more important is to be sure to do the shoulder-in with the same amount of angle in both directions rather than on three tracks one way and four tracks the other way. You want to be sure to develop your horse evenly in both directions.

To get the idea of shoulder-in, plan to ride a 10-meter circle in the second corner of the short side of your arena. Then, imagine that you discontinue riding that circle one stride after you start it. Maintain the bend that you established at the beginning of the circle, and send your horse straight down the long side of your ring instead. Your horse's hind legs stay on the track as if they were traveling straight forward parallel to the track, while his forehand is moved onto an inside track. Essentially, a shoulder-in

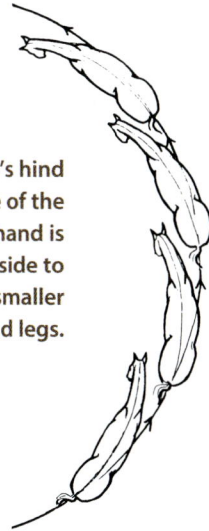

17.11 Your horse's hind legs stay on the line of the circle and his forehand is brought to the inside to describe a slightly smaller circle than his hind legs.

is a first step of a small circle but repeated on a straight line.

You can also practice on a circle. Here, your horse's hind legs stay on the line of the circle and his forehand is brought to the inside, to describe a slightly smaller circle than his hind legs (fig. 17.11).

THE AIDS FOR SHOULDER-IN

The aids for left shoulder-in are as follows:

1. **Seat:** weight on left seatbone.

2. **Left leg:** on the girth for the horse to bend around as well as to ask for engagement of the inside hind leg.

3. **Right leg:** behind the girth to help bend the horse around the inside leg.

4. **Left rein:** vibrate for inside flexion.

5. **Right rein:** steady and supporting to prevent too much bend in the neck.

6. **Both hands:** stay low and move to the left. They should stay equidistant from your body and move sideways on the same plane. Be sure that your inside hand (left) does not get drawn closer to the saddle and that your outside hand (right) does not cross over the withers. Move both hands enough to the left to lead your horse's shoulders in that direction so that you place his outside front leg in front of his inside hind leg.

SEQUENCE OF AIDS

As with any of the lateral movements that have a bend, always ask for the bend before you ask for the angle. First, ride well into the corner to bend your horse. If he doesn't want to bend in the corner, ride a small circle until he bends easily. Think about your bending aids while on the circle. When circling to the left, your weight is on your left seat bone, your left leg is on the girth, your right leg is behind the girth, you vibrate the left rein for flexion while supporting with the right rein to prevent your horse from bending his neck too much to the inside. The supporting outside rein is essential because horses are more flexible in their necks than through the rest of their bodies and would happily overbend their necks to the inside if you let them. For the shoulder-in to be correct, the bend must be uniform from poll to tail.

You'll know your horse is bending easily when you can soften the contact on the inside rein, and he feels like he'll stay bent pretty much by himself. Then, once your horse is bending well on the small

circle, start another one and interrupt it after the first step to continue down the long side while bent. Initiate this movement down the long side by looking straight down the track rather than between your horse's ears as you do on a circle, and increase your inside (left) leg to send your horse down the long side of the ring (fig. 17.12).

Once he is headed in the right direction, ask for the angle of about 30 degrees by bringing your two hands to the left. This will bring your horse's forehand in. Think of the angle that your horse's body makes to the track or the rail as a small wedge of pie. Keep your hands side by side and place them low. It's important that your hands are low because if they aren't, your horse's shoulders can escape underneath the reins rather than being influenced and displaced by them. Think of using an opening left rein to help keep your inside hand in front of your inside hip and

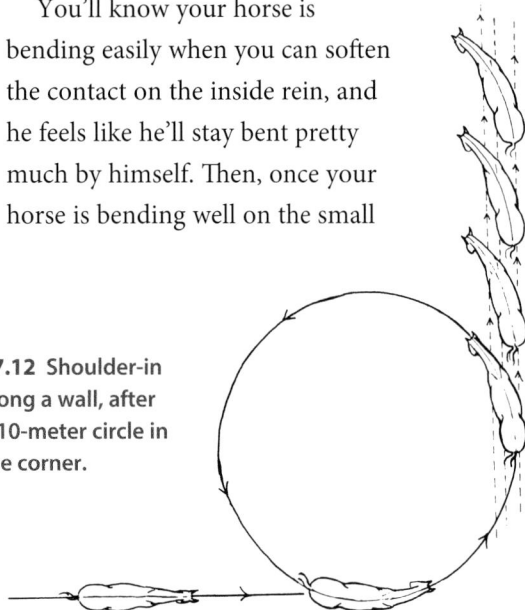

17.12 Shoulder-in along a wall, after a 10-meter circle in the corner.

17.13 In shoulder-in, the 30-degree angle your horse's body makes to the track is like a small wedge of pie.

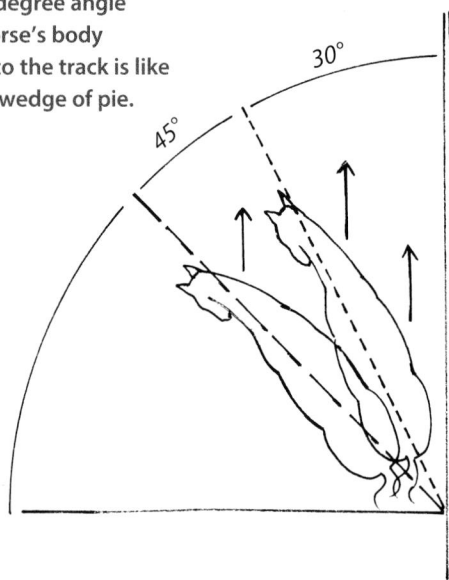

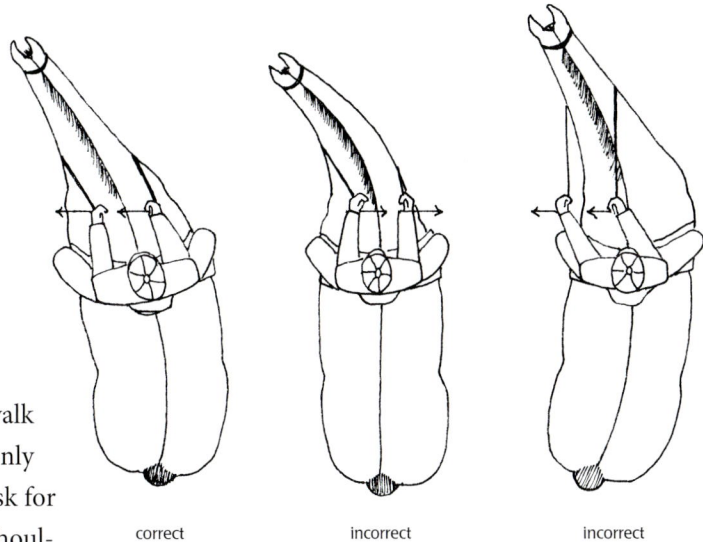

17.14 Rein aids for left shoulder-in. Both hands stay low, are equidistant from your body, and move sideways to the left on the same plane.

correct   incorrect   incorrect

bring your right fist toward your horse's shoulders to create the angle (figs. 17.13 and 17.14).

Shoulder-in can only be done in the walk and trot. When in the canter, you should only ride shoulder-fore (see chapter 9). If you ask for the greater degree of angle required for a shoulder-in while in the canter, you might destroy the purity of the pace by making it four-beat.

✳ HELPFUL HINTS FOR SHOULDER-IN

MAINTAINING THE TEMPO

One of your major goals in all of riding is to keep your horse's tempo constant, and this rule applies to shoulder-in as well. He should neither slow down nor speed up. Because the movement makes a lot of new demands on your horse, when he is first learning it, he might lose impulsion and slow down or get so worried that he rushes off.

These reactions usually happen because he's not yet supple or strong enough to cope with the increased engagement of his inside hind leg. So, for the time being, make one of the following adjustments to decrease the difficulty of the movement until your horse becomes more able and athletic. You'll find that depending on the

individual animal, some horses benefit from one exercise rather than the other.

1. Ask for less angle and bend by doing shoulder-fore instead (see chapter 9).

2. Ride shoulder-in for only a few steps. Straighten your horse and renew his desire to go forward by lengthening for several strides. Ask for only a few steps of shoulder-in again.

3. Ride shoulder-in at the walk. This exercise won't be helpful for the nervous horse who gets more tense when you ride on contact in the walk. Those "raring-to-go" types will do better in the trot because they'll have a forward outlet for their pent-up energy. For most horses, though, doing shoulder-in in the walk is a good idea because it gives you more time to get organized and apply your aids quietly.

MAINTAINING THE BEND

If your horse's hindquarters swing out toward the rail rather than staying parallel to it, he'll lose his bend and you'll be doing a leg-yield, not a shoulder-in. That's fine if your goal is to do a leg-yield with a straight body. But since one of your goals when doing shoulder-in is to engage your horse's inside hind leg, he needs to be bent through his body with his hindquarters parallel to the fence while he's going sideways.

You'll probably find that your horse will be perfectly happy to swing his hindquarters out towards the fence because by doing so he can evade the increased bending of the joints of his inside hind leg. You may actually be the cause of this evasion if you don't use your legs correctly. If you neglect to keep your outside leg back, it won't be in a position where it can control the haunches. To cut off this escape route, imagine that you "trap" your horse's outside hind leg and

17.16 If you tend to draw your inside leg back by mistake, exaggerate the correction. Visualize tucking it up into the curve behind your horse's elbow and letting it nestle there.

keep it from escaping by applying your outside leg behind the girth (fig. 17.15).

To absorb this concept of preventing the hindquarters from swinging out with your outside leg, think about just riding the hind legs *straight down the track* while moving the shoulders in. Do many transitions from a few straight strides along the track to a few steps of shoulder-in and back to straight ahead again. Concentrate on maintaining the exact same position of your horse's hind legs—parallel to the fence—at all times.

You also need to be careful with the position of your *inside* leg. If you draw it back instead of keeping it on the girth, you'll push your horse's hindquarters out as if you were actually asking for a leg-yield (fig. 17.17).

Use a mental image to help you keep your inside leg on the girth rather than letting it slide back behind the girth. I call this position of your inside leg at the girth an "engaging" spot because your leg needs to be placed there

17.15 To keep your outside leg back where it can control the haunches, think of trapping your horse's outside hind leg to keep it from escaping.

17.17 A & B The position of hindquarters in relation to the rail matters during shoulder-in. The shoulder-in ridden correctly has the horse evenly bent and moving on three tracks (A). If your horse's hindquarters swing out toward the rail rather than staying parallel to it, he'll lose his bend and you'll only be doing a leg-yield (B).

in order to engage or activate the horse's corresponding hind leg. If you tend to draw your leg back, exaggerate the image by picturing that you tuck this leg right up into the curve behind your horse's elbow and let it nestle into that spot (fig. 17.16). This should counteract the urge to pull it back, so that it will end up on the girth where it belongs.

In either case, once you realize that either of your legs hasn't done its job correctly, first ride your horse straight down the track. Do this by leading his forehand back to the track by bringing both of your hands toward the rail. Then make sure you've repositioned your legs so that they are side by side. Once your horse's body is realigned so that he's on a single track and parallel to the fence, you can have another go at riding the shoulder-in, and as you do it, "think" that you want to bring his shoulders in rather than push his hindquarters out.

Sometimes, rather than not having enough bend, a rider overbends her horse's neck to the inside. Remember that during shoulder-in (and all of the lateral exercises with bend, for that matter) the bend should be uniform from poll to tail. Often there's too much bend in the neck because a rider uses an unequal influence of the two reins. For instance, she uses too much inside rein without supporting with her outside rein. Or, she neglects to keep her hands side-by-side.

MAINTAINING THE ANGLE

Once you commit yourself to an angle with the rail, it shouldn't waver. Get a visual reference point for a steady angle by lining up your outside knee with a point at the end of your arena. Feel your knee being drawn to that point as if there were a line attached to it that was being reeled in by an imaginary fisherman (fig. 17.18).

Here's something else you can do to get a visual reference point for a steady angle. If your

17.18 In shoulder-in, get a visual reference point for a steady angle. Line up your knee to a point at the end of the ring, and feel it being drawn to that point as if by an invisible line attached to it.

riding area or ring is mostly dirt and has pretty heavy traffic, you probably have a gulley along the well-used track. On either side of this depression, there's a lip of dirt. Take advantage of this. Place your horse's hind legs in the gulley and put his outside front leg on the inside edge of the track. Glance down at your horse's outside shoulder to check that his outside foreleg steps exactly on the inside lip of the track with every stride. This leg should not move back into the track or go any further beyond the edge toward the center of the ring.

One of my students had a real challenge riding the shoulder-in with an angle of 30 degrees in both directions. She consistently asked for too much angle when she went to the right and not enough angle when she went to the left. She knew that she did this habitually, but that information wasn't enough for her to make the necessary adjustments.

She needed to develop a sense of where her horse's shoulders were in relation to the rail. To develop this awareness, we divided the long side of the ring into three parts. I had her ride the first third of the long side in shoulder-fore at a 15-degree angle. Then she increased the angle and did a shoulder-in at 30 degrees for the next part. Finally, she increased the angle to about 35 degrees and did a leg-yield for the last third of the long side. I acted as her mirror and gave her feedback on the various angles.

Sometimes we'd change the order of the exercises. In time she developed her perception of what she needed to do with her aids to create a specific amount of angle, regardless of the direction she was going. Eventually she was able to place her horse's shoulders anywhere she wanted.

CONTROLLING THE SHOULDERS

One of the most common mistakes that I see is a shoulder-in ridden as a "head- and neck-in." What I mean by this is that if you were watching, you'd see the horse's head and neck brought to the inside, but his shoulders either stay directly in front of his hindquarters or, even worse, they fall out toward the rail (fig. 17.19).

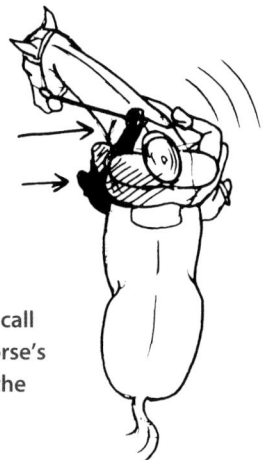

17.19 This is not shoulder-in. I call it a "head-and-neck-in." The horse's head and neck are brought to the inside while the horse falls out through the outside shoulder.

A horse is inclined to adopt this position more frequently when his soft side is on the inside. This is because he often doesn't step solidly into the rein and accept it on his soft side. Since he's not really connected to this rein, when you go to use it, he collapses away from it and just bends his neck. As a result it's impossible to influence his whole body (figs. 17.20 and 17.21).

Although this might be an odd concept to absorb, you'll find that it's actually easier for you to do a shoulder-in when your horse's stiff side is on the inside. I realize that bend is a requirement

17.20 Bekki and Alpen demonstrate different positions of the head and shoulders in these two photos. In both these pictures, Alpen's head is brought to the left at approximately the same degree. However, in the first photo, Bekki does not have control of the horse's shoulders and they bulge out to the right so that Alpen's right front leg is almost directly in front of his right hind leg. Also, because he is not stepping into the rein on his soft left side, he collapses away from it, bends only in the neck, and tips his head.

17.21 In this photo, Bekki has good control of Alpen's shoulders. She has successfully moved them to the left so that we see a shoulder-in being performed on slightly more than three tracks. Also, Bekki has created good engagement of the left hind leg and as Alpen steps into the left rein, his ears become more level and his head is straighter.

of shoulder-in, and it's more difficult to bend your horse on his stiff side, but because he steps into the rein and accepts it on his stiff side, it'll be easier for you to influence his shoulders.

When you use your hand to correct a part of your horse's body that should be controlled by your leg, you'll get a "head- and neck-in." For instance, you start a shoulder-in but then feel your horse's whole body wanting to move off the track toward the inside of the ring. You attempt to hold his hind legs on the track by using your inside rein as an indirect rein rather than keeping it in front of your inside hip.

Here's how this cycle unfolds: you ask for shoulder-in and your horse realizes he's going to have to do more work by engaging his inside hind leg. This is very physically demanding for him because not only does he have to bend the joints of his inside hind leg to a greater degree, but he also has to take that leg and place it underneath his body in front of his outside hind leg. In an effort to avoid this extra work, he steps toward the inside of the ring.

To be more specific, during left shoulder-in, he steps sideways to the left with his left hind leg rather than stepping toward his center. He is attempting to avoid the increased closing of the joints of this leg. You feel him coming off the track and your instinct is to bring your hands back toward the rail (to the right) to hold his body on the track.

This is not going to help. When you feel this happening, you need to treat the cause and not the symptom. The symptom is that your horse comes off the track toward the inside of the ring. The cause is that your horse is drifting to the inside to avoid the increased bending of the joints of his hind leg. So you need to direct your correction to his hindquarters rather than to his forehand. Insist that he keep his hind legs on the track by using your inside leg actively. Since your legs control his hind legs, the correction must be made by using your inside leg actively on the girth.

In clinics I often try to give a rider the idea of moving the shoulders in by allowing her to counter-flex her horse at the poll. I realize that by doing this her horse won't be bending correctly for a shoulder-in. But this is only temporary. At this point my primary concern is to teach her the feeling of controlling her horse's shoulders. Once she feels how she can move his shoulders by moving her hands sideways as I described in the aids for this movement on page 264, I have her go back to correct flexion and bend.

Sometimes your horse refuses to move his shoulders, and they just seem glued to the rail. You feel that you're using your hands correctly, but your horse's shoulders don't budge and it's difficult to get any angle at all.

The problem here might be that your horse lacks suppleness and mobility in his shoulders. So do some "shoulder-mobilization" exercises to improve the horse's ability to slide his shoulders left and right.

I described these exercises in detail in my "Hard To Steer" section in chapter 12. All of them can be done in all three paces. In each case, you ask your horse to flex at the poll (by vibrating the rein) in the opposite direction from the way you want his shoulders to move.

In other words, if you're going to slide his shoulders to the left, you'll want to first flex him to the right. You'll know you're gaining in the suppleness department when you can easily move your horse's shoulders around yet the weight of the reins in your hands doesn't get any heavier.

USING SHOULDER-IN TO INCREASE SELF-CARRIAGE

During each step of shoulder-in, your horse's inside hind leg moves in the direction of his center of gravity and he lowers his inside hip. Doing so causes his hindquarters to lower and his hind legs to carry more of his weight than before. As a result, his shoulders are relieved and his forelegs can step more freely.

One way for you to determine that you've ridden a good shoulder-in is to do several strides and then ask yourself the following question. "When I'm finished, does my horse feel like he's carrying himself because he's more balanced back on his hindquarters and lighter in my hands than he was when I started?" In other words, has your shoulder-in increased his self-carriage? You've done a good shoulder-in if your horse's balance is more "uphill" and less on the forehand after the shoulder-in than it was before you started.

Here's an image to help you achieve that desired effect. Do you remember that in chapter 15 I told you that one way of measuring the degree of self-carriage is to evaluate the relative height of the withers to the top of the croup? So, when you ride shoulder-in as an exercise to increase self-carriage, think of calling the movement "shoulders-up" instead. Picture your horse's withers becoming higher than his hindquarters. "Feel" a lighter rein contact as he comes into self-carriage because his entire forehand from the withers forward is raised.

Maybe your horse maintains his self-carriage pretty well while in a particular gait, but as soon as you do a downward transition, he falls on his forehand. If this happens, do the following exercise to teach him to stay in good balance throughout the transition.

Start by doing trot-walk-trot transitions. Ride down the long side of the ring while in a collected trot. Step into the walk and ask for shoulder-in at the moment of the downward transition. Then straighten your horse and pick up the trot again.

You can also do canter-trot-canter transitions. Ask for a transition to the trot and at the moment that your horse steps into the the trot, immediately ride shoulder-in for a few strides. Then straighten him and ask for the canter depart again.

SHOULDER-OUT

When schooling, you can do an exercise that is the mirror-image of shoulder-in. (I say "when schooling" because it is not used in competition.) I call this exercise **shoulder-out**, and I use it when I want to engage my horse's outside hind leg. For example, I might decide to do a shoulder-out prior to a canter depart if I have a horse that consistently picks up the wrong

17.22 To prepare to do shoulder-out, Amy first rides parallel to the long side on a line that is about three feet in from the track. She does this so that Brie has room to move her shoulders over.

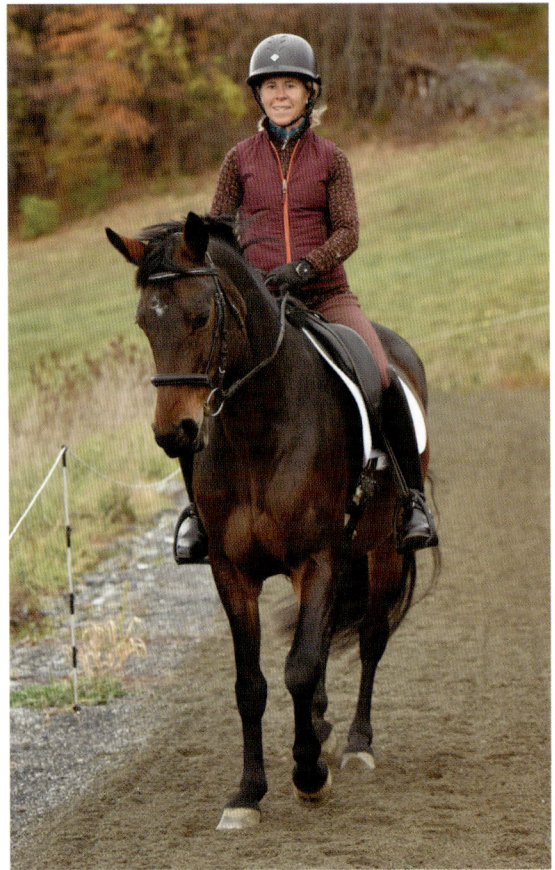

17.23 Next, she bends Brie around her leg that is closest to the rail. Finally, she brings Brie's forehand toward the outside of the ring by moving both of her hands in that direction.

lead because his outside hind leg—the strike off leg—is not engaged. I'll do shoulder-out to help activate that leg.

All of the same principals as well as the suppling and engaging benefits of shoulder-in apply to shoulder-out. It can be done only in the walk and the trot.

To do a shoulder-out, first ride your horse straight down a line that is slightly to the inside of the track around the ring. You need to do this so you'll have room to move your horse's forehand toward the rail (figs. 17.22 and 17.23). If you are riding to the left and you want to ride shoulder-out, flex your horse to the right and bend him around your right leg. Your weight is on your right seatbone. Your left rein supports; your left leg behind the girth helps bend your horse around your right leg. Both of your hands move to the right to lead your horse's shoulders in that direction.

HAUNCHES-IN

Haunches-in (also known as **travers**) is another exercise that you can do to help supple your horse and improve his balance and self-carriage. Doing haunches-in improves the mobility of the haunches by stretching and loosening the muscles and ligaments of the hindquarters. It also checks a horse's obedience to your outside leg. Haunches-in can be done in all three paces, and it can be performed on both straight and curved lines.

Once you know how to ride a shoulder-in, doing a haunches-in should be simple for you. Here's why. Remember when I told you to think of shoulder-in as the first step of a circle that is repeated on a straight line (p. 305)? Well, you can think of haunches-in as the last step of a circle repeated on a straight line. If you imagine the arc of a circle where it touches the track, you can see that shoulder-in and haunches-in are close relatives (fig. 17.24). If you ride a small circle and don't finish it by one stride, but instead keep the bend you have on the circle while sending your horse forward on a straight line, you have a haunches-in.

DESCRIPTION

Haunches-in is a lateral movement in which the horse is slightly bent around your inside leg. Specifically, when tracking to the left, your horse is bent around your left leg. His front legs stay on the original track of the long side and his hindquarters are brought in off the track

toward the center of the ring at about a 30-degree angle to the rail. His outside legs pass and cross in front of his inside legs and he looks in the direction he's moving.

With the horse's hind legs shifted toward the inside of the ring at a 30-degree angle from the rail, his outside hind leg is lined up directly behind his inside foreleg. So if you stand in front of a horse as he comes towards you in haunches-in, you see three tracks (fig. 17.25).

17.24 The horse's position in haunches-in.

17.25 Haunches-in showing a clear bend from poll to tail around Joy's inside leg. Wilkinson's outside hind leg is lined up directly behind his inside foreleg so only three tracks are visible.

THE AIDS FOR HAUNCHES-IN

The following are the aids for haunches-in when tracking to the left:

1. **Seat:** weight on left seatbone. Because your outside leg is behind the girth asking your horse's hindquarters to move over, it's easy for you to end up leaning to the right with your whole upper body. Concentrate on keeping your weight over your inside leg by visualizing moving your right seatbone toward the middle of the saddle.

2. **Left leg:** on the girth for the horse to bend around as well as to ask for engagement of his inside hind leg. Feel your horse's rib cage softly yielding away from your inside leg rather than bulging or leaning against it.

3. **Right leg:** behind the girth to help bend the horse around your inside leg and to take his hindquarters away from the rail.

4. **Left rein:** vibrate for inside flexion.

5. **Right rein:** steady and supporting to prevent too much bend in the neck.

6. **Both reins:** hold your horse's forehand on the track but the outside one is dominant and is supported by the inside rein.

Some people are reluctant to introduce haunches-in because they have spent a lot of time straightening their horses who like to carry their hindquarters to the inside naturally. They are concerned that if they ask the hindquarters to come in, they'll be encouraging this form of crookedness.

I have two thoughts on this subject. The first has to do with obedience: there's a world of difference between asking your horse to move sideways from a specific aid and letting your

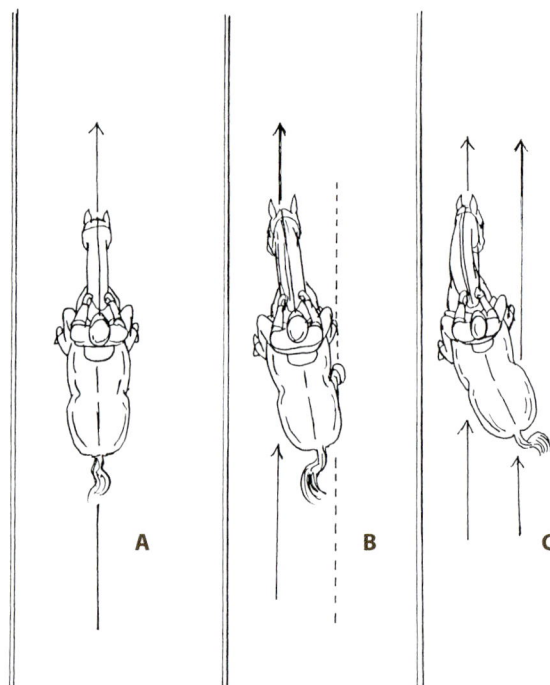

17.26 Haunches-in: traveling straight correctly, using both hind legs equally (A); traveling crooked on two tracks to avoid carrying weight behind equally (B); traveling on two tracks doing a correct haunches-in with bend through the horse's body (C).

horse take the initiative to move his hindquarters over. The other vital distinction is that during haunches-in, your horse is asked to bend through his entire body, thus making him engage his hindquarters. The crooked horse described above doesn't bend at all. His hindquarters are just drifting to the inside of the ring so he can avoid bending the joints of his inside hind leg (fig. 17.26).

SEQUENCE OF AIDS

You'll base your decision about whether to start haunches-in at the walk or the trot by using the same criteria that you did for starting shoulder-in. Specifically, if your horse maintains the regularity of his rhythm, stays in front of your leg, and seems calm, start in the walk because you'll have more time to get organized and think about how to coordinate your aids. If the walk isn't "**safe,**" start in the trot.

As with shoulder-in, be sure to ask for the bend before you ask for the angle. Otherwise, all you'll end up with is a leg-yield instead of a haunches-in. First, ask for bend in a corner. If your horse doesn't bend easily, stay on a small circle in the corner until he does. In your mind, run through the bending aids while on the circle as you did for the shoulder-in. Think about improving the bend by "embracing" or "enveloping" your horse's barrel with both of your legs. Feel the contact of your legs on your horse's sides all the way down to your ankles so you can "wrap him up" in between your legs.

Since I suggested that you picture doing a

haunches-in from the last step of a small circle before it intersects with the track, apply the "angle" aids just before you finish a corner or a circle. Add the angle by increasing the pressure of your outside leg and leading your horse's shoulders to the rail with an opening outside rein. This way you'll prevent the hindquarters from completing the entire turn as you start down the long side, thus doing a haunches-in.

While you're doing this, be sure to maintain flexion and bend to the inside. Look straight down the track.

HELPFUL HINTS FOR HAUNCHES-IN

MAINTAINING RHYTHM AND TEMPO

Sometimes when you introduce haunches-in, a horse loses his impulsion or his rhythm. He might also become worried and show his anxiety either by rushing off or "sucking" back. As in shoulder-in, any of these problems can occur because he's not yet supple or strong enough to cope with the increased engagement of his hind legs. If you feel him struggling either physically or mentally, decrease the difficulty of the movement by modifying it in the same way that you did for the shoulder-in:

1. Ask for less angle.

2. Ride only a few steps, then renew your horse's desire to go forward by turning onto a circle or by doing a few steps of a lengthening. Once he's "thinking" forward, ask for a few steps of haunches-in again.

3. Ride haunches-in in the walk as long as the quality of his walk doesn't suffer.

MAINTAINING BEND

It's absolutely vital that your horse stays bent during haunches-in. Otherwise, rather than riding an engagement exercise, you'll simply be riding a crooked horse whose hindquarters have drifted to the inside to avoid engagement.

If your horse resists being bent correctly when you start a haunches-in, circle first. Then, only do a few steps of haunches-in and quickly melt back onto a small circle before he loses his bend. It's better to do a couple of high-quality steps than to overface your horse and end up with many strides of a leg-yield. As your horse becomes more supple, you can gradually increase the number of haunches-in steps.

Another way that your horse can lose his bend is if you allow his front legs to deviate from pointing straight ahead up the track. Proper coordination of the two reins (the steady outside rein, which functions as a slight opening rein and leads the forehand toward the rail, and the vibrating inside rein, which supports this position) as well as a firm inside leg will keep his front legs traveling in the right direction.

While on a straight line, your horse's front legs should travel straight forward parallel to the rail, while his hindquarters are displaced onto an inside track. If his forehand starts to point toward the fence, it means he's losing the bend. Once the bend is lost, the exercise becomes a leg-yield.

So one way for you to determine that you're maintaining bend is to make sure that the position of your horse's front legs during a haunches-in is exactly the same as it is when you ride straight down the track—parallel to the fence.

In your mind's eye, hold the image of his front feet pointing straight down the track like a car's headlights that are lighting your way. If the headlights are misaligned, they'll point out toward the rail and they won't help you see your way straight ahead (fig. 17.27).

17.27 As you ask your horse's haunches to move toward the inside of the ring, make sure you maintain bend by keeping his front end pointed straight ahead, parallel to the rail. Imagine he has miners' lamps on his knees, and they shine straight forward.

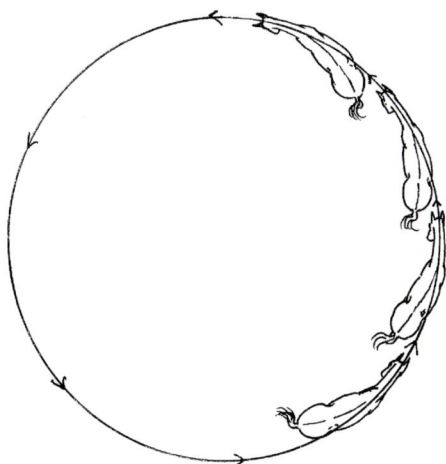

17.28 Haunches-in on a circle follows the same rules as haunches-in on a straight line. Specifically, the forehand stays exactly on the line of travel. The hind legs move to the inside to make a slightly smaller circle.

"At an angle greater than 30 degrees, it's difficult for a horse to bend."

• • • • •

You do a haunches-in on a circle in the same way as on a straight line. Your horse's front legs stay on the track of the circle, and his hindquarters are moved to the inside to make a slightly smaller circle. If his forehand starts pointing to the outside of the circle, the bend is lost, and, once again, you'll end up just doing a leg-yield (fig. 17.28).

I frequently see situations where a rider causes the loss of bend because she asks her horse to move his hindquarters over at too great an angle to the rail. She uses too much outside leg and she pushes her horse's hindquarters too far to the inside. At an angle greater than 30 degrees, it's difficult for a horse to bend and his only option is to straighten his body and do a leg-yield.

I'm not sure why this is such a common problem but I'm suspicious that the reason is that the rider can't see how far she's bringing her horse's hindquarters in from the rail when doing a haunches-in. She therefore tends to ask for more angle than she needs. It's easier to do a shoulder-in because all you have to do is look down at your horse's forehand to see the angle at which the shoulders are brought in off the track.

MAINTAINING THE ANGLE

Some people find it difficult to move their horse's hindquarters in with enough angle. Be sure you're not part of the problem. Remember that your horse's front legs should be on the track parallel to the fence. He should be slightly bent and flexed toward the inside of the ring. I say "slightly" because many riders crank their horses' forehands too much to the inside of the ring in an effort to keep them bent and, as a result, only the horse's barrel is left on the track. But by bringing the front end in off the track so much, it becomes impossible for the back end to come in at the required 30-degree angle away from the rail. After all, your horse's body isn't a pretzel!

However, as I mentioned above, a more likely scenario is that you ask for too much angle because you can't see where the hindquarters are. Sometimes you are too strong with your outside leg. Other times your horse sees an escape route from engaging his hind legs, and he happily swings his hindquarters in too far. Remember that if there's too much angle, you'll probably lose the bend and the purpose of the haunches-in is lost. Make sure your horse stays on three tracks with his inside fore and outside hind on the same track so that his hindquarters are at an angle of approximately 30 degrees away from the rail.

Use a person on the ground or a mirror to help you to learn this feeling of the correct angle. Remember this isn't a huge shifting of his hindquarters. Lining up the outside hind leg behind the inside foreleg is merely the displacement of a few inches. If you tend to ask for too much angle, compensate by underriding it. It's better to bend your horse and perhaps not have enough angle than to lose the bend by asking for too much angle and end up with a leg-yield.

FURTHER USES OF HAUNCHES-IN

Controlling the Hindquarters in Shoulder-In

Since the rider's outside leg must be behind the girth during haunches-in, I use this movement as a way to teach

17.29 To learn the feeling of controlling your horse's hindquarters with your outside leg during shoulder-in, alternate between a few steps of haunches-in and a few steps of shoulder-in.

her how to prevent the horse's hindquarters from swinging out when she's riding a shoulder-in. I ask the rider to alternate between a few steps of haunches-in and a few steps of shoulder-in without straightening her horse in between. Because her outside leg is clearly positioned behind the girth in haunches-in, she just keeps it in that exact same spot as she slides into shoulder-in. The bending aids are exactly the same in both movements. The difference is whether the front end or the back end of her horse is displaced off the track (fig. 17.29).

Developing Self-Carriage in the Canter

I often use haunches-in in the walk for horses that have a tendency to get strung out, fall on the forehand, and lose their self-carriage after a few strides of canter. Since the walk and canter are very closely related, I can often help the canter through good walk work. However, even though my objective is to improve the canter with this work, I make a special point of preserving the rhythm of the walk, which can be lost if you're not careful.

For horses with **"safe" walks** who always stay active and in a regular rhythm, you can proceed with the exercise in the following way. After warming up, walk around the ring in haunches-in. Stay in that position through the corners and the short sides until it feels "easy." (It's easy when you don't have to work hard to keep the bend.) You should almost feel as if your horse is bending all by himself. In fact, you should be able to soften by relaxing the tension on your inside rein and have your

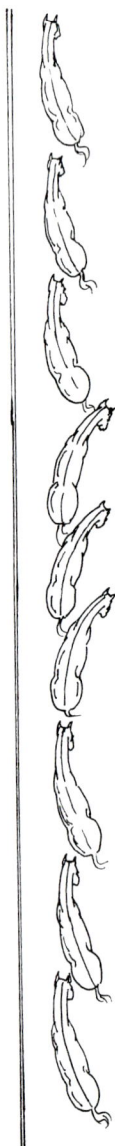

17.30 To improve self-carriage in the canter, ride haunches-in at the walk on a small circle. Arc out onto a larger circle, straighten, and do a transition from walk to canter. Canter a few strides, and before your horse loses his balance again, walk and resume the haunches-in position.

horse feel as if he'll stay bent without you having to hold him in position. When this happens, it'll feel as if your horse has gathered himself together and the contact will feel much lighter. Obviously, this should be done only with horses who are experienced and comfortable with haunches-in.

Once you have accomplished these "feelings" as you ride down the long side in haunches-in, try turning on to a small circle here and there while still riding haunches-in. Place your horse's front legs on the track of your circle and move his hind legs toward the inside so that they make a smaller circle than the front legs do. The addition of the circle makes the exercise more demanding than by just doing it the whole way around your ring.

Finally, when your horse feels very soft in haunches-in on this small circle at the walk, it's time to try the canter. While still in the walk, arc out onto a larger circle. Straighten him along the arc of that circle and do a normal walk-to-canter transition. Canter for just a few strides. Then, before he falls on his forehand and his balance degenerates again (sometimes it takes only five or six strides), walk and resume the haunches-in position. In this way, your horse learns to carry himself in the canter a few strides at a time (fig. 17.30).

HAUNCHES-OUT

Just as shoulder-out is the mirror image of shoulder-in, **haunches-out** (also known as **renvers**) is the mirror image of haunches-in. Consequently, it provides the same loosening, suppling and engaging benefits as the haunches-in.

To do haunches-out when tracking to the left, flex your horse to the right and bend him around your right leg. While his hind feet remain on the track, bring his forehand onto an inside track at about a 30-degree angle from the rail (fig. 17.31).

At this angle, your horse is on three tracks. Specifically, when tracking to the left, one track is made by the outside hind leg, the second track is made by the inside hind leg lined up directly behind the outside foreleg, and the third track is made by the inside foreleg. All of the same principles of haunches-in apply to haunches-out (fig. 17.32).

17.31 Haunches-out: Wilkinson is bent from poll to tail around Joy's left leg. This was her outside leg when she was traveling on a straight line, but now that she has bent her horse around it, it has become her inside leg. (Remember, "inside" and "outside" is determined by the bend of the horse—not by where the rail is.) Once her horse is bent, Joy moves Wilkinson's forehand about 30 degrees away from the rail. Since the horse's left hind leg is hidden behind his right front leg and we can only see three legs, Wilkinson is on three tracks.

17.32 The horse's position in haunches-out.

KEY POINTS

- The more advanced lateral movements are distinguished from the easier lateral movements (turn on the forehand and leg- yielding) because the horse is bent through his body as he moves sideways.

- Think of this formula when you ride these lateral movements: Bend + Sideways = Engagement.

- Shoulder-in supples, straightens, and improves self-carriage. Think of shoulder-in as the first step of a small circle that is repeated (maintaining the bend) along the straight line of the track.

- Haunches-in supples and improves self-carriage. Think of haunches-in as the last step of a small circle just before it joins the track that is repeated (maintaining the bend) along the straight line of the track.

18

Advanced

LATERAL MOVEMENTS

HALF-PASS

DESCRIPTION

With haunches-in firmly in your repertoire, it should be fairly easy for you to do a **half-pass**. I find it puzzling when a rider tells me that her horse can do a good shoulder-in and a good haunches-in but he can't do a half-pass yet. If a horse can do haunches-in, he can certainly do a half-pass, because this lateral movement is simply haunches-in done on a diagonal line across the arena instead of along a straight line or on a circle.

Half-pass is a lateral movement along a diagonal line in which your horse is slightly bent around your inside leg and his body is parallel to the fence, with his forehand slightly in advance of his hindquarters. His outside legs pass and cross in front of his inside legs, and he looks in the direction of movement (figs. 18.1 to 18.5).

You're already familiar with this idea of going forward and sideways along a diagonal line from the work you've done with leg-yielding. But what makes a half-pass so much more difficult

18.1 The horse's position in half-pass.

than a leg-yield is that you're now asking your horse to go sideways while he's bent around your inside leg. This bend makes the movement much more demanding.

You can do half-passes in all three paces to supple your horse, improve his self-carriage and lighten his forehand so that he can "dance" with greater fluency and grace.

PLACES AND PATTERNS FOR THE HALF-PASS

When you're in a large arena, you can do a half-pass from the long side to the center of your arena, from the centerline to the long side, or all the way across the diagonal. (See chapter 22 for arena charts.) Be sure that you do half-passes from, and to, specific points so that you work both hind legs equally.

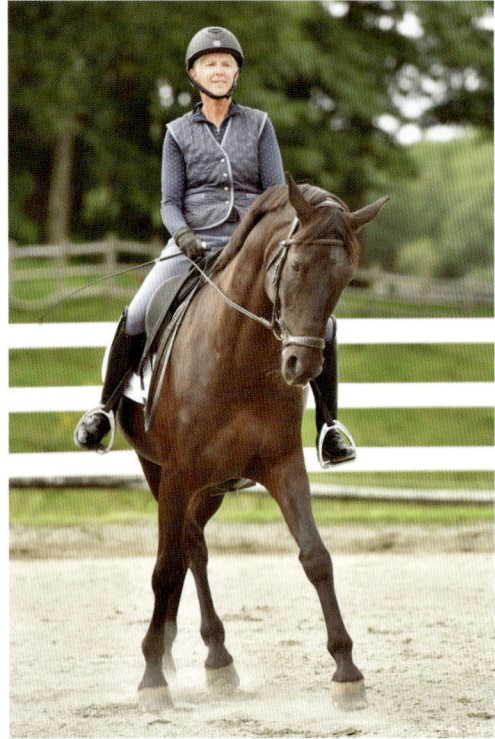

18.2–18.5 A half-pass sequence from the beginning of the long side to the centerline: in this half-pass to the left, Deborah (Deb) Dean-Smith bends Furstenten (Fursty) around her left leg. Fursty's body is basically parallel to the long side, but his forehand is slightly in advance of his hindquarters. His outside (right) legs cross in front of his inside legs and he looks in the direction he's going.

THE AIDS FOR THE HALF-PASS

The faids for a half-pass to the left are as follows:

1. **Seat:** weight on the left seat bone.

2. **Left leg:** on the girth for bend through the body, impulsion, and engagement of the inside hind leg.

3. **Right leg:** behind the girth to help bend the horse around the inside left leg and to initiate movement sideways.

4. **Left rein:** vibrate for inside flexion.

5. **Right rein:** vibrate for flexion.

Note: the left rein and left leg are responsible for maintaining the bend. The right leg supported by the right rein is responsible for the degree of sideways movement.

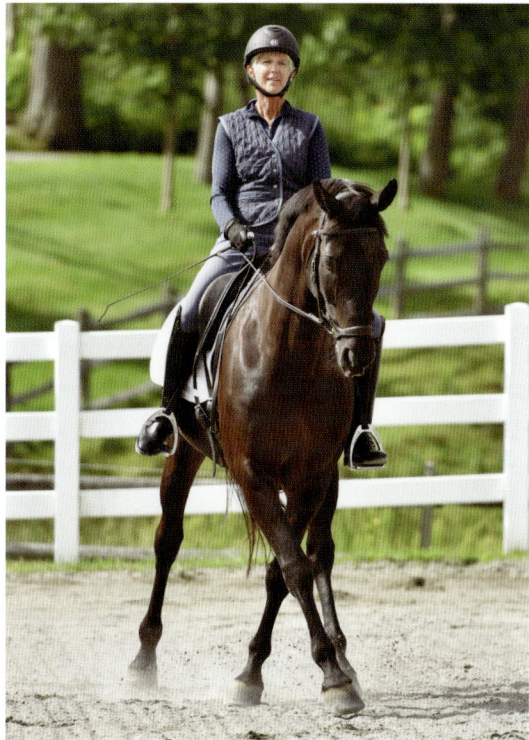

For our purposes we will limit the angle of the line you ride sideways to approximately 22 degrees from the rail. In a large arena (fig 18.6), for example, this angle would take you from the letter marked D, over to E; or E, over to G. It's also the angle that would be made if you did a half-pass along the entire diagonal from M to K or from H to F.

(More advanced horses in dressage competition are hardly ever asked to exceed a 30-degree angle, while at the highest level, the Grand Prix, the maximum angle required is 40 degrees.)

SEQUENCE OF AIDS

First, ride a small circle in the corner as you did before beginning a shoulder-in or haunches-in (see fig. 18.12). Next, upon leaving the circle, do a step or two of **shoulder-fore** to ensure that

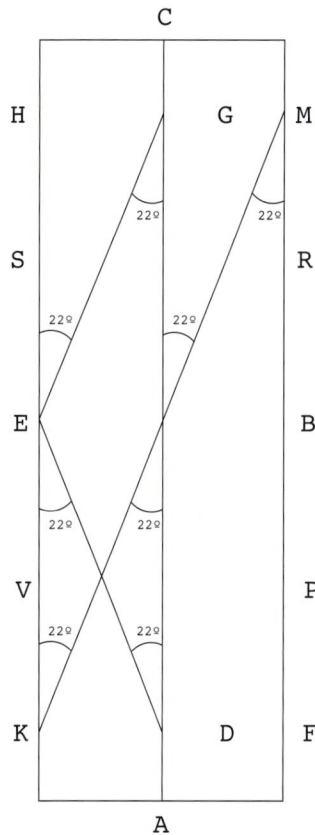

18.6 Some of the lines—with 22-degree angles to other lines—on which you can ride a half-pass.

your horse's shoulders will be slightly in advance of his hindquarters when you start going sideways. Then, initiate sideways movement by "stepping down" into the inside (left) stirrup and using your outside aids. One way for you to learn this feeling of "stepping down" in the direction of the half-pass is to imagine that you want to shift the saddle over to the left side of your horse's back.

There is another school of thought that recommends starting the half-pass without doing the step or two of shoulder-fore. Instead, teach your horse how to do the half-pass by first turning straight onto the diagonal line for a few strides. Then, keeping the forehand on the diagonal line, ask for a haunches-in. This is the half-pass.

The reasoning behind this different approach is that in shoulder-fore, the horse's inside front leg has to cross over and in front of his outside front leg. However, in a half-pass he does the opposite. His outside front leg crosses over and in front of the inside front leg. This change in the way the legs move can cause a loss of rhythm and impulsion.

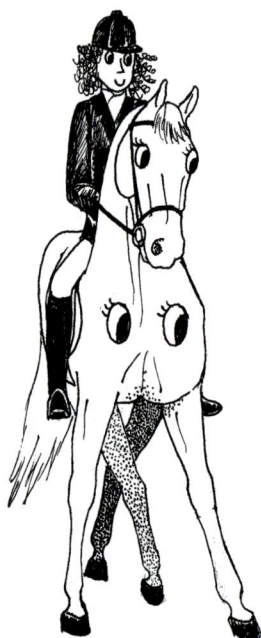

18.7 To help with the bend during the half-pass, pretend your horse has eyes in front of his shoulders, and make them "look" at the specific point you are riding toward.

I suggest that you try both methods to see which approach is easiest for your horse. In either case, while you're applying the aids, do some imaging to help ensure the correct bend and positioning of your horse's forehand. Pretend he has eyes in the front of his shoulders and make him "look" at the specific point that you're riding toward (fig. 18.7).

✳ HELPFUL HINTS

MAINTAINING IMPULSION

Some horses lose impulsion during a half-pass because their riders try to push them sideways too much. If this is what you tend to do, think of riding the movement "forward and sideways" rather than "sideways and forward." This idea, plus an active inside leg and a light, non-restrictive inside rein, will help you to maintain his activity. If your horse still struggles and feels like he's losing power, do only a few steps of half-pass and then ride him straight forward or onto a circle to renew the impulsion.

You can also help maintain impulsion by asking for less engagement. One way to do this is to decrease the bend. Another way is by going more forward and less sideways, so that rather than going from D on the centerline over to E, (or B), go from D over to S (or R). Either of these options will reduce the required amount of engagement. Then, when your horse becomes stronger and is able to maintain his impulsion, gradually increase the bend or resume going more sideways.

It can also be difficult for your horse to go forward and sideways fluidly and with energy if you lose your own balance by getting left behind the movement. This is happening if you notice that you are leaning to the right as your horse moves to the left. You might feel like you are getting left behind, and you've probably experienced this sensation before. Remember when you were first learning how to post to the trot? You most likely fell behind your horse's movement a lot. But then you got used to the forward momentum, and as you became more balanced, you were able to "go with" your horse's motion. In the half-pass, you need to "go with" your horse's motion when he's going sideways and forward, too.

In order to help you with this problem in the half-pass, try to place your body weight in the direction of movement. Visualize moving your outside seat bone more toward the center of your saddle. Or, practice sitting in the direction of the half-pass by doing the following exercise. You'll need a friend or instructor to help you.

Since you're doing a half-pass to the left, your helper should stand on your left. While sitting on your horse, close your eyes and without warning have your helper grab your belt on the left side of your waist and pull your body toward her. Have her do this several times until you memorize this feeling of moving your body over to the left. Then start a half-pass and recreate the feeling of being pulled sideways so that you can counteract the effects of getting left behind.

You can also end up getting left behind the movement if you use too much outside leg to send your horse sideways. When you use this leg too strongly, your body will be pulled to the outside. Don't fall into this trap of using your outside leg too hard, too often, or too far back on your horse's side. If your horse doesn't move away from your outside leg readily, try a "wake-up call." Give one good kick, or tap him with the whip, in a way that sends him sideways rather than forward. Then, expect him to go eagerly sideways from a polite leg. If he doesn't, repeat your warning until he believes you and obediently moves away from your leg when it's applied lightly behind the girth.

MAINTAINING THE TEMPO

Many riders find that their horse's **tempo** changes when they introduce the half-pass. The first thing you should do is check that the tempo is good before you even start. Keep in mind that tempo is controlled by your seat. Your horse should adjust his tempo to match the one designated by your seat; you should not succumb to the tempo that he offers.

So, if your horse goes faster, you can steady the tempo by tightening your stomach muscles. This action causes your seat to have a non-following, retarding effect.

If the horse gets slower during the half-pass, speed up the tempo by quickening the action of your seat. Do this by moving your seat faster than the tempo that your horse is going.

I haven't mentioned this "speeding up of tempo" with the seat before, because I don't want you to get into the habit of driving with your seat every stride. You'll end up on the same dead-end street as you will by using your legs constantly, where you do a lot of work and your horse soon gets dull to your aids. When you quicken the action of your seat in the half-pass, do it briefly to speed up your horse's tempo. Then go back to sitting quietly and in harmony with your horse at his new and improved tempo. If the tempo doesn't improve as a result of a brief increase or decrease in the action of your seat, try decreasing the angle of the half-pass, or do the half-pass in posting trot, until the tempo can be maintained easily.

MAINTAINING THE BEND

The most common fault that I see riders make when riding a half-pass is that their horses lose the bend. And without bend, the half-pass becomes a leg-yield. Usually a horse loses his bend in an effort to avoid the difficulty of the movement. When your horse has lost his bend, it's advisable to use the same exercise as you do when training shoulder-in and haunches-in. Do a couple of good steps of half-pass, arc onto a circle to renew your horse's bend, and then continue in half-pass for a couple more good steps. This is infinitely preferable to doing many more steps without bend.

It's also possible to lose the bend if your horse's front end isn't facing toward a specific spot. Place your horse's entire forehand so that it's positioned toward the place you're riding to and stick to it. You need to do this because if his front feet are not pointed exactly where you're

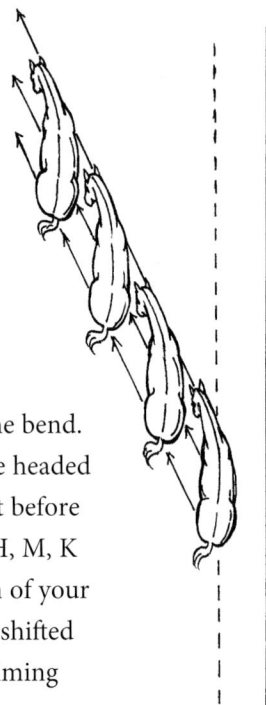

18.8 If you have trouble with your horse's positioning during a half-pass, think of the movement as a haunches-in on a diagonal line.

headed, you've lost the bend. For example, if you're headed toward the letters just before the corners, such as H, M, K or F, and the position of your horse's front feet has shifted so that they're now aiming directly toward the corner itself, or even toward the short end of the ring, it's a sure sign that the bend has been lost.

To help a student absorb this concept, I explain that a half-pass should be thought of as a haunches-in ridden on a diagonal line instead of a straight line. To emphasize my point, I first have her ride haunches-in along the rail. Once she gets comfortable with the aids and familiar with her horse's positioning along this straight line during a haunches-in, I tell her to imagine that she's working in a triangle instead of a rectangle.

All she has to do is ride haunches-in along the longest side of the triangle (the diagonal line) as easily as she rode haunches-in along the track by the rail. This is the half-pass. It's important, as I said earlier, to remember that the horse's front feet and ears must remain pointed at the exact spot he's headed toward (fig. 18.8).

PREVENTING LOSS OF ENGAGEMENT

For a half-pass to be effective, your horse must engage his hind legs. Often, it's not that easy to tell if your horse has escaped this engagement. A good test of engagement is to check if you could leave the half-pass and ride straight ahead parallel to the long side in a shoulder-in.

For example, do a few steps of half-pass across the diagonal, ride a few steps of shoulder-in, and then go back to half-pass again. Initiate the transition to shoulder-in by increasing the influence of your inside leg and driving your horse's inside hind leg toward your outside rein. Concentrate on the transition into the shoulder-in, and ask yourself if it's easy for you to go from one movement to the other. The answer to that question tells you whether your horse has maintained the engagement of his inside hind leg during the half-pass or merely stepped sideways as he would in a leg-yield.

He can escape this engagement if you don't keep him correctly positioned in relation to the rail on the long side. This correct alignment of your horse's body in a half-pass dictates that his bent body is basically parallel to the rail but his forehand is ever so slightly in advance of his hindquarters. If you find your horse's hindquarters either leading or trailing rather than being

positioned just slightly behind his forehand, that means there is insufficient engagement of his inside hind leg (figs. 18.9 to 18.13).

If your horse's hindquarters tend to lead, it's vital that you set him up with a step or two of shoulder-fore before you start the half-pass. Then take care not to push too much with your outside leg as you start moving sideways.

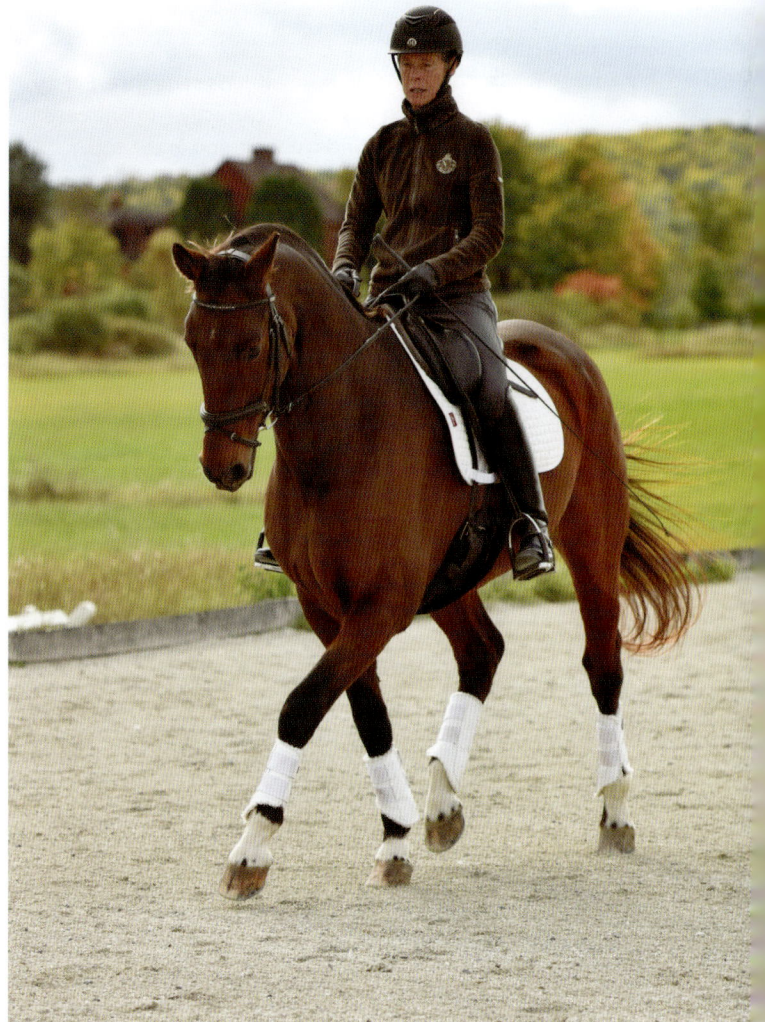

18.9 A half-pass showing correct alignment of Wilkinson's body. He is almost parallel to the long side of the arena and his forehand is ever so slightly in front of his hindquarters. This position encourages good engagement of the hindquarters—the purpose of the movement.

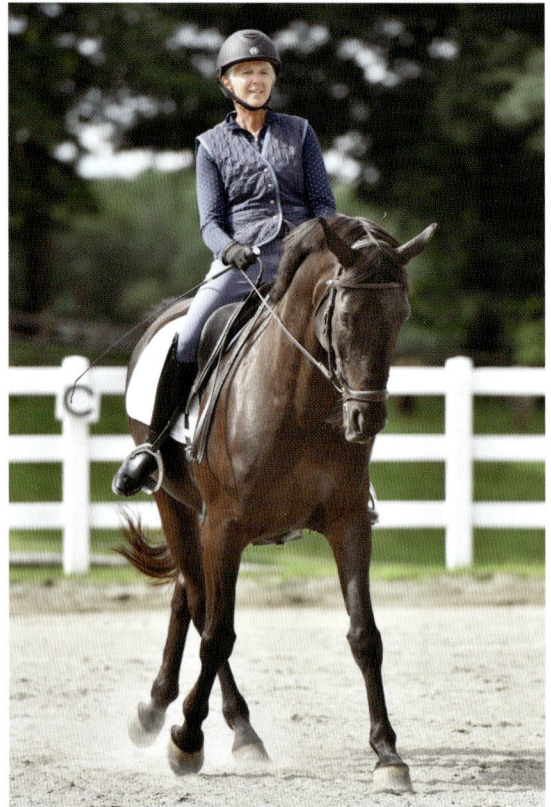

18.10 & 18.11 In this half-pass sequence, Fursty has not been positioned correctly—in one case he is overbent and crooked, and in the other, his hindquarters are trailing too far behind his forehand.

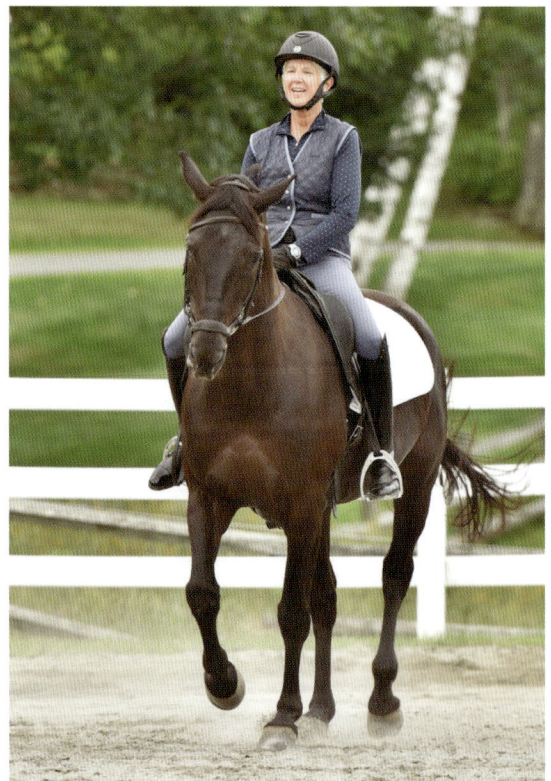

18.12 & 18.13 In this half-pass sequence, Fursty's haunches are leading because Deb has used too much outside leg. If the haunches are trailing or leading, there is insufficient engagement of the inside hind leg—the reason for the exercise.

If your horse prefers to trail his haunches behind his forehand, or his forehand gets too much in advance of his hindquarters, realign both ends of his body. Use a slight opening outside rein to hold his shoulders back and close your outside leg behind the girth to send his hindquarters over. As you work on the correct alignment of your horse's body, you'll probably notice that if he tends to trail with his hindquarters when going to the left, he'll probably want to lead with them when he goes to the right.

CORRECTION FOR A "TOO-MUCH-SIDEWAYS" HALF-PASS

If a horse doesn't go sideways to the proper degree, which is an angle of approximately 22 degrees (see diagram on p. 330), he can't be using his inside hind leg correctly. If he goes more sideways than forward at an angle much greater than 22 degrees from the rail, it means he's not listening to your inside leg—the leg that is responsible for the bend as well as sending him forward. By stepping sideways too much, he can avoid closing the joints of, and engaging, his inside hind leg. To be engaged, your horse must step under *and forward* with his inside hind leg. Focus on this leg and picture it stepping forward toward your inside hand with each step.

CORRECTION FOR A "TOO-LITTLE-SIDE WAYS" HALF-PASS

On the other hand, if your horse goes forward too much and doesn't cover enough ground sideways, he's also escaping engagement. When you first train your horse to do half-passes, an angle of less than 22 degrees from the rail or the centerline is fine. You can do it as a preliminary exercise to give your horse the idea of going sideways with bend, but eventually you want to make the angle sideways more sharp so that he travels at about a 22-degree angle to the rail.

Here's an image to hold in your mind's eye if you're having difficulty moving sideways at the proper angle. Pretend there's a magnet on the fence and your horse's body is made of iron. You are being drawn inexorably toward the fence by the force of the magnetic attraction (fig. 18.14).

You also need to be sure that your horse bends the same and goes sideways at the same angle to the fence in both directions. When his

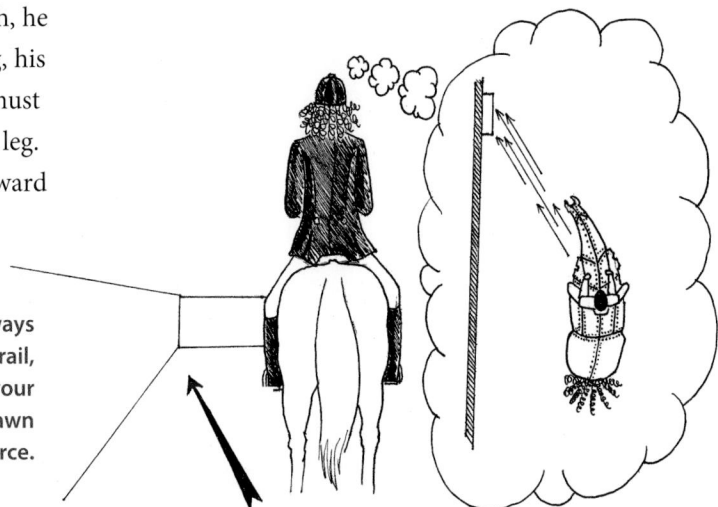

18.14 If you have trouble going sideways in half-pass at a 22-degree angle to the rail, visualize a magnet on the fence and your horse made of iron! Your horse will be drawn toward it by magnetic force.

hollow side is on the inside, it's easier for him to bend and he'll probably want to go too much sideways. However, when his stiff side is on the inside, it's more difficult to go sideways with enough bend. In order to be certain that you're always doing half-passes the same in both directions, check your bend and be sure to ride from and to specific points.

FURTHER USES OF THE HALF-PASS

I like to use the half-pass to point out to the rider just how much she can influence the various parts of her horse's body with her aids. I use it as an exercise to help her develop the ability to influence her horse's shoulders.

To do this, I'll have her start a half-pass and take both of her hands in the direction of the movement to guide her horse's forehand over. Next, while maintaining bend and sideways movement, I'll have her move both arms slightly away from the direction they are traveling. This will slow her horse's shoulders down. I'll once again have her put both hands in the direction of the half-pass to allow his front legs to go in advance. By doing this several times as she works her way across the arena in half-pass, she gets a chance to practice using the reins to control the position of her horse's shoulders—either allowing them to advance or slowing them down.

I have one caveat for you here, though. The exercise I just gave you is a wonderful rider exercise, but it's not necessarily a great exercise for the horse. This is because the ultimate purpose of a half-pass is to increase self-carriage. If you carry your hands away from the direction of movement for many strides, (that is, you move your hands to the right in a left half-pass), you'll succeed in bending your horse okay, but you'll lose self-carriage and put him on his forehand. Other than a stride here and there, your inside hand should remain in front of your inside hip and your outside rein should come toward your horse's neck so that both hands guide him over by moving in the direction of the half-pass.

I also like to use half-passes to help horses learn how to do clean flying changes. I'll explain how to do this in chapter 20.

TURN ON THE HAUNCHES

Another distant cousin to shoulder-in is the **turn on the haunches.** It's actually a closer relative to haunches-in. In fact, a haunches-in on a small circle is one of the exercises that I do to introduce the concept of the turn on the haunches to both horse and rider.

DESCRIPTION

The turn on the haunches is a 180-degree turn executed at a walk (fig. 18.15). The horse is bent in the direction of the turn and his forehand moves around his hindquarters until he is facing in the opposite direction. His forefeet and his outside hind foot move around his inside hind foot, which forms a pivot. As with all of the movements in the walk, care must be taken that the regularity of the rhythm is maintained. Even

18.15 The first steps of a turn on the haunches to the left.

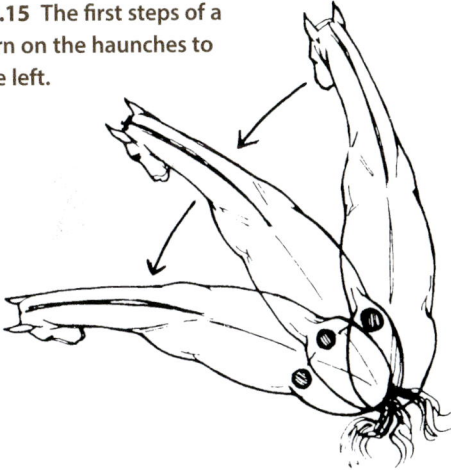

18.16 Deb prepares for a turn on the haunches to the left by shortening Fursty's stride while maintaining a clear four-beat walk. She also flexes him slightly to the left in preparation for the turn.

though it forms the pivotal point of the turn, the inside hind leg must be picked up and returned to a spot slightly in front of where it left the ground (figs. 18.16 to 18.22).

The turn on the haunches engages a horse's hindquarters and encourages good flexion of these joints. Earlier, I told you that when you execute a shoulder-in correctly, the end result is that your horse's body feels more packaged at the finish than when you started. The same holds true for a turn on the haunches.

In order to enhance your aids with an image, as you turn, picture your horse's hind legs stepping more underneath your seat and his body becoming a more compact package from poll to tail. As you ride each step of the turn, visualize the joints of your horse's hind legs bending as if he were doing some deep knee bends (fig. 18.23).

The turn on the haunches is also used as a safe way to introduce a walk pirouette to a horse who will later on be asked to do this

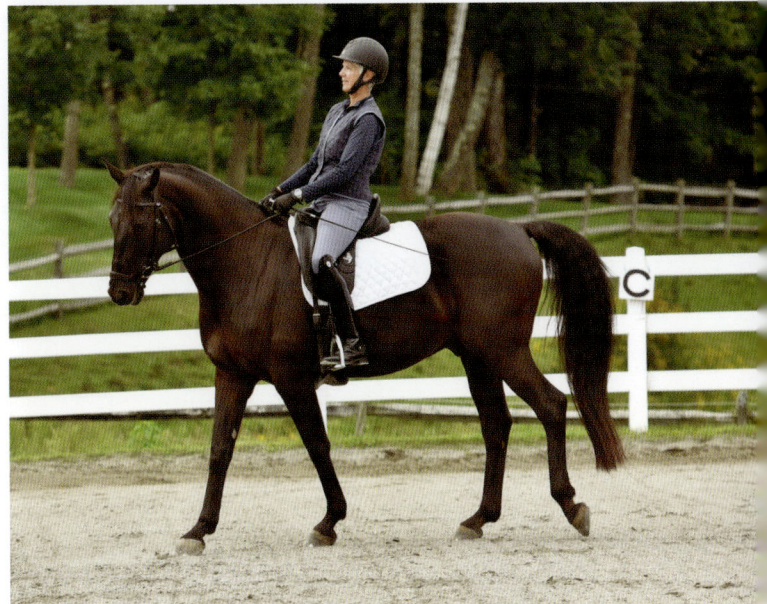

18.17 Deb starts the turn by putting her weight on her left seat bone, keeping her left leg on the girth, her right leg slightly behind the girth, and moving both hands to the left to lead Fursty's forehand around his hindquarters.

18.18–18.21 Deb keeps her horse nicely bent around her inside leg throughout the turn around the inside hind leg.

18.22 This well-executed turn on the haunches has improved Fursty's balance. His forehand is lighter, higher, and freer than before the turn. His poll is now the highest point and his nose is just slightly in front of the vertical.

THE AIDS FOR THE TURN ON THE HAUNCHES

The aids for a turn on the haunches to the left are as follows:

1. **Seat:** weight on the left seat bone.

2. **Left leg:** on the girth to promote bend through the body and engagement of the inside hind leg.

3. **Right leg:** place behind the girth to help bend the horse around the inside leg and to prevent his hindquarters from swinging out.

4. **Left rein:** vibrate for flexion.

5. **Right rein:** steady and supporting to limit the amount of bend in the neck.

6. **Both hands:** move in the direction of the turn (to the left) to lead your horse's forehand around his hindquarters. Your hands should stay side by side and equidistant from your body. Your left rein is used as an opening or leading rein while your right rein is brought closer to the neck to guide your horse's forehand around.

18.23 The turn on the haunches encourages good flexion of the joints of the horse's hindquarters. In order to help him engage, visualize these joints bending as if he were doing some deep squats.

18.24 In a turn on the haunches, visualize your horse in a marching band, his hind legs working like pistons in the regular rhythm of the walk.

more advanced movement. This is because the turn on the haunches has all the good qualities of a walk pirouette (desire to go forward, bend, and rhythm) but is less demanding for a horse both physically and mentally. However, the turn on the haunches differs from a pirouette because it is done from a medium walk, which is just slightly shortened prior to the turn, rather than from a collected walk as in the pirouette. Plus, in a turn on the haunches, the horse's hind legs are allowed to describe a small circle (about the size of a dinner plate), while in a walk pirouette, the inside hind leg should be picked up and put down on the same spot—obviously a more difficult movement.

SEQUENCE OF AIDS

When you're ready to ride a turn on the haunches, give the aids in this order. First, prepare for the turn by shortening the length of your horse's stride in the walk with a retarding action of your seat—the "**stilled**" seat I have mentioned previously. Do this by stretching up tall and tightening your stomach muscles so your seat doesn't follow along with the longer steps. Make sure that you keep your legs on in order to maintain the activity of your horse's legs as you still your seat. Next, bend him to the inside. Then, set him up for the turn on the haunches by riding in a slight shoulder-fore position. Finally, bring both of your hands in the direction you want to turn in order to guide your horse's forehand around his hindquarters.

✳ HELPFUL HINTS

USING HAUNCHES-IN AS PREPARATION FOR TURNS ON THE HAUNCHES

Haunches-in on a small circle is a very useful preliminary exercise before doing turns on the haunches. Asking for a "competition-size" turn on the haunches right off the bat is difficult for your horse. As a result, you risk losing one or more of the Basics such as his desire to go forward, his bend, or his regular rhythm in the walk. However, if you introduce the idea of a turn on the haunches by doing haunches-in on a circle, you have a greater chance of preserving these basic qualities.

18.25 To prevent my horse from jigging when I shorten his walk to prepare for a turn on the haunches, I imagine that his feet are in molasses and that he has to slowly and deliberately pick them up out of the "goo."

MAINTAINING RHYTHM

During a turn on the haunches your horse must maintain the rhythm of his walk at all costs. His inside hind leg should step in that rhythm and never stay on the ground as a pivot. So use some good imaging to help you with this. "See" your horse's hind legs working like pistons as they go up and down in a regular rhythm. Or, visualize that your horse is in a marching band and those hind legs stay in a well-marked rhythm as you gently guide his forehand around (fig. 18.24).

REDUCING TENSION

I've worked with some horses that get extremely tense as soon as you begin to shorten their walks. They'll begin to jig, or even think about rearing. For these horses, I stay in the medium walk rather than trying to shorten it, and ride several small circles in haunches-in with many relaxing breaks in between each series of circles. Doing several circles gives these tense horses time to settle into their rhythm and to realize nothing terrible is going to happen to them. Over time, I'll decrease the size of the circle in direct proportion to the degree of my horse's relaxation. In my mind I prevent these horses from jigging by pretending their legs are in molasses, and that they have to slowly and deliberately pick those legs up out of the "goo" and put them back down again (fig. 18.25).

ADJUSTING THE SIZE OF THE TURN

As with all work you do with your horse, maintaining his desire to go forward is one of the priorities (regular rhythm being the most important). If he loses this desire during the turn on the haunches and feels like he might even step backward, try riding one or two steps around the turn, then close your legs and ride him straight forward for a couple of steps. Continue alternating even if you go 360 degrees or more around, until you feel that your horse is happy to react by immediately going forward at any point during the turn.

> *"The outside rein is the rein that defines the size of the turn."*

• • • • •

Although it's much less of a fault than losing energy or stepping backward, sometimes the turn will be too large because you haven't placed enough emphasis on your outside rein. The outside rein is the rein that defines the size of the turn. To make the turn tighter, close your outside hand in a fist and firmly support with it. Pick a definite spot in the arena and mark it with an imaginary "X." Visualize keeping your horse's hind legs marching up and down on that spot.

Sometimes the turn is too large and it seems to take forever to bring your horse's forehand completely around. Often this is caused because you're restricting his shoulders by using an indirect inside rein away from the direction of movement. Some people use this in an effort to maintain the bend, but this is wrong. If you're doing a turn on the haunches to the left, both hands should move to the left to lead your horse's forehand around the turn.

You might also find that it takes too long to finish the turn if you lose your balance and get left behind the motion. This is the same sensation of falling to the outside that I discussed in the previous section on half-passes (p. 332). Your horse is moving to the left but your upper body gets shifted to the right. Or, you squeeze too hard with your outside leg, and your upper body leans to the outside as well.

Use the same corrections that we did for the half-pass. First, be sure your horse is responsive to your outside leg so you don't have to push too hard with it. Then, step down into your inside stirrup to encourage your horse to move under your weight while you think about moving your outside seat bone toward the middle of your saddle.

MAINTAINING THE BEND

Remember, if your horse loses his bend, there will be little engagement of his inside hind leg, so you need to make your bending aids more active. To do this, ask for flexion by vibrating your inside rein. Then lighten or ease the tension on the rein. Your horse should stay flexed to the inside by himself when you soften the contact.

While you're asking for flexion, use your active inside leg on the girth with the idea of pushing your horse's ribcage away from it and to the outside of the turn. At the same time, make sure that you remember to "trap" the outside hind leg so that it doesn't swing to the outside. Use your outside leg, which is placed behind the girth.

CONTROLLING THE HIND LEGS

Most of the mistakes I see in turns on the haunches revolve around how the hind legs step. Your horse's hind legs must maintain the regular rhythm of the walk and be picked up and put down slightly in front of the same place where they left the ground.

If your horse pivots on his inside hind leg as though he is screwing it into the ground, you've lost the rhythm of his walk. As you know by now, maintaining the regular rhythm is the priority, so this is a serious fault. If this is your horse's tendency, ride larger turns as a schooling exercise. Then when you do make the turn somewhat smaller, be sure to maintain the activity of your horse's inside hind leg by squeezing and releasing with your active inside leg. Also, soften your inside hand forward so you don't block or interfere with the stepping of his inside hind leg.

Then again, I often see a horse step toward the inside of the turn with his inside hind leg. Specifically, in a turn on the haunches to the left, his left hind leg steps sideways to the left as if he's leg-yielding away from your outside leg. A horse will do this to avoid the bending of the joints of his hind legs. Engage his inside hind

leg in preparation for the turn by riding shoulder-fore before you start. Then use an active inside leg during the turn to remind him to keep using it.

You can also do the following exercise as a check that you're maintaining control of your horse's inside hind leg. During the exercise, stay away from the rail so you don't run into any obstacles. First, walk your horse forward in shoulder-fore. When you're ready, do one step of a turn on the haunches, and immediately walk forward in shoulder-fore again. Make sure your horse's hind legs stay on whatever line you choose rather than drifting to either side of that line. Think about using your inside leg and driving it toward your outside rein as you move your horse's shoulders slightly to the inside. Then when you're ready, do another step of your turn and then proceed forward in shoulder-fore again.

Sometimes you'll manage to capture your horse's inside hind leg and prevent it from stepping to the inside of the turn, but you'll find that he'll look for an escape route by stepping to the outside of the turn with his outside hind leg. That is, on a left turn on the haunches, his right hind leg will swing out to the right.

Generally, this can be prevented by passively guarding and supporting with your firm outside leg. If your horse persists in swinging out with his outside hind leg, prepare for the turn by riding haunches-in before you begin. Try to keep the feeling of pushing his haunches to the inside of the turn as you make your way around the turn on the haunches. Keep in mind that this is only a schooling exercise to give your horse the idea of where to place his outside hind leg. In competition, or done correctly for maximum benefit, the turn on the haunches should always be started from the shoulder-fore position.

USING TURNS ON THE HAUNCHES FOR DEVELOPING SELF-CARRIAGE

With horses that have a bit of education, I've used turns on the haunches to develop self-carriage in all three paces. First, I'll have a student cruise around in the walk, trot, or the canter, and simply evaluate her horse's balance. How much weight is on his hind legs and how much is on his forelegs? What's the weight in the reins? How long is her horse's body from poll to tail? Then, I'll have her ride several turns on the haunches. Sometimes I'll even have her do turns of 360 degrees or more as long as she is keeping the rhythm and the bend correctly.

Next, she'll resume whatever pace she was in before and take a moment to reevaluate the horse's balance. If the turns on the haunches have been ridden correctly, the balance will be shifted somewhat toward the hind legs, the contact will be lighter, and her horse will be shorter and more "packaged" from poll to tail.

KEY POINTS

- The half-pass supples and improves self-carriage. Think of a halfpass as a haunches-in position ridden on a diagonal line across the arena.

- Turn on the haunches is an engagement exercise and a preparatory exercise for walk pirouettes. Think of it as a haunches-in position done on a tiny circle.

19

Shifting into Second Gear

MEDIUM AND EXTENDED GAITS

In chapter 8 you learned about lengthening your horse's strides and frame in the working trot and canter. The horse in training at the basic levels in dressage is able to show two "gears" in each of those paces. He can trot and canter and he can show a lengthening—a longer stride and frame—of those paces. Remember that during a lengthening, your horse covers the maximum amount of ground with each stride that he's capable of doing at his current stage of development.

In this chapter, I'm going to introduce two additional types of lengthenings that are more advanced: the **medium** and the **extended** gaits. Just as the lengthenings are the "covering-more-ground" expression of the basic **working** gaits, the mediums and extensions are the "covering-more-ground" expressions of the **collected** gaits which I described in chapter 16.

So this means that rather than only having two "gears" in the trot and canter, the educated horse is also able to show three more "gears"—collected, medium, and extended—in all his paces. As an analogy, you can think

that a lengthening is to a working gait what an extension is to a collected gait—the maximum lengthening of stride and frame that the horse can show at his stage of development.

DESCRIPTION

The medium gaits share certain qualities with extended gaits in that they are produced from a collected gait, but rather than being extended to their utmost, the horse's strides and frame are only moderately extended (figs. 19.1).

The medium and extended gaits are similar to lengthenings in two respects. The horse elongates his frame as well as covers more ground with each stride, as he does in a lengthening. He also maintains the same tempo that he had established in the collected gait.

Because of these similarities I often hear people use the words "**lengthenings**" and "**extensions**" interchangeably. This is incorrect because there is a very real difference between a lengthening of the basic working gaits where the horse's balance is more or less on his forehand

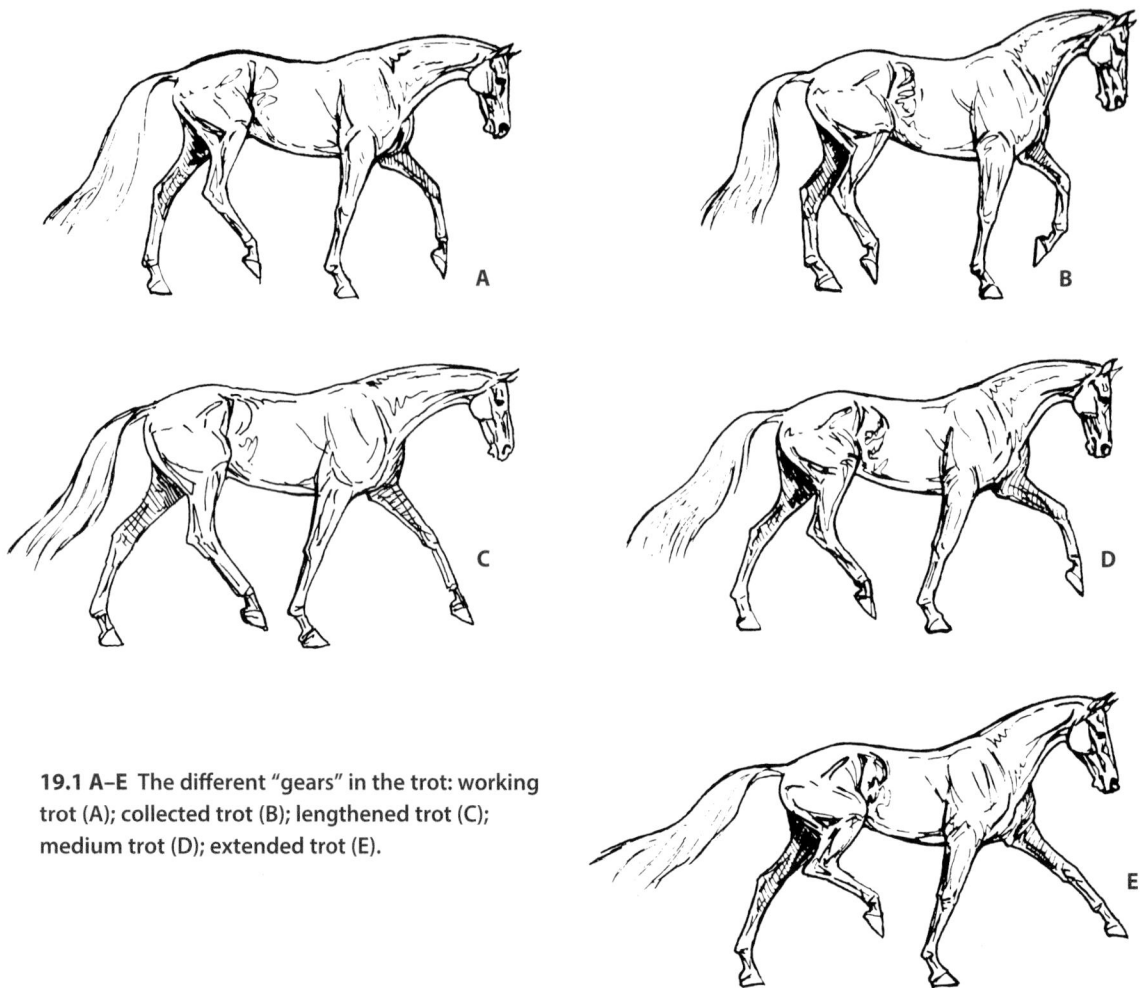

19.1 A–E The different "gears" in the trot: working trot (A); collected trot (B); lengthened trot (C); medium trot (D); extended trot (E).

and the medium and extended gaits, which can only be developed from a collected gait with a horse who is in self-carriage.

To help you understand the difference between a lengthening and a medium or extended gait, imagine that your legs are the horse's hind legs. Now, bend your knees just a little bit and then jump in the air. You'll probably get a few inches off the ground. The slight bend in your knees is equivalent to the amount the horse engages his hind legs in the working gaits. This minimal **engagement** of the horse's hind legs is the reason you're only able to generate a lengthening from a working gait.

Now, bend your knees a lot more, and jump again. You'll find that you can now spring a lot higher off the ground. The more the joints bend (or engage), the higher you can jump. This is how your horse is able to produce an extension from collection. Think of coiling the spring of the hind legs when riding a collected gait so your horse can propel himself, or "boing," into an extension (fig. 19.2).

During the collected gaits there is an increase

in the engagement of the hind legs, which causes the horse's center of gravity to shift more toward his hindquarters. As a result, the horse's balance is more "uphill." So it follows that the balance in mediums and extensions should remain uphill as well.

To sum up, the common denominator for the collected, medium, and extended gaits is the engagement of the hind legs, which causes a lowering of the hindquarters and results in a lightening and elevation of the forehand. I call this phenomenon **uphill balance**. Also, the length of the horse's strides and frame will vary, of course, becoming either shorter or longer depending on which "gear" you're in, but the tempo always remains the same.

In the collected gaits, the horse's balance is uphill: his strides are short and active, and they make an up and down arc; his frame is more compact than it is in the working gaits. In the medium and extended gaits, the horse's uphill balance is the same as it is in the collected gaits, but his strides are longer and his frame elongates.

Now, let's discuss the extended walk and look at how the medium and extended gaits differ in the trot and canter.

THE EXTENDED WALK

I am not going to cover the medium walk here (you have already learned this term in chapter 6, as the name for the basic walk). Years ago, the **USEF** had a walk called "medium," for more advanced horses, which was described as the

19.2 Think of coiling the spring of your horse's hind legs when riding a collected gait, so he can "boing" into an extension.

BOING!!

"gait between the collected and extended walk." This medium walk followed the same rules, as far as length of stride, length of frame, and self-carriage are concerned, as *medium* trot and canter still do. Specifically, in these gaits the horse must show a *moderate* lengthening of his stride and frame while his balance remains uphill.

Now, the USEF has "borrowed" the medium walk for use with younger, or uneducated horses, and it replaces the previously named "working" walk. Medium walk no longer falls under the same rules regarding uphill balance as medium trot and medium canter. The name was changed because the term "working walk" seemed to encourage riders to restrict their horses and "cram" them together, rather than letting them march on actively.

Keep it straight in your mind by thinking of it this way. We work young horses in the medium walk. We work more advanced horses in the collected and extended walk.

In the *extended* walk, the horse covers as much ground as possible without hurrying, and

19.3 In collected walk, Rowen remains on the bit as he marches forward with his head and neck raised and arched, showing self-carriage. Each step covers less ground but comes higher off the ground than at the medium walk.

19.4 In extended walk, Rowen covers as much ground as possible without hurrying. His hind feet touch the ground clearly in front of the hoof prints of the forefeet. He is allowed to stretch out his head and neck, but the reins do not become slack.

the hind feet touch the ground clearly in front of the footprints of the forefeet (figs. 19.3 and 19.4).

THE MEDIUM AND EXTENDED TROT

In the medium trot the horse goes forward with free, moderately extended steps. He lowers his head and neck slightly and carries his nose a little more in front of the vertical than at the collected trot (figs. 19.5 to 19.7).

In the extended trot the horse lengthens his steps to the utmost as well as lengthening his frame. His forefeet should touch the ground on the spot toward which they are pointing. They should not retract before being placed on the ground. (If this happens, it's usually because the rider restricts her horse with her hands and has not allowed him to lengthen his frame.)

THE MEDIUM AND EXTENDED CANTER

In the medium canter the horse goes forward with free, moderately extended strides. He carries his head a little more in front of the vertical than at the collected canter and lowers his head and neck slightly.

In the extended canter, the horse covers as much ground as possible with each stride, while remaining calm and in good balance. He should lower and extend his head and neck, and the tip of his nose should point more or less forward (figs. 19.8 to 19.10).

When training, I usually work on the medium gaits first. Once I know my horse has

19.5 Fursty remains on the bit with his neck raised and arched in collected trot. His steps are shorter than in other trots, but his hocks are well engaged.

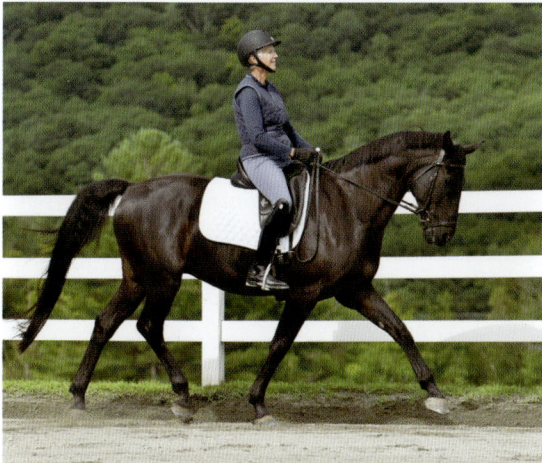

19.6 In medium trot, Fursty goes forward with moderately extended steps. His frame is slightly longer and his neck is somewhat lower than in collected trot, but his balance remains uphill rather than shifting onto the forehand.

19.7 Fursty lengthens his steps and frame to the utmost in extended trot.

19.8 In collected canter, Fursty remains on the bit and moves forward with his neck raised and arched. His strides are shorter than in the other canters, but they are active and energetic.

19.9 Fursty goes forward with free, moderately extended strides in medium canter. His frame is slightly longer and his neck is lower than in collected canter, but it's apparent that he stays in self-carriage as his body has the uphill look of an airplane taking off.

19.10 Fursty covers as much ground as possible while remaining in self-carriage during extended canter. Note the spread between his hind legs as he reaches well under his body to cover ground with long strides. He has lengthened his frame, lowered his neck, and the tip of his nose is slightly more forward than in collected canter.

THE AIDS FOR MEDIUM AND EXTENDED GAITS

Before asking for a medium or extended gait, first make sure that your horse's hind legs are sufficiently engaged in the collected gait to give him enough energy to be able to extend. If they aren't, you need to "coil the spring" of his hind legs by riding some good collecting half-halts (see chapter 16).

When the hind legs are engaged as the result of these half-halts, you will be ready to ask for an extension. The aids for medium and extended gaits are as follows:

1. Seat: use a driving seat that feels like you're sweeping the back of the saddle toward the front of the saddle.

2. Legs: press lightly with both legs to signal your horse to go forward over the ground in longer strides.

3. Reins: soften your hands a bit forward to allow the frame to become longer, but keep a contact with your horse's mouth and a bend in your elbows.

19.11 A & B Although the action of the horse's front leg might look extravagant in the extended trot in A, the extension is incorrect. Rather than showing good engagement, the action of the hind legs is backward. Because his back is stiff and his neck is short, he flips up the toe of his front foot, as discussed earlier in this book. The extended trot in B shows good engagement of the hind legs. The energy flows over the horse's back, through a long neck, and his nose is pointed toward the spot where his front foot will come to the ground.

the strength and understanding to maintain an even rhythm, constant tempo, and an uphill balance in the medium gaits, I begin to ask for the greater effort needed to do extensions.

Practicing the medium and extended gaits is valuable, not only as a way to supple your horse, but as a way to freshen him mentally and physically. For example, I intersperse them into my lateral work and collection exercises to relax his muscles and renew his desire to go forward.

✳ HELPFUL HINTS

INCREASING ENGAGEMENT WHEN DOING EXTENSIONS

It's not unusual to see a lack of engagement in extensions—even with a naturally big-moving horse whose strides are ground-covering and powerful. Sometimes, although the horse's strides get long, the action of the hind legs is backward: the hind legs push rather than come under the body to carry. Another common sight is the horse who widens or spreads his hind legs apart during extensions. In both cases the hind legs are pushing backward, rather than carrying, because of a lack of engagement (fig. 19.11).

To increase the engagement, start a half-halt (combine your driving aids, bending aids, and your **rein of opposition**) and "blend" that half-halt into the upward transition from the collected gait to the extension. This will remind the horse to keep his hind legs coming under his body. By "blend," I mean that you'll start the half-halt and continue to apply it while changing the emphasis of the driving aids or one of the other elements of the half-halt.

For instance, to blend the half-halt into the extension, you can gradually increase your driving aids over the course of three seconds. You can also keep the driving aids the same, but soften your hands a bit, or you might do a combination of both of these things.

You can also increase the engagement of the hind legs in preparation for extensions by riding some of the movements that you learned for improving **self-carriage** (chapter 16). For instance, ride a small circle to increase self-carriage, and then immediately after leaving the circle, ask for a few extended steps. Or, do some frequent upward and downward transitions from pace to pace. For each downward transition, remember to close both legs to drive your horse's hind legs more underneath his body. Once you feel him carrying himself better (and you'll be able to tell that he's doing so because his balance feels more uphill and he's lighter in your hands), ask for your extension.

Another way to increase engagement is to use the shoulder-in as an exercise to set your horse up for the extension. Ride a few steps of shoulder-in, do three or four steps of an extension, then go right back into shoulder-in. Repeat this pattern as often as you like. The first shoulder-in ensures that you start with engaged hind legs, and the transition back into the shoulder-in assists in the maintenance of that engagement. Don't feel like you have to extend for a long time; keep the extensions brief so you can do a few strides that are of a high quality rather than many strides that are not (figs. 19.12 to 19.14).

If your trainer has told you that this lack of engagement in extensions is a chronic problem for you (or perhaps you've seen it for yourself on a video), do some imaging to support all the actual exercises that I've just discussed. As you ask for the extension, focus solely on your

19.12 This extended trot down the long side of the ring lacks engagement. The loss of engagement can be seen as Rowen takes the load off his right hind leg by pushing backward and sideways to the right with it. (Compare this leg to its position in photo 19.14).

horse's hind legs. Visualize them staying close together and stepping well under his body as he extends.

This is what I did with my horse Zapatero, the reserve horse for the 1992 United States Olympic Dressage Team, who used to find it difficult to stay engaged during the extended trot. I practiced by riding the "perfect" test in my mind's

19.13 Riding the same line, Ally increases the engagement of Rowen's right hind leg by riding him in right shoulder-in. His right hind leg is lined up behind his left front leg; this position encourages Rowen to carry weight on his right hind leg.

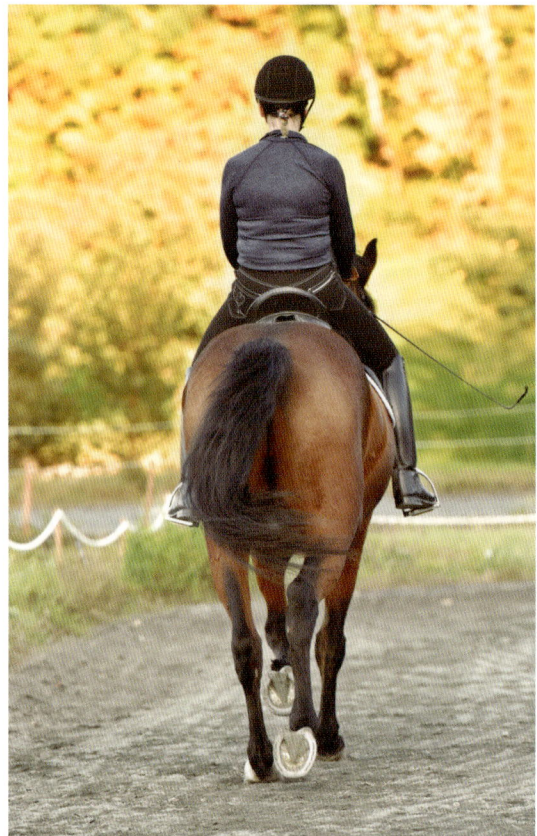

19.14 After a few steps of shoulder-in, Ally straightens her horse and immediately asks him to extend again. Here Rowen is able to carry himself in the extension because he brings his right hind leg directly under his body rather than pushing backward and sideways with it.

eye and I'd zoom my focus in on his hind legs only. I'd exaggerate the engagement by "seeing" him bending his hocks and bringing his hind legs so far under his body that he'd practically hit his belly with every step! (See fig. 19.15).

DEVELOPING BIGGER EXTENSIONS

If your horse does a good extension while correctly maintaining the tempo of the collected gait, but you'd like him to be more expressive—to float over the ground more with each stride—work on developing the energy in the collected gait. It's impossible for a horse to magically produce powerful strides out of "thin air." The magnitude of the extended stride is a direct result of the degree of engagement of the joints of the hind legs in the collected gait ridden right before the extension. Remember, the term "engagement" refers to the increased bending of the joints of the hind legs and of the lumbosacral area. When a horse engages his hind legs, his hindquarters lower and they support a greater proportion of the load. This engagement of the hind legs is a prerequisite for **thrust**—also known as **impulsion**.

Once again, you can use some of the movements and exercises that we did in the section on developing self-carriage (chapters 16 and 17) to engage the hind legs prior to asking for a bigger extension. The more you engage your horse's hind legs, the easier it'll be to ask for more.

1. While in trot, ride some steps of shoulder-in; in the canter, do some steps of shoulder-fore to engage the inside hind leg. Then straighten your horse and extend.

2. Do several trot-halt-trot or canter-walk-canter transitions to engage your horse's hind legs, and then ask for an extension.

3. Ride a 10-meter circle in either trot or canter and then ask for the extension as you leave the circle and go on to a straight line.

4. Go on a 20-meter circle and ride a shoulder-in (if you're in the trot) or a shoulder-fore (if you're in the canter). Be sure to keep your horse's hind legs on the original track of the circle. (If he even slightly decreases the size of the circle by drifting in toward the center during the lateral movement, he's avoiding the engagement of his inside hind leg.)

19.15 To increase engagement in extensions, in your mind's eye, zoom your focus in on your horse's hind legs. "See" him bringing them so far under his body that he practically hits his belly with every step.

Staying on the circle, straighten your horse from the shoulder-fore or shoulder-in position (which in this case does not mean literally straighten, rather that you bend him along the arc of the circle), ask for a few steps of an extension, and then collect the gait again in shoulder-fore or shoulder-in (depending on whether you're in canter or trot). Make sure you maintain the bend around your inside leg during the extension. Losing the bend is another way that your horse avoids the engagement of his inside hind leg.

KEEPING THE DIAGONAL PAIRS OF LEGS PARALLEL IN THE TROT

In any trot, the front and hind legs that make up the diagonal pairs should be parallel. In an extended trot, the legs should remain parallel. One way for you to learn how to see

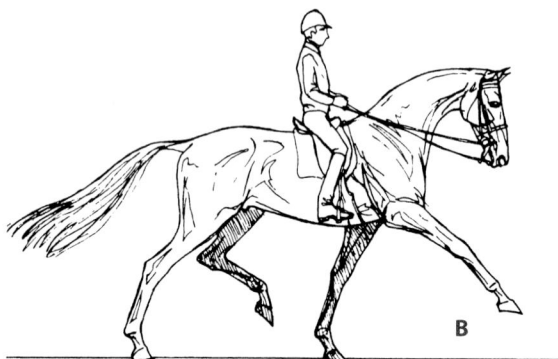

"parallelness" is to look at a photograph of a horse in trot and examine the diagonal pair of legs that is in the air. In a correct trot, you'd see that the upper part of the front leg (the forearm) and the lower part of the hind leg (the cannon bone) are parallel (fig. 19.16).

I often see a horse flinging out his front legs while his hind legs do very little. This is described in "dressage speak" as "promising more in front than delivering behind." This usually happens because the horse lacks engagement and connection; the freedom in his shoulders and the reach of the front leg is not coming from the power of the hindquarters. Instead, the horse "cracks" his back by breaking at a point just behind the withers and raises his front end without the corresponding lowering of the hindquarters.

Some people aren't sure if their horses extend more with their front legs than with their hind legs. If you have no ground person to instruct you, you can check that the diagonal pairs are parallel by having someone take a photograph or video of you while doing a medium or extended trot. If you see that the front legs are really reaching forward but the hind legs are dragging, indicating a lack of engagement and connection, direct your attention toward the hind legs to improve the trot.

19.17 During extensions, visualize your horse's hind legs engaging by pretending that he is sitting and snapping them forward like a Cossack dancer.

Give a half-halt to ensure the **connection** from back to front, and then do some engaging exercises such as shoulder-in, frequent transitions, and small circles in order to increase the impulsion from the hindquarters. Then, ask for an extension, being sure to soften your hands slightly forward so your horse can lengthen his neck.

Help the horse's hind legs become closer to parallel with the front legs by visualizing "taking the hind legs with you." "See" your horse coming forward and under more with his hind legs. Visualize the engagement of the hind legs and the bending of the hocks by pretending the horse is sitting and snapping the hind legs forward like a Cossack dancer (fig. 19.17).

MAINTAINING ENGAGEMENT DURING EXTENSIONS

When your horse is engaged and in **self-carriage**, which he should be in medium and extended gaits, the contact will be light. Even though you're doing an extension, you should still feel the lightness and **uphill balance** of the collected gaits in the medium and extended gaits. If you feel a great deal of weight in your hands when riding an extension, this is probably because there's a lack of engagement as described in the previous example. The feeling in your hands is the direct result of what's happening, or not happening, with the hind legs.

In other words, if the hind legs are not engaged, you're going to feel like you have to hold your horse up. Before you ask for the extension, you need to activate the hind legs so your horse is in self-carriage and, therefore, the contact is only the weight of the reins—pleasantly light.

> *"Always feel collection in extension and extension in collection."*
>
> ● ● ● ● ●

Quite often, a horse will start off in self-carriage but after six or eight strides, he loses engagement and ends up lying in your hands because he's no longer carrying himself. Perhaps the extra speed over the ground contributes to the loss of balance—the center of gravity gradually moves somewhat to the forehand. Maybe it's because he's not yet strong enough to maintain his engagement for so many strides. Whatever the cause, once you lose the feeling of self-carriage while extending, the horse's balance will shift to the forehand and he'll lean on your hands.

To sum up, remember this: always feel collection in extension and extension in collection! By this I mean you need to do an extension in an uphill, collected balance and you need to have the feeling of the barely controlled power of an extension when riding a collected gait.

The canter presents an added challenge to the maintenance of engagement. After all, even in a working canter when asking for minimal engagement, a horse generally chooses to be crooked and carry his hindquarters to the inside in order

19.18 Brie is crooked in the canter. Her hindquarters drift slightly toward the inside of the ring so that she can take the load off her inside hind leg. If Amy doesn't straighten Brie at this stage so that she learns to carry weight behind, she'll undoubtedly be crooked when asked to do extended canter.

to avoid bending the joints of his inside hind leg. He might do this as an escape route to carrying weight behind because he's lazy or weak. Or perhaps he simply hasn't been taught the mechanics of bending his joints and placing that inside hind leg toward his center through canter work done in shoulder-fore position.

Remember when you ride a shoulder-fore in left lead canter, you ask the horse's left hind leg to step in between the front legs by using your left leg on the girth while you displace his forehand to the left by bringing both of your hands slightly to the left.

If lack of engagement and crookedness is not dealt with at an earlier stage, it becomes even more obvious when a horse is asked to collect his gaits. After all, if he hasn't learned to carry weight with his inside hind leg when his center of gravity is more toward the forehand, he certainly isn't going to start when the work becomes harder in collected gaits when the center of gravity is shifted more towards the hindquarters.

If he's crooked and avoiding carrying weight behind in the collected canter, it's inevitable that he will "unload" and carry his hindquarters to the inside during an extended canter (fig. 19.18). To correct this fault, stay in a slight shoulder-fore position before, during, and after extensions.

KEEPING YOUR HORSE ON THE BIT

Not only can you lose engagement (and therefore, self-carriage) as just discussed, but you can lose the connection over your horse's back as well. For example, you're doing a collected trot around the ring and you feel like there's lots of impulsion in the trot. Because you feel so much power, you don't bother to prepare for the extension by blending a half-halt into the upward transition. Instead, you just close your legs to ask for the extension. As a result, your horse runs off his hind legs by pushing backward with them and his back becomes hollow (see fig. 19.11A).

If this happens to you frequently, it's essential that you once again blend or "superimpose" a half-halt into the upward transition to the extension—not so much to coil the spring of the hind legs as you did before to increase engagement, but to ensure the connection from your horse's hind legs over his back to his front end. Prepare for the extension by starting the half-halt while still in the collected gait and continue the half-halt right through the transition into the extension as I described earlier. Maintaining the half-halt through the transition helps the horse stay connected because you're asking the hind legs to come under the body rather than letting them push "out the back door."

I realize that blending a half-halt into the transition for an extension might necessitate sustaining that half-halt for a little longer than the three seconds that you're accustomed to. In fact, your half-halt might last as long as four to six seconds. But after that amount of time, be sure to soften the aids so the horse gets his reward. If you forget to relax, you'll be constantly driving and holding without giving your horse any relief, and he'll probably end up stiffening against your aids.

IMPROVING THE DOWNWARD TRANSITION FROM EXTENSION TO COLLECTION

My tips for improving the downward transitions refer only to negotiating the transition from the extended trot to the collected trot and from extended canter to collected canter. You probably won't have to do this in the walk because it's a slow pace, but since you can get barreling along at a pretty good clip in a fabulous trot or canter extension, you might need a little help bringing your horse back to the collected gait again. Your extension shouldn't gradually fade over the course of several strides. An observer should be able to pick a particular point where a distinct transition to the collected gait occurred.

Ideally you do this with a half-halt, but if your horse ignores you or takes too long to come back to the collected gait, sharpen up his response to your half-halt by doing the following:

Ride an extension and come to a full halt, using the same combination of aids that you use for the half-halt (seat, legs, and outside rein). You'll probably need to be a bit stronger with the aids initially in order to do this dramatic transition from the extension to the halt. But be sure not to be too harsh. When the horse responds by going from the extension to the halt within four or five strides, try a transition from an extended gait to the collected gait with a regular half-halt. If he doesn't shorten his stride to the collected gait within a couple of strides, don't just give him a stronger half-halt. Instead come to a complete halt again.

In other words, if he ignores the regular half-halt, don't make your half-halt stronger to accommodate his lack of reaction. Sharpen his response to the half-halt by doing a quick full halt. Remember that, as I told you way back at the beginning of this book, you want to "whisper" with your aids and have your horse "shout" his response (chapter 5). You don't want to shout with your aids and get a half-hearted response.

Another situation that often occurs during the downward transition is that your horse leans on your hands because he's lost his balance and his center of gravity shifts to the forehand. This can happen if you're too strong with the reins.

One solution to restoring engagement, which ensures that he stays in self-carriage and, therefore, light in your hand during the downward transition, is to step into shoulder-fore as you ask for the transition. Let the shoulder-fore slow him down and collect the gait rather than giving a half-halt. During the transition, use your inside leg to drive his inside hind leg diagonally toward his center and lead his shoulders slightly to the inside. The shoulder-fore engages your horse's inside hind leg and he'll have to carry himself. As a result, he won't need to lean on your hands for support.

KEY POINTS

- Medium and extended gaits are a more advanced type of lengthening. The horse remains in self-carriage and has the uphill look of an airplane taking off.

- In medium and extended gaits, both the frame and the strides get longer while the rhythm and the tempo stays the same as it was in the collected gaits from which it was developed.

- In medium gaits, the strides and frame are moderately extended.

- In extended gaits, the strides and frame are lengthened to the utmost.

- Since medium and extended gaits are developed from the collected gaits, the best way to improve them is by increasing the engagement of the hind legs while in the collected gaits.and the tempo stays the same as it was in the collected gaits from which it was developed.

20

FLYING CHANGES

L et's do a little "historic" review of how you've changed from one canter lead to the other with your horse so far. When I first discussed the working canter with your green (uneducated) horse in chapter 8, you did a **change of lead through the trot** when you wanted to switch from one inside foreleg leading in the canter to the other one. This meant that you'd do a few steps of trot between changing leads.

As your horse became more trained, I asked you to do **simple changes of lead** in chapter 16. This is a downward transition from one canter lead directly into a few steps of walk and then an upward transition to the other canter lead. Remember that if you don't hear or read the words "through the trot," you can automatically assume that the change of lead is a simple change through the walk rather than through the trot.

Now it's time to address a more advanced way to change your canter leads—the **flying change**. In a flying change, your horse stays in the canter the entire time, without walking or trotting. He switches his canter lead while he's in mid-air. He does this by changing which hind leg he places

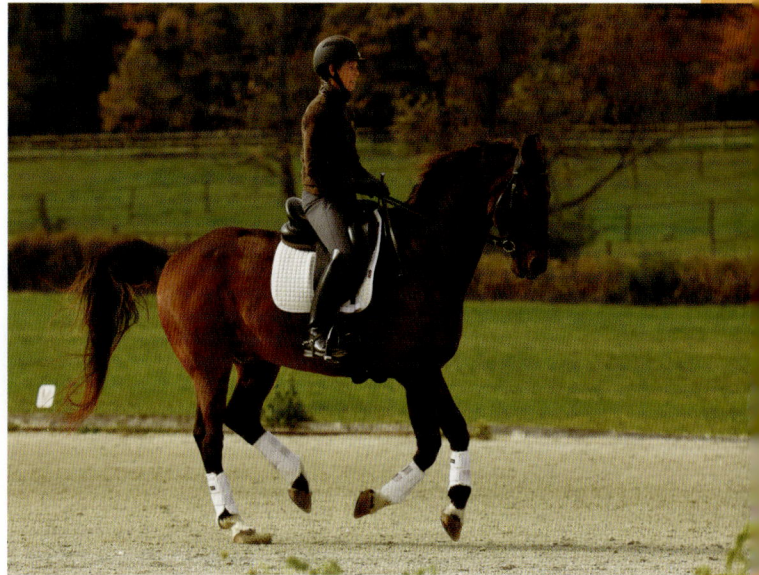

20.1 Wilkinson is coming across the diagonal in left lead canter. This is the first beat of the canter, which shows his right hind foot on the ground.

on the ground first after the period of suspension when all four of his legs are off the ground.

For example, when your horse is on the *left* lead, his *right* hind leg is the first beat of his canter stride. To negotiate the flying change of lead to the right lead, your horse must change the sequence of legs of a canter stride so that the first beat is made by the *left* hind leg as it comes to the ground (figs. 20.1 to 20.5).

20.2 The second beat of the canter, when the diagonal pair of left hind leg and right foreleg are on the ground at the same time.

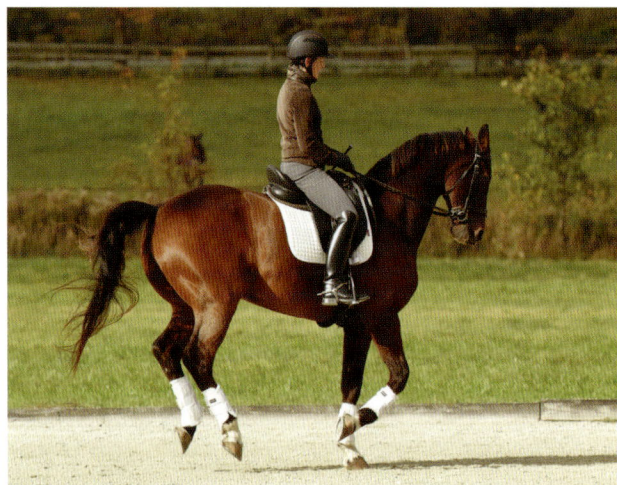

20.3 On the third beat of left lead canter, the left front foot is on the ground. This is the moment when the rider gives the aid for the flying change. This gives Wilkinson a second to recognize that the aid has been given so he can switch the sequence of his legs during the period of suspension, which comes as soon as his left front foot leaves the ground.

20.4 This photo has been taken just after the period of suspension. Wilkinson has switched his canter lead by placing his new outside hind leg—the right hind leg—on the ground first. This is the first beat of the new canter—the right lead canter.

20.5 The second beat of right lead canter, showing the diagonal pair of inside (right) hind leg and outside (left) foreleg on the ground at the same time.

In dressage, flying changes aren't required until the horse has acquired some degree of self-carriage, so a dressage horse is first asked to show flying changes in the tests that are of a medium degree of difficulty (Third Level tests). Western horses are asked to do flying changes at about the same stage of their training as are dressage horses—all should be able to walk, trot, and canter in balance, as well as lengthen and shorten their strides.

Most hunters, combined training horses, and show jumpers, however, learn flying changes earlier in their training. It's a distinct advantage to have a horse who can switch his leads quickly when changing direction around a course of jumps.

DESCRIPTION

In a flying change, a horse switches his canter lead during the period of suspension when all four of his legs are off the ground. In the higher levels of dressage, flying changes can also be done in a series. For instance, they can be done at every fourth, third, second, or at every stride. It is one of the most exciting movements to watch in dressage competition. When done in a sequence like this, they are commonly called "tempi changes." A horse can be trained to do four-tempi (every fourth stride), three-tempi, two-tempi, and one-tempi changes. But that is beyond the scope of this book, which focuses on cross-training your horse for improved performance with more fundamental dressage.

PREPARATORY WORK

Before schooling the flying changes themselves, you should spend many months laying a solid foundation by working on the following: simple changes of lead, self-carriage in the canter, and counter-canter.

1. Simple changes of lead. Before you try to do flying changes, you need to know that your horse is schooled enough and has sufficient engagement to be able to do clearly the downward transition from canter to walk. "Clearly" means that your horse doesn't do any "dribbly" trot steps in between the canter and the walk. If he's not balanced enough to do this yet, he's going to fall on his face when you ask for the flying change. In addition, for the upward transition he needs to be **"hot off your leg"** (see chapter 5) so that he reacts immediately when you ask him to go from the walk to the canter.

If you need to review how to ride transitions from the canter to the walk, and simple changes of lead, see page 278.

2. Self-carriage in the canter. You must develop and maintain the quality of your horse's canter. If your horse's canter is four-beat or it's too "flat," you need to improve it before you work on flying changes. This is important because a flying change is simply a canter bound, and the flying change itself should look like every other canter stride. Therefore, your horse should canter in some degree of self-carriage with big, "round," expressive bounds.

When a canter is flat, the horse doesn't get off the ground very much during the period of suspension. As a result, he'll find flying changes difficult to do because there won't be enough time for him to switch his legs. Sometimes, horses with flat canters end up doing a step of trot with their hind legs when they go to change leads because they can't figure out how to negotiate rearranging their legs if there's not enough "air" time. In this case, rather than switching canter leads with both hind and front legs at the same time, they change leads with their front legs while doing a step of trot with their hind legs. Then one stride later, the hind legs catch up to the front legs and also begin to canter on the new lead (fig. 20.6).

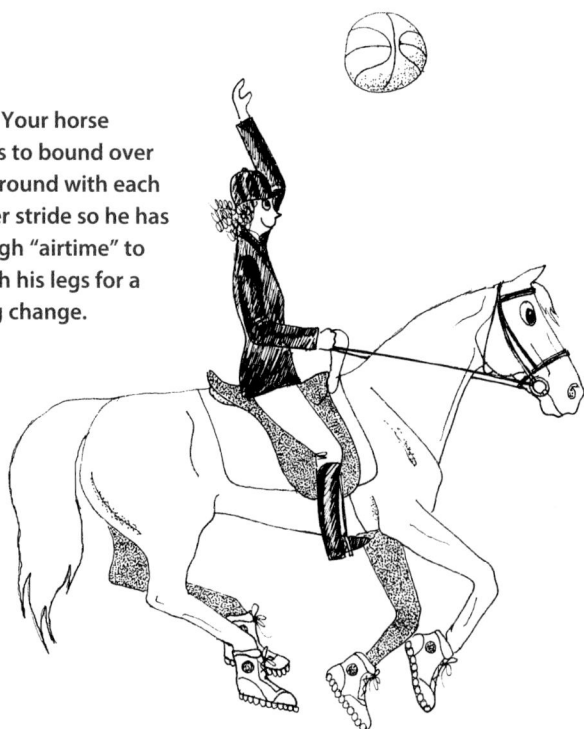

20.6 Your horse needs to bound over the ground with each canter stride so he has enough "airtime" to switch his legs for a flying change.

Once you have a pure three-beat canter, work on exercises that increase the self-carriage, such as shoulder-fore (remember that we don't ask for a shoulder-in with a 30-degree angle from the rail while in the canter), both on straight lines and on large and small circles; haunches-in on a small circle; and frequent canter-walk-canter transitions. When I say "frequent," I mean you can do as few as five strides of canter, five strides of walk, five strides of canter, then five strides of walk.

You can also improve self-carriage in the canter by giving **collecting half-halts**. You learned these half-halts in chapter 16. As you give one of these half-halts, drive your horse's hind legs further under his body as you always do during a half-halt. But, in this case, shorten the reins and increase the influence of your outside rein by using it more firmly so that your horse ends up covering less ground with each stride. As you close your outside hand in a fist, think about holding your horse almost on the spot in the canter during the three seconds of the half-halt. Then, go more forward over the ground for six or seven strides.

After the half-halt, your horse's balance should also be more **uphill**, It's important that you don't let him go back down on his forehand when you send him forward again. So make sure the reins stay short and that your horse doesn't pull them through your fingers in order to lengthen his frame and go back down on his forehand. Also, sit up tall and hold him in self-carriage by keeping your back erect and strong. Repeat this sequence of collected strides and shorter strides that are almost on the spot several times.

While asking for those short but very active and engaged strides, imagine you're convincing your horse to canter in a teacup (fig. 20.7). Do these transitions forward and back from the shortened canter to normal collected canter until your horse is easily adjustable and willingly responds to the "collecting half-halt" that asks him to canter almost on the spot.

Another way to determine that you've done good "collecting half-halts" is when you can feel that the canter has the same activity, rhythm, and tempo as it did before, but your horse does more strides per meter than he did prior to the half-halts. For example, if it normally takes a horse three to four canter strides to go through a corner, in a more collected canter he will cover less ground per stride and do it in five or six strides.

3. Counter-canter. As part of your "preparation-for-flying-change" homework, you'll need to develop a balanced counter-canter. (Should you need to review counter-canter, refer to page 134.) Work on it until you feel confident that you can ride counter-canter without tension on both circles and straight lines. Your horse should be able to do extensions in counter-canter as well as the transition back to collected canter without breaking to the trot or switching leads on his own. Ride the same exercise that I described in number two above, where you do transitions from collected canter to several shorter strides (canter in a teacup) to adjust your horse's center of gravity and create more self-carriage in his counter-canter.

20.7 When you want short but very active engaged strides in the canter, imagine you are asking your horse to canter in a teacup!

GETTING STARTED

I find the easiest place to introduce flying changes for most horses is on a small figure eight where each of the two circles has a diameter of about 10 meters. Ride the first small circle of the figure eight in canter, and when you come to the point where you're ready to start the second circle, do a simple change of lead. Then ride the other half of the figure eight in the direction of the new lead. Go back and forth between the two circles with simple changes of lead until you feel that your horse understands and almost anticipates the transition from one lead to the other. At this point, give the aids for a flying change instead of asking for a simple change of lead.

More often than not, your horse will do a clean flying change. When he does, stop immediately and praise him lavishly.

However, don't be surprised if your horse offers any number of alternative reactions to your request for a flying change. For example, he could do a clean change, but then rush off with excitement. When this occurs, you can either stay on the new circle and canter until he relaxes and slows down or do a downward transition to the walk. In either case, praise him generously for doing the flying change. Eventually, his exuberance will go away.

He might also do a flying change with his front legs without switching his hind legs or change his hind legs without switching his front legs. In both cases, he ends up doing a disunited canter. Don't make a big fuss about it. Just come back to either the trot or the walk. Then re-establish a true canter. Do a few more simple changes of lead between the two circles to remind him

about the task at hand, and then ask for the flying change again.

Then again, some horses don't do the flying change at all. They just canter merrily along on the 10-meter circle in counter-canter. In this situation, you can make your horse more alert by giving a slightly sharper outside leg aid or by tapping him with the whip a couple of times just before you give the actual aid for the flying change. But if you aren't making any progress after several attempts, you might want to abandon this exercise in favor of an alternative plan.

For example, forget about changing from one direction to the other because your horse might feel that this just complicates the issue. Instead, just ask for the flying change from the

THE AIDS FOR THE FLYING CHANGE

Since a flying change is merely another canter "bound," the most important prerequisite for a successful flying change is the quality of your horse's canter. Another factor that contributes to completing a successful flying change is the timing of your aids. Normally you give the aids when your horse's leading front leg touches the ground, immediately before the period of suspension. This is because it takes your horse a moment to understand and carry out your request for the change, which will be done during the period of suspension. When doing a flying change from left lead to right lead, the aids are applied as follows:

1. **Seat:** a forward push with your right seat bone.

2. **Right Leg:** squeeze on the girth to remind the horse to go forward.

3. **Left leg:** swing behind the girth to signal the new outside hind leg to strike off.

4. **Left Rein:** close your hand in a fist to stick your horse's new outside hind leg on the ground and to maintain his uphill balance. Imagine closing and opening that hand so quickly that you could snatch a fly out of the air and then let it go.

4. **Right Rein:** soften forward to allow the new leading leg to change.

counter-canter. The first pattern to try is to simply ride a large circle in counter-canter. Engage your horse's "new" outside hind leg by tapping him with the whip, and then ask for the flying change anywhere on the circle. (If you're circling to the left, and you're in right lead canter, carry the whip in your right hand so you can engage his right hind leg.)

You can also just go all the way around the ring in counter-canter. Stay in counter-canter for as long as you need to feel organized before you ask for the flying change, but do wait until you're on the straight line of a long or short side of the ring. It's more difficult for your horse to be correctly balanced for the flying change when he's in a corner.

✳ HELPFUL HINTS

DEALING WITH TENSION

Sometimes when you start schooling flying changes, you'll find that your horse gets tense because he's worried or confused about changing his leads. Because he's anxious, he might begin to anticipate the flying change and nervously offer it before you ask.

Never punish him if he does a flying change on his own. If you do, you'll only add to his anxiety. Just quietly trot or walk, and resume cantering on whatever lead you were on originally. Then, help him to stop "obsessing" about the flying changes by doing a lot of counter-canter without asking for any changes at all. While in counter-canter, you might alternate

20.8 If your horse gets tense because he's anticipating and worrying about doing a flying change, help him to relax by riding him in a deep frame in counter-canter as Joy is doing here with Wilkinson.

between riding him in a normal balance and putting him in a **deep frame** as described on page 227. The deep frame helps to loosen and relax his muscles, and in turn, his mind unwinds.

Once your horse is calm, simply finish the session with this relaxed counter-canter. In this way you won't have more tension to deal with the next time you school flying changes (fig. 20.8).

Many young horses get a bit excited when they start flying changes and can rush off. If I can, I always try to start these horses either in an indoor arena or within the confines of a well-fenced in area outside. The rail or wall acts as a sort of psychological barrier that backs the horse off and slows him down. To use this "barrier" to my advantage, I position my horse so I ask for the flying change when I'm cantering toward the solid wall or the railing rather than when heading toward a wide open space.

Sometimes an exuberant horse will speed up considerably after doing a flying change (often happily bucking!). In order to counteract this horse's excitement, I ask for the flying change and then immediately halt. Then I'll reward him with lots of pats or a treat. In this way my horse anticipates stopping for his reward rather than frolicking off enthusiastically.

HORSE IGNORES THE AID

When I introduced flying changes to Eastwood, I found that he was an interesting combination of nervous tension and dullness to my leg. He was worried about the flying changes, but he was slow to react to my leg aid. I made him hotter off my leg by doing a lot of simple changes of lead from the walk to the canter back to the walk and then to the counter-canter. If he wasn't quick to answer, I'd kick him once and then ask for the canter depart again.

As soon as he gave an electric response to my leg, I worked on relaxing him in the canter. I put him in a very deep frame and made sure his tempo didn't get too quick. We did lots of transitions to medium canter and back to collected canter in this frame to make sure he stayed relaxed yet still immediately responsive to my leg aids. When he was quick to my leg and relaxed, rather than dull to my leg and tense, I asked for a flying change.

I remember Gary Rockwell, World Equestrian Games bronze medalist, telling a story of a young horse he had in for training that just didn't understand the concept of doing a flying change with a rider on his back. He said this horse was perfectly happy doing counter-canter on the tiniest circle imaginable! Gary did all sorts of acrobatics to knock him off balance, thinking it had to be easier for the horse to change his leads than to stay in counter-canter. But this horse just kept cantering calmly around the small circle on the original lead. Interestingly enough, when Gary finally managed to get him to do his first flying change, a light bulb must have gone off in the horse's head. As soon as he realized that he was supposed to "swap" leads, the rest of his flying change education, including learning how to do tempi changes, came easily.

Now, Gary Rockwell is a lot more athletic than I am, and he was able to cleverly maneuver that horse into a position where he either had to change canter leads or he'd feel like he was going to tip over. But rather than doing all sorts of acrobatic contortions as Gary did, I usually use a pole on the ground or a low cavaletti to help give my horse extra "air" time, so it's easier for him to change the sequence of his legs during the period of suspension. If my horse approaches the pole on the left lead, I'll turn him with an opening right rein while he's in the air over the pole and ask for the flying change at the same time with my left leg behind the girth.

IMPROVING FAULTY CHANGES

Changing Late Behind

When a horse changes "late behind," he changes with his front legs first and then a stride or more later he finally changes with his hind legs. This is the most frequent mistake I see when riders begin to school flying changes, and it's a serious fault. In the beginning stages of training I might make a lot of compromises, but doing a clean change is the priority for me. For instance, I won't make an issue about whether my horse stays on the bit, is a little late to react to the aids, or gets somewhat tense. All of these things will go away in time. But I do insist that my horse change "cleanly," and I have several exercises for the horse that doesn't do so. Here are some of them:

1. I find that some horses don't change "clean" because they are not **"through"** the outside of their bodies (the side that will become the "inside" after the flying change). By "not through" I mean it feels as though they aren't connected because they've stiffened against the outside rein and their hind legs seem "paralyzed" and unable to jump under their bodies.

I had a horse like this in training several years ago who had been doing his flying changes late behind for over a year. This had become a very bad habit, and it was difficult to get him to change his established way of doing things. For the first six weeks of riding him, I didn't do any flying changes at all and just worked on his connection and "throughness" because he was so confirmed in this bad habit. I did a couple of

unusual things (chronic problems sometimes need drastic measures).

The first was to school him a lot in counter-canter but with one slight modification. Normally, when you do counter-canter, your horse is flexed at the poll toward the lead that he's on. Specifically, if he's in counter-canter while going to the right, he should be on the left lead and flexed at the poll so that he looks slightly to the left. Instead, I flexed this horse to the right when we were doing counter-canter on the left lead while going to the right. And I flexed him to the left when we were doing counter-canter on the right lead while tracking to the left. I asked for this counter-flexion at the poll by using an indirect rein as described in chapter 7.

When I began the exercise, I knew that he would try to evade the "throughness" by swinging his hindquarters in the opposite direction from my indirect rein aid. So I made sure that his body didn't drift sideways when I asked for counter-flexion at the poll—by firmly supporting with my legs and the other rein. The "guarding" effect of my outside rein and outside leg were particularly important here. I knew if I let my outside hand go forward, he'd pop his shoulder to the outside. And if my outside leg didn't control his hindquarters, they would swing off the line we were on as well.

No matter where I was in the ring—circles, corners, long sides—I checked that I kept his legs exactly overlapping whatever line I was on.

We went around and around in counter-canter in this position until he felt comfortable. I could tell this was happening when I felt two

20.9 & 20.10 In preparation for flying changes, Deb alternates every few strides between true flexion and counter-flexion. While doing this she is careful to keep Fursty's hind legs lined up directly behind his front legs so that his body stays straight and parallel to the long side.

things. First, I didn't have to work so hard to keep his body straight. I could relax the pressure of my "guarding" outside rein and leg, and he'd keep following the line we were on. And second, when I asked for counter-flexion, he'd answer my rein aid without stiffening against my hand.

Sometimes I rode around with him counter-flexed all the time. Other times, I alternated between counter-flexion and correct flexion every few strides (figs. 20.9 and 20.10). We did

everything in this position—circles, serpentines, diagonals, and shallow loops. Over the course of the six weeks, this horse began to feel very soft on the outside of his body. I imagined that when he was "through," he felt like butter on that side. When I finally asked for the flying change, it was clean. Today this horse does beautiful flying changes, including one-tempi changes. But it took several weeks of patient reschooling to change his habitual response.

The second drastic measure that I took with this horse was to supple him in the canter as described in chapter 10. However, in his case, I always suppled him away from the lead he was on (figs. 20.11 and 20.12). (I guess you could call this "counter-suppling" as opposed to counter-flexion!) In the beginning, I really had to pay attention that I used my "guarding" outside rein and leg to keep him straight. When he could finally bend his neck willingly while keeping the rest of his legs on the line of travel, I knew he was more "through" and was ready to attempt a flying change.

If you start the flying changes yourself rather than inheriting someone else's problem, you probably won't have to resort to such drastic measures. (By the way, if you're concerned about starting the flying changes yourself, get professional help. It's a lot easier to do them right in the beginning than to have to reschool a problem later.) But this is a good exercise to file away in your bag of tricks if you run into a reschooling problem with another horse.

In fact, you'll find that you can use it for much more than fixing late flying changes. For example, if you're trotting or cantering along and you feel your horse stiffen against your outside rein, counter-flex or "counter-supple" him until he feels softer. Or, if you're on a circle or corner, and you feel like your horse is becoming crooked because his shoulders are bulging or "popping" to the outside of the line you're on, counter-flex him at the poll to help make him **axis-straight**. When you counter-flex him, his shoulders will slide over to the

20.11 Fursty is in counter-canter (on the right lead while going to the left), and Deb is counter-suppling him to put him "through" by bending his neck away from the lead he's on—to the left.

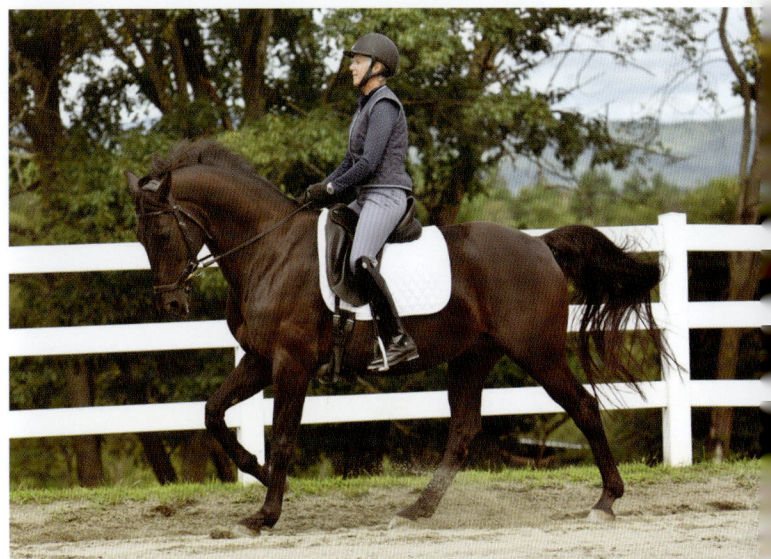

20.12 Once again Deb is counter-suppling her horse to put him "through" the left side of his body while he's in counter-canter. But in this example, she is also riding him in a deep frame.

20.13 Here, Fursty has become a bit crooked. His shoulders are popping out, and his hind feet do not follow directly in the tracks of his forefeet.

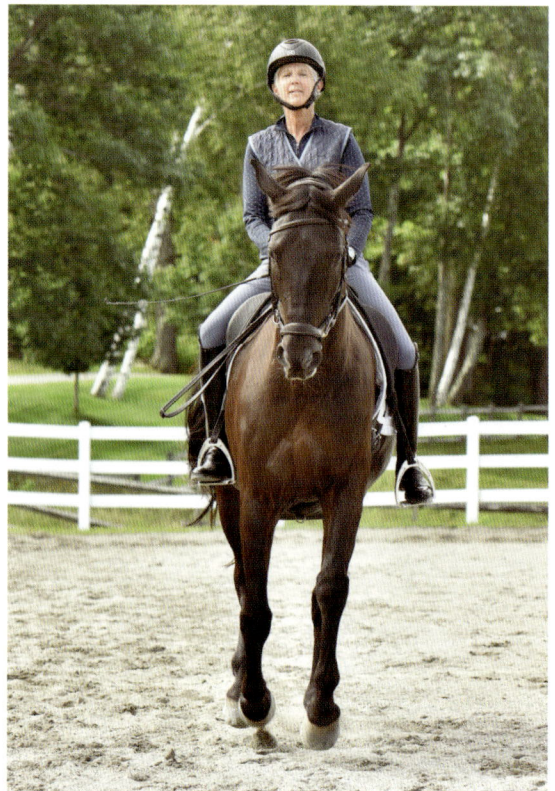

20.14 Deb straightens Fursty by counter-flexing him at the poll. By positioning him so that he looks very slightly toward the fence, his shoulders slide over so that his front feet are now directly lined up in front of his hind feet.

inside so that they're back in front of his hips (figs. 20.13 and 20.14).

2. You can use a similar throughness exercise to help fix flying changes that are late behind. Start a canter half-pass to the right. Go sideways for a few strides, and then continue to move to the right but begin to bend your horse's neck to the left. When he feels soft on his left side and doesn't resist the action of your left rein, straighten his neck and ride straight forward. Be

sure you straighten his neck completely before you ask for the flying change (fig. 20.15).

3. Another "throughness" exercise to help with late flying changes is to canter a serpentine of three or more loops. As you approach the center of the arena to start the second loop, slide your "new" (upcoming) inside leg forward on the girth. Once your leg is in this position, press with it and push your horse sideways for a stride or two toward your new outside rein. If your horse feels stiff in his rib cage and leans his barrel against your leg instead of moving away from it, don't continue onto the second loop of the serpentine. Instead, circle so that you stay on the first loop. Then, as you approach the center line again, push him away from your inside leg. You might have to do the first circle and ask him to move sideways several times before he softly bends around your new inside leg.

Don't be in a hurry to ask for the change. Your main concern should be that your horse "gives" in his barrel and feels like he's stepping sideways toward your new outside rein. When that happens, you can straighten his body, ask for the flying change, and work your way back onto the arc of the second loop of the serpentine. Go through the same process as you approach the centerline between the second and third loops of the serpentine (fig. 20.16).

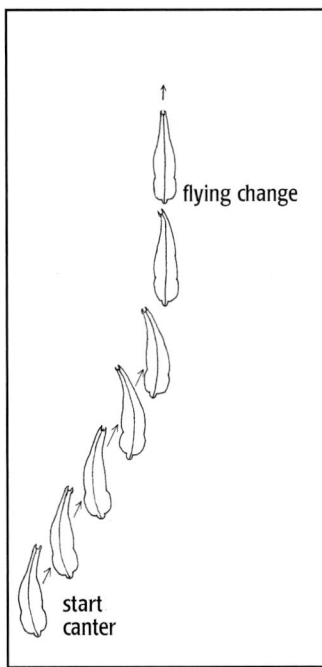

20.15 A "throughness" exercise to improve flying changes that are late behind: start a canter half-pass to the right, and gradually bend your horse's neck to the left. When he feels soft and doesn't resist the action of your left rein, straighten his neck, ride straight forward, and ask for the flying change.

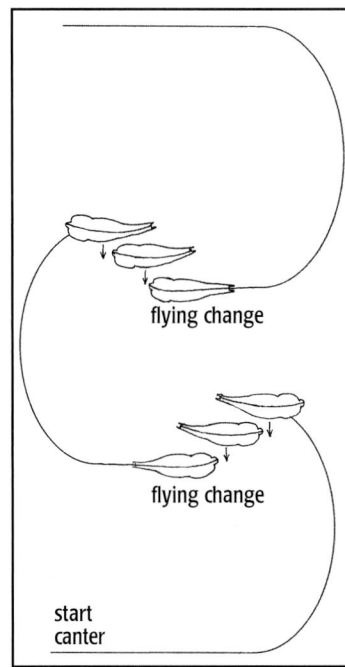

20.16 Canter a serpentine of three or more loops. As you approach the center to start the second loop, slide your "upcoming" inside leg forward to the girth, press with it, and leg-yield your horse for a couple of strides into your new outside rein. Then ask for the flying change.

4. Sometimes the cause of late changes isn't a lack of "throughness" but is the result of insufficient engagement of the inside hind leg—the leg that will become the new outside hind leg. So, if that's what you're running into, here are some "engagement-of-the-new-outside-hind-leg" exercises for you:

a. Do a half-pass in the canter to engage your horse's inside hind leg. Then, ride straight forward for a stride or two before you ask for the flying change. Since the old inside hind leg becomes the new outside hind leg (the strike-off leg) in a flying change, the more ready, eager and, therefore, engaged it is from the half-pass, the more likely you'll be to get a clean change (fig. 20.17).

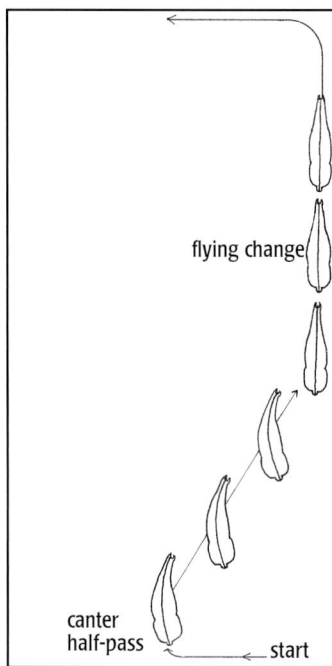

20.17 For late flying changes due to insufficient engagement, do a half-pass in canter, then ride straight forward for a stride or two before asking for the change.

flying change

canter half-pass

start

b. Ride a haunches-in in the canter on a small circle until you feel your horse lower his hindquarters and "sit down" behind. When he does, straighten him, leave the circle by riding straight forward, and immediately ask for the flying change. If you wait too long before you ask, your horse has time to shift his center of gravity toward his front legs, and you'll lose the benefits of the exercise.

c. Ride three **preparatory half-halts** that are directed to your horse's inside hind leg—the leg that will become the new outside hind leg. These half-halts are yet another variation of the ones you're used to doing in that they are shorter than the usual half-halt that lasts for three seconds. Each "preparatory" half-halt consists of a momentary closure of seat, legs, and hand. You close your legs, push with your seat, and close your inside hand in a fist.

Do three of these half-halts very quickly in a row in sync with the rhythm of the canter.

Since you want to engage the inside hind leg, give the half-halts when that leg is on the ground (during the second beat of the canter). That is the moment during which you can influence it so that it will be used more powerfully.

Then after three quick half-halts, ask for the flying change. It's even helpful to count out loud, "1-2-3- change," or, "now, now, now, change," each time the inside hind leg is on the ground, to get your timing. If you can't feel this moment, look at your horse's mane. It usually goes up during the second beat of the canter. Each time you count out loud, push with your seat, close your legs and quickly open and close your inside hand in a fist. Specifically, if you're changing from the right lead to the left lead, you'll be giving the half-halts on the right rein. At the fourth canter stride when you say the word "change," close your inside hand in a fist again at the same time that you bring your inside leg back to tell your horse to do the change.

d. If your "preparatory" half-halts don't engage your horse's new outside hind leg sufficiently, use the whip in a similar way. Ride around in canter and say "now, now, now" as you give three taps on the inside hind (the leg that will become the new outside hind). Tap as lightly or as vigorously as you need to get that leg active and "jumping." While tapping, imagine that the hind legs are so eager that they're begging to switch leads. If your horse's hind legs could talk, you'd hear them saying, "When? When? How about now?" with each tap of the whip. Do this several times and then finally go ahead and

20.18 To engage your horse's new outside hind leg (the "old" inside hind leg) sufficiently to prepare him for a flying change, ride around in canter and say, "Now, now, now," as you tap it three times with the whip. If the horse's inside hind leg could talk, you would hear it saying, "When? When? How about now?" You want it to be "begging" to switch the lead.

give the aid for the flying change—tap, tap, tap, change (fig. 20.18).

Here's another exercise to help to engage the horse's new outside hind leg.

Start by riding to the left about a yard inside the track in counter-canter (on the right lead). Bend your horse around your right leg and ask for haunches-out around that leg. This means that his forehand will remain a yard away from the track and his hindquarters will be moved toward the rail. He will be on three tracks, with his left hind leg lined up directly behind his right front leg (figs. 20.19 and 20.20).

Once your horse can do this haunches-out easily, keep his legs in the same position but straighten his neck by bringing it toward the

20.19 Here Joy prepares Wilkinson for the flying change by riding him a little off the track in haunches-out in the counter-canter. He appears to be nicely bent and flexed to the right.

center of the ring. Then, close your left leg and feel like you're pushing his left hind leg toward your right hand. You should be able to go easily back and forth from haunches-out with bend to straightening his neck. When he feels like he's stepping from your left leg into your right hand, ask for the flying change.

To ensure the straightness and the engagement of the inside hind leg while on the new lead, continue cantering forward in a shoulder-fore position after the flying change. This should not be too difficult; because of the haunches-out exercise you did before the flying change, your horse's legs are already lined up to do a three-track shoulder-in. So, all you have to do is decrease the angle slightly to get a shoulder-fore on four tracks. Keep his shoulders 15 degrees from the rail and use your active inside leg to hold his hind legs in the track.

Changing Late in Front

I also see horses who change leads behind first but are late to change in front. This situation doesn't concern me as much as the horse who changes late behind, because at least I know that this horse is thinking about his hind legs. In fact, usually when a horse does this, it's because the rider has restricted him with her new inside rein rather than softening it. It's definitely a challenge in rider coordination to be able to give a firm half-halt on the new outside rein while you ease the tension on the new inside rein.

I often have a student practice this when she is on the ground. To change from right lead to left lead, she closes her right (outside) hand in a fist and softens her left (inside) hand an inch

20.20 Joy keeps Wilkinson's legs and body in the haunches-out position as she straightens his neck with her left rein. Once he feels like he's pushed from her left leg into her right rein, she'll give the aid for the flying change.

or so forward. Then, she changes back from left to right by closing the left hand and softening the right hand. In the beginning, I suggest that she even exaggerate the forward movement of the inside hand. In this way she develops some muscle memory, so that it becomes automatic for her to soften the inside rein forward, rather than hang or pull on it, at the same time that she's closing the outside hand in a fist.

Late to Answer the Aid

Sometimes, you'll find that the problem isn't that your horse is late behind or in front, but that he's late to answer your aid. You give the aid and one or two strides after you ask, your horse finally answers with a clean flying change. This frequently happens in one direction more than the other. One solution is to mentally prepare your horse by giving your three "preparatory" half-halts before asking for the change as described on page 328.

You can also change the timing of your aid ever so slightly. Give the aid a fraction of a second earlier than you normally would, in order to give your horse an extra moment to mentally compute and physically respond to the aid.

Sometimes a horse gives a delayed reaction to the aid because the tempo of his canter is too slow, and it takes him an extra moment to respond to the aid. If you suspect that tempo is the issue, work on teaching your horse to canter more crisply. Do some transitions to medium canter to quicken the tempo, and when you come back to collected canter again, maintain the faster tempo. Mark this quicker tempo by speeding up the forward and back motion of your seat rather than just following along at the speed your horse chooses.

Keeping Your Horse Straight

I frequently see horses who aren't straight when doing flying changes. This crookedness can be expressed in a variety of ways—I'll discuss three of them here.

A horse may swing his hindquarters to the inside in the direction of the new lead. Sometimes this is because the horse is trying to avoid the engagement of his new inside hind leg. More often than not, however, the problem is created by the rider. If a rider pulls on her new inside rein during the change, not only will she turn her horse's neck to the inside, but the backward action on the rein will block his hind leg from stepping under his body.

Since he can't come under his body with his inside hind leg, he has a few options, none of which are desirable: he can be late behind in the change; he can change cleanly, but take a short step behind; or because it's difficult to come under, he can take the path of least resistance and swing his hindquarters to the inside. The rider needs to remember to soften her new inside hand forward as described in *Changing Late in Front* on page 332.

If it becomes a habit for her horse to swing his hindquarters to the inside during the change, it'll be helpful for her to do two things. First, close her new outside hand in a fist as she would do normally. Then move that hand laterally in the direction of the new lead as if asking for shoulder-fore. This rein action helps place her horse's forehand in front of his new inside hind leg.

Another expression of crookedness is when a horse does a straight flying change in one direction, but in the other direction his entire body drifts or even jumps sideways. You can prevent this by using your new inside leg firmly on the girth. In this way you can make a physical barrier that blocks your horse from jumping sideways during the flying change.

Yet a third form of crookedness is shown when a horse stays straight during the flying change but becomes crooked by swinging his hindquarters to the inside on the very next stride afterwards. He does this to avoid bending the joints of his inside hind leg and carrying weight on it in the canter. In this case, ride the change and immediately step into shoulder-fore for a few strides. That is, after a flying change from right to left, do left shoulder-fore until the horse learns that he must keep his new inside hind leg engaged and underneath his body (fig. 20.21).

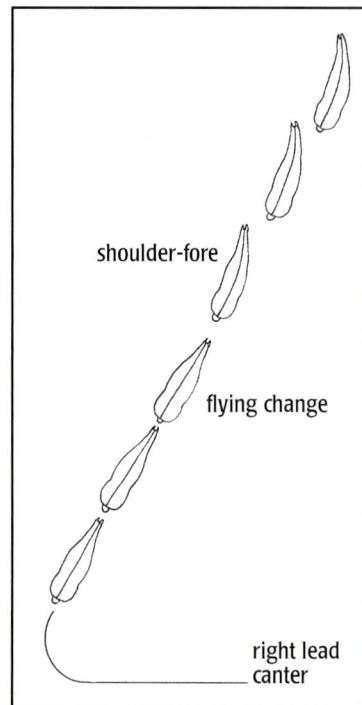

shoulder-fore

flying change

right lead canter

20.21 When your horse becomes crooked by swinging his hindquarters to the inside during and after a flying change, ride the change and immediately step into shoulder-fore for a few strides.

KEY POINTS

- In order to do a flying change, the horse reorganizes his legs during the period of suspension in the canter. The hind leg that he places on the ground first determines the canter lead he will be on.

- To prepare your horse to learn flying changes, work on simple changes of lead, self-carriage in the canter, and counter-canter.

- In the initial stages, your priority is to get a "clean" flying change where the hind and front legs switch leads during the same canter stride. Later on, you'll systematically add in other ingredients such as relaxation, straightness, roundness, and the immediate reaction to the aid.

- If you have a horse who changes late behind, focus either on "throughness" exercises or engaging his inside hind leg.

21

Typical Problems Solved by

USING "FANCY STUFF"

These "typical" problems that I'm going to address in this chapter are not necessarily more complicated than the ones you might have been faced with earlier in your horse's training, but because you are further along in your education (your horse, too) and have more information at your disposal, you have more tools to deal with them.

When you run into trouble during schooling, the symptoms may vary, but the cause is almost always the same—something in **the Basics** has gone awry. So, rather than repeatedly drilling a movement or exercise, look for the answer in the Basics. Run through a checklist of the qualities that should be a constant theme throughout all of your work. Ask yourself if your horse is relaxed, moving freely forward, in a regular rhythm, and is straight. Check that he's responding to your half-halts so you can first connect him and later ask for self-carriage. Then, when the Basics are in order, try the movement again (the Basics are all covered in Stage One).

I remember watching a clinic that Klaus Balkenhol (fig. 21.1), a member of the German dressage team that won the Olympic Gold Medal

in 1992, was giving to the American riders who were aspiring to gain a slot on the 1996 Olympic team. All of these riders were very accomplished and the horses were trained to a very high level. Yet the message that Mr. Balkenhol repeatedly sent home was that if they were having a problem with any movement or exercise, it was always caused by a fault in the Basics.

He didn't want them to make adjustments or corrections during the actual movements. Instead, he had these top riders concentrate first and foremost on relaxation, rhythm, suppleness, contact, impulsion, and straightness. Invariably, with the Basics as a priority, the quality and correctness of the movements improved dramatically.

DECREASING TENSION AND TIGHTNESS

In chapter 14, I talked about riding your horse in a **deep frame** at the beginning and end of your schooling session to warm him up and cool him down, as well as to help him stay connected if he

21.1 Working your horse in a deep frame, as Amy is doing here, is a great way to dissipate tension.

was struggling to stay on the bit in a particular movement.

I also mentioned that working in a "deep" frame can be used to dissipate tension, and I'd like to explore that idea a bit more here. Understand that when you train a horse, you're dealing with an inseparable mind and body connection. If your horse is tense, excited, or inattentive you can effectively quiet his mind by relaxing him physically. This approach is often more productive than simply trying to calm his mood by speaking to him in soothing tones.

If a horse is tense or tight, he holds his back rigidly, and this blocks the connection from

his hind legs to his forehand. However, when he's ridden deep, his back has to swing and as a result his whole body can become looser and freer. As his body relaxes, you can almost feel a horse take in a deep breath, exhale, and let go of his tension (fig. 21.1).

If your horse is a spooky type, deep is a great position for you to work him in. Take it from Holland's Anky van Grunsven, winner of the individual gold medal in the 1994 World Equestrian Games and 1995 World Cup, who relies on working deep with her timid and easily distracted Olympic Bonfire. She not only does a very lengthy warm-up in this frame, but she also does all of her advanced movements deep until just moments before she's ready to enter the competition arena. Even though you might not be headed for the World Championships or the Olympics, knowing how to put your horse deep can come in very handy in the many situations you encounter when he becomes frightened or defensive.

Generally, I start each schooling session with my horse deep. But I'll also return to this frame when I'm introducing a new exercise that will stress him mentally as he tries to learn it. I'll alternate between the exercise itself and riding him deep on a circle until I can re-establish relaxation. Then I'll resume the exercise.

One of my students, Kathy, was having difficulty keeping her horse relaxed when she did a series of flying changes across the diagonal. Her horse was fine doing the flying changes on the long side of the arena, but as soon as she started across the diagonal line, he began to get worried. So we worked him deep as part of his relaxation program.

Kathy started across the diagonal on the right lead and asked for only one flying change to the left lead. Immediately after the flying change, she turned onto a 10-meter circle to the left and put her horse deep in the canter. She stayed on that circle several times around until he finally relaxed. Then she rebalanced him and continued across the diagonal, asked for the next flying change to the right lead, and immediately circled to the right and put him deep again. After about a week of riding the flying changes on the diagonal this way, her horse began to relax because he expected to do the comforting canter on the

circle rather than anticipating the next flying change. Within a few weeks, she was able to ride flying changes in a sequence on a diagonal line with a calm and confident horse.

ALL MANNER OF CROOKEDNESSES

UNEVEN IN THE REIN

Riders frequently complain to me that their horses are hanging on one rein and won't take a contact with the other rein. This unevenness in the rein actually is a result of the horse's innate crookedness. On his stiff side, a horse steps into the rein and the contact can be quite firm. On his soft side, however, a horse avoids stepping into the rein, and the contact can be lighter, or even nonexistent. Your goal is to make your horse even in the reins so that you feel the same weight in both hands.

So what can you do to make your crooked horse straight so you feel the same amount of contact in each rein? Well, with a minor adjustment, the same half-halt that you learned in chapters 13 and 14 in order to **connect** your horse can also be used to make him even in the reins.

"Reversing" the Half-Halts

Let's say your horse is stiff to the right and soft to the left. When riding to the right, ride your usual half-halt where you drive the horse through your closed outside (left) hand. However, when riding to the left, you're going

21.2 Alpen's soft side is his right side. It's obvious that he is uneven in the rein because there is a firm contact on the left rein and slack in the right rein.

to reverse your half-halt. Send him forward through your closed inside hand—once again the left hand—and, if necessary, flex him a little to the outside (figs. 21.2 and 21.3). Your aids are essentially saying, "Step from behind into this light left rein and take a contact with my left hand...and stop hanging on the right rein."

Once your horse is consistently even in both reins, you can go back to riding normal half-halts through the outside rein in both directions. Horses change constantly during schooling. Always remember to ride the horse you have on

any given day—not the one you were riding last month or even yesterday.

When I first got Eastwood he was stiff to the right and soft to the left as in the above example. So, when tracking left, I reversed my half-halt—sending him through my closed inside hand—for a month or so. Then gradually I realized that his stiff and soft sides had changed in the course of training. So, temporarily I had to reverse my half-halt and drive him into my inside hand while riding to the right! Now, he's fairly even in my hands, but occasionally he'll collapse away from

21.3 Bekki fixes the uneven contact by reversing her half-halt. She drives Alpen forward through her closed inside (right) hand and flexes Alpen slightly to the outside. The horse has established a solid contact with the right rein here.

one rein so that the contact between it and my hand is too light, and he ends up hanging on the other rein. When he does this, I'll immediately give a half-halt through whichever is the light rein—the one he's not stepping into and taking a contact with—in order to remedy the situation.

RIDER-CREATED CROOKEDNESS

Eastwood was a fairly short-term project as far as getting him straight and even in the reins. I do have a student, however, who had to ride her horse with "reversed" half-halts in both directions for a solid year. I had her do this because she was the cause of the problem. She made her horse crooked by being heavy-handed with her inside rein in both directions. In response to her inside hand, her horse was happy to overbend his neck to the inside, collapse away from whichever was the inside rein, and pop his shoulders to the outside. Because this is what she did habitually, this felt normal to her. She had lost her perception of what it felt like to have her horse **axis-straight**. (Remember, axis-straight means the horse's spine exactly overlaps his line of travel.)

I told her to reverse the half-halts so she could get the idea of keeping his shoulders in front of his hips. She needed to become familiar with this feeling of his spine being truly straight and the contact being equal in the two reins.

So, except for a canter depart when her horse needed to be flexed to the inside, she used half-halts through her closed inside hand for everything else that she did with him. It took a long time for her to learn the feeling of keeping her horse axis-straight, but now she is able to give normal half-halts through the outside rein. And, even though it took her a while to learn the feeling of a straight horse, reversing the half-halt wasn't a big deal for either one of them.

USING HAUNCHES-IN TO STRAIGHTEN AND STRENGTHEN YOUR HORSE

Haunches-in can also be used as a straightening exercise for a horse who has one hind leg weaker than the other. I know it must seem like a contradiction to move a horse's hindquarters sideways in order to make him straight. But this displacement done on purpose by the rider is different from an evasion caused by a crooked horse. The crooked horse moves his hindquarters sideways, with no bend in his body, to avoid bending the joints of his weaker hind leg (figs. 21.4 to 21.6).

Do you remember the formula from our discussion of advanced lateral movements? Bend + Sideways = Engagement (chapter 18). During haunches-in there's a bend through the horse's body, so as he goes sideways with a bend, he has no option but to engage this hind leg (fig. 21.7).

In addition, the leg that steps under his mass—the outside hind leg—has to "weight-lift." So the haunches-in becomes a strengthening exercise as well. As this weaker hind leg becomes stronger,

21.4 In this photo, Brie is crooked. She has moved her hindquarters ever so slightly sideways to avoid bending the joints of her inside hind leg and carrying weight on it. Her hind feet do not follow directly in the tracks made by her front feet.

the horse is able to use his hind legs more equally, and it's easier to make him straight.

If I have a horse who habitually carries his quarters to the right, I'll ride him with his hindquarters slightly to the left regardless of where I am in the ring. This means placing him in haunches-in when I ride to the left, and haunches-out when going to the right. I do this because the horse whose hindquarters are always to the right isn't carrying as much weight on that right hind leg and is letting his left hind leg do most of the work. I need to reverse this tendency by placing his right hind leg under his body. This way it has to carry weight until it becomes strong

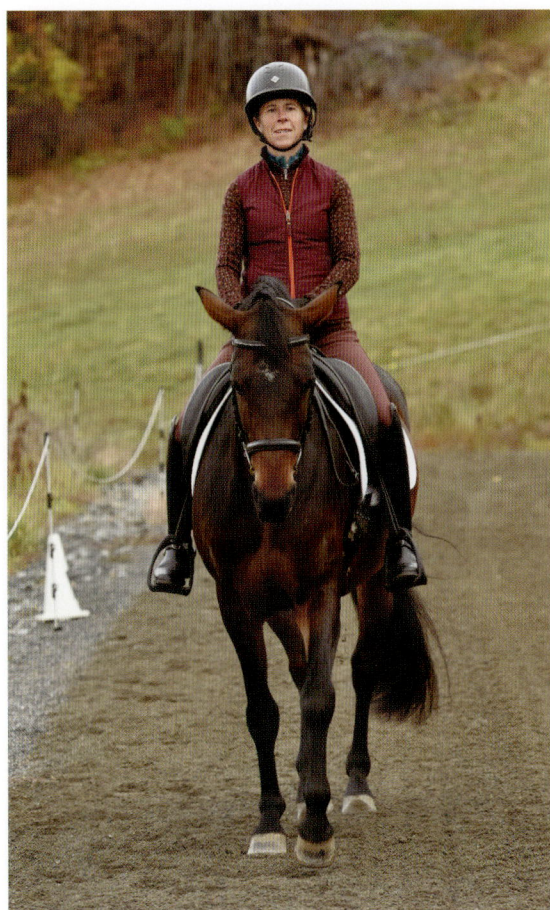

21.5 A requested very slight haunches-in–in this case, the sideways displacement is useful (in an engaging way) rather than harmful (in an "unloading weight," or evasive, way), because Brie is bent around Amy's inside leg. The position of Amy's outside leg is behind the girth to help with the bend and to specifically ask Brie's hindquarters to move in off the track.

21.6 A true haunches-in: Amy has increased the angle that Brie's hindquarters are moved in off the track. She is still doing a good engagement exercise, because Brie maintains a uniform bend from poll to tail around Amy's inside leg.

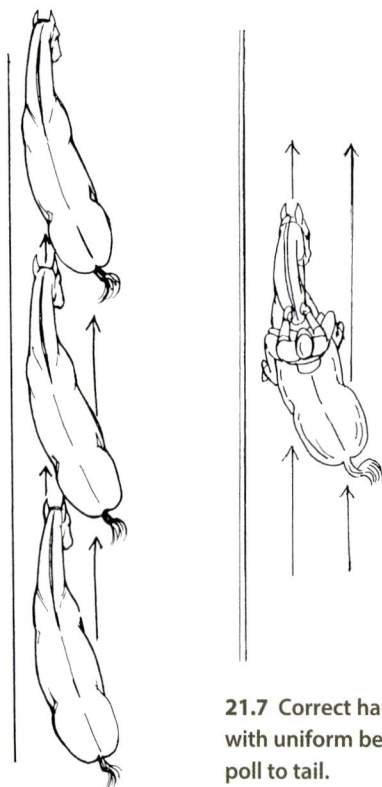

21.7 Correct haunches-in with uniform bend from poll to tail.

21.8 To correct the tendency to carry her hindquarters to the right, and, therefore, avoid carrying weight with the right hind leg, Amy places Brie's hindquarters a little bit to the left as a straightening and strengthening exercise. Here, as they go to the right she puts Brie in haunches-out.

enough for the horse to be happy to use it willingly (figs. 21.8 and 21.9).

I remember a horse that I had in for training that was incredibly crooked in this way. As soon as I picked up a contact, his haunches would swing to the left. All horses have some tendency to be crooked, but this horse had developed very unevenly because his rider had never straightened him. So, it was physical therapy time!

For three weeks, when riding to the right in the walk, trot, and canter, I rode him in a very subtle version of haunches-in on circles and straight lines—just enough positioning to put his left hind leg ever so slightly underneath his body. When riding to the left, I rode a slight haunches-out position in the walk and trot or a shoulder-fore position in walk, trot, and canter.

All of my efforts and every position I used were designed to keep his left hind leg under his body so that it had to carry weight. I knew that the left hind had become stronger when I picked up the reins one day and this horse adopted a slight, right haunches-in position on his own. His willingness to carry weight on his left hind leg proved to me that it was getting as strong as his right hind leg. At that point I abandoned those particular physical therapy exercises and began to school him more like a normal horse (fig. 21.10).

21.9 When they change direction and go to the left, Amy still wants to keep Brie's right hind leg underneath her body, so she rides her in haunches-in. As long as Brie's right hind leg is under her body and lifting her weight (even if she only moves it over an inch or two), it will get stronger.

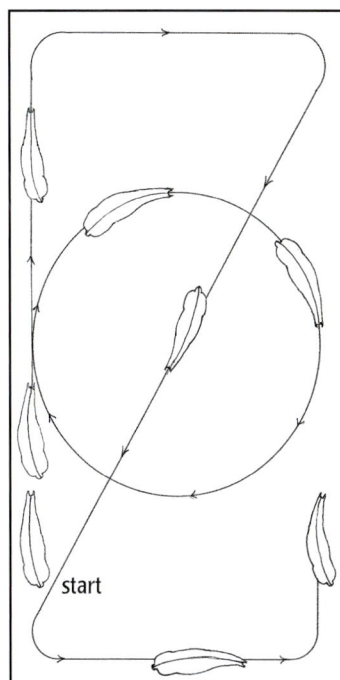

21.10 To strengthen your horse's left hind leg, move his hindquarters slightly to the right no matter where you are in the ring—going right, changing direction across the diagonal, circling, and even going left.

USING SHOULDER-IN TO MAINTAIN BALANCE AND IMPROVE EXTENSIONS

Use shoulder-in to help you when you ride movements during which your horse habitually loses his **self-carriage** and falls on his forehand. For instance, when you ride an extended trot or canter and then find it difficult to do the transition back to the collected gait because your horse's balance has shifted toward his front legs. Try riding shoulder-fore or shoulder-in to keep his shoulders "up" in the moment of the downward transition. For this exercise you don't need to extend for a whole long side. Ask for the extension for five or six strides. Then rather than using a half-halt to collect the pace, put him in a shoulder-in to engage him and keep his balance back toward his hindquarters for the downward transition. Then repeat the sequence again.

You can also use shoulder-in to develop your horse's medium and extended gaits and make them more expressive. Remember that the degree of extension that a horse can do is directly related to the degree of collection he has prior to the extension. Think of it this way. A spring that is only gently coiled won't have much thrust. But a tightly coiled spring will have more power when it's released.

So ride several steps of shoulder-in to coil the spring of your horse's hind legs. Then straighten him and ask for the extension.

CROOKEDNESS SHOWS UP MORE IN COLLECTED AND EXTENDED GAITS

Remember that it's important, all through your training from the very beginning, to always ride your horse axis-straight in order to make the hind legs equally strong. If you don't, you'll end up having problems sooner rather than later, and certainly in the collected and extended gaits.

Here's an example of the way a rider allows one hind leg to become weaker and the consequences of doing so. She keeps her horse axis-straight when she rides in one direction, but lets his haunches drift to the inside when she goes the other way. As a result, over time the hind leg that deviates toward the inside of the ring, as opposed to stepping directly under the horse's body, gets weaker because it's not carrying an equal amount of weight. This can seem fairly subtle in the beginning. But eventually, when the physical demands on that leg are increased as they are in a collected gait, the weaker hind leg can't cope with the added burden, so the horse becomes even more crooked by carrying his hindquarters off to one side.

Then when he's asked to do something like a trot extension, he shows his weakness. His stronger hind leg is more engaged, comes under his body correctly and has more pushing and carrying power than the weaker leg. As a result,

21.11 By standing behind Rowen, it's easy to see that he prefers to carry more of his weight with his left hind leg. While circling to the right, he is carrying his haunches slightly toward the inside of the circle so he can "unload" his right hind leg. You can see this because neither of his hind feet is going to step into the track of the corresponding front foot.

he makes a greater effort with this stronger leg, making him look uneven behind.

You may have wondered all along if your horse has one hind leg weaker than the other. Well, the reality is that most horses do. You can probably assume that one side of your horse is stronger than the other, just as you're stronger on one side of your body than the other. This becomes quite apparent in the collected and extended gaits.

Have someone stand directly in front of, or behind, your horse as you walk, trot, and canter on both a straight line and on a circle. That person can tell you which direction your horse chooses to carry his hindquarters. If they drift to the left, he's unweighting the left hind leg because it's weaker. If he carries his hindquarters to the right, then the right hind leg is the weaker one (figs. 21.11 to 21.13).

If you have a horse that is noticeably stronger with one hind leg than the other, strengthen the muscles by using them. Insist that he carry the weaker hind leg under his body regardless of the direction he's going. If his left hind leg is weaker, ride a shoulder-fore or shoulder-in when you go to the left, and ride haunches-in or shoulder-out when you track to the right (fig. 21.14).

Doing these exercises as I've described places his left hind leg underneath his body all the time so it has to do some "weight lifting." You can do them as a series of exercises every day. Or you can do a very slight version of these exercises

21.12 Ally continues the circle to the right and brings her right leg back to place Rowen in haunches-out so he has to carry weight with his right hind leg. This leg steps directly in the track of his left front leg. This position helps his right hind leg become stronger.

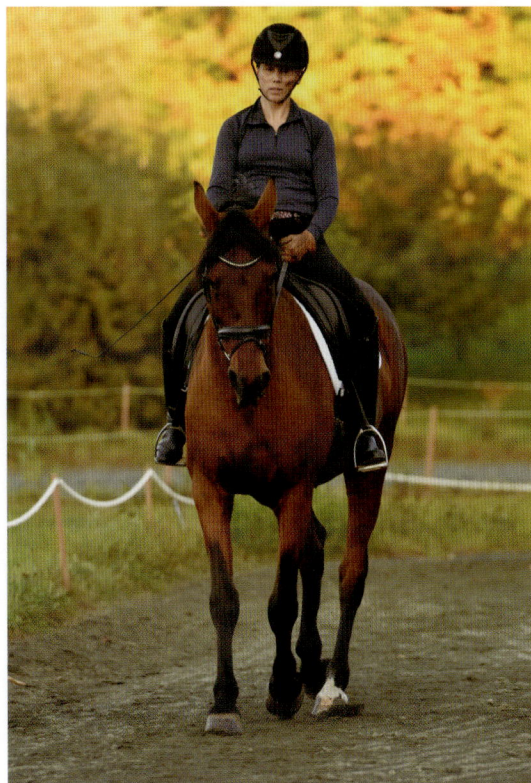

21.13 To strengthen Rowen's right hind leg so that he's more willing to carry weight on it, Ally places her horse in haunches-in while tracking left. Once again, this position makes him "weight-lift" with his right hind leg.

21.14 Now Ally works on strengthening Rowen's right hind leg by placing him in right shoulder-in as she makes a circle to the right. Every step he makes with his right hind leg stepping under his body will help to make that leg stronger.

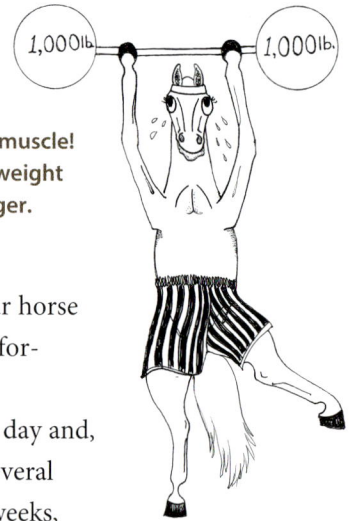

21.15 Use makes the muscle! Asking a hind leg to "weight lift" will make it stronger.

demanding that your horse do the exercises for forty-five minutes.

Do a few the first day and, over the course of several days to a couple of weeks, build up to a series of exercises. Also, within each session, make sure you give your horse lots of breaks to a walk on a loose rein so he can relax his muscles. Plan to intersperse extra "play days" in between days of hard work. Keep in mind that with all "weight-lifting," muscles repair and get stronger when they're given an opportunity to recover—on rest days and play days.

FAULTY TRANSITIONS TO AND FROM THE CANTER

Before I show you how to use some of the dressage exercises that you know or improving the transitions both upward to and downward from the canter, I want to make a point about the canter aid itself. It's important that you get into the habit of using your outside leg—the one that actually signals the depart—in a quick windshield wiper-like motion. If you haven't trained the aid in this way from the beginning, you can run into problems later on in schooling.

For example, let's say you want to start teaching your horse how to do a half-pass in

during your entire ride. For example, you could always place his weaker left hind leg an inch or so to the inside of the left front leg no matter what line or figure you're on, or which direction you're traveling (fig. 21.15).

But understand that there's a fine line between strengthening muscles and straining them. Sometimes you don't know if you've gone over that line until it's too late. At that point your horse lets you know because he will become markedly resistant, or even sore. To avoid this scenario, work on making his muscles stronger gradually and systematically rather than suddenly the trot. So, you give the leg aids to initiate the half-pass and instead of going sideways, your horse hops into the canter because he thinks that's what you're asking for. You need to realize that the leg aids for a half-pass and the aids for a canter depart are very similar. There has to be a way for your horse to differentiate between them.

In both cases, your horse is flexed to the inside, your inside leg is on the girth, your weight is on your inside seat bone, and your outside hand is closed in a fist. So what's the difference? In a half-pass your outside leg stays behind the girth to help with the bend and to move him sideways, while in a canter depart, it swings back and forth once to give the signal to canter.

Also, if you get into the habit of holding your leg back and waiting for your horse to react to the canter aid, you're going to have difficulties if you ever decide to go further with his training and do flying changes in a sequence. When you do a series of flying changes, your legs have to move quickly. Your horse must respond immediately so you can do them on the fourth, third, second, or even every stride. You might as well train your horse with the correct canter aid from the beginning rather than have to reschool him later on.

IMPROVING THE UPWARD TRANSITION TO THE CANTER

In chapter 12 on problem solving, I gave you some ideas on how to help a horse who was picking up the wrong lead. Now that you have more tools in your arsenal, I can give you some other exercises to help with canter departs.

Sometimes you'll ride a horse who picks up the wrong lead because his outside hind leg isn't sufficiently engaged. So alert his outside hind to be ready to strike off into the canter by directing two or three quick **preparatory half-halts** to it as a call to attention. Your half-halts ask the question, "Are you ready, outside hind leg?"

In this case, rather than maintaining your half-halt for three full seconds, each preparatory half-halt lasts for only a moment. Start in either the walk or the trot. Then half-halt in the rhythm of the gait by pushing with your seat, closing your legs, and closing your outside hand in a fist each time you feel your horse's outside hind leg on the ground. (You'll be able to feel when it's on the ground because your outside seat bone will feel like it's being pushed forward or up.) Then on the next stride, after the three quick half-halts, ask for the canter depart.

To help with the timing of the aids, say out loud in the rhythm of whichever gait you're in prior to the depart, "1, 2, 3, canter" or "Half-halt, half-halt, half-halt, canter."

You can also do an "engagement of the outside hind leg" exercise by doing a few steps of shoulder-out, in the walk or the trot, on a circle or a straight line. Position your horse's hind legs one meter in from the original track of the circle or line, bend him around your outside leg, and lead his forehand toward the outside by bringing both of your hands in that direction. While you're doing this be sure to drive his "old" outside hind leg (this leg has now become the horse's "inside" leg since you've changed the bend) under his center with your active "old" outside leg. Then, straighten him by re-establishing the correct bend and quickly give the aid for the strike-off before you lose the engaging effects of the shoulder-out (see fig. 17.23).

You can even use haunches-in to help with the departs. You might wonder why this is okay to do since I've already said that horses like to be crooked in the canter by swinging their hindquarters to the inside. Well, there are two things to consider here. The first is that when a horse places his hindquarters to the inside to avoid bearing weight, he loses the bend through his body. As a result, he can avoid engagement because he doesn't have to bend the joints of his hind legs. But because he's asked to bend through his body in a haunches-in, he has to bend the joints of his hind legs and engage them.

In addition, I won't be asking you to maintain the haunches-in position during the actual moment of the depart. You just use the haunches-in prior to the depart to put your horse more "through" the inside of his body. Then, straighten him before the transition. For example, start in the walk in haunches-in on a straight line; arc onto a circle and go back to a line—all in haunches-in while walking. When your horse feels very soft, straighten him, and immediately ask for the canter.

IMPROVING THE DOWNWARD TRANSITION FROM THE CANTER

Now let's look at how you can use some dressage exercises to improve the downward transition from the canter to the trot.

One of the most common problems I see with a horse learning to do downward transitions from the canter to the trot is the horse who rushes off rather than ending up in a balanced trot. Your instinct will probably be to pull on the reins to slow him down. As I've discussed before, this may well decrease your horse's speed but, unfortunately, it'll also stop his hind legs from coming forward. As you know, once his hind legs stop coming under his body, his back goes down, and his head and neck come up. So you might manage to keep your horse from running off, but he'll no longer be connected!

There's an exercise to teach your horse to keep his hind legs underneath him during the downward transition from the canter. Go on a circle in the canter. Then, ask for the transition to the trot. During the first stride after the transition, ask for shoulder-in on the circle. By doing a good shoulder-in and engaging his inside hind leg, he won't be able to rush off. As soon as you're at a manageable speed going sideways, you can go straight forward again.

Sometimes you'll find yourself asking for a downward transition from the canter, and you feel like you're being totally ignored. Your horse just won't listen to your **stilled seat**, and he keeps cantering merrily along.

Once again, don't resort to pulling on the reins. Instead, send him steeply sideways in the canter by pushing his hindquarters away from the lead you are on (if you're on the right lead in the canter, push his hindquarters to the left with your right leg). If he's leg-yielding at a 35-degree angle, your horse will find it impossible to stay in canter and he'll eventually fall into the trot. Then you can praise him, go back to the canter, and ask for the downward transition again. Ride the leg-yield at the same time that you still your seat until you can use your seat alone to get the downward transition.

COMBINING TWO SETS OF AIDS TO IMPROVE BALANCE

At this point you've learned how to ride many movements. In addition, you know how to give half-halts not only to put your horse on the bit but also to increase his self-carriage. The next step for you is to do both of these things at once. (Don't panic. It is possible!) By combining two sets of aids, you can ride the movements and maintain good balance at the same time.

In the beginning you might feel uncoordinated. You know the feeling—like you're trying to pat your head and rub your stomach at the same time. But eventually you'll rely on this blending together of two sets of aids because you'll discover how much easier it is to maintain your horse's balance rather than to have to correct him every time you do something different.

The half-halt and the movements themselves should become dependent on each other. The half-halt improves the quality of the movements and the movements themselves make your horse more athletic.

For instance, you normally use a certain amount of seat, leg and hand to ask a horse to come on the bit in the working gaits. If you use

a greater degree of those three elements, you ask for more self-carriage. And, if you want an extension, use more driving seat and legs—compared to the amount of restraining outside hand—than you would to do a **connecting half-halt**. When you want to do a downward transition at the end of this extension, apply your legs as usual, but still your seat, and use more outside rein to collect the gait.

As far as all the lateral movements are concerned, you first produce "connection," then "direction." Begin each movement with a half-halt that produces balance and roundness, then emphasize whichever aids within the half-halt you need to send your horse in the direction you want. For instance, more inside leg pressure moves him into shoulder-in, while more outside leg pressure moves him into a half-pass.

You want to become adept at doing this because it's reasonable to expect your horse to lose his balance every time you do any kind of a transition. Simply put, any time there's any sort of a change, there's a potential loss of balance. When you change from one pace to another, lengthen and shorten, go from a single track to a two-track exercise and back to a single track, or change from one bend to the other, you can assume your horse might lose his balance. This loss of balance can express itself in a variety of ways. Your horse can drop his back and become hollow. Or he might fall on the forehand, rush off, or lean on one or both reins. Any loss of balance should trigger you to give a half-halt.

Think of every situation where there's a potential loss of balance, and **blend** or "superimpose" a half-halt on top of those critical moments. Rather than waiting to correct your horse after the fact, prepare him for what's coming up by riding a half-halt a little bit before, during, and for a step or two after you begin each new movement. Obviously, to do this, your half-halt will last longer than the standard three seconds I described in chapter 13. In fact, it's not unreasonable for this half-halt to last five or six seconds.

Here are some examples of how to blend two sets of aids at once.

TRANSITIONS FROM ONE PACE TO ANOTHER

Let's first have a look at transitions from one pace to another. To maximize the physical benefits of a transition and to make your horse more comfortable for you to ride, the transition should be done on the bit. Think about what your signals say to the horse. Your transition aids just tell your horse to change from walk to trot, or canter to walk, for example. They don't tell him to stay connected or in good balance. It's not the transition aid's responsibility.

Staying connected is the half-halt's job. So, if you're having difficulty keeping your horse on the bit during a transition, you need to do two things at once: a half-halt and the transition aid. The half-halt says "stay on the bit" and the transition aid tells your horse to change from trot to canter, for instance. When both sets of aids are applied at the same time, you're telling your horse to "do a transition on the bit." Start the half-halt first, and somewhere during those three seconds increase

your legs for an upward transition or tighten your stomach muscles and still your seat for a downward transition (figs. 21.16 to 21.19).

Remember that your horse's balance and connection during a transition can be no better than it was during the steps just before the transition. So if he's hollow, on the forehand, stiff, or leaning, first use a preliminary, three-second half-halt to rebalance him. Then give another longer half-halt, which you'll blend into the aid for the transition to keep him balanced throughout.

Make sure your horse doesn't anticipate the transition and do it when you start the half-halt. He has to wait for the actual aid. For instance, let's say your goal is to go from canter to trot with your horse on the bit. You start the half-halt and before you get a chance to blend it into the aid for the downward transition, your horse breaks to the trot on his own. If this happens, you need to tell him he's wrong. Otherwise, he'll start to make his own decisions. For example, you might be in the canter, and you give a normal three-second half-halt for the purpose of making him rounder. Before you know it, your horse slips into the trot on his own!

This miscommunication can be particularly inconvenient in competition. Maybe you know the feeling. Even though you'd like to make an adjustment to improve your horse's balance in the canter, you don't dare disturb the status quo because you're afraid he'll anticipate, or misinterpret, your signal and make a costly mistake by falling into the trot.

To correct this in training, give some three-second half-halts while cantering and touch him

21.16 Maeve and Bekki are in trot here and Bekki is about to ask Maeve to do a transition to the right lead canter. Because she's not properly connected in the trot, it will be impossible for her to do a canter depart on the bit. Note the inactive hind legs, the concave-looking back, the high neck, and the stiff poll and jaw.

21.17 Maeve's balance, frame, and connection during the first stride of canter can be no better than they are in the steps just before the transition. Because Bekki didn't connect her with a half-halt while they were still in the trot, Maeve is hollow and disconnected in the canter.

21.18 Compare Maeve's shape and balance in these next two photos with the two previous ones. She and Bekki are in the trot preparing to step into the right lead canter. Maeve is nicely on the bit and Bekki wants to keep her there during the transition to the canter. To do that she has to blend a connecting half-halt into the aids for the canter. Bekki starts the half-halt by closing her legs, pushing with her seat, closing her left hand in a fist, and using her right hand to keep Maeve softly flexed to the right.

21.19 Bekki maintains the connecting half-halt and asks for the canter depart by bringing her left leg behind the girth at the same time. By giving both sets of aids at once, she is telling Maeve to stay on the bit as she transitions to the canter.

with the whip to remind him to keep coming from behind in the canter rather than trotting. Do a few half-halts without a transition. Then when you know he's listening and waiting, give a half-halt and blend it into the aid for the downward transition. Then go back to the canter and do a few half-halts without a transition. Keep alternating until you trust that he's really paying attention to you.

What if your problem with downward transitions is even more basic than the maintenance of connection and balance? Maybe the bottom line is that your horse is not paying attention to you. If that's the case, you need to give short preparatory half-halts rather than blending a long, connecting half-halt into the aid for the transition. In the section on faulty canter departs, (p. 402) I explained how to engage the outside hind leg—the strike-off leg—for the canter depart by giving three quick preparatory half-halts when that leg is on the ground. You can also use quick preparatory half-halts to set your horse up for downward transitions.

For all downward transitions, you need to direct your quick half-halts to the *inside* hind leg because that is the leg that has to work harder, and engage more, on circles and corners. Close your eyes and feel when the inside hind leg is on the ground, by noticing when your inside seat bone is being pushed forward. (It might feel to you as if it's being pushed up, rather than forward).

This is the moment when you give your preparatory half-halts by pushing with your seat, pressing with your legs, and closing the fingers of both hands. Each time you apply this quick half-halt, say out loud "now, now, now," or "one, two, three." Then on the fourth step, close your legs and hands again but still your seat to ask for the downward transition.

If you want to go from canter to trot, direct your half-halts to the inside hind leg. When that leg is on the ground, half-halt three times in the rhythm of the canter, and say "now, now, now, trot." Do the same for other downward transitions. For example, when you want to go from trot to walk, direct your half-halts to the inside hind leg, and in the rhythm of the trot say, "now, now, now, walk." When you want to go from the walk to halt, direct your half-halts to the inside hind leg, and in the rhythm of the walk, say "now, now, now, halt."

TRANSITIONS FROM A SINGLE TRACK TO TWO TRACKS

Now, let's have a look at how you can combine two sets of aids to keep your horse on the bit as you start a lateral movement. Let's say you're riding to the right and you want to do a leg-yield to the left with your horse on the bit. First, insure the connection over your horse's back by giving a half-halt while you're still on a single track. Close your legs, close your left hand in a fist and, if necessary, vibrate the right rein. Then continue to give the half-halt as you add in the aids for leg-yielding to the left. Keep your weight centered and your left leg on the girth, but slide your right leg slightly behind the girth. Your left hand is supporting and remains closed in a fist while your right hand continues to vibrate to ask for a little flexion.

CHANGES OF BEND

Suppose you want to do a figure-eight. Each time you go from one circle of the figure-eight to the other, you have to change your horse's bend. Because of this change, there's a risk of upsetting his balance.

To avoid any stiffening, losing the connection over his back, or falling on the forehand, super-impose your half-halt over the change of bend in the following way. Two or three strides before you change direction, close your legs (your inside leg is on the girth and your outside leg is behind the girth), close your "old" outside hand in a fist and ask for flexion by vibrating with the "old" inside hand. At the point where the two circles are tangent, keep your legs on but switch their positions so that your "new" inside leg is on the girth and your "new" outside leg is behind the girth. You'll also need to change the action of your hands. As your old inside hand becomes your new outside hand, close it in a fist. As your old outside hand becomes your new inside hand, ask for flexion by vibrating this rein. Once the change of bend is completed, relax the aids.

You can use this same technique for changes of bend between each loop of a serpentine. Start your half-halt a little before you ask for the change of bend and continue to apply it until a stride or so after the change of bend is completed.

KEY POINTS

You now have more tools in your "bag of tricks" that you can use to help solve some common training problems. For example, you can:

- Help your horse relax by working him in a deep frame.

- Make your horse take an even contact with both reins by reversing the half-halt and asking him to step into the light rein.

- Straighten your horse and strengthen his weaker hind leg by using shoulder-in and haunches-in.

- Improve canter departs with engagement exercises such as preparatory half-halts, shoulder-out, and haunches-in.

- Improve the downward transitions from canter to trot with shoulder-in and leg yielding.

- Maintain good balance by blending half-halts into the aids for different movements.

22

Putting It All Together:
How to Organize a Logical, Systematic,

DAILY WORK SESSION

In chapter 11, I gave you a sample schooling session that you could do with your horse once he is well-grounded in the Basics. If you have been working along with me since then it's time for me to give you some examples of how to incorporate what you've learned in your work in a logical, organized way that is conducive to the development of your horse's physical well-being and his ability to carry out what's asked of him.

It's not, for instance, very sensible to start working your horse in shoulder-in and half-pass and then finish up with leg-yielding! Leg-yielding helps to loosen, stretch and relax your horse's muscles, so it belongs in the warm-up to prepare him for the more advanced work. Shoulder-in, haunches-in, and half-pass are exercises that collect the gaits and should only be done *after* your horse is thoroughly warmed up.

Think of each of your daily schooling sessions as a story unfolding. Like any good story, there should be a beginning, a middle, and an end.

The way you warm up your horse at the beginning of your ride is important because it sets the tone for everything that follows. You really can't continue productively with your work if your horse's body is tight or he's tense and inattentive.

The middle of the session starts with a review and refinement of established work as well as occasionally introducing new ideas. You should always have a plan before you start, but be flexible enough to modify your program depending on what surprises come at you on any given day. You know the kind of day I'm talking about: rollerbladers in fluorescent tights are zipping down the road by the ring, and all the horses are bouncing around like bumper cars. This is probably not a great day to start flying changes!

And, of course, you should carefully cool your horse's muscles down at the end of your ride. A good finish ensures that you won't have to deal with a stiff or sore body the next day. Plus, psychologically, ending up on a good note leaves everyone satisfied and with a positive "to be continued" feeling.

THE BEGINNING: WARM-UP

Students often ask me how long a warm-up should last and what work is appropriate during this period. The answer to the first question is "as long as it takes." The main goal of the warm-up

22.1 Think of each of your daily schooling sessions as a story unfolding. Like any good story, there should be a beginning, a middle, and an end.

is to loosen and supple your horse's body and make him calm and attentive. If your horse starts out stiff, tight, or tense, you'll have to do a lengthy warm-up. If he's relaxed, supple, and agreeable, the warm-up can be as brief as five or ten minutes.

THE WARM-UP FRAME

Spend the first five to ten minutes of your ride walking energetically around on a loose rein. At this point your horse can carry himself in any frame he chooses. This is simply the time for him to begin to adjust to your weight. Since he

may have been standing around in the stable for hours, these few minutes give him the opportunity to move freely forward.

Once you pick up contact, however, you should **connect** him. I'm not saying **collect** him, mind you—merely put him on the bit, with his hind legs stepping well under his body, his back raised, and his head and neck stretching toward your hand. Your horse's center of gravity will be toward the forehand, and you should ride him in the deep frame that I described in detail in chapter 14. (See photo 14.21 on p. 259.) This frame accomplishes two things at once. You'll warm up his cardiovascular system as well as stretch the muscles over his back and top of his neck to the maximum, so it'll be easier to school him in a round frame.

I recommend this deep frame during the warm-up because generally I think it's a mistake to do your first trot and canter on a loose rein. Riders who do this believe they're giving their horses a chance to limber up before serious work. I agree that you'll be warming up your horse's cardiovascular system, but you won't be loosening up his muscles correctly for the frame he'll eventually be working in.

Warming up on a loose rein is akin to you preparing yourself to touch your toes by walking around for ten minutes with your back arched. All your back muscles become shortened and contracted, and you'll find it difficult to stretch them enough to comfortably reach your toes on the first effort.

WARM-UP EXERCISES

So now you know what frame to put your horse in during the warm-up, but you also need to know what you should do for work. At the beginning of the warm-up, check that your horse is forward, straight, and moving in a regular rhythm in all three paces. After these prerequisites are established, make sure that your horse is listening and responding to your half-halts since that's the key to dealing with all his balance issues—both mental and physical. Be sure to do this check not just once but throughout the entire warm-up.

In the sample training session that I gave you in chapter 11, school figures, leg-yields, and lengthenings made up the "heart" of your story or the middle of your session. But now that your horse is more educated, these movements are incorporated into the warm-up.

Mix and match these movements so your warm-up doesn't take any longer than necessary. For example, you can ride a serpentine of three loops in the trot and lengthen the strides around the middle loop. Or you might start on a very large circle, decrease the size of the circle by spiraling in on a gradually decreasing arc, and go sideways in a leg-yield back out to the original circle. Then when you're back on the larger circle, lengthen and shorten for a few strides.

School Figures

Let's talk first about school figures in the warm-up. They help your horse to become more flexible by bending him laterally. (He's already bent longitudinally because you've warmed him up in a deep frame.) So practice circles, serpentines, shallow loops, and figure eights. All these figures should be large enough for your horse to do them comfortably, because it's too early in your ride to ask him to cope with doing small circles.

Make sure your horse is bending equally in both directions. Compensate for any one-sidedness by bending him on his stiff side and not letting him bend too much on his soft side.

The other important thing to remember when riding school figures is to be sure you're absolutely accurate. You may ask why you need to be so precise if you're not going into a dressage arena to be judged. Well, there are actually several reasons.

First, you want to develop your horse's ability to stretch or shorten the muscles on both sides of his body equally well. Horses tend to make circles and loops larger when they are circling with their stiff sides on the inside. They do this because it's difficult to elongate the shortened muscles on the outside of their bodies.

Second, you also want to encourage your horse to use his hind leg on his soft side better so that it becomes as strong as his other hind leg. When horses circle with their soft sides on the inside, they "cut in" on the circle to avoid carrying weight on their weaker inside hind leg.

Third, any strides the horse takes that bulge out from the line of the circle, or follow a straight line for more than one step, allow him to lose the bend and the engagement of the inside hind leg.

Last, when your horse cheats on circles in any of the ways just described, he's being mildly disobedient. By allowing him to do so, you're setting a precedent for him to make other decisions on how to evade the difficulty of work.

So, use reference points to make sure that you're riding accurate school figures. At the end of this chapter, I'll give detailed instructions on how to ride school figures with precision.

Leg-Yielding

Although I don't recommend doing advanced lateral exercises in the warm-up, it can be very useful to do some leg-yielding for a few minutes. Remember, leg-yields differ from the rest of the lateral work like shoulder-in, haunches-in, and half-pass in that there isn't any bend through the horse's body—just flexion at the poll away from the direction of movement.

Leg-yielding allows your horse to stretch and loosen muscles physically, as well as mentally answer some obedience questions. As you alternate between having your leg on the girth to placing it slightly behind the girth, you're asking some important questions. "Are you paying attention?" "Will you go forward when my leg is placed on the girth and immediately sideways when my leg is moved behind the girth?"

I find leg-yielding particularly useful for my older horses after they've had a day off. I know from experience that "rigor mortis" has probably set in after their rest day! (Since most of our horses have Monday off, when they're stiff we say that our horses are feeling "Tuesdayish" even if it happens to fall on a Friday.) So, I'll almost always do some leg-yielding in the walk to get rid of the "Tuesdayish" feeling before I even do my first posting trot. As I ask my horse to go sideways, I visualize his muscles stretching, loosening, and elongating so that by the time I trot, he feels buoyant and supple (fig. 22.2).

Lengthening and Shortening

Lengthening and shortening the stride in working trot and canter also supple the horse physically and mentally. Physically, these exercises develop the "rubber band effect." Can your horse stretch and compress his body smoothly and easily? Mentally, they ask vital questions like "Are you hot off my leg and willing to go forward?" and "Are you attentive to my rein and back and willing to slow down?"

Tuesdayish

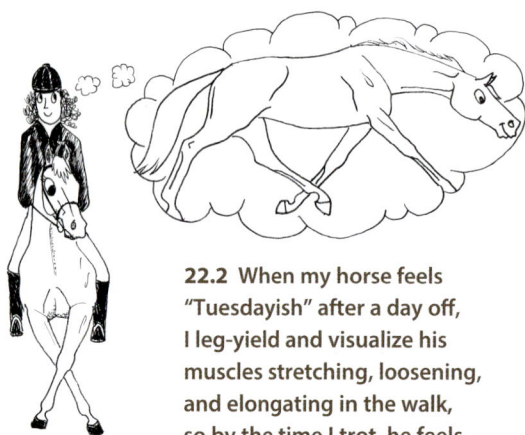
22.2 When my horse feels "Tuesdayish" after a day off, I leg-yield and visualize his muscles stretching, loosening, and elongating in the walk, so by the time I trot, he feels buoyant and supple.

But if this is a normal work day, warm up your horse until his body is loose and supple and he is concentrating on you. Then, you'll be ready to review and confirm established work as well as perhaps introduce something new.

ORGANIZING THE MIDDLE OF YOUR SESSION

REFINING OLD WORK AND INTRODUCING NEW EXERCISES

Most of your schooling session will be about confirming, refining, and improving balance in established work. I probably spend ten minutes or so reviewing work from the day before, and then I strive over the next fifteen to twenty minutes to get "a little bit more" **self-carriage** in all my established work through half-halts. If all is going well, I'll spend the last few minutes before my cool-down introducing something new.

I don't try to teach my horse anything new when the work isn't going well. When I do start something new, I don't expect him to do it perfectly. As long as he makes an effort, that's good enough. I reward him and finish the session. I always want to end on a good note, even if it means I have to go back to doing something very simple like leg-yielding or a lengthening. That way we go back to the barn feeling satisfied and start the next day with a positive outlook.

On the one hand, you should always have a plan when you work your horse so you can go a little further with your training every session.

As I explained in chapter 11, if you're riding a young horse (five years old or less), the warm-up is pretty much all you'll do in an entire session. The session itself can be as brief as twenty or thirty minutes. Young horses need to develop their ability to concentrate as much as anything else. So it's desirable to do short periods of work with frequent breaks. You want to bring your horse back to the barn as fresh and eager as he was when he came out.

Also, if your goal for the day is simply to exercise your horse, just do the warm-up and then go for a hack. Remember how important those "play-days" are to your horse's emotional and physical well-being.

But you should also be willing to abandon your program in favor of a simpler agenda if your horse is distracted, bewildered, or tense.

THE MAIN GOAL—
HOW TO IMPROVE SELF-CARRIAGE

If you've read this book from the beginning, you'll know by now that when I talk about self-carriage I'm referring to the loading of the hind legs—the change in balance caused by the lowering of the hindquarters and the resulting raising, lightening, and freeing of the forehand.

So, what can you do to improve self-carriage? Riding smaller school figures than you did in the warm-up, doing lots of transitions, and practicing lateral movements with bend are all exercises that will help you to improve your horse's balance. Remember that these self-carriage exercises belong in the "middle of your story" rather than at the beginning in the warm-up where you must be careful not too ask your horse for too much before he's ready.

Ride smaller circles and serpentines with several loops, making sure your horse doesn't evade the bend by swinging his hindquarters in or out, or by leaning in on your inside leg. The tighter arcs will change your horse's balance and promote self-carriage because they demand an increase in the bending of the joints of his inside hind leg.

If you're riding a horse that's just beginning to develop collected gaits, reduce your large 20-meter circles to 15-meter circles. Once your horse can cope with the demands of 15-meter circles, gradually (over the course of several months) decrease your circles to 12 meters and then 10 meters. If you ask your horse to do smaller circles than he's ready for, he'll find some sort of escape route. You're better off doing larger figures correctly than smaller ones incorrectly. If your horse has to cheat on small circles because he hasn't been systematically developed to the point that he can deal with the greater demands of bend through his body and engagement of his hind legs, doing smaller circles is counterproductive.

Frequent transitions from pace to pace as well as within the pace also contribute to self-carriage. The key word here is frequent. By riding many transitions, particularly those where you skip a pace, such as walk to canter and canter to walk or trot to halt and back to trot, you'll shift your horse's center of gravity more toward the hindquarters.

With the exception of leg-yielding, which has no bend, all lateral work with a bend will help you work toward self-carriage, as these lateral movements demand an increased bending of the joints of the hind legs. Be sure to pick exercises that are appropriate for your horse's level of training, or you'll run into the same difficulties that you'd encounter by prematurely asking for very small circles.

Remember to give frequent half-halts to maintain or restore balance—either before, during, or after any of these exercises that you're doing to promote self-carriage. With every half-halt, you'll add hind legs up to a restraining outside hand. Your driving aids send the hind legs further under the body while your closed outside hand captures that energy. Because the "door is closed" in front, there's an increased bending of the joints of the hind legs. As a result, the horse changes his shape and balance as his hindquarters lower and his center of gravity shifts more toward his hind legs.

PROGRESSIVE LEVELS OF TRAINING

If you're still confused as to what kind of work to do in the middle of your session, take a look at the dressage tests. They offer a guideline for training that is systematic and progressive.

In dressage in the United States, all the levels starting at Training level and progressing through First, Second, Third, and Fourth as well as the International Levels of Prix St. Georges, Intermediare I, Intermediare II and Grand Prix are designed to show a progressive development of strength and self-carriage. Although this book focuses on the work required through Third Level, I think it's interesting to take a moment to look at all the levels in order to get a feeling for the big picture (fig. 22.3).

In the United Kingdom the levels have different names: they start at preliminary, go through novice, elementary, medium, advanced medium, advanced, and then on to the International Levels described above. This book covers the movements required through advanced medium level.

Depending on your horse's talent, physique, gymnastic ability, and attitude, you can reasonably expect to advance from one level to the next in approximately six months to a year.

22.3 Dressage tests are designed with the systematic development of the horse in mind, and can, therefore, be used as guidelines to training.

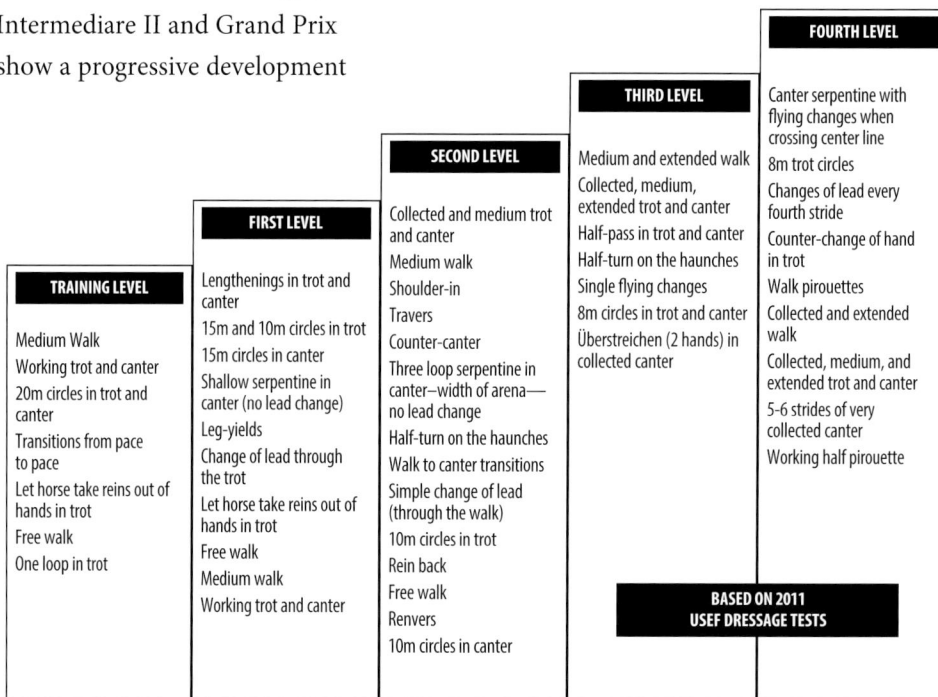

TRAINING LEVEL

Medium Walk
Working trot and canter
20m circles in trot and canter
Transitions from pace to pace
Let horse take reins out of hands in trot
Free walk
One loop in trot

FIRST LEVEL

Lengthenings in trot and canter
15m and 10m circles in trot
15m circles in canter
Shallow serpentine in canter (no lead change)
Leg-yields
Change of lead through the trot
Let horse take reins out of hands in trot
Free walk
Medium walk
Working trot and canter

SECOND LEVEL

Collected and medium trot and canter
Medium walk
Shoulder-in
Travers
Counter-canter
Three loop serpentine in canter—width of arena— no lead change
Half-turn on the haunches
Walk to canter transitions
Simple change of lead (through the walk)
10m circles in trot
Rein back
Free walk
Renvers
10m circles in canter

THIRD LEVEL

Medium and extended walk
Collected, medium, extended trot and canter
Half-pass in trot and canter
Half-turn on the haunches
Single flying changes
8m circles in trot and canter
Überstreichen (2 hands) in collected canter

FOURTH LEVEL

Canter serpentine with flying changes when crossing center line
8m trot circles
Changes of lead every fourth stride
Counter-change of hand in trot
Walk pirouettes
Collected and extended walk
Collected, medium, and extended trot and canter
5-6 strides of very collected canter
Working half pirouette

BASED ON 2011 USEF DRESSAGE TESTS

You might get "stuck" at one level longer than another; just watch your horse's progress. You'll be able to tell when he's ready to go on by the ease with which he performs the requirements at each level. In the long run, training progresses more quickly and smoothly if you don't force your horse to conform to some preconceived timetable. One of my students bought a six-year-old who had not been started correctly, so she had to spend over a year and a half working at First Level to establish and confirm his basics. But then once her horse had a solid foundation, he easily learned everything in Second through Fourth Levels over the next year!

So let's have a look at how each successive level builds upon the work from the previous level (figs. 22.4 to 22.9). The purpose of the tests at the lowest level, Training Level, is to establish that the horse's muscles are supple and loose, and that he moves freely forward in a distinct and steady rhythm, accepting contact with his rider's hand. At Training Level you are only required to show that your horse accepts a contact with your hand—he doesn't necessarily have to be on the bit; you're asked to show medium walk, working trot, and working canter as well as the transitions in between each pace. You'll ride some large curved lines like 20 meter circles and shallow loops.

You are also asked to show that your horse will "take the reins out of your hands" in the trot as he seeks the contact forward and down to the ground while maintaining balance and regular rhythm. This movement proves that

22.4 The Training Level horse's muscles are supple and loose, and the horse accepts a contact with the rider's hand. Brie carries about 60 percent of her weight on her forehand. This horizontal balance is apparent because her withers and croup are basically level.

22.5 At Training Level, the horse should "take the reins out of your hands" in the trot while seeking the contact forward and down to the ground. The rider determines just how much her horse can stretch by the amount of rein she feeds out. Be sure not to offer more than the horse will take, because you always want to maintain a contact with the mouth rather than letting the reins get slack.

22.6 At First Level, the horse shows greater thrust from behind than at Training Level. Here Brie's frame is shorter, she is connected over her back, her balance is more toward her hindquarters, and her neck is slightly raised and arched.

22.7 At Second Level, a horse clearly accepts more weight on the hindquarters and accordingly the neck is raised and arched to a greater degree than a First Level horse.

the horse is relaxed and is moving forward into the rider's hand rather than being forced into a frame by being pulled in from front to back.

At First Level, the tests are designed to show that in addition to the requirements of Training Level, the horse has developed **thrust** from behind (pushing power) and is connected over his back **(throughness)**, as well as showing the beginnings of a shift in his center of gravity toward his hindquarters (self-carriage).

These changes are achieved by connection, or expressed another way, **putting your horse on the bit**. Your trot circles progressively become as small as 10 meters and you're asked to do 15-meter circles in the canter. You are also

required to show lengthenings in the trot and canter, leg-yielding in the trot, and a gentle loop in counter-canter.

The purpose of the Second Level tests is to confirm that the horse, having demonstrated that he has achieved the thrust required in First Level, now shows that through additional training he accepts more of his weight on his hindquarters and shows the power required at the medium gaits. At this level he should be reliably on the bit. A greater degree of straightness, bending, suppleness, throughness and self-carriage is required than at First Level.

This is the first time you'll be asked to show real self-carriage by being required to do a

22.8 Relaxing the inside rein on a circle at the canter (doing a one-handed *überstreichen*), demonstrates the balance of the Second Level horse. Brie has obviously maintained her self-carriage and the quality of the canter.

22.9 The horse in Third Level balance is accepting even more weight on the hindquarters and as a result the forehand is raised. You can also see more compact "package" from poll to tail.

collected as well as a medium trot and canter. Your canter circles are reduced to 10 meters and counter-canter loops are tighter, demanding greater engagement. New movements include shoulder-in, travers, and renvers at the trot and a turn on the haunches at the walk. Up until this point, changes of canter leads have been done through the trot. But now you'll be asked to show simple changes of lead going from one canter lead directly to the walk and then after three steps immediately to the other lead.

In previous years, you were also asked to do a one-handed *überstreichen* on a canter circle to demonstrate your horse's self-carriage. And although the one-handed *überstreichen* is no

longer in the Second Level tests, it's still an important part of your horse's training. Let me explain this German expression: you'll extend your inside hand forward up the horse's neck for three to four strides while maintaining contact on the outside rein. During this exercise, your horse should maintain his self-carriage, rhythm, bend, and quality of his canter. Done correctly, this movement demonstrates that your horse is truly connected with a half-halt and, therefore, steps from behind through your outside hand.

Both *überstreichen* and "taking the reins out of your hands" are part of the tests that I told you to use to check the honesty of the half-halt (see p. 224). Since the half-halt is so much a part of my students' training programs, they always get the highest points possible on those movements!

At Third Level, the horse must show rhythm, suppleness, acceptance of the bit, throughness, impulsion, straightness, and self-carriage in each movement. This is particularly important during the transitions to and from the movements as well as in the medium and extended gaits themselves. There must be a clear distinction between these gaits. This is the first time you'll be asked to show three clear "gears" in the trot and the canter—collected, medium, and extended. Although it's interesting to note that even at this level only medium and extended walk is shown. The committee that created these tests is only too aware of how easily the walk can be ruined, so they take great care not to introduce the collected walk too early.

New movements include half-passes at the trot and the canter and a flying change in each direction. The rider is also asked to show that her horse is in self-carriage in collected canter by doing a two-handed *überstreichen*. The rider extends both her hands up the crest of the neck toward her horse's ears. If the horse is carrying himself and not relying on the rider's hand, his frame and balance stay the same as she does this.

Although Fourth Level is beyond the scope of this book, you will probably be interested to know that the tests are designed to confirm that the horse has acquired a high degree of suppleness, impulsion, throughness, balance and self-carriage while always remaining reliably on the bit. His movements are straight, lively, and cadenced (a steady tempo with marked accentuation of the rhythm and emphasized springiness), and the transitions precise and fluid.

At this level the horse is also asked to show all three gears—collected, medium, and extended—in trot and canter. New movements include walk pirouettes, working pirouettes in the canter, and flying changes of lead every fourth stride.

If you compare horses at the successive levels in terms of their progressively changing balance, you'll see that even though the First Level tests do not specifically ask for collected gaits, the horse at this level is carrying himself somewhat more than the Training Level horse. And the Second Level horse is more in self-carriage than the First Level horse.

Not only is self-carriage a goal for dressage horses, but it also helps horses in other fields do their jobs successfully. For example, to avoid fatigue and wear and tear on their limbs over long distances, endurance champion Becky Hart asks her horses to work in a Second or Third Level balance. Before Dennis Reis even starts to ask his horses to perform roll backs, he ensures success by asking for the balance required at Third Level. And I can guarantee you that Anne Kursinski's jumpers are rocked well back onto their hindquarters at a Fourth Level balance to have the power and thrust necessary to propel themselves over the obstacles on a Grand Prix jumper course.

THE CONCLUSION: THE COOL-DOWN

You'll finish your ride with a cooling-down period. This is as important as your warm-up. You certainly wouldn't jog five miles and then immediately sit in an easy chair even though you'd probably love to do just that! If you did, your muscles would contract, and you'd probably feel pretty stiff and sore the next day. The same common sense applies to schooling your horse. Allow him to stretch and loosen his body in the same deep frame you used for the warm-up. He should trot or canter around with a feeling of harmony for awhile and then walk on a loose rein before he returns to the stable feeling relaxed and satisfied with himself (fig. 22.10).

I say he should stretch "for awhile" because the length of time is going to vary, depending on what's happened during your session. On a normal day, a couple of minutes of working him deep is going to be plenty. Not only is this good for your horse's muscles but once he learns that this final stretch means he's finished for the day, you can use this routine to dissipate any tension that might have crept in while you were teaching him something new.

For example, when I start anything new with Woody, it's a given that he'll get worried and I'll have to ride him deep for longer than normal. I know that this is just his personality and that once he understands and becomes adept at the new exercise, he becomes calm and even proud of his new accomplishment. So I always wait until the very end of my session before I start

22.10 Before you let your horse "relax," allow him to stretch and loosen.

new work. Then, after practicing the new movement briefly, I go right into the deep frame in the posting trot. This way Woody knows we're done and his tension doesn't escalate.

Another example of when "a while" may have to last more than a couple of minutes happened when one of my students, Nikki, started flying changes with her very sensitive Thoroughbred, Rupert. When Nikki gave her horse the aid to change, she applied it a little too strongly. Rupert did, in fact, do the flying change, but he thought it was so exciting that he took off afterwards, bucking exuberantly. Needless to say, Nikki "bought some real estate" (although she was quick to reassure me that it was the softest landing she ever had!), and that startled her horse even more. So, after she remounted, she cantered him in a deep frame until he was thoroughly relaxed. We wanted to be sure there wouldn't be any skeletons in his closet the next time we worked on the flying changes. (By the way, he does lovely, relaxed flying changes now.)

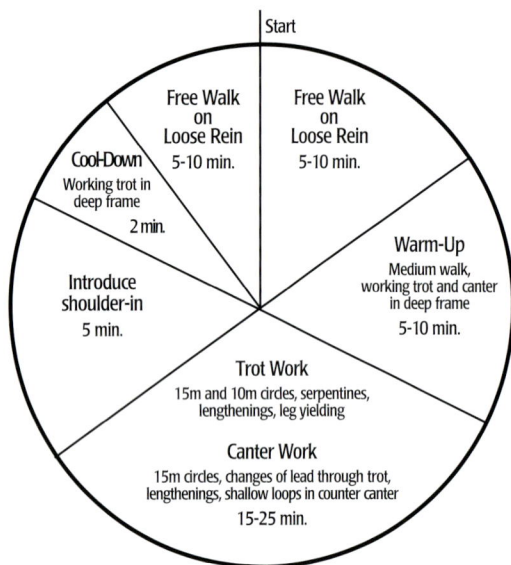

22.11 Sample schooling session: First Level.

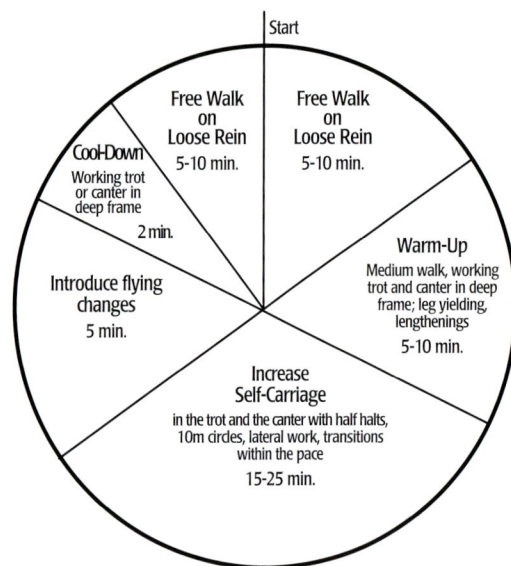

22.12 Sample schooling session: Third Level.

TWO SAMPLE SCHOOLING SESSIONS

I'll give you a couple of sample schooling sessions—one for the horse working at First Level (Novice in the UK) and one for the horse at Third Level (Medium in the UK). In between each new exercise, always give your horse a short break by walking on a loose rein. Remember, these are merely examples of how to put things together in a logical sequence. They are not "the Gospel"! Some horses get bored if you don't challenge them with new work, while others take comfort in the familiarity of a routine.

For the First Level horse (fig. 22.11):
5-10 minutes: free walk on a loose rein.

5-10 minutes: medium walk, working trot posting, and working canter in both directions in a deep frame on straight lines and 20-meter circles.

15-25 minutes: trot work including 15- and 10-meter circles, serpentines, lengthenings, and leg-yields. Canter work including 15-meter circles, changes of lead through the trot, lengthenings, and shallow loops that require a little counter-canter.

5 minutes: introduction of shoulder-in.

2 minutes: working trot in a deep frame to stretch and relax.

5-10 minutes: free walk on a loose rein.

Third Level horse (fig. 22.12):
5-10 minutes: free walk on a loose rein.

5-10 minutes: medium walk, working trot

posting, and working canter in both directions in a deep frame on straight lines and 20-meter circles. Then shorten the reins a bit and add in leg-yields in the trot and lengthenings in the trot and the canter.

15-25 minutes: use half-halts, 10-meter circles, lateral work in the trot (shoulder-in, haunches-in, and half-pass) in both directions, and transitions within the trot (collected, medium, extended) to increase self-carriage and collect the trot. Use half-halts, half-passes, counter-canter, and transitions within the canter to increase self-carriage and collect the canter.

5 minutes: introduction of flying changes.

2 minutes: working trot or canter in a deep frame to stretch and relax.

5-10 minutes: free walk on a loose rein.

RIDING ACCURATE SCHOOL FIGURES

I stressed earlier how important it is to ride precise school figures. To get a feeling for the correct size and shape of these figures, we'll go into both a small and a large dressage arena where we have specific dimensions and designated placement of letters. Once you have a feeling for the dimensions and flow of a truly round circle by riding it in a prescribed area, it's a lot easier to recreate this feeling in an open space.

If you don't have access to a regulation dressage arena, measure the distances out in a field and put some markers where the letters should be. Mark off the perimeter with fence poles or simply mow the grass shorter to form a rectangle. You don't need expensively made letters, either. Buy some traffic cones at a sporting goods store or fill some plastic gallon containers with sand so they don't blow away, then mark them.

The key to riding school figures accurately is to have very specific reference points and to always look two points ahead. As you approach one reference point, look over to the next one, and as you approach that point, look toward the next one. Pretend you're playing the child's game of "connect-the-dots." See all the reference points in your mind and then connect them while maintaining correct bend.

If you have trouble seeing distances, get out on the arena on foot and pace them off until you develop an eye for them.

THE SMALL ARENA

A small arena is 20 meters wide and 40 meters long—twice as long as it is wide. The arena is divided in half lengthwise by the centerline. Each of these halves is again divided lengthwise by the quarterlines. Since the arena is 20 meters wide, each of these sections is 5 meters wide. The two quarterlines are 10 meters apart. The centerline is 10 meters from either long side. Each quarterline is 5 meters from one long side and 15 meters from the other long side.

The middles of the long sides are marked by the letters B and E. The middles of the short sides are marked by A and C. The corner letters are all 6 meters from the corner. (That's right! I said 6

STANDARD ARENA

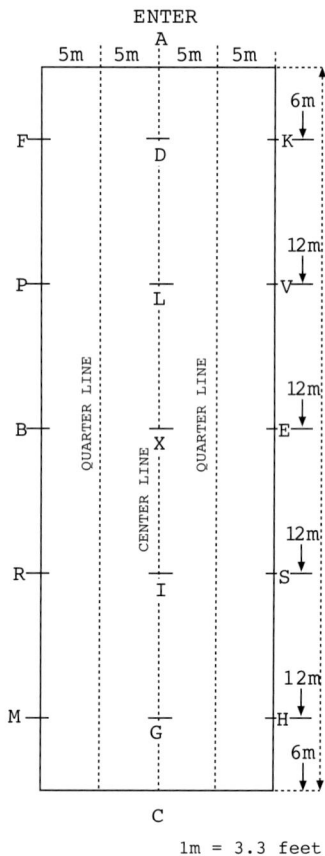

SMALL ARENA

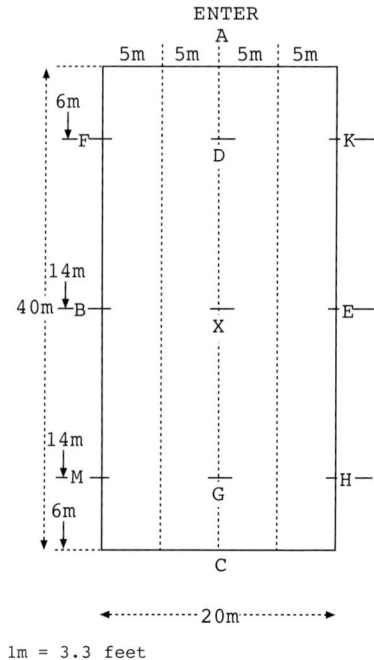

22.13 Arenas for dressage: standard and small.

1m = 3.3 feet

SMALL ARENA

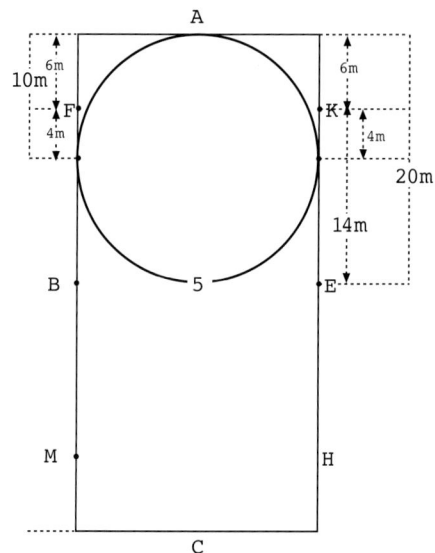

22.14 Small arena: correct 20-meter circle at A.

SMALL ARENA

22.15 Small arena: correct 20-meter circle between B and E.

meters—not 10. No wonder your 20-meter circles always look like eggs. You've been aiming for the corner letter all this time!) See fig. 22.11.

The four reference points for a 20-meter circle at the end of the small arena are: 1) A or C; 2 & 3) 4 meters past the corner letters (so that you are 10 meters from the corner when you touch the long side); and 4) X (which is located on the centerline between B and E). See fig. 22.14.

The four reference points for a 20-meter circle at B or E (in the middle of the small arena) are: 1) B or

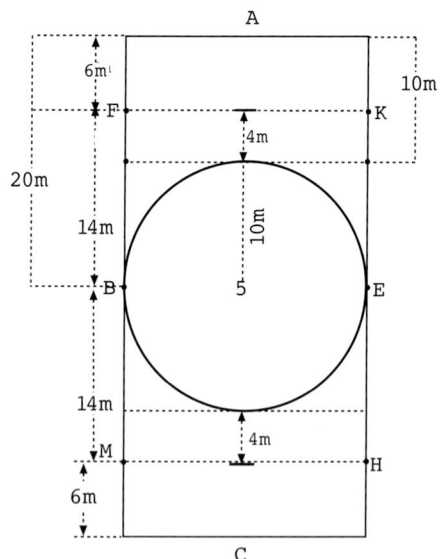

SMALL ARENA

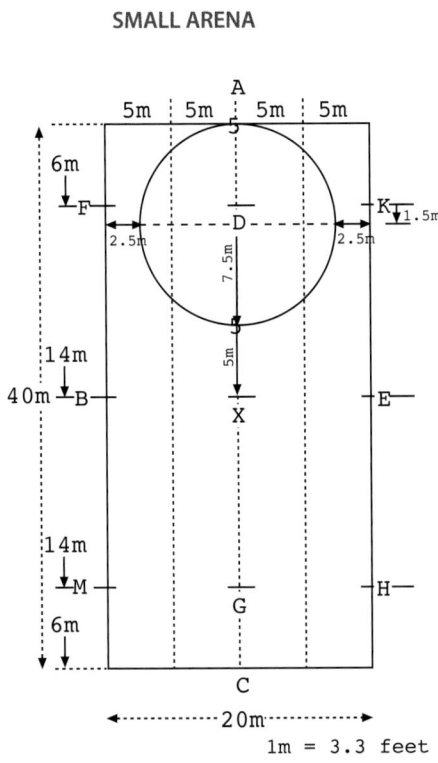

22.16 Small arena: correct 15-meter circle at A.

SMALL ARENA

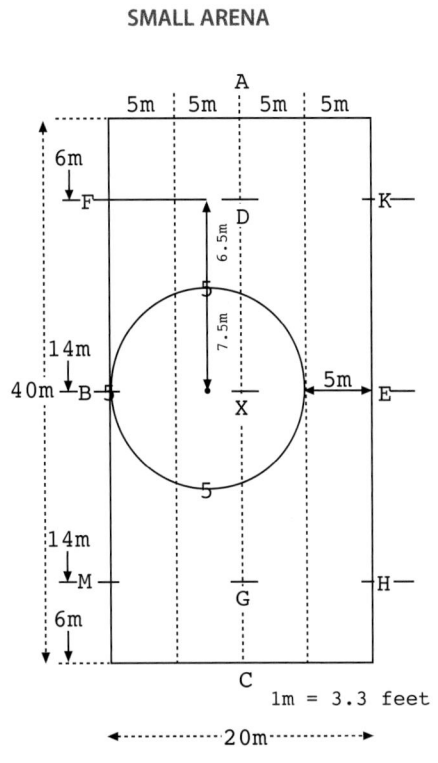

22.17 Small arena: correct 15-meter circle at B.

E; 2) the centerline 4 meters above D (10 meters from A); 3) B or E; 4) the centerline 4 meters above G (10 meters from C). See fig. 22.15.

The four reference points for a 15-meter circle starting at A or C are: 1) A or C; 2) 2.5 meters in from the rail and 1.5 meters above the corner letter (so you are 7.5 meters from the corner); 3) 5 meters from X; 4) 2.5 meters in from the rail and 1.5 meters above the corner letter (so you are 7.5 meters from the corner). See fig. 22.16.

The four reference points for a 15-meter circle starting at B or E are: 1) B or E; 2) 7.5 meters above an imaginary line connecting B and E (hit this point when you are 2.5 meters past the first quarterline); 3) the far quarterline across from B or E; 4) 7.5 meters below an imaginary line connecting B and E (hit this point when you are 2.5 meters before the first quarterline also). See fig. 22.17.

THE STANDARD ARENA

A large or standard arena is 20 meters wide and 60 meters long (see fig. 22.13). Since the width of the small and large arena is the same, the same distances for the centerline and the two

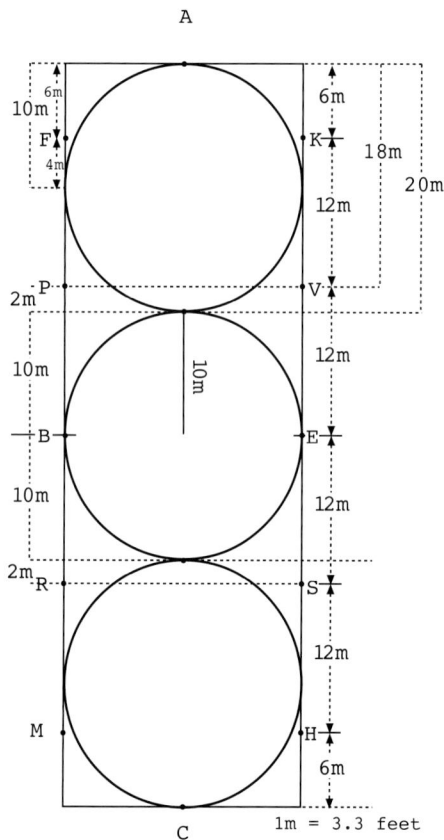

22.18 Standard arena: correct placement of 20-meter circles. (Note that the reference or tangent points for the circles at A and C are 4 meters beyond the corner letters.)

22.19 Standard arena: correct 15-meter circle at A.

quarterlines apply. In addition, the corner letters are still 6 meters from the corners, the middles of the long sides are marked by B and E, and the middles of the short sides are marked by A and C. The main difference is that all the other letters are twice that distance, or 12 meters, apart. Therefore, an imaginary line drawn from M to H is 6 meters from the short side and an imaginary line from R to S is 18 meters from the short side.

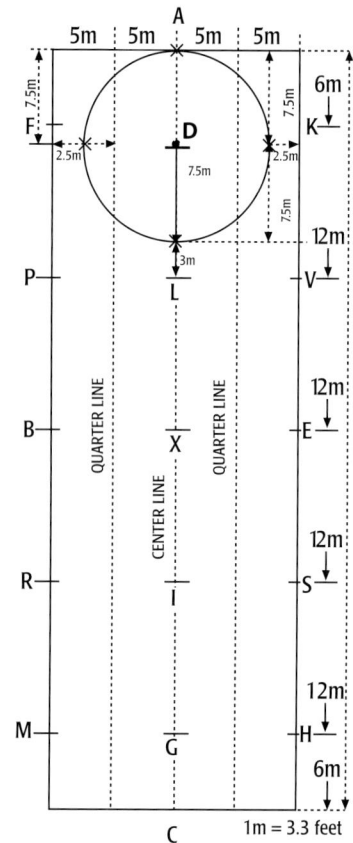

Because the large arena is three times as long as it is wide, you can fit three 20-meter circles end to end in it.

The four reference points for a 20-meter circle that begins at C are: 1) C; 2) 4 meters past M (so that you're 10 meters from the corner); 3) 2 meters past the R to S line; and 4) 4 meters above H (so that you're 10 meters from the corner). Remember, always look two points

STANDARD ARENA

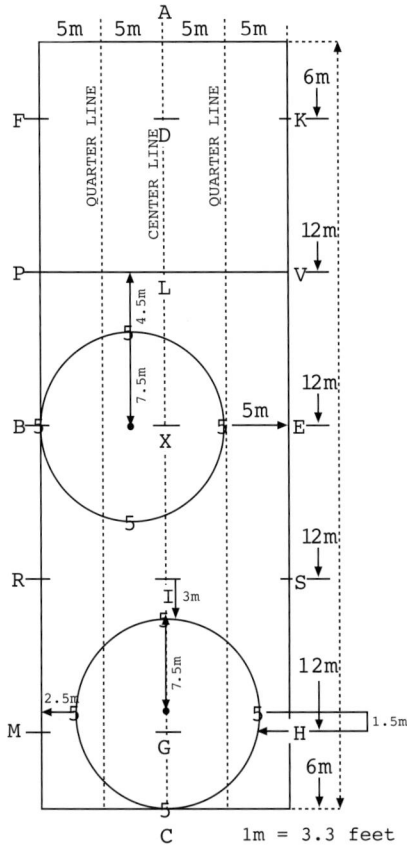

22.20 Standard arena: correct 15-meter circle at B and C.

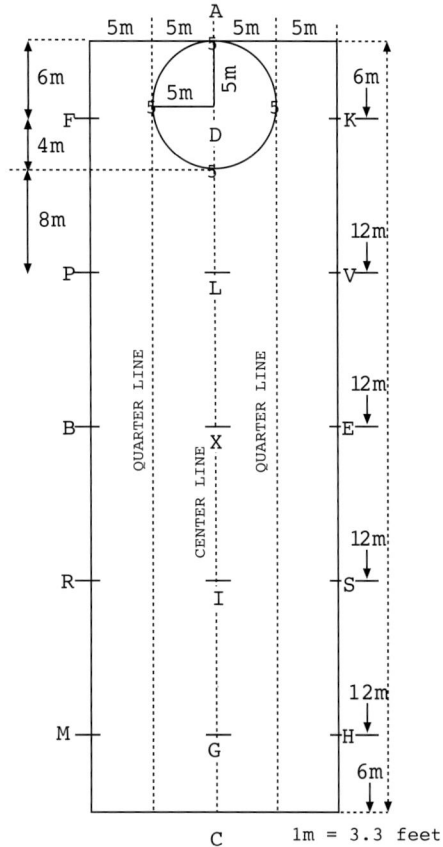

22.21 Standard arena: correct 10-meter circle at A.

ahead and then "connect the dots." See fig. 22.18.

The four reference points for a 20-meter circle in the middle of the standard arena are: 1) B; 2) 2 meters shy of the P to V line; 3) E; and 4) 2 meters shy of the S to R line. See fig. 22.18.

The four reference points for a 20-meter circle at A are: 1) A; 2) 4 meters past K; 3) 2 meters past the P to V line; and 4) 4 meters above F (so that

you're 10 meters from the corner). See fig. 22.18.

For a 15-meter circle at A in a large arena, your reference points are: 1) A; 2) 2.5 meters in from the rail and 1.5 meters above the corner letter (so you are 7.5 meters from the corner); 3) 3 meters shy of the P to V line; 4) 2.5 meters in from the rail and 1.5 meters above the corner letter (so you are 7.5 meters from the corner). See fig. 22.19.

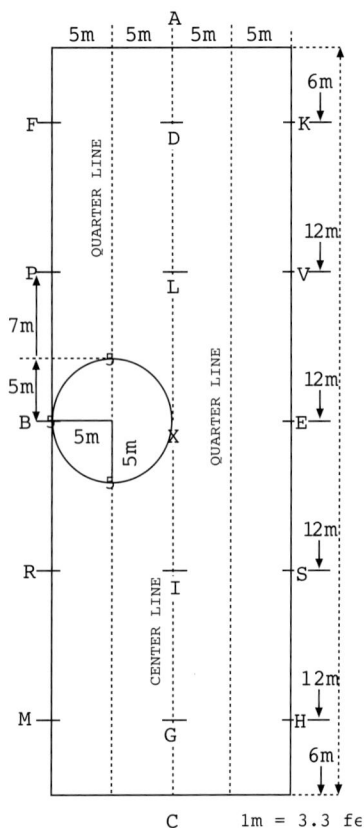

22.22 Standard arena: correct 10-meter circle at B.

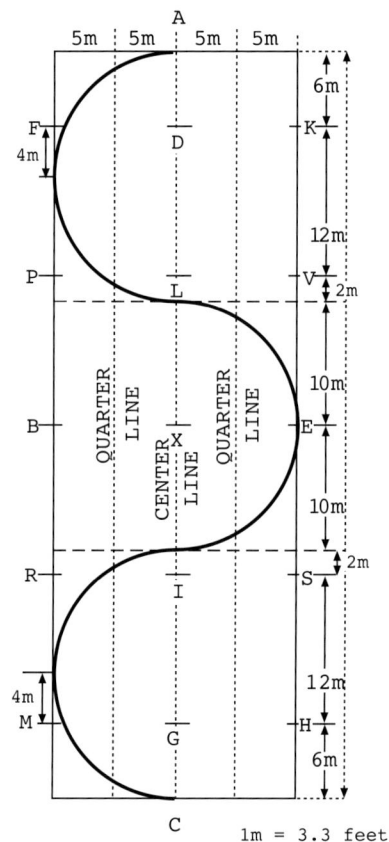

22.23 Standard arena: a serpentine.

For a 15-meter circle at B in a large arena, your reference points are: 1) B; 2) 4.5 meters shy of the P to V line; 3) the far quarterline; and 4) 4.5 meters shy of the R to S line. See fig. 22.20.

For a 10-meter circle at A in a large arena, your reference points are: 1) A; 2) the quarterline (aim for a point one meter before the corner letter so you hit that point when you are 5 meters from the short side); 3) 4 meters above

D; 4) the quarterline (once again, aim for a point one meter before the corner letter so you touch that point when you are 5 meters from the short side). See fig. 22.21.

For a 10-meter circle at B in a large arena, your reference points are: 1) B; 2) 5 meters above the B to E line; 3) the centerline at X; and 4) 5 meters above the B to E line. Riders often make offset 10-meter circles in competition and lose points. Their 10-meter circles are round, but the circles are displaced toward one end of the arena. See fig. 22.22.

A three-loop serpentine in the large arena consists of three 20-meter half-circles. Remember that circles and serpentines don't go into the corners. The serpentine itself begins and ends at A or C. If you begin at A, go into the corner before A and after you finish the serpentine at C. But as soon as you come to the beginning point (A or C), arc off the track and aim for your next reference point.

Follow the reference points for a 20-meter circle at A, and when you get to the centerline, switch direction and follow the reference points for the 20-meter circle in the middle of the arena. Once again when you reach the centerline, switch direction and follow the points for the 20-meter circle at C. In each case, change the bend before you change direction. See fig. 22.23.

Along the same lines, you can ride a shallow loop down the long side. In this case, your reference points are: 1) H; 2) the quarterline across from E; and 3) K. If you're tracking left, arc off the wall at H with left bend. When you're midway between H and the quarterline across from E, begin to bend your horse to the right. When you are midway from the quarterline to K, smoothly change the bend back to the left. Don't allow the horse to be drawn back to the wall before the letter. Ride precisely to each point. See fig. 22.24.

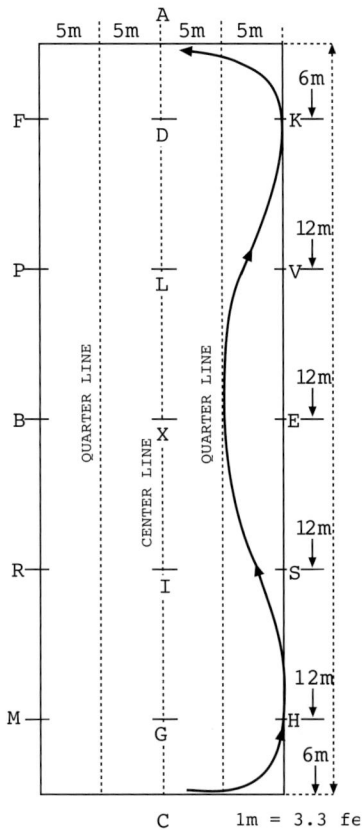

22.24 Standard arena: a shallow loop.

KEY POINTS

- The length of time it takes to warm up your horse will vary depending on a number of factors. The bottom line is that the warm-up should last as long as it takes to loosen and supple your horse's body and make him calm and attentive.

- Ideally, the warm-up should be done in a deep frame so that there is a solid connection from back to front and the right muscles are being worked.

- Exercises that belong in your warm-up include school figures, leg-yields, and lengthenings.

- The heart of your session will be used to review and refine old work with the goal of increasing self-carriage in all of the gaits and movements.

- Improve self-carriage with collecting half-halts, frequent transitions, smaller circles, and lateral movements that have a bend.

- Always finish your session by doing something your horse enjoys and does well so that you end on a satisfying note.

- The cooling-down period should also be ridden in a deep frame so that the horse's muscles are stretched and loosened and he won't be stiff and sore the next day.

- As you progress through the levels of training, think of your goal as the systematic development of self-carriage, so that your horse can do his job more athletically and be more of a pleasure to ride.

PHOTOGRAPHER'S NOTE

Photographs for this edition of *Dressage 101* were taken by Jayson Benoit of Round Robin Farm in Tunbridge, Vermont. Most were shot on location at the farm, with assistance from Jayson's wife, long-time eventer and riding instructor Bekki Read. Three generations of the Read family have owned and operated Round Robin Farm over the past 70 years, most recently (since 2017) at the new beautiful 200-acre site in the hills of Tunbridge. The family has long promoted the Connemara breed and has run a summer overnight riding program for over 40 years, coaching thousands of young riders in horse care and the skills of dressage and eventing. Year-round activities at the farm also include boarding and riding opportunities for all ages. For more information, visit roundrobinfarm.com.

It has been a great pleasure and honor to be part of this special project in tribute to Jane Savoie's memory and life's work. We are especially grateful to all the models for their contributions of time, skill, patience, and enthusiasm. These included: Lexie Evans, Lakewin Evans, Bekki Read, Allyson Tessier, Eliza Haun, Carole Ann Tullar, Adeline Tullar, Joy Congdon, Deborah Dean-Smith,, and Amy Halley. Carole Ann Tullar and Deborah Dean-Smith also appeared in the previous edition of this book. A special thanks as well to those who welcomed us to their farms for these shoots.

ACKNOWLEDGMENTS
From the Original Edition

Editor's Note: These Acknowledgments were composed by author Jane Savoie for the original edition of this book. Some details do not apply to the new edition, but we have included them in their entirety as originally written.

A project like this book is rarely done alone and this one is no exception. It's my distinct pleasure to thank all of the talented people who helped me with their time, effort, skill and support.

To the gifted riders and gracious owners who generously allowed themselves and their horses to be photographed showing both the "do's" and the "don'ts:"

Michele Bump
Carole Ann Cahill
Lynda Cameron
Jamie Cripps
Deborah Dean-Smith
Amy Foss
Christopher Hickey
Ruth Hogan-Poulsen
Gerri Jenkyn
Renate Kundrun
Claire Talbot
Kelly Weiss

To my husband, Rhett Savoie, for his skill behind the camera and his unfailing patience during this massive project. Rhett, you can finally walk through the living room again without having to tiptoe through the wall-to-wall carpet of manuscript pages, photographs, and illustrations.

To my publisher, Caroline Robbins, who sweated shoulder to shoulder with me for six years over the creation of these books. During that time she worked tirelessly as my editor, conscience, supporter, and most importantly, my friend. I could always count on her to be the voice of reason when I couldn't see things clearly.

To Martha Cook of Trafalgar Square Publishing for her many contributions to this project. She wears many hats and they all fit comfortably. Thank you, Martha, for all your efforts but especially for your special ability of always making me feel that I was your most important project even when you were buried in something else.

To Lynn Palm Pittion-Rossillon and Anne Kursinski for agreeing to write forewords for Book One and Book Two, respectively. I consider it a great honor as I have tremendous admiration for both the skill and training philosophies of these two women.

To the following trainers who I have had the very great privilege of working with:

Linda Jaskiel-Brown, for introducing me to the joy of dressage

Robert Dover, my "brother," for being the major influence in my education by teaching me the priniciples as well as the art of dressage

Cindy Sydnor, whose elegance I constantly strive to emulate and whose teaching style set the pattern for my own

Pam Goodrich, for helping me to think creatively

The late Herbert Rehbein, for his pure genius on a horse

Sue Blinks, for inspiring me with her loving approach to training. She's a shining example that excellence and kindness do, in fact, go hand in hand.

To Susan Harris, for generously allowing us to use her brilliant drawings from her book *Horse Gaits, Balance and Movement.*

To Patty Naegeli, whose lighthearted illustrations not only educate but also remind us that riding is supposed to be fun.

To my dear friend Ann Kitchel, who graciously allowed me to take over her arena at Huntington Farm during the photo shoots.

To all my friends who supported and commiserated with me through each "final" rewrite. I love you all.

GLOSSARY

aids (signals): The various combinations and actions of the seat, legs, and hands that allow you to communicate nonverbally with your horse.

axis-straight. Refers to the straight horse's spine, which should overlap his line of travel. *See* **straight/straightness.**

Basics, the. Rhythm, forward, and straightness. The Basics are the foundation for all correct work.

behind the leg. The horse doesn't respond promptly to light leg aids.

blend (half-halt). Combining the half-halt with another aid in order to keep the horse **on the bit** and maintain good balance during an exercise or movement.

bend. Refers to lateral bending. When the bend through the horse's side is correct, it conforms to the arc of whatever curved line he is on.

bridge. The connection over the horse's back that allows the unrestricted flow of energy from back to front.

cadence. A steady **tempo** showing marked accentuation of the rhythm and emphasized springiness.

change of lead through the trot. A downward transition from one canter lead into a few steps of trot followed immediately by an upward transition to the other canter lead.

collect. To gather your horse together so that he carries himself in a balanced way. A horse is collected when his center of gravity shifts more toward his hind legs and this is because he has engaged his hindquarters. This causes the hindquarters to lower and carry more weight so that the forehand lightens and appears higher than the hindquarters.

collected gaits. A walk, trot, and canter that show the horse **on the bit,** with the hind legs engaged and clearly in **self-carriage.** He covers less ground with each step than he does in the **medium** gaits, but his hind legs arc higher off the ground because the joints bend more markedly.

collecting half-halt. A short, simultaneous action of seat, legs, and hands that is used to improve the **self-carriage** of the horse. The collecting half-halt is only effective when a horse has first been put **on the bit** through the use of a **connecting half-halt.**

connect/connection (on the bit). When a horse is connected from back to front, energy can travel from the hind legs, over the back, through the neck, into the rider's hands and then be recycled back to the hind legs.

connecting half-halt. The primary three-second half-halt that is used to put your horse **on the bit.** Apply the driving aids, close the outside hand in a fist and (if necessary to keep the neck straight) vibrate the inside rein for three seconds. All other half-halts are variations of this basic one. *See* **collecting half-halt,**

increasing half-halt, preparatory half-halt, reversed half-halt.

contact. When the horse stretches forward into the bit and accepts the taut rein as a means of communication with the rider.

counter-canter. An obedience and suppling movement in which the horse is asked to canter on what is considered the "wrong" lead (i.e. while going to the right he canters on the left lead).

counter-flexion. Flexion at the poll to the **outside.**

counter-suppling. An exercise that puts the horse "through" the **outside** of his body. The rider quickly but smoothly bends the horse's neck to the outside as she closes her outside leg while supporting with her **inside** rein and leg.

deep/deep frame. A horse whose silhouette shows the hind legs coming under the body, a raised back, a long neck, a low poll, and the nose ever so slightly behind the vertical but looking as if it is stretching toward the **contact.** A good position for warming up, cooling down, and teaching the horse to stay **connected** if he tends to come above the bit in an exercise.

driving seat. The action of the seat that is used to send the horse forward or speed up the **tempo** of a **pace**. To use a driving seat, stretch up and push with the seat as if you are trying to move the back of the saddle toward the front of the saddle.

elastic contact. A desirable quality of contact. Elastic contact is made possible by the opening and closing of the elbows, allowing for the forward and back movement of the horse's neck in the walk and canter and for the up and down movement of the rider's body during posting trot.

engage/engaging/engagement. The bending and flexing of the joints of the hindquarters so that the angle between the bones is decreased. As a result, the croup lowers and the hindquarters bear more weight.

extended gait. At the trot and canter, a pace in which the horse, maintaining his **rhythm** and an **uphill balance,** lengthens his frame and covers as much ground as possible with each stride. At the walk, a pace that covers as much ground as possible without hurrying, showing greatest push from behind and maximum reach so that the hind feet touch the ground clearly in front of the footprints of the fore-feet. The rider allows the horse to stretch out his head and neck but keeps a contact with his mouth.

extension. *See* **extended gait.**

flexes. (Joints of the hind legs). *See* **engagement.**

flexibility. The horse's ability to bend through his side equally easily to the left and to the right; the ability to move joints freely.

flexion. Refers to bending in the joints, specifically the poll and jaw.

flying change. A change from one canter lead directly to the other canter lead; the flying change takes place during the period of suspension in the canter.

forward. One of **the Basics.** The direction the horse moves over the ground (i.e. forward as opposed to sideways).

frame. The outline or silhouette of the horse's body, showing his posture.

free walk. A pace of relaxation in which the horse is given a loose rein and allowed complete freedom to lower and stretch out his head and neck.

front to back. The wrong way to ride your horse; trying to force or manipulate the horse into a round frame by overuse of the hands.

gaits. The "gears" within each pace (i.e. extended walk, working trot, or medium canter). *See* **paces**

half-halt. A hardly visible, almost simultaneous, coordinated action of seat, legs and hands that increases attention and improves balance and harmony. *See* **collecting half-halt, connecting half-halt, increasing half-halt, preparatory half-halt, reversed half-halt.**

half-pass. A **haunches-in** on a diagonal line; the horse is slightly bent around the **inside** leg, his body is parallel to the rail with his forehand slightly ahead of his hindquarters. The outside legs pass and cross in front of the inside legs and he looks in the direction of movement.

haunches-in (travers). The horse is slightly bent around the rider's inside leg. His front legs stay on the original track of the long side and his hindquarters are brought in off the track toward the center of the ring at about a 30-degree angle to the rail. His outside legs pass and cross in front of his inside legs and he looks in the direction he's moving.

haunches-out (renvers). This is the inverse movement of the haunches-in, with the tail to the wall instead of the head. Otherwise the same principles and conditions are applicable as in haunches-in.

head to the wall. A position for **leg-yielding** in which the horse is **flexed** toward the rail, the forelegs remain on the track, and the hindlegs are moved away from the rail at about a 35-degree angle.

horizontal balance. The horse's natural state of balance, with the center of gravity toward the forehand. He carries approximately 60% of his weight on his front legs and 40% of his weight on his hind legs. In horizontal balance, the withers and croup are basically the same height and the topline is parallel to the ground.

hot off the leg. The horse reacts promptly and enthusiastically to light leg aids; in front of the leg.

impulsion (thrust). The horse gives the impression of carrying himself forward and springing off the ground. The elastic springing off the ground begins in the haunches with a bending of the joints of the hindquarters and culminates in very energetic gaits.

in front of the leg. *See* **hot off the leg.**

increasing half-halt. A modification of the basic **connecting half-halt.** It is used when the horse is either ignoring the half-halt or stiffening against the **outside** rein during the half-halt. Start with a light connecting half halt and increase the pressure of all the aids over the course of three seconds. *See* **connecting half-halt.**

inside. Refers to the direction or side toward which the horse is **bent** and/or **flexed.**

lateral walk. A rhythm fault in the walk in which the foreleg and the hindleg on the same side move almost on the same beat, so that there is no longer even spacing between the four steps that make up a stride of walk. This irregularity is a serious deterioration of the walk. *See* **rhythm.**

leg-straight. The hind feet follow in the exact same tracks as those made by the front feet. *See* **straightness.**

leg-yield. A lateral movement in which the horse's inside front and hind legs clearly cross in front of his **outside** legs. The spine is straight, but there is flexion at the poll away from the direction of movement. *See* **two-track movements.**

lengthenings. An exercise preliminary to extension. The horse lengthens his stride and frame while maintaining **rhythm, tempo,** and balance.

medium gaits. At the trot and canter, a pace at which the horse shows a length of stride and frame between that of **collection** and **extension.** He shows a more **uphill balance,** more forward and upward thrust, and more reaching than in the **working** gaits. The movement is rounder than that of an extended gait. At the walk, a free, regular, energetic yet calm walk of moderate lengthening. The hind feet touch the ground in front of the footprints of the forefeet.

moving from the hind legs into the hands. *See* **connected; on the bit.** Correctly ridden from back to front so that the **frame** is round.

on the bit. The horse moves actively from behind through a **supple** back and accepts a light **contact** of the rein with no resistance. He yields in the jaw and poll to the rider's hand, has a **round** outline, and willingly responds to the rider's aids. *See* **connection, round.**

outside. The side of the horse's body opposite from the direction toward which he is bent and/or flexed.

over the back. *See* **through the back.**

paces. The walk, trot and canter. *See* **gaits.**

packaged. Connected, on the bit, in a **round** shape.

preparatory half-halt. A quick, simultaneous action of seat, legs, and hands that is done to prepare the horse for a transition. The half-halt is timed so that it is given when the hind leg you want to engage is on the ground—that is, the **inside** hind leg for a downward transition and the outside hind leg for a canter depart.

psychocybernetic. Refers to the part of the subconscious mind that is responsible for the goal-striving behavior of human beings.

putting on the bit. Using a three-second **connecting half-halt** to make your horse round.

rein effects. The different ways that the reins are used to communicate. The five rein effects include: opening rein, indirect rein, direct rein of opposition, indirect rein of opposition in front of the withers, and indirect rein of opposition passing behind the withers. *See also* **contact.**

rein of opposition. The outside rein.

renvers. *See* **haunches-in.**

reversed half-halt. A three-second half-halt that is used to correct the horse that is too light on the **inside** rein and too heavy on the outside rein, so that he takes an even contact with both hands. The legs and seat are used in the same way as they are in the basic connecting half-halt, but the inside hand closes in a fist and the outside hand vibrates to ask for a little **counter-flexion.**

rhythm. One of **the Basics.** The order of the footfalls or the "beat" of the pace (walk: 4-beat; trot: 2-beat; canter: 3-beat).

round/roundness, round outline, shape, or frame. The shape of the horse's outline or silhouette when the hind legs step well under the body, the back is raised, supple and looks convex, the neck is long and arched, and the horse stretches toward the **contact.** *See* **connection; on the bit.**

safe walk. A walk that always stays active and absolutely regular in **rhythm.**

self-carriage. The horse carries himself without balancing on the rider's hands. *See* **collection.**

shoulder-fore. A lateral movement that can be used as a **straightening** exercise. The horse is slightly bent around the **inside** leg and the forehand is brought in off the rail so that the inside hind leg steps in between the tracks of the front legs.

shoulder-in. A lateral movement that can be used as a **straightening, suppling** and **collecting** exercise. The horse is flexed to the **inside** and slightly bent around the inside leg. The forehand is brought in off the rail at approximately a 30 degree angle so that the inside hind leg is lined up directly behind the outside foreleg. The inside foreleg passes and crosses in front of the outside foreleg; the inside hind leg is placed in front of the outside hind leg. The horse looks away from the direction in which he is moving.

shoulder-out. A schooling exercise that is the mirror-image of **shoulder-in.** The horse is ridden on a line that is slightly to the inside of the rail. He is bent and flexed toward the rail and his forehand is brought closer to the rail. All of the same principles of shoulder-in apply.

silhouette. The horse's outline or **frame.**

simple change of lead. A downward transition from one canter lead directly into a few,

clear steps of walk, followed by an upward transition to the other canter lead.

single track. See **work on a single track.**

stilled seat. The aid that is used to signal the horse to slow his **tempo,** steady his **rhythm,** decrease his length of stride or do a downward transition. It is done by stretching up and tightening the abdominal muscles so that the seat stops following along with the horse's motion.

straight/straightness. One of **the Basics.** A straight horse is straight on lines and bent along the arc of curves, with his spine overlapping the line of travel and his hind feet stepping into the tracks of the front feet.

supple/suppleness. Pliability; free from stiffness or resistance; the ability to smoothly adjust carriage (longitudinally) and bend (laterally) without loss of flow of movement or balance.

suppling. An exercise used to reduce tension, loosen stiffness, teach acceptance of the rein, improve bending, or enhance connection.

tail to the wall. A position for leg-yielding in which the horse is ridden slightly to the inside of the track, is **flexed** away from the rail and the hind legs are moved towards the rail at about a 35 degree angle. *See also* **head to the wall.**

tempo. The rate of repetition of the **rhythm.**

throughness. The quality of being on the bit, **connected,** and having a **round frame;** the **supple,** elastic, unblocked, **connected** state of the horse's musculature that allows unrestricted flow of energy from back to front as well as the recycling of that energy back to the hind legs.

through the back. Over the back; a horse can only be through his back when he is on the bit. The back swings and looks convex rather than tight and hollow. *See* **throughness.**

through the horse's neck. A horse can only be "through his neck" when he is **on the bit.** The neck looks long and gracefully arched. *See* **throughness.**

thrust. See **impulsion.**

transition. Any sort of change, including from one **pace** to another, within a pace such as to and from a **lengthening**, or from movement to movement such as from working straight **forward** on a **single track** to a **leg-yield.**

travers. *See* **haunches-in.**

two track movements. *See* **work on two tracks.**

turn on the forehand. The horse yields away from the rider's leg when he's at a standstill. His front legs remain more or less on the same spot while the hindquarters make a 180-degree turn around the forehand, so that the horse ends up facing in the opposite direction.

turn on the haunches. A 180 degree turn done at the walk. The horse bends in the direction of the turn and his forehand moves around his hindquarters. His forefeet and his outside hind foot move around his inside hind foot, which is picked up and put down slightly in front of the spot where it left the ground.

überstreichen. A clear release of contact, where the horse maintains **self-carriage,** rhythm, **tempo, straightness,** and the quality of the pace. In a one-handed überstreichen, the rider extends her inside hand forward up the horse's neck for three to four strides while keeping the **contact** on the outside rein. In a two-handed uberstreichen, the rider extends both of her hands up the crest of the neck toward her horse's ears.

uphill balance. The balance created by increased **engagement** (bending of joints) of the hind legs. The bending of the joints of the hind legs causes the hindquarters to lower. As the hindquarters lower, the forehand lightens and the horse's silhouette gives the appearance of an airplane taking off. The **self-carriage** shown by a horse in **collected, medium,** and **extended gaits.**

work on a single track. Work done going straight forward with the hind feet following in the tracks of the front feet, such as straight lines, school figures (circles, serpentines, figure eights, shallow loops), and transitions.

work on two tracks. Work done with the horse going forward and sideways at the same time such as **shoulder-fore, shoulder-in, shoulder-out, haunches-in, haunches-out,** and **half-pass.**

working gait. The trot or canter in which the young or uneducated horse shows good balance. In the trot, the horse moves energetically in a regular 2-beat **rhythm** and his hind feet step into the tracks made by the front feet. In the canter, he moves energetically in a regular 3-beat rhythm and his **inside** hind leg reaches well under his body.

INDEX

Page numbers in *italics* indicate illustrations.

horse's suitability for, 27
  to improve rider's seat, 26–36
  as riding from the ground, 15–17, *16*
Longitudinal flexion, 136, 205
Loops, shallow, 354–55, 371, *371*. *See also* Serpentines

M

Magnet visualization, 289, *289*
Marching band visualization, *294*
Medium gaits
  described, 314
  canter, 302–3, *303*, 303–4
  defined, 61
  in dressage training levels, 361
  evaluating, 65
  vs. lengthenings, 116–17
  trot, *71*, *300*, 302, *303*
  walk, 67, *67*, 69–71
Metronome image, 121, *121*
Mistakes, coping with, 44–45
Mistral, Kip, 23
Mounting, standing still for, 64
Mouth, rein effects and, *83–84*. *See also* Contact

N

Neck
  as barometer of hind legs, 212, *212*
  in connection, 217–19, *217–20*, 223, 224, *225*
  in counter-canter, 129–30
  following motion of, 86–91, *87–91*
  lengthening of, 213–14
  in lengthenings, *122–23*
  muscling of, 224, *225*
  overflexion of, *220* (See also Behind the bit)
  raising of, 177
  in straightness, 55–58, *55–58*, 100, *100*, 101
  suppling and, 162–63, *163*, 167
Negativity, avoiding, 40–42

O

Obedience
  to aids, 255
  counter-canter as, 125–28

in halt, 64
  school figure accuracy as, 355
Obsessive thoughts, dealing with, 40–42
On the aids, 197. *See also* Half-halts
On the bit. *See* Connection
Opening rein, *93*, 94, 154–55, *155*
"Opening the front door," 123–24, *124*
Outside rein. *See also* Inside/outside aids
  acceptance of, 213–14, *214–15*
  in half-halts, 201–3, *203–4*, 210–12
  as rein of opposition, 202, 249

P

Paces. *See also* Canter; Trot; Walk
  described, 61–62, 65–66, 80
  canter overview, 76–79, *76–79*
  energy in, 71, 76
  vs. gaits, 61
  transitions between, 105, 348–50, *349*, 357
  transitions within, 105, 357
  trot overview, 71–76, *71–74*
  walk overview, 67–71, *67–70*
Pacing, in walk, 70, *70*
"Packaged." *See* Self-carriage
Patience, required for training, 44–45, 243–44
Physical therapy, dressage as, 8–9
Piaffe, *234*
Pirouette, walk, 291, 294
Play days, 170–71, 356
Pleasure riding, 4, 12, 221
Plumb line alignment, of rider position, 25, *25*, 28, 38, *38*, 108
Podhajsky, Alois, 23, 216
Poll
  flexion of, 103–4, *103*, 136–37, *137*, 168
  suppling of, 168–69, *168–69*
Positive affirmations, 39–42
Posting trot
  in developing lengthenings, 120
  diagonals in, 145, 147
  elbow mobility in, 89–90, *89–90*
  horse's rhythm and, 73–74, *73*, 151
  rider balance in, 42–43
  in warm-up, 172

Preparatory half-halts, 215, 328, 331, 345–46, 350
Psychocybernetics, 96
Punishment, 6, 50, 175, 321
Pushing power, 360
Putting the horse on the bit. *See* Connection

Q

Quarter Horses, 243
Quick fixes, pitfalls of, 43

R

Racehorses, 44–45
Read, Bekki, 373
Rearing, 91
Rebalancing, 122, 123, 130, 199, 205
Reference points, arena letters as, 365
Rein aids/effects. *See also* Contact; Reins
  bit-to-elbow alignment in, 83, *83–84*
  direct rein, 92–94, *93*
  "hand-riding," 223, *224*
  indirect, 92–94, *93*, 103, *103*, 163, *165*
  opening rein, *93*, 94, 154–55, *155*, 276
  outside rein, 201–3, *203–4*, 210–12, 213–14, *214–15*, 249
  restraining hands, 62
  teaching of, 15
Rein back, 111–16, *112–14*, 178, 181, *181*, 253–54
"Rein yielding," 152
Reining horses, 233, 362
Reins. *See also* Rein aids/effects
  chewing out of, 225, *226*, 228, 359–60, *359*
  leaning on, by horse, 184
  pulling on, by rider, 42–43, 62
  riding without, 28
  securing for longeing, 17, *17*
  uneven contact on, 335–37, *336–37*
Reis, Dennis, 12–13, 362
Relaxation
  deep frame for, 333–35, *334*
  as finish of half-halt, 203, 210
  flatwork for, 176–77
  of rider, 42
  in warm-up, 171–72
Renvers. *See* Haunches-out

Resistance, 46, 49, 165, 184–85. *See also* Training problems

Restraining hands, 62

Reversed half-halts, 215, 335–38, *336–37*

Rewards, 6, 175, 322

Rhythm
    as basic principle, 47, 65–66, 80
    of canter, 76–79, 131
    in lateral work, 295, 297
    in leg-yield, 153–54
    in lengthenings, 116
    as prerequisite for half-halts, 201
    of trot, 73–75
    in walk, 69–70, 159–60, 278–79

Rib cage, giving in, 101, *101*

Rider position. *See also* Seat aids
    balance in, 24–26, *25–27*, 35–38, *38*, 42–43, 285
    behind the motion, 296
    in canter, 38, *38*
    crookedness related to, 55–60, *55–58*, 337–38
    in half-pass, 285
    improving, 36–38, *36–38*
    for an independent seat, 108
    in leg-yielding, 141–43, *142–43*
    longe exercises for, 26–36, *29–35*
    straightness in, *54*
    in transitions, 28, 36, 65–66, 90

Riders
    attitude of, 24, 39–46, 175
    coordination in, 187
    self-evaluation for, 24–26

Riding areas. *See* Arenas

"Rocker" exercise, 181

Rockwell, Gary, 322

Round frame. *See also* Connection
    described, 10, 217–19, *217–20*
    half-halts and, 205, *205, 214–15*
    poll flexion in, 136

Round Robin Farm, 373

Rubber band image, 119, *119*

Running away, 177–78

Rushing
    after downward transitions, 109, 346
    flatwork for, 177–78
    in flying lead changes, 321–22

vs. lengthening, 120
in rein back, 114

S

Saddle seat disciplines, 25, *26, 61*, 108

Saddles, longeing with, 17–19, *18, 20*, 28

School figures
    accuracy of, 354–55, 365
    arena layouts and, 365–71
    benefits of, 222, 252–53
    size of, 357
    in warm-up, 354–55

Schooling areas. *See* Arenas

Schooling sessions
    breaks during, 175
    cool-down from, 175, 228, 363
    examples of, 364–65, *364*
    to improve self-carriage, 357–58
    new movements in, 356, 363
    planning of, 170–71, 175, 352, 372
    strengthening exercises in, 344
    training levels and, 358–62, *358–61*
    warm-up for, 171–73, *171–74*, 228, 335, 352–56, *356*
    work phase, 174–75, 356–62

Schutof-Lesmeister, Ellen, 23

Scissors exercise, 33, *34*

Seat, independent. *See also* Seat aids
    development of, 26–36, *29–35*
    in different riding disciplines, 25–26, *25–26*
    rider balance in, 24–26, *25*, 42–43
    rider position for, 108

Seat aids
    horse's responsiveness to, 346–47
    influence of, 65–66
    in setting tempo, 285–86
    "stilling" of, 65, 106–7, *107*
    in transitions, 106–7, *107*

Second Level, 360–61, *360–61*

Seesaw image, 129, *129*

Self-carriage
    described, 11–12, 233–35, 237–38, *237–40*, 244
    balance in, 219, *219*, 221, *221*
    benefits of, xiv, 9, 231, 362
    connection and, 235, *236*, 241–44, *243–44*

contact and, 84
developing, 254, 278–79, 356–58
in extended gaits, 309, 311–12
feel of, 240–41
lateral work for, 222, 256, 260–61, 290, 298, 341–42
prerequisites for, 241–42
strength required for, 242–43

Self-esteem. *See* Confidence

Self-talk, 39–40

Sensitive horses, 49–50

Serpentines, 326–27, *327*, 354–55, 357, *370*, 371

Short steps
    benefits of, 75, 179, 186, 222
    vs. collection, 247, *248*, 252
    rider position in, 36

Shortening, of paces
    balance in, 36, 67
    benefits of, 28, 179
    vs. self-carriage, 233–34
    for suppling, 186, 355
    in warm-up, 355–56

Shoulder rolls exercise, 30, *30*

Shoulder-fore
    described, 156–60, *157–58*, 261
    for developing straightness, 60, 192–96, *193–96*
    for engagement, 95
    as four track movement, 133, *134*, 259, *259–60*
    for improving the canter, 178
    to mobilize shoulders, 187
    as preparation for half-pass, 284

Shoulder-in
    described, 262–63
    aids for, 263–65, *265*, 266–67, *266*, 270
    benefits of, 260–62, 287, 307, 341–42, 346–47
    on circles, *263*
    faults in, 268–71, *268–69*
    with haunches-in, 278, *278*
    quality of, 257, *257–58*, 262–68, *262–64, 266*
    in self-carriage, 271
    vs. shoulder-fore, 156
    as three-track movement, *134*, 259, *259*, 261, *261*